A
DAILY GUIDE
TO MIRACLES

A
DAILY GUIDE
TO MIRACLES

And Successful Living
Through SEED-FAITH

by Oral Roberts

SPIRE BOOKS

FLEMING H. REVELL COMPANY

OLD TAPPAN, NEW JERSEY

ISBN 0 8007 8300-X
Copyright © 1975 by Oral Roberts
Published by Fleming H. Revell Company
All rights reserved

COPYRIGHT © 1975
BY PINOAK PUBLICATIONS
TULSA, OKLAHOMA
ALL RIGHTS RESERVED

Printed in the United States of America

CONTENTS

THIRD WEEK

I DISCOVERED THE SOURCE THAT NEVER FAILS AND I CAN BRING HIM ALIVE IN YOUR LIFE

FOURTH WEEK

HOW I DISCOVERED THE FANTASTIC JOY OF GIVING AS A SEED I SOW RATHER THAN AS A DEBT I OWE

FIFTH WEEK

THE GREATEST THING YOU CAN EVER LEARN IS . . . HOW TO EXPECT A MIRACLE!

SIXTH WEEK

GOD'S GREATEST MIRACLE IS YOUR PERSONAL SALVATION

SEVENTH WEEK

HOW I OVERCAME THE QUESTION: HAVE MIRACLES CEASED? AND HOW MIRACLES CAN OPEN UP TO YOU

EIGHTH WEEK

THE INFALLIBLE WAY I DISCOVERED OF HELPING YOU TO RELEASE YOUR FAITH TO GOD

NINTH WEEK

HOW YOU AND I CAN TALK TO GOD AND HE CAN TALK TO US

TENTH WEEK

HOW I LEARNED TO HAVE A KNOWING THAT GOD WILL MAKE A WAY WHERE THERE IS NO WAY

ELEVENTH WEEK

HOW YOU CAN STOP FAILING AND START SUCCEEDING

TWELFTH WEEK

WHY YOU MUST STRUGGLE AND HOW TO FIND THE SEED OF AN EQUAL BENEFIT

THIRTEENTH WEEK

**GREATER IS HE (GOD) THAT IS IN YOU
THAN HE (THE DEVIL) THAT IS IN THE WORLD**

ORAL ROBERTS—
As Seen By A Friend And Admirer

By Dr. L. D. Thomas, Jr.
Pastor And Senior Minister
First United Methodist Church
Tulsa, Oklahoma

When I travel and say I'm from Tulsa, usually the first question I am asked is: "Do you know Oral Roberts?" A friend of mine recently visited the Bahamas and said, "While I was eating, the waiter asked me where I was from. I told him, 'Tulsa . . . you probably never heard of it.' He shot right back, 'Oh, yes, that's the home of Oral Roberts, isn't it?'" Tulsa is known everywhere because of Oral.

Yet, most people know very little about the man himself, so I am grateful for this opportunity to tell you a few things about Oral Roberts that you cannot see on a TV screen or grasp from public appearances. During the past ten years, as pastor of First United Methodist Church in Tulsa, I have been closely associated with Oral both personally and publicly, and the better I have gotten to know him the more I have admired and respected him as a man.

Oral Roberts is a close personal friend. He knows how to be a friend better than any person I know, for when he is in your presence he is capable of giving himself almost 100% to you. He is genuinely interested in you and your concerns and you are able to feel it when you are with him. I am convinced that herein lies one of the secrets to his phenomenal success. Because he is able to almost completely lose himself for others, God is able to use Oral as an instrument for His healing power to others.

During my second year as pastor of First Methodist, Tulsa, in the course of a friendly conversation with Oral I asked him, "If I were your pastor what one thing would you want most from me?" He looked me straight in the eye, set his jaw and said without hesitation, "I would want to know that you cared! I would want to know that you were genuinely feeling with me and my family, and daily lifting us and our problems up to God in prayer." This was truly a turning point in my own ministry, for in that moment I saw that the important thing which Jesus wants us to grasp is not so much "Doctrinal Theology" as it is "Relational Theology." What happened to me and my congregation as a result of this is another story altogether, but the point is it was because Oral Roberts was able to get "inside my skin and feel with me" that God could use him to reveal to me the truth that I needed

11

most and that turned First Methodist from a dying downtown church into a growing, exciting, alive fellowship of caring Christians.

Oral Roberts is also a community man. In fact, he is one of the best boosters of our city, not only as a religious leader but in the business community as well. He serves on the boards of some of our leading businesses and institutions, including one of our largest banks and public utilities. Before entering the ministry I practiced law for twelve years and was General Counsel for Consolidated Gas Utilities Corporation, and I can truthfully say that I have met few men in my life who have the ability to go directly to the heart of a business problem as quickly as Oral Roberts. At first, this is amazing when you consider that Oral's background and training was for the ministry, not business; but when you get to know the man you begin to see that this is simply another natural result of his whole approach to Christianity and life; for to Oral, Christianity is not a formal, stylized religion but a whole way of life that touches everything we do. He expects God to use him as an instrument for business decisions exactly the same as he expects God to use him as an instrument for healing the hurts and pains of others; and the good news is—God does! I know of nothing that is needed more in the business community of America today than this; God is just as interested in our business and financial affairs as He is in our religious lives on Sunday. And, it just could be that Oral Roberts will be the man that God uses to reveal this to the business community in America. No wonder that Oral is the most sought after man for our civic, charitable, and community drives. No wonder that he has been selected as the outstanding citizen of Tulsa, for he never passes up an opportunity to let God use him for the good of our community.

Oral Roberts is an outstanding educator. This, too, is amazing but when you get to know the man you realize he is not only interested in man's soul but he is concerned about the whole man—mind, body and soul. In Tulsa, if you really want to see a miracle, all you have to do is go to 81st and Lewis and look at one of the most amazing institutions in the whole history of higher education: Oral Roberts University. No other school has ever come close to it in reaching top rank so quickly, both academically and athletically. And those of us who know Oral Roberts think "we ain't seen nothin' yet." For example, while most private universities are having a struggle just to keep the doors open, Oral recently announced plans for new medical, dental, and law schools; the school of medicine to be in operation by 1978. Oral truly lives what he preaches, "God can bless only what we risk for Him!"

Finally, in my opinion, Oral Roberts is the one man most responsible for a genuine spiritual revival in our time. During the terrible 60's—one of the most tragic declines ever in both the church and the moral fiber of America—here was a man who refused to join the pessimists. Wherever he could, he stood up and shouted as loud as he could, "God is alive!"

When I entered the ministry in 1959, there were barely a half dozen good books on the Holy Spirit. Now throughout the church, the work of the Holy Spirit is the most talked about and the most exciting thing that is happening in the church and in people's lives today. And the man most responsible for this, in my opinion, is Oral Roberts.

I thank God for Oral Roberts. I thank God for his emphasis upon a living God who is concerned about each one of us personally. I thank God that Oral has allowed God to use him as an instrument for a spiritual revival in our time that is giving new life to the church and new life to our nation. I thank God that he has written this new book which embraces the concepts of his ministry and offers us *A Daily Guide To Miracles And Successful Living Through Seed-Faith* from the pen of the man who has more personal knowledge about both than any other living man. I hope that every person who reads it will catch something of the spirit of the man himself. If so, our world will be a much better and more exciting place to live.

Why I Wrote This Book For You

EVERY time I get a miracle I am so thrilled I feel I could shout . . . or cry . . . or just fly away.

But it brings an ache to my heart too. An ache for all those years I didn't know God cared about me, and for all those years I had no miracles, not a single one.

And I get another kind of ache, deeper and more hurting inside me. It's this: Every day when I open my mail and read what people are going through . . . their problems, heartaches, needs . . . I want to reach out my hands, wrap my arms around them and say, "Listen, there is a God. He loves you. He has many miracles for you. Don't you understand God has miracles for YOU?"

I ache because I can see many of them are like I was, they've been down in their hurts and ills so long that expecting a miracle from God has never occurred to them.

I ache too because almost every person I meet shows by his eyes, or the look on his (or her) face, or the way his body moves, or the spirit he gives off, or by the negative phrases he uses . . . that he would give anything in the world to have a miracle from God, even a tiny one, if he only could believe God was concerned about him . . . or if he knew what to do . . .

SO . . . I told God that I was going to search the 28 years of my ministry, and asked Him to help me find the KEYS I had gotten from Him and used countless times . . . keys that brought His miracles into my life when I needed and HAD TO HAVE THEM!

That's what I said to God; that's what I asked Him.

Then I had an unusual *impression* to hit me in the pit of my stomach. *WHY DON'T YOU go through your notes, your diaries, your sermons, your experiences . . . and look for different weeks when you found God's way to miracles. Break each week into days. Get three months of these—91 whole days—and let the person reading them live them with you. Then ask them to repeat their reading four times a year . . . then they will have it burning inside them. I promise you they will get the miracles they are looking for.*

15

NOW I HAD GOD'S WAY TO DO IT. I thought at first it would be easy, but it was hard. I mean HARD!

I asked my darling wife Evelyn to help me remember, and as she did she would often throw up her hands and say, "Oh, Oral, it's too painful to live this all over again." Or she would say, "Honey, don't forget that miracle we experienced when we did . . ." and she would relate the incident.

I got the first week written, seven full days. Then the second, and on through five. The next eight seemed forever. I worked from dawn to dusk some days until my writing hand cramped and my shoulder hurt.

But as I neared the end of the thirteenth week I forgot about the cramps in my hand, I was soaring in God's assurance that He was going to show you new things . . . you would understand them . . . AND your miracles would start happening.

Then . . . I read the chapters, week after week—the entire 91 days —over and over. Searching for something I may have missed. Looking for the times I may have gotten carried away and had raced too much. I stayed at it until . . .

Deep inside me I could hear the inner voice:

> *You've done it! It's going to do the job I want done. The miracles are going to happen!*

So . . . you've got virtually the whole of my life . . . going back to when I was just a little boy . . . my teen-age years . . . my middle years . . . and now my 57th year . . . through it all, M-I-R-A-C-L-E-S.

Even though I wrote it, I found myself wishing I had it back there earlier in my life. I know now it would have opened me up sooner to miracles for my everyday life. It would have truly been A DAILY GUIDE TO MIRACLES AND SUCCESSFUL LIVING—THROUGH SEED-FAITH.

That is exactly what it is for you. Thank God it is, and thank God it's going to do great things in your life . . .

NOW . . . here's exactly what I want you to do to get these ideas to working fantastically for you.

First: Don't fight me. Cooperate by simply reading it day-by-day. God has called me to be His servant and prophet to help you. Let me be me, and let me help you through this book. What I'm saying is very personal and I ask you to take it personally . . .

Second: As you read and start seeing that what I'm saying is real and alive to you, be a *partner* together with me to find God's best. To be on top, not on the bottom. To be the head, not the tail. To succeed, and not fail. My *partnership* with you can be worth a lot to you . . . because I am a servant of God and a prophet of His to you . . .

Third: Don't quit on me or on yourself. Start with the first week. Take the first day and read it. Devour it. Then take the seven days just like I wrote it. Then at the end of the week say, "Now what is God saying to me?" Then say, "God, show me how to apply this." Then believe He will—and He will!

Finally: And this is very important to you, get the "Key" phrases, *things I want you to say to yourself.* Say them until they are part of you, like they are to me. They are Keys that are really GIANTS to open doors, to release you, to fill you with God's good things, to bring you miracles until you shout or cry for joy! Do this, will you??

OK . . . Here it is, my seeds of faith for your life. As I've worked and planted them I've tried to visualize you picking up this book, holding it in your hands, reading, stopping . . . reading, smiling, crying, meditating, believing, receiving, and finally knowing that you know that you know that you know . . . GOD IS THE GREATEST POWER YOU HAVE AND HE'S IN THE MIDDLE OF THE N-O-W of your needs!

Your partner always,

Oral Roberts

P.S. I urge you to keep A DAILY GUIDE TO MIRACLES with your Bible all the time. Compare what the book says with what the Bible says . . . compare . . . compare. Then you'll see, you'll understand Seed-Faith will never fail to work miracles in your life . . . you will feel God's presence and know His guidance. And I haven't a doubt but that you'll enter into God's rhythm of successful living. **It will happen to you!**

A
DAILY GUIDE
TO MIRACLES

FIRST WEEK

These Ideas Lifted Me Out Of Failure And They Will Help You Too

SUNDAY

Key: DEVIL, YOU CAN'T TOUCH ME—I AM GOD'S PROPERTY

or

The Truth About You, The Devil And God

WHY keep on struggling and knocking yourself out with extra worry and anxiety just because something has gone wrong and something is falling apart that is precious to you?

I ask you . . . "Why?"

You say, "Oral Roberts, are you out of your mind? Haven't you ever had things go wrong . . . things to get so bad . . . bills to pile up . . . sickness to strike . . . trouble to come in and almost make you go under?"

Have I? How many times! And how often bad things hit at me now. Sometimes the devil hits me so hard that I feel like I can't raise up my head. My inner man wants to lie down inside and there seems to be NO WAY OUT FOR ME . . .

    or for my family . . .

        or for my ministry . . .

            or for the people I'm trying to minister God's healing power to.

But I *know* Jesus. I *know* who my SOURCE is. I know Jesus Christ of Nazareth as my personal Lord and Savior, as the Baptizer of my soul in the Holy Spirit, as the ONE who will supply all my needs with many miracles. I *know* HIM! In spite of having to struggle, of getting weary with doing, or feeling like the Lord may sometimes forget I exist, I am learning the greatest secret in the world and it is . . .

to expect many miracles from my Savior.

I want to talk real plain to you about *you,* the *devil* and *Jesus Christ,* and the exciting new concept that . . .

YOU ARE GOD'S PROPERTY

Here's how you can do what God wants you to do and then expect many miracles:

FIRST: Believe the truth about the devil and his purpose toward you, and the truth about Jesus Christ of Nazareth and His purpose TOWARD YOU.

That truth is stated by Jesus himself in St. John 10:10:

The thief (devil) *cometh not* (comes), *but for to steal* (from you), *and to kill* (you), *and to destroy* (you): *I* (Jesus) *am come that they* (you) *might have life, and . . . have it more abundantly.*

There is a devil and you've got to believe that. Jesus called him a *thief* and says he comes to steal from you, to kill you, to destroy you.

Believe that. Don't shrug it off. Don't just fall back and say, "I can't understand it." You are not told to understand it. Jesus tells you to believe it.

Then Jesus tells you to believe Him, that the reason He came is to give LIFE to you . . . and to give it to you MORE ABUNDANTLY.

Look. You can draw a line right down the middle. Put the devil with all his badness on one side, and Jesus with all His goodness on the other, and with you in the middle—like this:

The devil   YϕU   Jesus Christ
                                                                   of Nazareth

On one side of your life is the devil. On the other side is God, and you are in the middle.

The devil is a bad devil.
God is a good God.
There is no goodness in the devil
and no badness in God.
The devil is totally bad . . .
and God is totally good.
On the one side is the devil with his terrible badness, and on the other side is God with His infinite goodness.

The devil hates you but God loves you. God is greater than the devil and God can command the devil to take his hands off you. You need to grasp that with your understanding. And you need to quit blaming God and at the same time start putting the blame where it belongs—on the devil.

Listen.

The devil comes to steal from you: your faith, your love, your hope, your desire to trust in God, your earning power, your right relationship with your family and others, your health and well-being, your expectation for miracles. You name anything good in life, or anything good coming across your path, and it's the devil's business to try to steal it! He's trying to steal from you right now. I'm telling you on the authority of Christ, our Lord.

Know what the devil is trying to do to you. The devil is trying to kill you—to actually destroy everything good about you, every good from happening to you, to stop any good from coming to you, to get you down in your spirit, down in your mind with depression, to get you down in your body with weakness and disease. The devil is trying to ruin you, to keep you from advancing, from receiving the money you need, from prospering and being in health physically and mentally and spiritually. The devil hates you and he is literally trying to destroy your life. This is why the Bible says:

Resist the devil and he will flee from you (James 4:7).

"Resist the devil!" This means, stand up to him; don't give an inch; *take charge.*

On the other hand, Jesus tells you the reason for His coming to this earth, dying on the cross, rising from the dead, ascending back to heaven and sending the blessed Comforter—the Holy Spirit, who is Jesus' own other self, the unlimited form of His presence and power in the NOW. It is to GIVE YOU LIFE...MORE FULL AND CONTINUING.

Believe that.

Stop ignoring or doubting it.

Believe it.

Think on it.

Know it.

Say this great living truth:

> JESUS CAME . . .
>
> JESUS CAME TO GIVE ME LIFE . . .
>
> JESUS CAME TO GIVE ME LIFE MORE ABUNDANTLY . . .
>
> ME!
>
> ME!

Remember—the devil and Jesus don't mix! Their purposes don't mix! Their *works* don't mix! Believe and know this so you can doubt what the devil tries to tell you, and trust in God.

SECOND: Believe you belong not to the devil but to God; therefore . . .

> YOU ARE GOD'S PROPERTY . . . NOT THE DEVIL'S.

Jesus said of the devil, "[Ye have] nothing in me . . ." (John 14:30). So you can say, "The devil has nothing in *me*."

Say, "I don't belong to the devil. I AM GOD'S PROPERTY."

Say, "I will *resist* the devil's efforts to steal the good things of life from me, to kill me with his oppression of sickness, poverty, fear, anxiety, a down spirit, a negative attitude."

Say, "I will resist the devil's efforts to destroy the things God has for me to receive."

Say, "I believe Jesus Christ. I believe He has come to fill me with His life, His love, His faith, His hope, His Spirit, His power."

Say, "I believe Jesus has come to bless me, to heal me, to prosper me, to guide me, to open up my inner man, to teach me to love and give, to plant seeds of faith because . . .

"I am God's property!"

Say these statements over and over—say them out loud until they become a part of you. (I do this all the time and it really works.)

When you know you are God's property, it puts you in a take-charge position. When you are hurting, when you may not even know what to do or where to turn, you can know there is a God and He loves you because you are God's property!

Recently I preached a sermon on the theme: "I BELONG TO GOD; THEREFORE, DEVIL, TAKE YOUR HANDS OFF GOD'S PROPERTY! . . . ME!" I didn't know at the time there was a young girl sitting there listening who would soon be physically attacked by a rapist. I only felt I **had** to say what God wanted me to say:

"You belong to God; therefore, tell the devil to take his hands off God's property."

God anointed me to say this over and over, my spirit and voice rising until you could feel the presence of God all over the place.

A few nights later this particular young woman was waylaid in a dark area. As the man put a knife to her neck, threatening to kill her if she didn't yield to him, she remembered WHO SHE WAS, WHO SHE BELONGED TO, and she said, "YOU CAN'T DO THIS TO ME. I AM GOD'S PROPERTY."

Each time he would try to force her she would say, "YOU CAN'T DO THIS TO ME. I AM GOD'S PROPERTY!"

Suddenly three strangers appeared from out of the darkness and the rapist ran. Later the police captured him, and while questioning him he confessed why he had not criminally assaulted the girl before the three men appeared and frightened him away. He told the police, "It was strange but when she kept saying, 'YOU CAN'T DO THIS TO ME; I AM GOD'S PROPERTY,' something came over me and I couldn't do anything except threaten her. Something happened inside me."

I personally know the power of stating in faith, "I belong to God. Devil, take your hands off God's property."

When praying for a person, either in person or on our television program, as I reach out my hands toward the viewer, or in personally praying through my letter back to one who has written me for prayer, I often say, "DEVIL, TAKE YOUR HANDS OFF GOD'S PROPERTY!" Where's the Scripture for this? St. Paul says it clearly in 1 Corinthians 6:19,20.

> *What? know ye not that your body is the temple of the Holy Ghost* (Spirit) *which is in you, which ye have of God, and ye are not your own? For ye are bought with a price* (Christ's own shed blood): *therefore glorify* (honor) *God in your body, and in your spirit, which are God's.*

(Please read this Scripture again prayerfully and carefully—let it sink in.)

Don't you see God wants you to believe you don't belong to the devil, you are not the devil's property but God's? Don't you see the Holy Spirit is IN you, and you don't belong to yourself, but to Him? Don't you see that Christ actually died for you and, therefore, in your body AND spirit, which are God's, you are to submit to Him and trust yourself to Him?

You, my dear friend, are unique and irreplaceable.

Did you know that?

You are God-bought, God-filled, God-owned!

You may be tempted by the devil to believe your battle is with God—that God isn't mindful of you, or concerned about you, or doesn't love you, or doesn't want to prosper you or to give you physical and spiritual health and wholeness. Well, Jesus calls the devil a LIAR and the FATHER OF LIES (St. John 8:44).

Believe there is a devil and believe he is a thief, a murderer, a destroyer, and a LIAR!

Your battle is not with God but with the devil, your adversary (1 Peter 5:8). Your weapons are not of the flesh, but they are spiritual (2 Corinthians 10:4). These weapons God has given you are:

the power of the measure of faith (Romans 12:3) . . .

the power to love and power to hope (1 Corinthians 13:13) . . .

the power not to fear but to believe (2 Timothy 1:7) . . .

and He has given you the knowledge that you are not the devil's property, but God's! (1 Corinthians 6:19). But don't ever forget—even though you have these weapons—the devil is a coward and he will not fight fair. He is not going to come up to you and say, "Good morning, this is the devil. I have come to tempt you today. I have come to trick you. I have come to deceive you. I am your adversary and I'm out to do you in . . ."

NO!

His strategy is deceitfulness, cunning, craftiness, subtlety—he hits below the belt. He is out to destroy you. And by yourself you're no match for him. But let me tell you something more precious than gold: You are "mighty through God to the pulling down of [the devil's] strong holds" (2 Corinthians 10:4). You don't belong to the devil but to our God, the mighty Source of your total supply. And our God is mightier than the devil.

> *Greater is he* (God) *that is in you, than he* (the devil) *that is in the world* (1 John 4:4).

David said, "The battle is the Lord's." Therefore, you must learn these great truths, make them a part of your being, until you know they are absolutely true.

I know it!

And I want you to know it . . . for yourself!

THIRD: DON'T LET OUTWARD APPEARANCES DECEIVE YOU. In other words, don't let the devil trick you into believing something is good when it's bad, or bad when it's good. As St. Paul said, "We are not ignorant of his devices" (2 Corinthians 2:11).

For example, I am told that a shot of heroin makes you feel very good, at least seemingly, for a few hours. You think if it makes you feel good, why shouldn't you continue it? But, you see, the devil is a liar. He's trying to deceive you. The truth is, you may feel good for a few hours or for a few times, but later you will feel wretched and wrecked for years, or maybe your whole lifetime . . . or it may ultimately destroy you.

I've dealt with many who told me they knew this about heroin, yet believed the devil and not God. The devil gave them an excuse to trick themselves. And in every case I had to start by showing them that the devil and Jesus are different, their works don't mix. These people had to come to the point of turning back to God and telling the devil, "Take your hands off God's property . . . ME!"

Something people are frightened of is sickness, and now especially cancer. The President's wife—Mrs. Betty Ford's experience with cancer has awakened a lot of people to these dangers. What I want to remind you of is that sickness of any kind is not sent from God but from the devil. It's the devil trying to steal your health. If the devil can't get your whole body he will try to take part of your body, an arm or a leg or an important organ.

If the devil can't take all your earnings away, he'll try to take part. If he can't get your job, he'll try to lay you off for a month or more. If he can't get all your money, he'll try to make inflation take it. In fact, there are so many different and cunning ways the devil tries to get at you. If you try to face him alone, you can't possibly win—for the devil is stronger and smarter than you are, or I am, or all the humans in the world.

So . . . **your only chance is to remember that you don't belong to yourself, or to the devil. You belong to God.** You are God's property. The devil knows this too . . . he believes and trembles (James 2:19). Did you know that? But if you don't know it, the devil is not going to tell you. The moment he finds out that you know you belong to God, half of your battle is won. And when you say, "Devil, take your hands off God's property . . . ME," you have begun to drive the devil out of your life and away from you and to get yourself under God's great protection.

HOW THIS WILL WORK TODAY AND EVERY DAY
ALL THROUGH YOUR LIFE

In your day-by-day life, the little things that seem so ordinary are really the groundwork for bigger things from the devil . . . OR FROM GOD.

You need to know and remember things like these:

Such as the devil putting in your mind the thought of an unkind word about yourself which he tempts you to say to yourself, or to a loved one, or to someone else . . .

Or, such as starting to develop a bad attitude at your work which may cause a demotion, or a layoff, or even the loss of your job or position . . .

Or, such as doing little things leading to the beginning of a breakdown in your health: not taking care of yourself, letting tension and fear build up, being angry too long and too often, not putting in the seeds of faith in the form of your giving of love, kindness, time, talent, money . . .

Such as forgetting about miracles and God's great concern to give you many miracles.

On the other hand, these are the little things you *can* do toward God:

Such as being positive in your attitude, believing for the best to happen . . .

Such as seeing the good things in yourself, your loved ones, and others . . .

Such as keeping a good attitude which can lead to a promotion, or being kept on in bad times, or even a new and better job or position . . .

Such as keeping on a more even keel or balance, not permitting the devil to steal your peace of soul and mind, refusing his suggestions to get mad and try to hurt someone. In short, you must go . . .

from planting bad seeds which are multiplied back in bad things . . .

to planting good seeds, however small, every day . . . good seeds which are multiplied back in good things.

Start believing Jesus rather than the devil. Believe that each good seed you plant will be multiplied and sent back in God's own *way* and *time* and in exactly the way you need your miracle from His hand.

I want you to feel to the depths of your soul the loving care God has placed in my heart for you—and I want you to feel my belief and faith that God wants the devil to take his hands off God's property . . . you . . . and your loved ones.

I remind you, and will keep on reminding you, to tell the devil:

"I AM GOD'S PROPERTY. YOU CAN'T TOUCH OR DESTROY ME!"

———————◆———————

All day long today say:

"Devil, you can't touch me; I am God's property."

"Devil, you can't touch me; I am God's property." Any time any negative thing begins to happen or you are tempted to do wrong, say it:

"Devil, you can't touch me; I am God's property." Now stand up to him every time he tries to get at you.

YOUR GOD-GIVEN KEY FOR TODAY

Say again:

"Devil, You Can't Touch Me; I Am God's Property."

MONDAY Key: GOD CARES ABOUT ME

or
How I Found The Miracle That Loosed My Stammering Tongue And Opened My Diseased Lungs

The first day I attended school I was 6 years old. It was a little one-room school in the country with one teacher and about 25 children from the first through the sixth grades.

We were each asked to stand and tell our name. As each child ahead of me stood and called out his name I waited my turn. I shook with fear. My mouth dried up, my throat closed, my heart pounded. You see, I stuttered. What was fairly easy for the other children was hell to me.

Finally, when the teacher looked at me and nodded, I opened my mouth but nothing came out. I tried and tried to say, "My name is Oral Roberts," but the words wouldn't come. All the pupils laughed. That would not have been too serious for I had been laughed at by kids for my stuttering before—*but the teacher laughed!*

The effect upon me, a preacher's kid who was already held in a certain kind of contempt, was catastrophic. My whole world fell out from under me. The psychological impact turned me from a bright, laughing child into a frightened, inferior little human being for the next 12 years of my life—and in some ways, until I was 30. For the next 12 years . . .

I DREADED TO TALK—TO OPEN MY MOUTH

I hated people who made me talk and hated them more when I tried to talk, stuttered, and they laughed.

My name is Oral. When I was older I learned it meant the *spoken word*. But it meant humiliation to a sensitive child, driving him into himself so he was hidden on the fringes of life, peering around the corner at the other children as they talked and laughed and had a good time.

WORDS FROZE IN MY THROAT

One day while trying to recite orally the multiplication tables before the class, I broke down and burst into tears. I knew them forward and backward but the numbers stuck in my throat. The students howled in glee. The teacher sent me from the room to get a glass of water. "That will help you," she said.

But it didn't.

At 15, nearly 6'2" tall, I entered high school. One day my father was telling one of my uncles a feeling he had about me, his stuttering son. "Someday Oral will preach," Papa told Uncle Willis. "He will preach the gospel."

My uncle, who didn't dislike me but was rather amused with me because he enjoyed hearing me stutter, replied, "Oral will never preach; why he can't even talk."

Suddenly I wanted to run and run and run—going as far away from people physically as I already had inwardly.

And I did run.

I stayed gone nearly a year. I suppose I never would have come home but I was suddenly struck down with tuberculosis. My basketball coach carried me home and I said to my Papa, "I have gone the last mile of the way."

As I lay on the bed, hemorrhaging to death, I remembered something my mother had said to me years before. A group of little boys were teasing me, trying to get me to talk and then laughing at my stuttering. They had chased me all the way home jeering, "Let's hear you talk, Oral. Let's hear you talk." My mother sent them away, pulled me upon her lap, put her arms around me, and said:

"Son, someday God will loose your tongue and you will talk. I prayed for God to give me a blue-eyed, black-haired little boy who someday would preach the gospel — and He gave me you."

"Me, preach?"

"Yes," she said.

"But how will I ever preach; I can't even talk."

"You'll see," she said.

Now lying on the bed, my dreams of someday being a lawyer and governor of Oklahoma, my body wracked with pain, my tongue frozen in my mouth, I let the tears flow and I cried, "Why has this happened to me? What have I done to deserve it? Other kids can breathe, talk, run, play, and be normal. Why me? WHY? WHY? WHY?"

There I lay, the hope of my parents for me to follow in their footsteps and preach the gospel, hopeless — and feeling absolutely lost and confused.

AT FIRST I WAS SCARED I WOULD DIE
THEN I WAS AFRAID I WOULDN'T

I turned my face to the wall and away from the doctors who said they could only offer a diet of raw eggs beaten in milk, and bed rest . . . the unseen forces of the world out there were against me . . . and God, whoever or whatever He or It was. Worn out, disillusioned, despairing, I gave up. (They had not yet discovered miracle drugs for tuberculosis back there in 1935.)

The moment I settled into utter despair, the prayers and dreams for me took on new power. Jewel, my sister who lived in a nearby town, felt a strange urge to come to my bedside. Before, she had cried for me. Now she was driving toward our little house with a message "from above."

SEVEN WORDS CHANGED MY LIFE

When she came in and looked at me I was a mass of skin and bones, going in less than five months from a healthy 163 pounds to 120. At 17 years of age I was lying there, trying to breathe easy so I wouldn't break my lungs loose into another hemorrhage, and hoping nobody would ask me to talk. I looked up into my only living sister's face, and she spoke seven words. And I suddenly forgot to hate, I forgot to despair, I forgot my feelings of being utterly lonely and alone, I forgot my helplessness. And that moment Jesus Christ of Nazareth came to me.

Jewel said, "Oral, God is going to heal you."

I managed to say, "Is He, Jewel?"

With a knowing that I later learned was faith personified she replied, "Yes, He is."

I thought:

> *God knows my name, Oral, and what it stands for. He knows
> ME. God knows me!! I am a somebody, a person, not just a
> preacher's kid who stutters and is doomed to die before his
> time. God cares about me. Me!!*

That evening my parents said it was now or maybe never and they
knelt and prayed by my bedside. When the nurse and my mother
finished and sat back, my father continued praying where he was
kneeling at the foot of the bed.

As I looked upon Papa's face, I saw Jesus in his countenance and I
became aware that Jesus was looking at me—and loving me. I had
never seen such faith, such love.

Involuntarily, I began talking to Jesus, asking for His help and His
salvation. A sensation of warmth began at my feet, slowly coming up
through my body, working through my burnt-out lungs, then into my
vocal cords, then exploding inside me. It drew the hate and bitterness
and despair out of me just as poison is drawn out of an infected wound. I
was engulfed with Jesus' presence. I was not healed at that moment.
My breath was still labored, my stammering was still there when I
talked. Something, however, had happened—something I've never lost.

The next thing I knew, the door opened and my older brother,
Elmer, 13 years older than I and with whom I had never been close,
walked in. He said, "Oral, get up; we're going to take you to a man who
is praying for the sick."

"I can't get up, Elmer." I answered.

"I'll carry you," he said.

I ended up in a crowd of over a thousand waiting for the preacher
to touch them and offer prayer for healing. As Elmer and my parents
set me down in front of him, holding me up, a pair of hands brushed
my head lightly and I heard these words:

> "Thou foul tormenting affliction, come out of this boy, in the
> name of Jesus Christ of Nazareth."

A burning sensation struck my lungs and swept up through my
throat so quickly that instantly I was out of their protecting arms,
walking, talking, laughing, crying. The preacher put a microphone in
front of me and said, "Tell us what is happening."

A dam burst inside me, the words coming forth in currents so
swift I ran my words together. I breathed as if breathing was the most
normal thing in the world. Gradually I gained control and calmly talked
to the crowd, telling them that Christ had come to me, I was going to
get well, I was going to preach the gospel, and never again would
stuttering and tuberculosis destroy me.

From the deepest part of my being, words which I had heard
while being carried by my brother welled up in me crystal clear:

> *Son, I am going to heal you, and you are to take My healing power to your generation.*

My healing took a year. At times I thought I had lost it. The hurting in my lungs was stubborn, so was my stuttering. My mother sensing my struggle said, "Oral, do you remember when the power of the Lord came over you and you could talk and breathe normally?"

"Oh, yes," I replied.

"Hold that picture in your mind and heart and your complete healing will come." And it did!

From that hour the change began that has never left me. I still stutter some, particularly when I am excited, and my lungs still hurt occasionally after strenuous preaching and praying for people. But I do not doubt my healing. For I can talk. I can breathe. And . . .

I know
    that I know
        that I know
            that I know
                that I know
                    that I know.

Seven words changed my life: "Oral, God is going to heal you." Suddenly I knew GOD CARED ABOUT ME . . . ME! I knew I was somebody — not just a preacher's kid who stuttered and was doomed to die before his time.

I want you to get this down deep inside you, live with it every day — for this is where miracles begin:

GOD CARES ABOUT YOU!

Yes, YOU — in spite of what you have done . . . or have not done . . . or who you are . . . or are not — GOD CARES ABOUT YOU! BELIEVE THIS: GOD CARES ABOUT YOU!

Say it to yourself again and again:

"God cares about me."

"God cares about me."

Learn to repeat it again *every time* you begin to feel low:

"God cares about me!"

This is a fact of life you can't afford not to bring inside you to expand you.

YOUR GOD-GIVEN KEY FOR TODAY
"God Cares About Me!"

TUESDAY Key:
JESUS LIVES AT MY HOUSE

or

The Strange Thing That Happened In My Illness Which Made Me Recognize Jesus When He Came To Me

I've been told by people who study such things that:
We become like unto that which we adore.

They say the thing or things we choose to adore—or the person or persons we choose to adore—will determine what and who we become and finally are.

If this is true (and who can doubt it?) we have to ask ourselves, "What, or who is it I adore?"

Well, during my five months flat on my back my parents kept the name and person of Jesus before me. I was a captive audience. They had a habit of awakening before daylight each morning and lying in bed for 15 or 20 minutes talking to Jesus and to each other about Jesus. They talked to Jesus in a personal way. It recalled scenes in my childhood when they talked to Jesus as if He were a member of our family and I thought He lived at our house.

There was something about the way they talked to Jesus that was authentic. It was conversational, it was loving and real, and I discovered myself listening in.

Actually, they carried on a running conversation about Jesus, or to Him all day. I could not escape it. It was in the tone of their voices, the look in their eyes, the feeling they gave, their mannerisms—all of it made me feel, **my parents know Jesus Christ personally. He is here! He lives in this house!**

I began to believe in Jesus before I believed in God. The name of God was a threat. He seemed more like a terrible judge, while Jesus appeared friendly, tender, caring and absolutely able to do anything.

It was apparent my father and mother were like the ONE they adored. And gradually I began to adore Him. *Adore* might not be the exact word, but I liked Jesus. He was believable and desirable.

My stammering made my parents feel for me and offer me all the protection they could, even to finishing sentences I could not complete. My tuberculosis devastated them. Their deepest concern, however, was me—the inside me that needed God—to awake to Him and come to the point where I would earnestly joyously cry, "Jesus, I want You as my Lord. I want Your salvation. I want to belong to You."

There were many times of stillness. First, because I was sick and lonely. Second, because gradually I was adoring Jesus until I was beginning, ever so slightly, to be like Him. I would be still and quiet for hours. No matter how hurt or how high my fever or how scared I was, I would listen. And I would think about Jesus.

The night I saw Him in my father's face I instantly recognized Him and cried, "JESUS!"

That was many years ago but the process continues. Through it I have come to know who I am, and what I am. A stillness runs deep in my character. I listen to Jesus a lot. I now find I listen to Him while I am doing other things. There seem to be two paths for me: one, I am listening to Jesus, communing with Him, talking to Him; two, I am preaching, or teaching, or counseling, or doing business, or jogging, or carrying on a conversation, or eating—it matters not, I am traveling both paths simultaneously.

JESUS HAS BECOME MY BREATH, MY SPEECH, MY LIFE. IN THE DUAL PROCESS OF LIVING FOR HIM IN BOTH THE SECULAR AND SPIRITUAL REALM OF THIS LIFE, MY THOUGHTS ARE NEVER FAR FROM HIM. HE IS THE MOST REAL PERSON I KNOW AND I KNOW HIM BETTER THAN I KNOW ANYONE ELSE.

Jesus can actually live at your house—be your constant companion. He said, "I will never leave thee" (Hebrews 13:5).

Say to yourself:

"Jesus lives at my house."

"I will let His presence there influence everything I do and say."

"I won't get angry."

"I'll be kind."

"I'll think of the other person and his problems and needs and be considerate and not judgmental. Since Jesus is here and with me each moment, my life will be a constant reflection of Him."

———

Say it again now: "Jesus lives at my house." If you really learn to live in that truth you'll never be the same again. You two (Jesus and you) will really go places together.

Now once again, "Jesus lives at my house."
My address is:

_____

(Please fill in your address.)

YOUR GOD-GIVEN KEY FOR TODAY
"Jesus Lives At My House."

WEDNESDAY

Key:
GOD WANTS ME TO PROSPER
AND BE IN HEALTH

or
The Greatest Discovery Evelyn And I Ever Made About
Health, Prosperity, And Spiritual Blessings

This conversation was recorded live on television.

EVELYN: Do you remember the morning when you found 3 John 2, Oral? Do you remember that day?

ORAL: Will I ever forget! I was hurrying out early that morning to make a class at Phillips University. I had a wife and two children and was trying to support them and go to school. I always had a habit of reading a little in the Bible every morning. But I forgot that morning and I ran out to catch the bus and then I stopped and ran back in, grabbed up my Bible, and it just fell open to that little book in the New Testament, 3 John—verse 2. There it was. I had read the New Testament over one hundred times, and had never noticed that verse.

EVELYN: What does it say?

ORAL: Well, it says, "Beloved, I wish above all things that thou mayest prosper and be in health, even as thy soul prospereth."

EVELYN: Do you remember what you said when you found it?

ORAL: I yelled and I said, "Evelyn, where are you; where are you?" And you were back in the kitchen, and said:

"I'm here. What do you want?"

And I rushed back. I said, "Look here, look here, here in the Bible!" And you said, "What is it?"

So I read, "Beloved, I wish above all things that thou mayest prosper and be in health, even as thy soul prospereth." And do you remember what you said?

EVELYN: Oh, I remember. I said, "Oral, is that in the Bible?"

ORAL: I said, "It sure is. It's right here."

EVELYN: And you know what I said? I said, "Well, you have read the Bible a hundred times, and if it's there, why didn't you find it before?"

ORAL: I said, "I don't know." But you also said, "Do you believe it?" I said, "Well, of course. I have to believe the Bible. I have to believe that." We had been down so low in our finances. We were so low that if we had died, they would have had to jack us up to bury us. All the furniture in our whole house didn't cost $300. I'd put my elbows on my dining room table and the thing would fall over in my lap.

EVELYN: Well, don't tell how bad it really was.

ORAL: Well, I did tell you that I could certainly believe it, but I didn't know it was in the Bible before.

EVELYN: Right. Now we had actually given to the Lord. We had always paid our tithe. Well, really I had paid my tithe before I married you, and you had paid yours. Then when we established a home, that was one of the things we decided to do together, to pay our tithe. That was one thing we did before we paid anything else. But we had never learned, really never been *taught*, that you can expect something back from God. And we've found that a lot of people don't know this. They give and they give, but they have never been taught to receive.

ORAL: Well, what I hadn't learned was that I wasn't to pay God as a debt I owed. And that's what *paying* tithes implies. We try to pay but we can't pay because **Jesus paid it all on the cross.** I hadn't learned Seed-Faith giving. I hadn't learned to give as a seed I plant.

EVELYN: That's true.

ORAL: And certainly I had not learned to receive back from God.

EVELYN: Well, it was such an exciting event in our house that morning. Remember, you didn't even go to school that day.

ORAL: No. (Don't tell the students around here at ORU though.) I didn't go to class all day long. You and I just walked and talked and cried and laughed and praised the Lord.

EVELYN: Then you said, "Evelyn, now this means that we're *supposed* to prosper. The Lord wants us to."

ORAL: And then I asked you, "Do you believe that if I ask the Lord for a new car, He would give us one?"

EVELYN: And I said, "No, Oral, I really don't." And I didn't. I had not been able to get it into my thinking that the Lord actually wanted our needs met.

ORAL: But you know, you bring something to my mind. Even though I did not know at that time, I had planted a seed of faith. You remember we were driving an old nineteen-hundred-and-something Chevrolet. And one day, shortly before this, I was backing out of our driveway and backed into my neighbor's car.

EVELYN: Yes, I remember.

ORAL: And I put a big dent in his car. And the first thought I had was, *Oh, well, he'll never know about it.* And then I said to myself, *Oh, but I'll know. I'll know.* So I parked my car and I got out and I knocked on the door of my neighbor. And this big man came to the door and said, "Yes?"

And I said, "Mister, I just ran into your car."

He said, "You did?"

I said, "Yes, and if you will go down and have an estimate made, I will pay for it."

He was kind of embarrassed and he said, "Oh, go on, go on."

But I said, "No, no. I'll do it."

He said, "Go on, go on."

So in a few days, I was out mowing my lawn.

EVELYN: That was one of the rare times.

ORAL: Now, darling, you don't have to get personal.

EVELYN: Well, it is true.

ORAL: I was mowing my lawn and this neighbor leaned over against the fence and said, "Hey there, young man, I've been noticing that old car of yours. You need a new car, don't you?"

And I said, "Well, that's an understatement."

He said, "How would you like to have a new car?"

I said, "I'd like it."

"Well," he said, "I'll tell you what to do. I'm a car dealer."

I said, "You are?" I didn't even know that.

He said, "You bring your car down and I'll sell it at the highest price, and then I will let you have a brand-new car at my cost."

And do you know, he was a Buick dealer!

EVELYN: And we didn't know that at the time, did we?

ORAL: No. When I grew up, the Buick was the ultimate for people like us. We drove the smaller more economic brands, but we thought some day we'd have a Buick. So we went down there, and this man . . .

EVELYN: Now wait a minute. You have forgotten part of the story. He took us to Minnesota to drive a Buick back.

ORAL: Yes, but what I do remember was the little mountain between. He sold mine high and sold his low, and I got a brand-new Buick for just a few dollars difference.

EVELYN: Well, you see, the Lord used him as an instrument to meet our need.

ORAL: Yes, and we were driving that new car back from Minnesota where he had gotten it from a dealer.

EVELYN: And we hadn't gone far when I said, "Stop the car, Oral. Stop the car."

And you said, "Well, what's wrong?"

And I said, "Now look. This is really the answer to that 3 John 2 that you read to me. Because the Lord said He wanted us to prosper. And, Oral, this is the first step. The Lord will really do what He said He would do." Honey, I don't know if you knew it, it meant a great deal to me. (At this point Evelyn bursts into tears.)

ORAL: Well, you don't have to cry about it.

EVELYN: I know. But I never really knew before that God was our Source. That we could really look to Him. And He would, He really would supply needs.

ORAL: Now you're getting me to crying.

EVELYN: But you know, when we stopped that car and had prayer and dedicated that car to God, that was the seed, Oral, the seed of faith for ORU. That very day. That was the seed. Because if we had not learned that God wanted to meet our needs, how could we ever have taught other people that God would meet their needs too? Just suppose we had gone out to some old army barracks someplace, and put that kind of building on this campus when we started to build Oral Roberts University!

ORAL: I'd have died.

EVELYN: Yes, you would, because you have always said God wants the best.

ORAL: That's right. I can't offer Him the second best. Evelyn, every time I try to do something for God the second or third or fourth best, I don't get anywhere. I only do well when I give Him my best.

EVELYN: Well, I just praise Him for that verse of Scripture. Because everything that has happened to us since that day started with that verse of Scripture you read.

ORAL: "Beloved, I wish above all things that thou mayest prosper."

EVELYN: This is God's highest wish for us.

ORAL: And we didn't know He wanted us to prosper.

EVELYN: No, we didn't. And I just praise Him every day for that verse and so many other verses like it throughout the whole Bible.

(See my book, SEED-FAITH COMMENTARY ON THE HOLY BIBLE.)

ORAL: And then He said, "I wish above all things that thou mayest prosper and be in health." You see, this is something else we didn't know at that time — that God really wanted to heal the sick. ". . . that you may be in health, even as your soul prospers." I had come to believe, you know, your *soul* could prosper. But now I realized that God wanted to prosper my body and my financial needs and take care of me and be my Source. I began to understand that. And of course this is what we are trying to share with our friends and with our students. In fact, Evelyn, you spoke to a group of young students here who are engaged.

EVELYN: Yes. I have spoken to several groups, and really I tried to help them through the Seed-Faith concept because one of their main questions was about finances now and after they marry. And I told them the thing I really know. And that is, if they will plant seeds of faith and ask the Lord to multiply them back and really look to Him as the Source of their supply, God will meet needs. I know this.

ORAL: He will prosper them.

EVELYN: I wish somebody had told me this when I was 18 or 19.

ORAL: But aren't you glad we found it out as a young married couple ourselves?

EVELYN: Oh, I'm so grateful to the Lord that I found out when I did.

ORAL: And we know it better now than ever.

(End of live television discussion.) Here's what happened next— Evelyn and I didn't get a chance to talk about it on the TV program.

WHAT YOU PREACH IS TOO BIG FOR ONE TOWN

A few weeks later I was washing our new car when Mr. Gus walked over.

"Mighty pretty car, isn't it?" he said.

"Yes, Mr. Gus," I said. "It is the nicest car I've ever owned, thanks to the Lord and you."

"Oral, this is the beginning of great things for you."

"I hope so."

"I know so. You won't be preaching to small crowds much longer."

"How is that?" I asked him.

"Son, I'm going to tell you something you probably already know in your heart. You'll soon be leaving Enid."

"Leaving Enid? Why?"

"Because what you preach is too big to be kept in one town. The world is waiting to hear it. Big crowds will be hearing you preach in a few months."

I thought to myself, how can this man know so much about God? About me? About the world?

"I've sold cars for many years and made a lot of money," he continued, as if he were answering my unspoken questions. "That's because I have faith in what I'm doing. As I told you before, I'm not a churchgoing man. But there is one thing I know: A man has to have faith in anything he does. I know you have faith in the Lord. No one can hear you preach, or know you personally, and doubt that. But you can have even more! Believe in what you preach. Believe in your prayers. Believe in the Lord and His power! Someday, Oral, you'll be the most powerful voice for God this country has ever known!"

Then Mr. Gus walked away, leaving a young preacher staring after him, speechless.

FAITH IS WHERE YOU FIND IT

God uses many different instruments to teach His lessons to us. He used a little captive maid to show Naaman, the famous Syrian general, the way to recover from his leprosy (2 Kings 5:3).

He used a shepherd lad to deliver the children of Israel from the giant Goliath and the Philistines (1 Samuel 17:40).

He used a virgin to bear the humanity of His only begotten Son (Luke 2:7).

He used an unlettered fisherman to be His Son's chief apostle (Mark 1:17).

In my case God used an unchurched man, whom I might never have met except that I damaged his car and stopped to tell him about it, to teach me that miracles still happen in the HERE and NOW.

"GOD WANTS ME TO PROSPER—AND BE IN HEALTH."

Now say to yourself:

"God wants me to prosper and be in health."

"God wants me to prosper and be in health."

Say it until it explodes in your mind and life. Things will change for you.

YOUR GOD-GIVEN KEY FOR TODAY

Now, once more, say it!

"God Wants Me To Prosper And Be In Health."

THURSDAY Key: JESUS IS AT THE POINT OF MY NEED

or
Discovering The Key Issue Gave Me A Balance I Never Had Before

Jesus is oriented toward the human being. We could say Jesus is oriented toward the human family and still be correct. But it's different when someone says:

"God loves all the human family,"

than when he says:

"God loves YOU."

Both statements are true. God *does* love all people. But when that love is crystallized and individualized for your life it becomes infinitely more precious and desirable. It means . . .

GOD IS IN THE MIDST OF LIFE . . . YOUR LIFE!

He is always in the midst of your life. And you are more important to Him than even His universe. You are more important to Him than your car, or your house, or anything you possess.

Here I discovered the *key issue* that gave me a balance I never had before—that God is in the midst of *your* life and He values it above everything else.

Do you recall the important incident in the life of our Savior when He was traveling with His disciples through a cornfield on the Sabbath day? His disciples were hungry. Having nothing to eat, they took the ears of corn and rubbed them in their hands so they could get the kernels (Luke 6:1). The enemies of our Lord, the Pharisees, being very religious but not spiritual (being outwardly pious but inwardly selfish and antisocial), said, "You've broken the Sabbath. Rubbing the ears of corn together constitutes work. You are not to do any work on the Sabbath; therefore, you have broken the Sabbath."

Jesus said, "Which one of you if he found his ox in a ditch on the Sabbath would not go and get him out?" (Luke 14:5). Then Jesus made this statement:

> *The sabbath was made for man, and not man for the sabbath* (Mark 2:27).

No greater statement was ever made by our Lord in connection with His concern and care about you and me as individuals. The great Sabbath day, with its rules and regulations which dated back to the days of Moses, is not greater than man. The hunger of these individuals was more important to Jesus Christ than strict religious observance of the Law of Moses. In contrast, the Pharisees had made the observance of the Law more important than life itself.

Jesus pointed out that man is more important than any special religious day. He said that every day is made for man . . . including the Sabbath. The Sabbath is made for man (Mark 2:27). Whatever accrues to man's benefit is important, even though it might happen on a so-called holy day. In our Lord's view . . .

EVERY day is a holy day.

Every day is a day in which to enjoy life.

Every day is a day to worship God.

Every day is a day in which you are the center of HIS love and He is the center of yours.

Every day He is concerned about the details of your existence, even numbering the hairs on your head (Matthew 10:30).

JESUS CHRIST IS PERSON-CENTERED. HE CARES ABOUT YOU! HE IS ALWAYS IN THE MIDST OF YOUR LIFE . . . HE IS AT THE POINT OF YOUR NEED. THIS IS THE KEY ISSUE THAT WILL GIVE YOU A BALANCE FOR YOUR LIFE . . . JUST AS IT HAS FOR ME!

You have needs—and that is a fact. You have loved ones in trouble.
You have physical problems that are a weight and thorn to you. You
may have financial problems. Whatever it is, the key issue is: "Jesus is
at the point of your need."

Now say it aloud:

"Jesus is at the point of my need."

Don't stop saying it. Today and every day you have a need to repeat it
to yourself until it becomes a part of your life-style.

YOUR GOD-GIVEN KEY FOR TODAY

"Jesus Is At The Point Of My Need."

Now, write it in right here:

_____

_____

FRIDAY Key:
I WILL OWE NO MAN ANYTHING BUT LOVE

or
What I Learned About Integrity And Life In Paying My Bills

Just prior to my launching out in 1947 into the healing ministry
to which the Lord had called me, I attended a healing revival where,
from all outward evidences, the evangelist's chief emphasis was on
raising money. He spent one full hour raising an offering in one service.

I know, for I timed him.

It made me sick at heart.

I knew the healing ministry was of God, that of all ministries it is
the most neglected, the most needed, and the most abused. The healing
ministry of Peter and John, of Paul, of Philip and Stephen in the New
Testament stand out as the greatest soul-winning ministries of all time.
I knew in my heart that a ministry patterned after their ministries
would bring millions to God.

But the evangelist's improper emphasis on money cancelled much
of the good he accomplished in the meeting. The people felt let down;
and many ministers, including myself, were justifiably disappointed
and critical.

God had laid His hand on me, saying:

"From this hour you will heal the sick and cast out devils
by My power."

I wanted to obey God but I had a very poor example of this ministry before me. Many of my friends had been disappointed in this evangelist and they naturally supposed I would be like him.

No one knows how close I came to saying, "Lord, I just can't do it. This example is so bad, and everyone will judge me in the light of this evangelist's actions. I can't bear the burden."

Instead, Evelyn and I talked it over. She said, "Oral, people may not believe you are sincere and honest at first, but if you conduct your ministry sincerely and honestly, someday people will know it and will receive you."

I knelt before the Lord and made a twofold consecration:

1. I would never enter the pulpit without feeling the presence of God.
2. And I would touch neither the gold nor the glory.

MY VOW IS TESTED

This vow was severely tested in one of our very first crusades. It was November 1947. I was preaching a crusade in a city auditorium in Kansas. There was a great spirit in the meetings and the people were responding to the invitation to accept Christ as Savior and Lord, and many were receiving healing for their illnesses and problems. There was only one thing wrong—the crusade expenses were not being met.

I took it as a personal failure of my ability to trust God. I allowed it to develop into a matter between God and me. The more I thought about the rent coming due and not having enough funds on hand to pay it, the more disturbed I became. I felt if I could not trust God for finances, how could I trust Him for people to be saved and the sick to be healed? If the Lord had really sent me to the people with the message of His healing and delivering power, I reasoned, and if He expected me to be His instrument, I had every right to expect sufficient funds to be raised to meet the obligations incurred by the ministry.

I could not bear to think of closing the crusade and leaving the city with the bills unpaid. I would sell every personal thing I had—my car, my clothes, everything, if need be—to pay those bills. Anything less was a contradiction to all I was and stood for in integrity and faith.

In spite of my thoughts, nothing changed. The crowds were large and enthusiastic, the spirit was high, and the results were miraculous. Still, each night we fell further behind in the crusade budget.

One evening I was behind the curtain waiting to be announced to preach. My brother Vaden was standing near me. All at once something broke within me and I said to him, "I am through."

He said, "What's wrong?"

I said, "I don't have the faith and God is not helping me."

He said, "Well, Oral, this is a wonderful crusade."

I said, "Yes, but we can't pay the bills, and you know that Papa always taught us to be honest and pay our debts. Vaden, I have done everything I know to do. I have preached the gospel, prayed for the sick, and people have come to God. Now we can't even pay the rent on this building. I can't continue and be honest.

"I am through.

It is all over.

I am going home."

Vaden left and soon returned with Evelyn. She was as white as a sheet. She knew when I said something I meant it. And there behind the curtain she put her arms around me and said, "Oral, I know it's hard but you can't quit now. The services are too good and the people are turning more to your ministry every day."

"Evelyn, you know my vow. You and I both promised God that we would never touch the gold nor the glory, but we have to have enough to meet our budget. You know it and I know it. I have prayed to God but He has not heard me. If I am to continue in this ministry God will meet our needs. If not, I am going home."

She said, "Oral, why don't you go out there and tell the crowd how you feel? Maybe they will do more."

I said, "No. God knows my needs. If I can't trust Him for this, how can I trust Him for the other things?"

She said, "Aren't you going to preach tonight?"

I said, "No, it's all over."

She and Vaden left. Pretty soon I heard her talking to the crowd. For a moment it startled me. She had never done this before. In fact, she always said, "When I stand up in front of an audience my mind sits down." But this time she was really talking.

I looked through the curtains. The people were looking at each other and wondering what the evangelist's wife was doing in the pulpit. Moving over to where I could see, as well as hear, I heard her say:

"Friends, you don't know what it means for me to stand up here tonight in my husband's place. And I am sure you don't know him as I do. He has come here by faith. No one is responsible for the financial needs to be met except him and God. He has preached and prayed for you and your loved ones each evening, but tonight he feels like quitting. Some of you have not realized your responsibility in supporting this ministry and we can't even pay the rent on the building. Whatever you may think of Oral, there is this about him that you must know. He is honest and if he cannot pay the rent he will not go on. He will not blame you. He will take it as a sign that God does not want him to continue his ministry, and he will stop. I know God has called him and that he must continue to obey God. I am asking you to help him. Together we can save this ministry."

As she spoke, big tears splashed down her face, and I felt smaller and smaller.

"What kind of a man am I," I asked myself, "who would quit when the going gets tough?"

This and other questions raced through my mind. Still, I could not change my mind. It was a point of integrity. God had called me, and my needs had to be met. I had heard of others leaving unpaid bills behind, bringing a reproach on the ministry. I would either pay the bills or I would not preach.

I heard Evelyn say, "Maybe some of you don't know we are in need. Perhaps you are waiting for my husband to say more about it. He won't say any more about it, for his trust is in God. Now I'm going to do something I've never done in my life. I want some man here to lend me his hat. I'm going to take a freewill offering for the rent."

Several men volunteered their hats. Evelyn selected a big-brimmed, black one. Holding the hat close to her, she bowed her head and prayed. I could tell she was embarrassed. Still, she was determined to save my ministry.

Then she said, "All right, now, the Lord and you must help us. Not just for people here who have need of healing, but for people in other places and lands. I am coming among you to pass the hat. I ask God to help you do your part and to bless you for helping us."

Oh, how small my faith was that night. I did not expect Evelyn to succeed. It seemed I had swung too far from the shore and it was time I was striking for home. The devil whispered, "Well, you have sunk pretty low when you have to let your wife take the offering. It's time you gave up."

I FELT I WAS NEAR TOTAL DEFEAT . . .
THEN THE HAND OF GOD TOUCHED ME

Listening to the devil and knowing Evelyn felt like dropping through the floor, I knew I was near total defeat. I actually was blaming God. The truth was that by not remembering who is the Source for my TOTAL supply I was letting God down . . . and myself.

We needed only $300 to finish paying the auditorium rent. But because we didn't have $300 it was as large in my mind as a sum ten times larger. It was at this moment that the hand of the Lord touched me. This is a sensation that is difficult to put into words, but I always know and recognize it when it comes to me. It is this touch that changes me from Oral Roberts, just an average human being, to a God-anointed man.

Suddenly a man stood up in the audience and asked Evelyn for permission to say a word. He was a Jewish businessman who had been attending the services and we had taken a meal in his home. He had been deeply impressed with the crusade and we were praying for him.

He said, "Folks, you all know me. I am not a Christian; but if I ever am, these people (gesturing toward the platform) have what I want. I have some money I owe the Lord. I'm starting this offering with $20."

Evelyn just stood there and waited. Suddenly a large red-haired woman stood and said, "I'm ashamed of every one in this audience, especially of myself. I'm the mother of several children. We have lots of needs and the Lord has helped us get many of these needs met through His servant, Oral Roberts. Now you listen to me; I want every one of you to do what I'm going to do." Then she opened her purse, pulled out a worn dollar bill, put it in the hat, and sat down. In a few moments people were standing and saying, "Mrs. Roberts, bring that hat over here."

As Evelyn went through the crowd, holding out the black hat with the big western brim, I was thoroughly ashamed of myself. When she had finished with the offering, I had the courage at last to step to the platform. I was conscious that every eye was upon me. I had no idea whether enough had been raised to meet the rent, but a new feeling was taking possession of me. My wife had done something few wives would have had courage to do for their husbands. I knew she had not done this only for me. A team of wild horses could not have pulled her up there. She had willingly gone before the people because she felt the ministry, which she knew God had given me, was endangered. I was proud of her and ashamed of myself for letting doubt and fear creep into my mind.

When the need was fully met I knew that it was an answer from God to me personally. It was also a gentle rebuke. When I stepped forward to take over the service I made no reference whatever to what Evelyn had done, feeling that I could only atone for it by taking my Bible and again preaching the gospel and praying for the people. I read my text and began to preach. I tell you I felt like a Niagara of power released. I knew that the tide had changed. This meeting ended with a packed house and with the audience standing en masse, urging us to return for another crusade.

I call God as my witness that I have maintained the vow I made many years ago — to touch neither the gold nor the glory. I have never gone before the people to preach without feeling the direct presence of God and taking Him with me. Neither have I touched the gold nor the glory.

On several occasions I have been offered large sums of money to pray for the healing of certain persons. Many times while I have been praying for the sick in the healing line people have thrust rolls of money into my hand or pocket. Each time I have handed it back.

Ministers have brought me sums of money, sometimes as much as a thousand dollars, from their people who either wanted to be healed or who had been blessed already through my ministry. Again I have refused to accept it. Some of these ministers reported to their churches, and even to our congregations, that this was what convinced them that there are some ministers today whom money could not sway.

A wealthy man signed his name to a blank check and told me if I would pray for his dying child, I could fill in the check with any amount I desired and the check would be honored. I turned him down. (Of course I prayed for his child anyway.)

I have never accepted any sum of money or any other gift offered to me in connection with my praying for someone to be healed. I do not mean to suggest that the people who have offered me money privately are trying to buy their way or that they are selfish. They merely want to show their appreciation, or in some cases they want to do something to get my ministry of prayer in their behalf.

But I feel that to take the money would be to violate my pledge to God. This way I remain free. No man controls me. I "owe no man anything, but . . . love" (Romans 13:8). I can look into the face of every person who seeks my prayers and say, "I have coveted no man's silver, or gold" (Acts 20:33).

Now, say to yourself: "I will owe no man anything but love." If this idea unfolds to you in its fullness and comes alive in your spirit, all your financial circumstances will change. You will be free of obligation and bondage to any person.

YOUR GOD-GIVEN KEY FOR TODAY

Say again:

"I Will Owe No Man Anything But Love."

SATURDAY

Key:
SOMETHING GOOD IS GOING TO HAPPEN TO ME

or
Why I Tell People: Something Good Is Going To Happen To You!

Recently as I entered an airport terminal in a large city a man rushed up to me with a big smile on his face. "Aren't you Oral Roberts?" he asked.

"Yes, I am," I replied.

"Look, just keep saying it!" he said.

"Keep saying what?" I asked.

"You make my day when you say on television, **Something GOOD is going to happen to you!**" he said. Then he told me some good things that God had brought into his life since he began to believe God would do it.

A doctor friend of mine wrote me the other day and said, "Just as your television program was coming on the air, my 90-year-old mother came in to watch. And you were saying, SOMETHING GOOD IS GOING TO HAPPEN TO YOU! She straightened up to her full five feet and said, 'Let 'er happen, Sonny!'"

Anybody can dwell on his problems until he gets so low that the devil can climb on his shoulders and keep him down. But faith in God changes your perspective. An attitude of expecting something GOOD to happen to you will not only "make your day" but also revolutionize your life. Looking to God as your Source brings . . .

the mountain-moving,

problem-solving,

need-supplying

power of God into your life!

It's like the old boy who had a flat on a country road at night, and he didn't have a bumper jack. Looking around, he saw a light in a distant farmhouse. He said, "That farmer will probably have a jack."

So he trudged about a mile to the farmhouse. All the way he was building up a morbid expectancy.

I wonder if that farmer has already gone to bed?

I understand farmers are a little suspicious of strangers at night. In fact, I've heard they sleep with a shotgun by their beds.

He had better not chase me off his property!

By this time the man had reached the farmhouse. He knocked on the door. The farmer stuck his head out and asked, "What do you want?"

"You can just keep your old jack!" the man blurted out.

Humorous—perhaps, but sometimes don't we act as if we think God is *not* willing to give—*not* ready to help us? And by our attitude of doubt and negative anticipation, rob ourselves of God's gifts?

Our miracle can only begin when we cease being negative and start being positive, when we recognize that part of the problem is inside us. That regardless of how much power God has, miracle power will never fully be effective in our lives until we cooperate . . . until we fully expect something good to happen.

———————

Now say:
"SOMETHING GOOD IS GOING TO HAPPEN TO ME."
Unless you come alive and are responsive to the fact that something good *REALLY IS* going to happen, you'll miss some of God's best. Good things will happen and you'll miss the full blessing and impact for what you need today.

YOUR GOD-GIVEN KEY FOR TODAY

Now, once more say:

"Something Good Is Going To Happen To Me."

FIRST WEEK

SUNDAY	DEVIL, YOU CAN'T TOUCH ME; I AM GOD'S PROPERTY
MONDAY	GOD CARES ABOUT ME
TUESDAY	JESUS LIVES AT MY HOUSE
WEDNESDAY	GOD WANTS ME TO PROSPER AND BE IN HEALTH
THURSDAY	JESUS IS AT THE POINT OF MY NEED
FRIDAY	I WILL OWE NO MAN ANYTHING BUT LOVE
SATURDAY	SOMETHING GOOD IS GOING TO HAPPEN TO ME

SECOND WEEK

How God Will Open Your Eyes To The Laws Of Seed-Faith Which Will Never Fail You

SUNDAY Key: GOD'S WAY WILL BE MY WAY

or
How You Can Learn God's Way Of Doing Things . . . That They Are Based On Eternal Laws . . . Laws So Exact And Perfect They Always Work For You

ONE day in the early '50s while I was driving through a beautiful well-watered valley in the Pacific Northwest, seeing the harvests of the fields and the farmers gathering and selling and prospering, many Scriptures in the Bible came alive to me:

While the earth remaineth, seedtime and harvest . . . shall not cease (Genesis 8:22).

Whatsoever a man soweth, that shall he also reap (Galatians 6:7).

He that ministereth seed to the sower both minister bread for your food, and multiply your seed sown (2 Corinthians 9:10).

If ye have faith as a grain of mustard seed, ye shall say unto this mountain, Remove hence to yonder place; and it shall remove; and nothing shall be impossible unto you (Matthew 17:20).

It is more blessed to give than to receive (Acts 20:35).

For God loveth a cheerful giver (2 Corinthians 9:7).

Surely blessing I will bless thee, and multiplying I will multiply thee (Hebrews 6:14).

Give, and it shall be given unto you; good measure, pressed down, and shaken together, and running over, shall men give into your bosom. For with the same measure that ye mete withal it shall be measured to you again (Luke 6:38).

But my God shall supply all your need according to his riches in glory by Christ Jesus (Philippians 4:19).

Concerning giving and receiving (Philippians 4:15).

Beloved, I wish above all things that thou mayest prosper and be in health, even as thy soul prospereth (3 John 2).

Scripture after Scripture poured through my mind. Scriptures I knew and believed and which I had practiced to some extent but never in a conscious, planned, and *focused* way.

I saw where I had missed it. I started rereading my Bible, all of it; not once, but many times. When I clearly saw an idea about God, I tried it. It worked every time. Not always quickly but given time and a little patience, it never failed to work. Pretty soon a pattern formed, a way of life. I saw it and began to work at it with my whole self. I saw God had a way of doing things. Yes, God has a way of doing things!

GOD'S WAY OF DOING THINGS IS BASED ON ETERNAL LAWS . . . LAWS SO EXACT AND PERFECT THEY ALWAYS WORK

At first I called it MY BLESSING-PACT COVENANT WITH GOD. I made a pact with God to learn His way of doing things and to do them — then I asked Him to bless me. I began doing it and expecting miracles from both expected and unexpected sources.

At first I asked for finances since my work suffered too much from financial lack. And the letters from my friends and partners indicated that they too were suffering with bills piling up and no money to pay them. The church put very little emphasis on God helping you with your finances. It was a spiritual emphasis which was good but too often it left out the physical needs, such as health and prosperity.

HOW I CHANGED MY METHOD OF GIVING

I began to give differently from my past practice of tithing. I loved tithing and still do. But I discovered it was more of an Old Testament form of giving, which is not really giving but more like paying a debt. Paying God. Paying a debt to God. Not paying tithes was a form of robbing God (Malachi 3:8,9). Still God blessed the tither, including me. The trouble was I was not taught to receive back or to *expect* miracles. So I tithed but not with an exuberant faith that God would meet all my needs.

Then Jesus opened my eyes, not as I see so clearly today, but enough for me to start giving through my Blessing-Pact with Him. I began to understand that whatever I gave, God would send back . . . multiplied. He would send it either from sources I usually drew from or from sources totally unknown to me, but He would send back more than I had given.

It worked. Oh, how it worked for me . . . and for those who accepted their Blessing-Pact Covenant with God as I led them in practicing it.

I was getting close to who my Source was but it was not clear enough yet.

I was, through my Blessing-Pact Covenant with God, giving and expecting from both expected and unexpected sources.

Notice in the past I had been expecting not from THE SOURCE, but sources. In other words, wherever I received from, or whomever I received from as a result of my giving, I counted as another source. But not as THE ONLY ONE SOURCE: GOD. These were instruments of God of course, but they often proved unreliable and left me frustrated. Worst of all, they left me saying, "Why, God, why?" I was questioning God and sometimes blaming God . . .

I can sympathize with anyone who blames God, or who asks, "Why?" I've done it too many times, all to my detriment.

Thank God a million times I finally found the real meaning of what I was getting close to: I found the Three Keys of Seed-Faith. (I'll tell you what they are further in this book.)

I FOUND GOD'S WAY OF DOING THINGS HAD
THREE KEYS . . . YES, THREE KEYS . . .

I'll always be grateful to God for leading me a step at a time. First into tithing, then beyond tithing into a Blessing-Pact in which I gave, expecting my giving to be given back and added to by both expected and unexpected sources. Without these I might never have gotten into the MIRACLE OF SEED-FAITH which I am totally convinced IS God's way of doing things through His Son Jesus Christ, our Savior, and then through His followers, for the meeting of all our needs — and for leading us into becoming real disciples, daily, of our Lord.

From my study of the Holy Word of God I realized it wasn't a variety of sources through which God would bless me but one Source only: GOD HIMSELF. The change that discovery made in my attitude which so often got negative and bad was revolutionary . . . it was *miraculous.*

Yes, I live a miracle life. Miracles happen to me. I get at least one new miracle every day. I don't doubt any more that I will receive miracles: little ones, middle-sized ones, big ones, an unending series of them. That's the truth and I'm getting things done that are hard to believe. You almost have to see them to believe them. But not one of these miracles is an accident, or a onetime thing, or a sometime happening. Each is repeatable. Each is dependable in its coming to me. Best of all, the same kinds of miracles are beginning to happen to tens of thousands of others who are learning GOD'S WAY OF DOING THINGS SO THAT AS THEY DO THEM, THEY KNOW THEIR MIRACLES WILL COME AND KEEP COMING UNTIL THE DAY THEY LEAVE THIS WORLD FOR HEAVEN.

The covenant I made with God is my Seed-Faith Covenant based entirely on the life of Jesus Christ. I've had to change some of my ways of doing things, as I've already indicated. I am glad I did because now I am into God's multiplication of seed sown—seed that I sow in faith to God, the Source of my total supply. Experiencing the miracles of multiplication in my life, and seeing others experiencing it beyond their fondest dreams, is truly an experience of healing for the whole man. For what I'm talking about takes away the inborn fear that "giving" means taking something away, leaving us diminished. It brings you into a simple, childlike faith that only what you give does God multiply back for the meeting of your needs.

———•———

WHEN YOU LEARN GOD'S WAY OF DOING THINGS, AND DO THEM, YOU DISCOVER WHO YOUR SOURCE IS, AND YOU FIND YOUR GREATEST SUPPLY BY GIVING TO HIM, AND THEN EXPECTING MANY MIRACLES FROM YOUR SEED-FAITH LIVING . . .

So say to yourself until you know it by heart:
"I will learn God's way of doing things . . . and DO them that way. Then I will ask Him to bless me and expect Him to do it."

YOUR GOD-GIVEN KEY FOR TODAY

"God's Way Will Be My Way!"

MONDAY Key: GOD IS MY SOURCE

or
How I Really Began Understanding Who My Source Is . . . And Ways I Learned To Trust In Him And Him Alone

In the Blessing-Pact Covenant with God I had the *beginning* of the most powerful idea in history for a follower of Jesus Christ. And even though Jesus gave me a little knowledge at a time, leading me a step at a time, I was faithful in trying to personally do exactly as I saw in the Bible.

Everything I said about the Blessing-Pact was true although many —particularly high religious leaders—misunderstood it, and often violently opposed it, including talking and writing against it. But they couldn't stop it. Once a group of such leaders met with me and tried to tear me up, telling me that in offering the Blessing-Pact I was not preaching the gospel.

Becoming very upset I said, "What I am preaching is THE gospel of Jesus Christ. Thousands are receiving Christ, are being filled with the Holy Spirit, are being healed, and through the Blessing-Pact they are for the first time seeing that God is a totally good God and is concerned for their finances and everyday needs, as well as for their souls."

They wouldn't listen and accused me of deceiving the people. I said, "But it works. It brings God into the NOW of a person's actual needs."

Words flew, bitterness developed. Finally I grew impatient. I said, "If you really mean what you said about what I'm preaching about the Blessing-Pact as a means of God supplying people's needs, then I will walk out of here this minute and I will never enter your churches again as long as I live."

The leader saw I meant it. When he made one more statement I said, "I meet people from your churches. They write me or talk to me about their needs. They have trouble in their homes, in their employment, in their finances, in their relationships with people; they are sick, they hurt, they are full of anxiety and fear, they are often so discouraged they want to give up. You intimate to them that if they'll just come to church on Sunday and go through the forms, they'll be saved and go to heaven. Well, I have news for you. There's more to Christianity than that. I'm a loyal church member but God has shown me that my trust in Him and my loving people and helping them get their needs met IS EVERYTHING. And it means I am becoming a disciple, or daily follower of the Lord."

Then I said, "The only church people I know who are getting their needs met, and experiencing miracles constantly in their lives, are those who believe God is in the *now*. And every one of them is practicing some form of a Blessing-Pact with God, maybe not in the terminology I use, but certainly the principles are the same. Besides knowing they are going to heaven they are experiencing the kingdom of heaven in their lifetime." The meeting finally ended on a good note and we are still friends today.

But I believe if God is not in the NOW, He has never been. If He can't supply your needs on earth, He can't do it in heaven. I agree there are specified needs God will meet only in the Resurrection but I also believe—and KNOW—the resurrection at least starts in this life! I've learned this from my own experience.

HOW I DEVELOPED A DEEPER UNDERSTANDING OF SEED-FAITH
IN THE MIDST OF A PERSONAL CRISIS WHICH THREATENED
TO DESTROY THIS MINISTRY

I really began to understand God is my Source when I was desperate with my needs and had no one to turn to, no place to run and hide. God had to become my Source of total supply or I was finished. I was in the midst of traveling the world in crusades, of building a university for God based on His authority and on the Holy Spirit, and carrying on a nationwide radio and television program.

In the midst of it God spoke to my heart to return to the church of my youth to which He revealed to me He was going to give a great renewing in the Holy Spirit. After much prayer and soul-searching I obeyed God, and was graciously received.

The Scripture God gave me for this move was:

> For a great door . . . is opened unto me, and there are many
> adversaries (1 Corinthians 16:9).

A great door opened for my ministry of healing but there was much opposition from people everywhere who had formerly been my friends. In one month at least one-half of my partners left me. Our finances decreased almost fifty percent and I had to go to the bank and borrow to pay those working in our office and teaching at ORU. Bitter letters poured in saying I was backslidden and that I had sold out the power of God, and that the church I rejoined was—well, I won't mention the many hard things they said.

These were good people who didn't try to think for themselves, but followed their denominational leader's point of view. It was a failure to understand that God can speak to one of His followers, and that person can hear and obey. I suffered untold vilification and loss. Really, in another month everything might have been gone—the University, my whole ministry.

But I knew God. I knew He was telling me His plan. I knew out of my need I must plant a new seed. I was coming into an understanding of Seed-Faith that would bless millions—I knew in my heart. However, how was I going to know it not only in my heart but in my head, in my intellect, and how would I apply it? That was the question.

ONE DAY I HAD IT OUT WITH GOD: WAS HE GOD TO ME,
OR WAS HE NOT?
WAS IT ALL OVER FOR ME OR WAS THERE MORE HE WANTED
ME TO DO?

God has spoken to me many times, sometimes clearly, audibly— other times from His Word, from a sermon, from His presence with me, from what I heard or saw someone do, and in other ways that are hard to explain. One way He has spoken to me is in an idea from His Word that emerges over the months and years. An idea that won't go away. It's there inside me constantly, taking deeper root and growing until I have to do something about it.

This time it was the idea that I had to make GOD MY SOURCE OF TOTAL SUPPLY. There were many instruments He would use but none of them was my Source. Before, I had been able to see God as my Source but I also saw other sources such as my crusades, the University, the television, my partners, and help from unexpected sources. These too were sources to me. Therefore, when one of them dried up or stopped, I had one less source. What hurt me so badly now was that so many of them were dissolving and I was being left alone. From out of the depths of my soul the idea that had been growing there came to full harvest:

THERE IS ONLY ONE SOURCE: GOD

Philippians 4:19 hit me hard: "But my God shall supply all your need according to his riches in glory by Christ Jesus."

This is the first Miracle Key of Seed-Faith: GOD IS MY SOURCE OF TOTAL SUPPLY.

This means He will supply all my needs. And He will supply them not depending on the economy being good, or depending on my former partners, or depending on my old methods of doing God's work or anything else—my supply would come from God my Source according to HIS RICHES, HIS LOVE FOR ME, HIS POWER TO HELP ME, HIS WISDOM TO GUIDE ME.

God became so big to me I saw I had no need or problem that could not be solved. God was bigger than all my needs put together. But only *He* was that big. Any other source I could turn to was too small, too apt to change or fail me.

About that time Richard, my son, began to sing for me with his fine young God-given talent. He sang a song titled "How Big Is God?" and as I listened I nearly burst inside as I felt God growing bigger in me.

Whether everything fell or stayed alive really made little difference. Instantly it hit me . . .
God is so big He cannot fail,
so wise He cannot make a mistake,
so strong He cannot let me down,
and too good to do me wrong!

I began to feel new confidence, new strength pouring into me, a new *knowing* that all I had to do was obey God and God as my Source would be with me in every way . . . *all* the way.

I also began to realize God was not married to or bound by methods but by His own eternal principles. Some of my methods so beautifully used by God had run their course, but my principles were His and I must never try to change any of them. Methods, yes; principles, no. And this was my position as 1967 came to a close and I stood among the falling remnants of the method I had been using for 20 years in the healing ministry.

I pondered God's way up till then.

1. God had given me a lifelong command to take His healing power to my generation. Methods must change, but my command was eternal with me. I would, as long as I had life, pray for the healing of the people.

2. God had put me on television and the method I was using started in 1954 and had swept through America's living rooms with a revelation to millions that God still heals people today. And hundreds of thousands had been helped through the particular method I used.

3. God had told me to build Him a university, to build it on His authority and on the Holy Spirit—to raise up my students to hear His voice, and to go to the uttermost bounds of the earth. Their work was to exceed mine and in that God was pleased.

4. God had given me a special command to answer people's letters with a compassion and a faith for their needs.

5. God had led me to publish books, magazines, tracts—numbering into the millions each year.

6. Above all, God had filled me with His Spirit and told me the time had come to emphasize its charismatic dimensions to people, and particularly to the church. He said I was to be one to bring His healing power to the sick body of His bride.

None of this was to change except some of the methods. I've always been able to change, not for change sake, but when change was needed. Most people, however, fear any change. They seem to think change means taking something away—being diminished in what they are or what they have. They think they will lose something. In my study of Seed-Faith in the Bible I saw that those using it, as shown by Jesus, did not fear changing their methods of doing things. If they had, the little boy who gave his lunch to Jesus, the disciples who loaned their boat to Jesus, the widow who gave God her last two pennies, would never have experienced their Seed-Faith being miraculously multiplied in their lives, and through them, multiplied to meet the needs of others. They never would have learned to become good disciples of Jesus.

The fact was they thrilled at learning new ways from Jesus, the Master, of giving **not as a debt they owed but as a seed they sowed,** and of daring to believe God would multiply back their seed sown.

That was a direct and divine revelation to me at a time of almost complete desperation in my life and ministry.

What did I do? I obeyed God! I changed my methods but held on to the principles He had given me when I began this ministry in 1947.

THE FIRST CHANGE HAD TO DO WITH GIVING

We were givers. I was a giver. My Blessing-Pact Covenant with God was still in effect but a strange thing had happened. I had let it partly lapse when my crusades ended in 1968. For an entire year, as I waited on the Lord to direct me for the methods He wanted me to use in the future, I failed to emphasize the Blessing-Pact.

Bob DeWeese, my associate evangelist, said, "Oral, the Blessing-Pact is probably the greatest concept you have given the people to get their needs met. It has helped thousands of people through the years that I've been with you. I feel the people are being cheated if you don't reestablish it and reemphasize it among your partners."

Bob was a man who never spoke to me on vital matters until he had thought things through and felt deeply about them.

Soon after that my longtime associate, Lee Braxton, talked to me of what the Blessing-Pact had done among the people, how they had talked to him, and of the tremendous benefits to him and his family. He too felt I should, as he said, "put it on the front burner again." Lee has a way of saying things that always strike home.

Evelyn also talked to me reminding me of personal needs we had faced that appeared completely impossible and that the Blessing-Pact had been God's key for us. "Why are you not saying more about the Blessing-Pact?" she asked me.

Patti and Richard, who were just launching their marriage, made the Blessing-Pact a cornerstone of their future. In fact, only by practicing it they had been able to save their marriage which since has blossomed into a beautiful "medley."

My son-in-law Marshall Nash and my daughter Rebecca talked to me. Marshall, a struggling young businessman at that time, said that only through the Blessing-Pact had he had the courage to start AND TO CONTINUE. He cited incidents of doors opening which would never have been opened had he and Rebecca not practiced the Blessing-Pact. His partner Doug Mobley used his Blessing-Pact so effectively that he had inspired Marshall beyond his own plans and they laid plans for growth spiritually in their relationships and finances, which today are coming to pass beyond even what they could ask or think. Both say, "Our giving to God has kept us going as young builders when many others went under."

"BROTHER ROBERTS, HAVE YOU GIVEN UP THE BLESSING-PACT?"

Then a brother in Christ came out of nowhere, it seemed, reminding me of his conversion to Christ through my ministry some 15 years before. He was a bankrupt young man spiritually, financially, physically, and everything else. Right out of the Korean War he was almost completely broken. He said, "Not only did Christ save my soul and give me a healing as you preached in the crusade, but also I got an understanding of the Blessing-Pact that showed me how God was interested in me as a person, how He was concerned about my needs, and how I could prosper in good times and bad."

Then he said, "The Blessing-Pact has sustained me through all these years. Not once has it failed to work. I'm stronger than ever before. My career is doing extremely well. I love God more than ever. Yet I'm troubled. The past several months Abundant Life (our monthly magazine) has carried almost nothing about the Blessing-Pact, whereas before, you had something on the Blessing-Pact in every issue to inspire people like me."

"Brother Roberts," he said, his eyes filling with tears, "the Blessing-Pact has become my way of life, God's way for me to share my life with Him in His plans, and the key to meeting my needs. Why have you not been preaching it the past months? Have you given it up?"

I said, "Given up my Blessing-Pact? Never! I guess I've said no more because I thought I had said too much and people perhaps thought that was my only concern."

He said, "Well, the Blessing-Pact pulled me out of a life that had hit bottom and it has put me on top and kept me there. Even though I have grasped its principles and it's working in my life, I still love to hear you talk about it. After all, God gave it to you first for people today and I love to get any new thoughts He gives you."

I knew these various individuals had been sent to me. They were not speaking on their own but God was stirring my soul to move forward again, and the Blessing-Pact was His key.

This time I understood something not revealed to me before. This was to find in the Scriptures exact terms which anyone could understand. *Blessing-Pact* was clear to me and clear to those close followers of my crusade ministry. Outside them it was a term hard to understand.

So again I went back to God and His Holy Word. I put in up to 12 hours a day with my Bible, my study and prayers. Then the Lord focused my attention on Philippians 4:19, the key Scripture for the Blessing-Pact. I thought there was nothing more I could find in it but I read it again and again, and kept on reading it, including the verses before and after it. I stayed with it. I could feel God's presence tingling through me. I knew I was getting close to something very important.

Then it hit me: GOD IS MY SOURCE. Not sources in the plural but SOURCE in the singular. Never again was I to say your giving will be multiplied by sources both expected and unexpected. I would say God will use many different instruments but He alone is THE Source, THE Eternal Fountain itself.

GOD HAS GOT TO BE FIRST IN YOUR LIFE

Not the instrument He uses, not even the blessing of supply itself —but God, and God alone. The truth kept expanding: **Give God who is your Source your best, then ask Him for His best.** Look to God for your supply. GOD IS THE SOURCE OF YOUR TOTAL SUPPLY. God. God. God.

This means God is now *my* God. I must not be so over-awed by God that I cannot think of Him in the most personal terms. Not simply God of the universe, God of the human race, God of eternity, but God of Oral Roberts, my God.

St. Paul said, "My God."

Jesus said, "My God."

Jesus taught us in the Lord's Prayer to say "Our Father," or "My Father."

God is a Person to me, *my* God very personal, very near, and caring for me in my humanness.

God is *with* me.

He is *in* me.

He is *for* me. (Psalms 56:9 says it: God is for me.)

He is for me; therefore, who can successfully be against me. (Romans 8:31 says it clearly.)

He is over, above, around and underneath me (Deuteronomy 33:27).

He covers me with His presence (Psalms 91:4).

My God shall supply all my needs. That says a lot. That says it all. My God shall supply . . . He shall supply. God is in the business of supplying my needs. All of my needs. This makes God the Source of my total supply, not merely the Source of supply for some or part of my need, but ALL of it.

"For my God shall supply all my need according . . ." According to what measure or power? "According to his riches in glory by Christ Jesus."

According to God's riches, not man's—but God's riches. According to Jesus Christ who sat where I sit, who felt what I feel, who returned to heaven as the unlimited Christ, freely restored with all the riches of His Father in heaven.

So because I have made Him MY God, as my God HE WILL supply ALL my needs according to HIS RICHES in glory by CHRIST JESUS. I have found a Source for my life, and for all my need for my days on earth, and for all eternity.

It's so stupendous, so great it almost boggles my mind. Yet it is true, absolutely true. God is my Source, my Source of total supply, for all my need.

I am linked with God and God is linked with me in the bonds of an everlasting love and faith. I believe in God, He believes in me. He is my God, I am His child, His disciple or follower. He is my God who will supply. He won't merely say it, He will do it. His supply is here with me in the NOW, if I can only understand that it is. It is here with me because He is *my* God, my God who supplies ALL my need.

This means everything to me, to my peace of soul and peace of mind. It calms and relaxes me to know who my Source is. I don't feel alone anymore like I used to. My need is His need now, His supply is mine. He is here with me and in me, and the measure of His supply for my need is according to His riches—not any man's—by Christ Jesus in heaven.

God as my Source is . . .
>   my Lord and Savior . . .
>   my hope and whole life . . .
>   my protection and guide . . .
>   my total supply . . .
>   my all in all . . .

GOD IS THE SOURCE OF YOUR TOTAL SUPPLY

This means you start with God . . . you stay with God . . . and you end with God. In every situation you remember WHO YOUR SOURCE IS (Philippians 4:19).

An immediate effect on me was to look back on the 20 great years of traveling in the healing ministry and to realize it still burned in me. Nothing had changed except the crusades as they had been carried on were over. That method, so long anointed and right for me and millions, now had to give way to another God-ordained method.

Who was my Source for this new method?

God.

Who would be my Source of total supply for merging the old method with the new and carrying it on to help even more people?

God my Source of total supply.

A feeling of relief, release, and peace filled me. A knowing came into my heart about my future ministry. I knew it would go. Not yet did I know the method or direction, but I knew my Source was in charge. I was His property and I would attempt to do what He laid on my heart.

———◆◆———

THERE IS ONLY ONE SOURCE—GOD!
HE IS THE SOURCE OF YOUR TOTAL SUPPLY—
OF MY TOTAL SUPPLY.

Say it. Say it. Say it now. Say it again. Say it an hour from now. Say it through the day. Say it when you are in bed. Say it when you are awake. Keep on saying it until it lives in your spirit, your understanding . . . until YOU ARE ACTUALLY DOING IT DAY AFTER DAY. Make it a part of your consciousness and subconsciousness.

The seasons have a rhythm of always coming—SO LET THIS BE A RHYTHM OF YOUR LIFE.

YOUR GOD-GIVEN KEY FOR TODAY

Now say again and again:

"God Is My Source."

"God Is My Source."

"God Is My Source."

TUESDAY

Key:
I WILL PLANT SEED AND GOD WILL
MOVE MY MOUNTAINS . . .

or
A Conversation I Had With Jesus About Making My Faith Like
A Seed I Plant And Causing Mountains Of Need
To Move In My Life

(This happened while I was up in the Prayer Tower alone with God.)
If ye have faith as a grain of mustard seed, ye shall say unto this mountain, Remove hence to yonder place; and it shall remove; and nothing shall be impossible unto you (Matthew 17:20).

Jesus said those words and now it was as if He had sat down with me in the special room I have in the Prayer Tower and was talking of them out of His heart to mine—almost like a conversation. Here is how I felt the sense of our conversation was—not verbatim, just the sense of it.

Jesus: *Son, when I tell you to have faith as a grain of mustard seed I am talking about Seed-Faith or having faith as a seed you plant.*

Me: Lord, I always thought You were saying that if we could have even a little faith it would grow until it would be big enough to move our mountains. I thought the mustard seed was the smallest seed in Your time in Palestine but when planted it became the largest tree of all.

Jesus: *Yes, all that is true. However, there's much more, something more fundamental to the eternal laws of the Father. From the beginning of creation of earth and man, eternal laws of seed-time and harvest were given. In My coming to show people what the Father is like, to demonstrate His love, and His principles, and finally to give My life on the cross and rise again to be alive forevermore . . . I have come to remind men of this eternal law of sowing and reaping, or of giving and receiving.*

Me: Lord, is planting seed what You call giving, and is reaping the harvest from the seed what You call receiving? Is that what You mean?

Jesus: *Exactly.*

Me: Then the seed of giving is the seed of faith! And the seed has to be planted BEFORE we can speak to our mountain of need to be removed! The Seed-Faith comes first! Then, and only then, do you speak to your mountain of need!

[This was a whole new thought to me. Although giving was a key part of the Blessing-Pact, it had not become quite clear that giving was the SEEDING for our miracle (Key Number 2) from which God our Source would multiply back with such an increase it would be bigger and more powerful than our mountains of needs and problems. Many times I had prayed—even pleaded—for God to move my mountains.

NOW I REALIZED MY GIVING WAS THE SEED OF FAITH ITSELF AND I COULD DIRECT THIS SEED TO MOVE A SPECIFIC MOUNTAIN OF NEED

It was powerful, logical, scriptural, workable, believable! And I took it as the very truth of God and of nature itself. For did not every farmer know this as a fundamental truth? Did he not prepare the soil and put in seed first—BEFORE he expected the God of the harvest to multiply the seed back far greater than what he had planted? Did not every woman who raised a garden, or flowers in her yard, first put in the seed? Of course!

And this rocked me! In the Blessing-Pact, hadn't I personally been giving of myself first and urging the people to do so? Yes, I had. The seed part, though, was a fresh revelation.]

Jesus: *Son, study My sermon on the mount and especially the core of it and you will see that giving is the heart of all I taught the people.*

Then He directed my attention particularly to St. Luke 6:38:

> *Give, and it shall be given unto you, good measure, pressed down, and shaken together, and running over, shall men give into your bosom . . .*

THIS IS WHAT I NOW CALL "SEEDING FOR YOUR MIRACLE" — THE SECOND MIRACLE KEY OF SEED-FAITH

He then directed me to notice that the Golden Rule is something we are to DO . . . and DO FIRST. ". . . as ye would that men should do to you, do ye also to them likewise" (Luke 6:31). (I began to understand that the thrust of His entire teaching in the Sermon on the Mount was on what we do first, such as being pure in heart, forgiving first, making peace first, hungering and thirsting for righteousness first, seeking the kingdom of God first, and giving *first.* It was thrilling for me to see all this.)

Me: Jesus, I notice in the Old Testament, giving was usually based on receiving first and you gave after you received. You received then you gave. Actually the law of tithing is based on receiving ten parts of something, then giving the tenth part back to God. It was a debt owed to God. You *paid* your tithes. This is the essence of Malachi 3:8,9, isn't it?

Jesus: *That is correct. I came to pay that debt that no man could fully pay. On the cross I paid it all with My life given as a seed I sowed. I am the seed of David that the Father promised to be the Messiah, the Christ. Since I gave My life on the cross and paid the debt for every man, I restored giving to its original purpose in the beginning.*

Me: Jesus, what is that purpose?

Jesus: *In the beginning it was first seedtime followed by the harvest (Genesis 8:22). In nature, this has never changed. In the times of the prophets in the Old Testament, this law was practiced many times, such as what the prophet Elijah did with the hungry widow of Zarephath (1 Kings 17). But when Israel became a nation the children of Israel had to be taught God's ownership, such as the firstborn son was God's, the tenth dollar was God's, the seventh day was God's, the seventh year all the land was to lay idle. And the fiftieth year was to be the year of Jubilee when all land in Israel which had been sold was to be restored to the original owners, all slaves freed, all debts cancelled. It was the Father's way of teaching them His ownership of them.*

All these things, including the tithe, were to pay God but no man could fully pay.

Israel robbed God of the tithe, of the seventh day, and of the other things representing His ownership. It became a burden greater than they could bear so God decided to send Me, His only begotten Son, the seed of David, to pay the full price of redemption and restoration. Now since My death and resurrection (My seed-time and harvest) giving is not a debt you owe, not something you pay . . . for I have paid the debt. Giving under the New Testament is a seed you sow.

Me: As a Christian, a follower of You, my giving is no longer a debt I owe but a seed I sow?

Jesus: *Yes, I fulfilled the old law of tithing by paying the full price on the cross. The cross is the seed of My life, the seed I gave which was multiplied back to Me by the Father raising Me from the dead, increasing My life far more than it was when I was a man. Do you see this?*

Me: Yes! Yes! It takes away the dread of having to pay, of acting from fear, from obligation. Many times I've given because I was urged to from a sense of obligation, of its being something I owed. So there was little or no joy in my giving, it was more of a forced type of thing. I am afraid I've given when it wasn't really in my heart. My best giving was when I wanted to give from sheer joy.

Jesus: *Remember, the New Testament says, "God loveth a cheerful giver" (2 Corinthians 9:7).*

Me: Well, Lord, my giving has not always been cheerful.

Jesus: *I know. But remember, too, My words: "It is more blessed to give than to receive" (Acts 20:35).*

Me: Lord, I've often wondered what You meant by these words, especially the term *more* blessed.

Jesus: *I mean it is more PRODUCTIVE to give than to receive. For giving is the seed, the seed is what reproduces. The seed is reproduced in the harvest which is many times greater than the original seed planted.*

Me: More productive. Yes, I see that when I give, it is an expression of faith I have that the seed will be multiplied. Is that right?

Jesus: *Yes, that is correct. Faith is what causes you to sow seed; otherwise you would not sow seed at all. It is a seed of faith because it takes faith to believe the seed will be multiplied. And because the seed is multiplied . . . the return is greater than your giving . . . it is more blessed, or more productive, to plant your seed than it is to receive.*

Me: Then it is not what I receive that is multiplied, but what I plant or give?

Jesus: *Yes. When you have a mountain of need, seed for your miracle. If you can have the courage to plant the seed—which is giving something of yourself first—then the seed will germinate and breathe through the soil of your life, becoming a plant full of fruit, or produce. The seed will give you power to speak to your mountain of need, to command it to be met in full, and nothing will be impossible unto you.*

Me: Jesus, are you saying that Seed-Faith will actually move my mountains?

Jesus: *Absolutely. I clearly said this in Matthew 17:20.*

Me: Nothing shall be impossible unto *me?*

Jesus: *Nothing, that is in My plan for you as My child and My disciple— nothing can ever be impossible to you when you have faith as a seed—when you put in Seed-Faith first.*

[Thoughts were bursting forth inside me—(Key Number 1: **God is my Source of total supply**). My giving is a seed of faith I sow (Key Number 2: **Seeding for your miracle**). Jesus paid all my debt through the seed of the cross. I am no longer under the bondage of giving out of obligation or of a debt I owe to God, which is the old tithing way. I am a seed-sower. As I give, God will give to me good measure, pressed down, shaken together and running over. This is even MORE than I had seen in the Blessing-Pact. This was a step further. Then another question arose in my mind:]

Me: Lord, I've always been taught when I give I am not to expect anything back. Here, You are saying to plant seed and to expect a harvest—that if I give, I will receive.

Jesus: *You are not to expect from the one or from those to whom you give. Your giving is always unto God although it is put to use on earth and for some person or group. Your expectation is to be from your Source. You give to your Source and you expect back from your Source.*

Me: Then I'm not to be concerned about the response of the ones I help by my seed-sowing. I'm to give whether they ever give back to me or not. Is that right?

Jesus: *That is right, the reason being they are not your Source. Only God is your Source. Those you help may or may not give to you but God your Source will never let you down. He will never fail to multiply your seed sown. That's why He wants you to give, so He can carry on His work and so He can give back to you to meet your needs.*

Me: Lord, many years ago You gave me the phrase, EXPECT A MIRACLE. I've shared it thousands of times. Is that what You mean I'm to do when I have seeded for my needs?

Jesus: *Yes, that is THE THIRD MIRACLE KEY OF SEED-FAITH (Mark 11:24). When you give, sowing your seed of faith to God your Source, you are to expect to reap from it; you are to reap the harvest. The harvest cannot be fully explained in natural terms, it is a miracle. Since God is the God of the harvest He will send the miracle for every seed you sow. Since He will send it, you must look for it and expect it. Unless you expect it, when God sends it you will not recognize it and it will pass you by. At that time you will be apt to ask, "Why didn't God help me?" when He did all the time.*

Me: But in expecting a miracle from the seeds of faith I sow I must expect only from God my Source.

Jesus: *Yes, God is the only unchanging, wholly reliable Source. It is God who will supply all your need according to His riches in heaven by Me. I became poor when I became a man, not for My sake but for man (2 Corinthians 8:9). I emptied myself of My former glory in heaven, I laid aside My riches, I became poor. At times I had no place to lay My head. But in My resurrection and ascension back to the Father as the Unlimited Christ, I was restored to My former glory and riches (Ephesians 4:8-10). I am not poor anymore. This is why the Father said He would supply all your need according to His riches in heaven by Me — Christ Jesus. All the riches in heaven are in Me. I am unlimited in My riches, My ability to supply all your need. What I need is your seed, your giving first. This is your giving God something to work with. This is your seeding for miracles. It means after you seed, start expecting a miracle and keep on expecting until it comes.*

Me: Lord, why is it that the miracle of supply sometimes comes quickly but other times it seems to take so long?

Jesus: *Because the times and seasons are with the Father only. He operates on His timetable, not yours. He knows the best time, the best way, to send your harvest. Again, this is why I say* **if you can have faith as a seed.** *It takes faith to plant a seed, it takes the same faith to believe it will ultimately become a harvest and be returned to you manyfold. My Kingdom is based on faith. As My word says, "The just shall live by [their] faith" (Romans 1:17). And, "Without faith it is impossible to please [God]" (Hebrews 11:6).*

Me: Lord, I recall that St. Paul wrote in Galatians 6:9 that there is a "due season" for seed sown.

Jesus: *St. Paul stated that the New Testament or New Covenant, is based on Seed-Faith. He said, "Whatsoever a man soweth, that shall he also reap" (Galatians 6:7). Good seed or bad seed, each will bring forth its own harvest. Good seed will produce a harvest of good things to you, bad seed a harvest of bad things to you. Then Paul added, "Let us be not weary in well doing: (or in your giving and seed-sowing) for in due season we shall reap, if we faint not" (Galatians 6:9).*

> *If you sow good seeds, God your Source will set His time and way for you to reap. That will be your due season to receive it. So don't give up your expecting a miracle, wait upon God. His due season will come. Be aware that He cares for you, He will supply all your need.*

Me: Lord, this almost overwhelms me. I've been doing it in my Blessing-Pact Covenant and teaching it to others. I've received many miracles. But I sense You are taking me deeper. What You are really saying is to make a Seed-Faith Covenant with God and the three keys are miracle keys:

Key Number 1: Make God my Source—put Him first in my life.

Key Number 2: Give, and give first . . . put the seed of faith in . . . seed for my miracles.

Key Number 3: Expect a miracle—not from those I help or give to, but from God my Eternal Source.

Jesus: *Yes, those are the Three Miracle Keys through which the Father will meet all of man's needs according to His riches in heaven by Me.*

Me: Lord, here I am waiting on God for my future ministry to help the people. There are many mountains of need facing me, and facing them. From this hour I make my Seed-Faith Covenant with God. I will endeavor with all my heart to practice the Three Miracle Keys and teach them to all who will hear me. And I will start by counting the next thing I give as a seed I sow . . .

And I did. And I got the beginning of the biggest miracle of my life.

I also began to get the attention of people in need who, as they heard of the Seed-Faith concept, started to feel hope for long-needed miracles.

———◆———

"I WILL PLANT SEED—GOD WILL MOVE MY MOUNTAINS."

"I don't have to beg God to do this. I can remember this truth by remembering the Golden Rule."

"I will give FIRST and joyfully and expect God to do the rest!"

YOUR GOD-GIVEN KEY FOR TODAY

"I Will Plant Seed—God Will Move My Mountains."

WEDNESDAY
Key:
GOD IS THE MULTIPLIER OF MY SEED SOWN

or

How One Family Raised Themselves From Poverty To Prosperity . . . And Can Truly Say, "We Are Alive And Prospering"

I kept hearing from a family who were in the depths of poverty. And they asked for my prayers. Each time I would write them back I would drop a few thoughts on Seed-Faith. Then they got a copy of my book, MIRACLE OF SEED-FAITH, and read it through in just a few hours and then read it again and again.

Well, we wrote back and forth for quite some time. Then I began to sense that they were catching on to what I was saying to them about "seeding for a miracle for their poverty." Then WHAM! I got a letter that was almost unbelievable! Prosperity was coming in like a flood. I wanted to know more so I sent one of my associates to their little home out on the plains of Texas.

Later my associate told me, "I listened with open mouth as they told their story . . ."

Here's the way David and Barbara Dzuik told it:

DAVID: We weren't on the verge of bankruptcy. We *were* bankrupt. I was teaching school and making a little over $4,000 a year. As our family grew the bills started piling up. Then inflation hit. And to make a long story short, we were not making it. I quit teaching and tried to get into something where I could support our growing family.

I went from one job to another not knowing what I wanted to do. I worked with a starch plant and in an automotive center, a sugar mill, farmed with my brother, and last was trying to sell insurance. I wiped out at that real fast. I wound up in the hospital with severe stomach pains. The diagnosis was peptic disease suspected but unconfirmed.

BARBARA: I had been crying when I picked up an **Abundant Life** magazine that someone had sent us. With David in the hospital and three small children who needed clothes and food, and the bills piling up, I didn't know where to turn. David hadn't made more than $35, in the past four months. Not only were we broke, we were deeply in debt. No wonder I was crying. What do you do? Get a divorce? Shoot yourself . . . or what?

As I thumbed idly through the magazine I ran across an article telling about the building of the new Worship Center on the Oral Roberts campus. I was deeply impressed by the article, particularly where it said, "Give what is impressed upon your heart . . ." because we had been writing to Brother Roberts and reading his book, MIRACLE OF SEED-FAITH, and we were really interested in the concept. But how do you give when you are so far in debt that you just know there is no way out?

DAVID: Well, when I got out of the hospital I can tell you things looked black. My parents came to our rescue temporarily by asking us to paint their house. So we rolled up our sleeves and went to work just to get money for food.

All during this time we were reading MIRACLE OF SEED-FAITH and trying to absorb Brother Roberts' concept of Seed-Faith living. We had read lots of books on success, positive thinking, and prosperity, but none of them ever "took." MIRACLE OF SEED-FAITH was different. We saw in it a powerful three-point formula to lift our level of living:

> Look to God as your Source . . .
> Plant a seed, and . . .
> Expect a miracle!

There were so many things in this book that we could identify with, especially the place where Brother Roberts says:

"God always has me to start with zero . . ."

That's where we were—ZERO—and in debt.

We continued writing to Brother Roberts back and forth, but for weeks nothing changed—nothing but our thinking. The Bible-centered principles of Seed-Faith began to bore into our minds.

BARBARA: Even our attitudes toward one another changed. For the past five years we had struggled so hard financially. Together we had committed "credit card suicide." Before we realized we were heavily in debt. I wanted to go back to teaching school as I had when we were single. But David didn't want me to work—I had my own little class right at home. So I found myself blaming him for the mess we were in. But now I realized that is wasn't all his fault. We had both made mistakes.

DAVID: Our house painting job didn't last long and soon I was looking into several job-career possibilities. They all looked good but nothing worked out. So I started helping my brother farm.

BARBARA: In debt as we were, I couldn't get the Worship Center off my mind and the phrase: "Give what is impressed upon your heart . . ." Still I didn't want to say anything to David until we could at least see daylight. But that phrase kept going over and over in my mind.

So one day before David left for the fields I said, "David, when you go out to plow today I want you to think about how much we should give as a love gift to the Worship Center." And he said, "OK." That night when he came home we talked about it and I said, "What have you decided?" And he told me. And I said, "Well, I feel we should give more than that."

DAVID: When she gave me the sum she had in mind, it was an amount I'd never possessed at one time in my entire life. I was flabbergasted to say the least. I wasn't against it because Barb and I had really talked about Seed-Faith giving. And we were convinced in our minds that nothing is impossible with the Lord. If it was done, He would have to do it anyway. So at this point it seemed to sink into our hearts as well as our minds, and I said, "OK. Let's do it. He can bless us to give a large amount just as easily as a small amount."

BARBARA: So I wrote again. And I told Brother Roberts exactly how it was. I told him according to our tax records we had made only $4,500 that year and had to borrow more to live on. But we still felt in our hearts that God wanted us to make a commitment of this special amount. I wanted to impress on Oral Roberts that we were still poor as far as money goes, but our faith was at the boiling point and we were looking to God as our Source, planting the seed by faith and expecting a miracle. His letters back to me were nothing but faith-builders. He would say things like:

> "God can move a mountain . . ."
> "Keep your faith—even your little faith . . ."
> "Don't let these problems get you down . . ."
> "Needs exist to be met . . ."

And he would quote the Scripture about the grain of mustard seed in Matthew 17:20.

He also told me in his letters how much he had prayed that God would multiply the seed gift ten times or more. So I held on to that. His letters made me believe that God could literally move our MOUNTAIN OF DEBT.

DAVID: During this time my brother passed away. He had never married and lived with my parents, so I had the opportunity to farm his portion of land.

I wasn't exactly a novice farmer. I had farmed part-time with my family so I was aware of the innovations of farming that we have now. But with the full responsibility of this land I knew that we had to put our trust completely in the Lord. God really became my partner and my Source. I learned the hard way to listen to Him. When I planted the way He impressed me to, we had bumper crops. When I listened to other people, I failed.

BARBARA: Sometimes it was frustrating to go against the really seasoned farmers. But God worked on every crop. Our wheat! Oh! You know how the wind blows in Texas. Well, our wheat went through it. The wind blew it and the hail pounded it. And here again, we had borrowed the money to plant the seed. David said, "Barb, we're not going to make it. There is about one grain to the inch—it's ruined. We won't get 15 bushels an acre."

But to me, I'd never farmed, and I thought, "Boy! it looks beautiful!" But then came the water problem. We have only three wells and there was just not enough water to water all the crops like we should. And even worse, we had only three inches of rain that year. Yet, our wheat yielded not 15, but 55 *bushels to the acre!* You talk about multiplication! We planted one bushel per acre and harvested 55! Now we know from personal experience that GOD IS A MULTIPLIER OF THE SEED SOWN!

DAVID: Everything we had read in MIRACLE OF SEED-FAITH was falling into place . . . looking to God as our Source, planting the seed, and expecting the harvest—the "due season" that the book talks about. Our wheat was so superior that we sold it as "seed" and saved some to plant for our own crop next year.

BARBARA: We still weren't quite out of the woods. We still owed the credit company money for what we had borrowed to plant our wheat, for food, shelter and clothes. And when we were about to get our "return" it seemed everything went wrong. Our freezer went out, we had to have tractor tires—well, we just needed everything. And when our money began to come in from our bountiful harvest—you'll never believe this—I was tinkering around with the idea of paying off our bills and getting the things we needed first. Then I'd pay the Seed-Faith money I'd promised. But a very dear friend said, "Barbara, I wouldn't mess around with God's money if I were you."

Well, that did it. We gave to our Source FIRST. We planted a seed of the exact amount of dollars that God told us . . . and we gave it as the first money that came into our hands. And the miracle is, GOD MULTIPLIED THAT SEED MORE THAN TEN TIMES! To us—David and Barbara Dzuik, who had never had a bumper crop of anything but bills—not only did we get our seed back, but ten times over!

DAVID: I don't think Barbara or I either one thought about it at the time, but somewhere in that book it said, "Plant a seed to match your need" and that is what we did without realizing it.

BARBARA: And I want to say that God went even further—beyond helping us with our hopeless finances. He has brought us into a right relationship with Him spiritually. As much as we needed Him to multiply our seed for our desperate financial needs, our spiritual needs were even greater. This closer walk we now have with God is precious beyond words.

DAVID: I can say AMEN to that.

After this, David and Barbara came to a lay seminar on the campus of Oral Roberts University and came forward to start another Seed-Faith project and to focus upon another need that had developed in their lives. As they stood there in front of that great audience I said, "Are you the REAL David and Barbara that I have been writing to?"

"We sure are! . . . AND WE ARE ALIVE AND PROSPERING." I said, "Well, we read your story and we carried it in the December 1974 issue of **Abundant Life**."

Then Barbara said, "Brother Roberts, we didn't have *any* money when we came into Seed-Faith living and we were without a lot of other things. But as we stand here today, we are part of a great miracle —the miracle of Seed-Faith!"

Almost involuntarily, they turned toward the audience and started talking excitedly to various people who were seemingly not grasping the joy of seed-sowing.

They didn't say much but it had a powerful effect. The people rose and gave them a standing ovation.

As they turned to go I said, "Let me shake your hands again—I just want to shake the hands of people who have come alive to Jesus Christ and have discovered that what He says to do really works in the NOW!"

I can see them now as they shook my hand. Starting to walk away, they stopped and looked back and there was enough joy on their faces which, if we could have bottled and given away, would have filled the hearts of millions.

———◆———

Say this:
  "God is the Multiplier of my seed sown."

  "I've got to let these vital points sink into my mind:
    Keep my faith in my Source—even my little faith . . .
    Let God impress me what, where, and when to plant . . .
    My needs exist to be met, and God will meet them!"

YOUR GOD-GIVEN KEY FOR TODAY

Now say it to yourself over and over: •

"God Is The Multiplier Of My Seed Sown."

THURSDAY
Key:
IT IS MORE PRODUCTIVE TO GIVE THAN TO RECEIVE

or

How One Gift Evelyn And I Made Was Multiplied Seven Times In Less Than Twenty-Four Hours

I used to wonder what Jesus meant when He said:

It is more blessed to give than to receive (Acts 20:35).

It seemed contrary to real life. I received such a blessing when I received something. Our needs were so many that any small gift thrilled us. It was a joy to *receive*.

Only occasionally did I experience the same joy by giving as I did when receiving. Overall it appeared to me to be the opposite of what Jesus said. To me, it seemed to be more blessed to RECEIVE than to GIVE.

Then one day when I was still a young pastor I began to see what Jesus meant. While facing a need I had a deep impression that I should give a certain amount of money to God's work. After I gave it, I felt a warm glow all over even though now I had even less money to meet my need than I had before. All I felt was pure joy. Somehow I forgot about my need until a man knocked at my door at 2 o'clock in the morning.

"Pardon me," he said, "but I had to come back and see you." (He had been present earlier and observed your giving.) "When I reached home and started to bed," he said, "the Lord began dealing with my heart. You didn't mention your needs but only the needs of God's work. For two years I have given very little and all at once it came home to me about my own need to give. I don't know why but I had an almost irresistible feeling that I should give this to you."

He handed me a sum seven times more than I had given! It was the exact amount Evelyn and I needed to continue living in the house we were in. This was our most urgent need.

When I started thanking him, he replied, "Don't thank me. I'm a wheat farmer and I know by experience that the yield I get from my land is in direct proportion to the seed I plant."

As he was closing the door he said, "Brother Roberts, this is just seed I've been needing to plant for a long time."

In his heart, this man had been withdrawn from the church for two years. His seed-giving was also withdrawn. Like the seed-money Jesus told about in the parable on giving, it was "buried." (See Matthew 25:14-28.) He had let his beautiful farm run down. Worse, he had gotten caught up in playing the stock market. He couldn't cope with the fluctuation of the market on a daily basis and he lost thousands of dollars.

After he started giving again and assumed his proper place in the church, everyone saw a profound change take place in his life. He quietly resumed tending his farm, he found a new joy in being with his family, and he became one of the most enthusiastic men in the church that I have ever met. He became a man of strength to all of us. He is still a partner with me today. He still practices SEED-FAITH. His last letter was full of praises to God for showing him how to live.

As I reflected on how God multiplied my gift seven times over, I began to realize what Jesus meant when He said, "It is more blessed to give than to receive." I understood the reason why:

**It is more productive to give than to receive
for what we receive is not multiplied . . .
only what we give!**

This is a thrilling truth . . . and it works! Ask yourself: "Do I have any buried seeds that I can plant so God can multiply them?" As you think of them, list them here:

_____

_____

_____

and watch for results!

YOUR GOD-GIVEN KEY FOR TODAY
Say:

"It Is More Productive To Give Than To Receive!"

FRIDAY Key: I WILL HAVE A SEED-FAITH PROJECT

or
How Your Pockets Full Of Needs Can Be Full And Running Over

(This story has got more people into Seed-Faith living than any I've ever given.)

People often ask me why I am so excited about Seed-Faith. "What is there about it," they ask, "that you never tire of talking about it . . . of doing it?"

Without fail, my mind always goes back to the fifth chapter of St. Luke where Jesus told the greatest story of Seed-Faith I have ever read. This story grips me. I have had our chief artist at ORU to paint it for me and I have it hung on the wall of my bedroom by my bed—it is the last thing I see at night and the first thing I see when I awaken. So you can see it is pretty important to me.

I want to take you by the hand and put you in this story, as I have put myself. Do you know why? Because it deals with POCKETS FULL OF NEEDS and how they can be FULL AND RUNNING OVER. If that doesn't grab you, I don't know what can. It not only grabbed me but I am still in its grip—so here goes.

The story begins with Jesus preaching to a large audience and right in the middle of it he stops and sees POCKETS FULL OF NEEDS of a single individual, and those needs occupy Jesus' full attention.

Even though Jesus was preaching to a multitude, He looked over and saw one individual fisherman washing his nets. I love that. He sees you . . . He sees me. His eyes turned toward the one fisherman and then to his companions.

The crowd was so big they could neither see Him nor hear Him well. And when He looked over and saw these fishermen—He saw something else—**He saw their empty boat.** And He said, "Lend Me your boat." Now you may wonder why He did this. Was He concerned only about the multitude—that He would have a place to stand up and preach? Surely He was concerned about them. But in my mind I ask the question, "Was He also concerned about the men who had an empty boat?"

It's very, very evident that He did not see a FULL boat. He noticed an EMPTY boat. And He called upon men who were washing and mending their nets, which were now old and broken, men who had desperate needs, men who were commercial fishermen. That's the way they fed their families. And now the boat is empty. The nets are old and broken. And they're the ones He called upon. And get this:

HE OFFERED THEM WHAT I CALL A
SEED-FAITH PROJECT

Maybe you can think of a better term. I can't. "Lend Me your boat." These men didn't even know Jesus as their personal Savior at the time they loaned Him their boat. He borrowed it EMPTY and He had in His mind to give it back FULL!

There's nobody in the world like Jesus, to ask you for something out of your need, and then send it back full. I love Jesus! I offered Him a thin wasted body full of tuberculosis and a stammering tongue. At the age of 17 that's all I had, AN EMPTY BOAT—AN EMPTY LIFE— and He gave me back my tongue and He gave me new lungs.

I may not succeed in convincing you today, but Oral Roberts is *convinced.* I'm sold on Jesus Christ of Nazareth and His way of Seed-Faith.

PUSH OUT A LITTLE FROM THE SHORE

So He said, "Lend Me your boat." Then He said something else. He said, "Push Me a little from the shore." This was so He could stand in the boat and people standing on the shore could see Him and He could project His voice. They could hear Him.

It's strange about Palestine—your voice carries much farther than it does here in the States. I've been there many times and something about the air carries your voice like a PA system. So He preached and the people listened.

Then they rowed Him back to shore. He dismissed the crowd and all that was left were these fishermen who had loaned Him their empty boat. Would He forget them? Would He say, "Thank you, fellows?" No. He did better than that. He said, "Come on. Get into the boat with Me. Launch out into the deep and let your nets down for a catch."

You see, it's evident that He had them in mind all the time. It's evident He was the only one there who had any concern about empty boats, rotten nets, and hungry men—the only one there who was concerned about the empty boats being filled and the old empty nets being filled with fish—and the only one who would do something about it EVEN IF IT TOOK A MIRACLE.

Well, you might know who spoke up. Old Peter broke right in and said, "Well, now, Lord, we've been out there. We've toiled all night and taken nothing."

What Peter was saying was, you fish in the sea of Galilee at night for the waters are crystal clear. If you fish during the day and throw your net over, the fish see the net and they rush away. You fish in the dark of the moon when the fish cannot see the net. And Peter is saying, "Now, Lord, I am an expert. I've observed all the rules of fishing. I've done it right. We've toiled all night and taken nothing. Nothing works."

If there is anything that is just like human beings today it is that we reach the place too often where we say, "Nothing works. Nothing I do is right."

DOES EVERYTHING SEEM WRONG?

Have you been there? I have. I've been there so many times. "No matter what I do, it seems wrong." "I work with my loved ones and I can't get many of them to listen." "I work with my body and I can't get it well." "I work with my finances and I can't get in the black." "My marriage—it just falls apart in spite of all I do." Isn't this what we say? This is what Peter and his men are saying: "We've toiled all night and taken nothing," meaning, "Nothing we do works."

They were discouraged. They were lonely. They were defeated financially. But thank God! They had loaned Christ their boat. **They had given to Him out of their need.** And I want to stress that. They didn't have a lot. I don't know why, but usually God doesn't have much success with people who have a lot. I wish that were not true. I wish people who have a lot of this world's goods could feel God 'dealing with them. But it seems like we humans won't do that. We've got to get down with some great need in our life.

I was like that. Why didn't I give my life when I had a whole body? I ran from God. That's how silly I was. I ran from Him. I only paid attention to Him when I couldn't breathe easily anymore, when I was hemorrhaging to death with tuberculosis. Maybe you are at that place today. Maybe the reason is different, but the need is just as deep. And deep down in your heart you feel that just maybe God can help you.

FOCUS YOUR NEED ON A DESIRED RESULT

I believe these disciples approached their problem correctly from a logical point of view. "Let's fish at night in the dark of the moon. Let's keep the rules of fishing." They did. And they failed. Now, THEY HAD TO HAVE A MIRACLE. And Jesus said, "I want you to launch out during the day. Let's break the rules . . . I don't want you to fish in the old way. I want you to believe in miracles. I want you to believe that . . .

> God is not dead . . .
>
> God is concerned about you . . .
>
> God saw you put in that seed of faith."

You know what He asked them for? The best they had . . . their means of livelihood—their boat. He asked them to give out of their *need.* Away with the idea, "Well, when I get a lot I'll do so and so . . ." The Bible doesn't teach that. But there was something more important. He told them to give and to focus on their need, to direct it for *a desired result.* Yes, for a desired result!

What was their desired result? To catch fish, because that's the way they fed their families. Without catching fish they were going to fail to support their families, to get their needs met.

You know, it's awfully easy when you get down to feel that nobody knows and nobody cares—not even God. How do I know? Because I've been there many times. People look at me and say, "How can you be there?"

You try doing what God has called ME to do and you might begin to see. It's a thrill, but it's tough too. This is how I know there are miracles. I need a miracle every day.

But the fishermen argued with the Lord. I really don't think it's so bad to argue with God. You are human. You are not God. You don't understand. I don't understand. And I ask, "Why, God? Why do you tell me to do this or that or the other thing?"

My precious mother, who has gone on to heaven, taught me two priceless things: One, she always said, "Oral, keep little in your own eyes and you'll bless the world." And the second was, "Obey God." She drilled that into me. Whether you understand or not, just obey. So I don't believe God requires you and me to understand. But He does require obedience.

FIND THE DEPTH WHERE THE MIRACLE IS

Jesus said, "Launch out into the deep and let down your net." The fishermen were saying, "We've toiled all night and taken nothing." They are at a standstill. Jesus is simply saying, "Obey Me. Obey Me. Obey Me. Do what I tell you. Do what I tell you."

Do you know who you are talking to when you deal with Christ? You are dealing with the Man that scooped out the bed for the ocean, that flung the stars from His fingertips, that hung the earth on nothing, and put the fish in the sea. And He can tell them when to strike the net! You are dealing with THE MAN. You are dealing with Jesus. Have you ever realized how great He is?

Finally, they got the message. They said, "Nevertheless, whether we think so or not, we are going to do what You say. We are going to do it according to Your *word*. We'll let down the net."

They launched out and Jesus said, "Put the net over into the deep. Go to the deep." You see, **there's a depth where the miracle is.** There's a depth in everything that I give and everything you give. You cannot give haphazardly. This is why I say, get yourself a Seed-Faith project so you can put your Seed-Faith to work and focus it toward a desired result. I don't believe that you can just pitch in a few dollars here or there. You can't just donate a few hours of your time, toss a haphazard prayer toward someone with a deep need, or just give of your talent in a loose way. I mean, there's got to be a purpose. You've got to purpose in your heart (2 Corinthians 9:7). And there's a DEPTH for you, and you'll know it. Forget all your past failures and believe God and He will give the miracle.

So the fishermen launched out into the deep—not the shallow— but when they had reached their depth, the Lord said, "Right here. Throw your net over." And they did. And it was daylight. The fish knew what they were getting into. But they couldn't help it. Jesus, who created the fish said, "Hit that net. Hit that net. Hit that net." And they hit it. They hit it. They hit it. They filled it and the fishermen began to pull the net into the boat. When they got it into the boat it was too heavy with fish and the boat began to sink, and the net began to break. That is what I call . . .

A NET-BREAKING, BOAT-SINKING LOAD!

All these fishermen knew at this point was that they *finally* believed His word—and He gave the miracle. And they got so much that they had to call other boats over to help them. And old rough, earthy Peter fell down on his knees and cried out, "Lord, Lord God, I'm not even right with You. I'm a sinful man."

But Jesus simply said, "Peter, just get up and follow Me and I'll make you a fisher of men."

BIG SEED FOR BIG NEEDS

Bob DeWeese was in Tulsa a short time ago. He lives in Florida now but he was my associate evangelist for 24 years, until he retired. He is a wonderful man of God and we are very close even now.

Some time ago he had given a Seed-Faith gift to this ministry but he didn't tell me what it was for. So when he was back in town he wanted to see me. He found out from my son Richard that I was out at the airport ready to leave town. So Richard called and had me paged and when I got on the phone Richard said, "Don't leave till we get there."

I said, "What's the matter?"

Richard said, "Bob DeWeese has got to see you."

I said, "Well, I'll be right back in a day or two."

"No," he said, "he's got to see you today."

So they came out to the airport and Bob handed me a Seed-Faith gift. And I said, "Bob, you just did this a few weeks ago." Then I opened the envelope and saw the amount and said, "This is too big—this is too big for you, Bob." And I handed it back.

Bob said, "No."

I said, "What's going on?"

And he said, "You know the other Seed-Faith gift?"

"Yes."

"Well, there was a man who owed me two thousand dollars and he wanted to pay it, but didn't have the money. Then last week he came over and paid it in full." Then he said, "Now I have another need and I want to plant some seed for God to send it back in the form of my need."

Bob DeWeese is a man that's really a man of God and I believed him. And he said, "Just get on the plane and go, Oral," and he was grinning from ear to ear.

And I thought, "Oh, God, to be obedient!" Bob knows and I know and God knows that *men* will give in to your bosom.

GOD IS GOING TO MAKE PEOPLE DO SOME THINGS FOR YOU
THAT THEY CAN'T HELP

For instance . . . I received a letter from a man in Canada while we were building Oral Roberts University. I'd never met him and he had never met me. And by the way he wrote, I'll probably never get to meet him. But in his letter was a check for several hundred dollars. I tell you, to build and operate a university takes all kinds of gifts and I was thrilled—until I read his letter. He said:

Dear Oral Roberts:

Enclosed is a check [for so much] to help you build Oral Roberts University. But don't get the wrong idea. I'm not sending this because I like you. I've heard you only once and I was not impressed. You may be wondering why I'm sending this gift . . . (I sure was) . . . it's because God showed me that you are to build Him a university and build it on the Holy Spirit. And He told me to make a sacrifice and to send you this check. And so I'm doing it —not because I like you, but because God said so.

Now there's a lot to what this man did. It took me back to St. Luke 6:38 where Christ said:

Give, and it shall be given unto you; good measure, pressed down, and shaken together, and running over shall men give into your bosom . . .

In other words, they can't help it. This old boy was caught there. He didn't have to *like* me, but he had to send the check. There was no way out.

I believe what I'm saying so much that I just thrill when I think of it, and yet it breaks me up. I just want you to know that I stake my life on the principles of Seed-Faith. If I were to die this minute every word I've said I would give my life for it.

Get into Seed-Faith and then get to your depth. In everything you do, whatever you give, give it for a desired result. And then don't tell God when or how to give you the desired result. Oh, you can tell Him but He isn't going to listen. At least God's never listened to me, because I have told Him a thousand times how to do it, when to do it, and where to do it. But I can guarantee you God hasn't answered me once in these ways. He ALWAYS answers but always in HIS way and His time and when it happens I have to admit it is better than the way I tell Him. Now can you believe that? Here's where the act of faith comes in. You've got to believe it and keep on believing it, day after day and month after month. God will do it. Say it: "God will do it." Say it again: "God will do it."

At this point in this message from Luke 5, I usually stop and present a SEED-FAITH PROJECT to my partners. At the seminar here at

ORU a few weeks ago our project was putting Bibles into the prisons of the nation, also Canada, and other countries that were interested. The response from wardens and prison chaplains has been overwhelming. The first million Bibles we printed were gone. Another million were being printed, all by faith. I had put ten of my sermons on THE MIRACLES OF CHRIST AND WHAT THEY MEAN TO YOU IN THE NOW in the back of the Bible. I did this bec: use we had discovered it kept some of the more violent prisoners from tearing up the Bible, because they were curious about what I had to say to them about Christ's miracles for their lives.

Well, I offered the partners present (some 2,000 of them) to take a number of these Bibles as their own SEED-FAITH PROJECT, to ask God for their "depth" of the amount they were to give as a seed of faith, then do it with joy. The response was electric. They almost climbed over the seats to come forward and tell me the *depth* God had given them—the number of Bibles for which they would sow a Seed-Faith gift.

This Seed-Faith project enabled us to obey our Lord's command, "I was in prison, and ye came unto me" (Matthew 25:36). Also, we were giving the partner a project for his Seed-Faith so God could meet his needs. From that day mail has been pouring in from those partners telling of the "NET-BREAKING, BOAT-SINKING LOAD" of miracles God is multiplying back to them. It is fantastic! The Scriptures are coming to pass in their lives, and in Evelyn's and mine, for we took our Seed-Faith project too.

In virtually every seminar we have we offer a specific Seed-Faith project because seed must be planted *before* God can multiply it back (2 Corinthians 9:10).

Also, before I attempt anything, I give *first*. I give out of my need. And I focus my giving for a desired result. This is the way I live my life for God as a disciple, a follower of Jesus. It has become the rhythm of success for me. Every success traces back to seed I'd planted either of my time, or talent, or concern, or prayers prayed for others, or good thoughts sent forth, or a piece of money given—any seed I sowed in loving, joyous faith toward God my mighty Source.

This explains also why on our radio and television programs I don't ask for money. Rather, I offer something free and without obligation—a Bible or a book or something else of value that will enrich your life spiritually. It is a seed I sow. The secret is: I am giving it out of my heart, out of my need, and for a desired result from God my Source.

Then God causes people to give to our ministry. It never fails when I do it according to the "depth" God inspires me to give. Then the miracle He has stored up for me, or for this ministry, will always come. This never fails to work for me or for Seed-Faith people.

Say:

"I WILL HAVE A SEED-FAITH PROJECT."

Now here's what I want you to do:

1. Get yourself a *Seed-Faith project*.
2. When you decide what it is to be—*focus* your thinking on the result you want to see—get a faith image.
3. Don't start *too big!* Find your "depth"—you'll know when it's right.
4. Work at your Seed-Faith project—keep notes—when you have received the desired results, start another Seed-Faith project!

You'll be thrilled as you see it working. Pretty soon it will become natural. God keeps His Word!

Now write down what you decide upon for your first SEED-FAITH PROJECT.

_____

Once again:

YOUR GOD-GIVEN KEY FOR TODAY

"I Will Have A Seed-Faith Project."

SATURDAY

Key:
I WILL PLANT SEED AWAY FROM MYSELF TO LEARN TO RELY ON MY SOURCE

or
Here's How You Can Make Your Losses Into Gain . . .

In the correspondence I carry on with people in virtually all walks of life, I recently dealt with a young couple who had borrowed money to start a little business. They had done well enough to pay the note down to $300. Then the bottom dropped out. The $300 coming due might as well have been thousands, it was so far beyond their ability to pay.

It was at this time they began writing me. I had just dealt with several people who had lost their jobs, some who had lost loved ones, and in each situation I had assisted them in applying the Three Miracle Keys of Seed-Faith.

The Scripture I used with all these who wrote me at that time was Philippians 3:7-10:

> *But what things were gain to me, those I counted loss for Christ. Yea doubtless, and I count all things but loss for the excellency of the knowledge of Christ Jesus my Lord: for whom I have suffered the loss of all things, and do count them but dung, that I may win Christ, And be found in him, not having mine own righteousness, which is of the law, but that which is through the faith of Christ, the righteousness which is of God by faith: That I may know him, and the power of his resurrection, and the fellowship of his sufferings, being made conformable unto his death.*

Here St. Paul in this Scripture deals with losses and with knowing the power of Jesus' resurrection over what He had lost on the cross: His own life. Then Paul says, "That I might know Him in the power of the resurrection—or—that I might know Christ in His multiplying power, the power that multiplies back to me that which I have lost."

THIS COUPLE HAD ONLY $30

As I indicated, the couple had paid this note down to $300. You would think the people who held the note would help them—and they had—but they had financial problems too.

Owing ten times what they had left, the couple faced bankruptcy. At this time I got their letter and they were desperate.

I usually don't hear from a person until he's nearing the point of desperation. I don't resent that because it was at my own point of desperation that I began to seek God for help. Apparently we are not aware of God's light until we face some great darkness. His strength doesn't appear important to us until our own weakness leaves us with our back to the wall, or flat on our back. I think it's wonderful that a person will, when he's in trouble, start remembering who his real Source of supply is, and call upon Him.

Well, this couple wrote that they had been watching our Sunday morning telecasts and had heard me say there is an eternal principle in the Bible called Seed-Faith, that God is your Source, that you give and give first—making it a seed of faith you plant, then expect a miracle. I thought, they have been listening pretty well.

Then they said it all sounded good but intellectually they couldn't grasp the idea of giving first because in owing $300 and giving the $30 they had, they would lose both the $300 AND THEIR LAST $30. They would be diminished even more.

Since I had been through this many times myself, and hundreds of times with others, I knew exactly why Seed-Faith would appear to them this way. I wrote back and said, "First of all, you've got to start with who or what your Source is. Is your source yourself, is it the people who hold your note, or is it GOD? Somehow," I said, "you've got to come to know God as your only Source. You must turn your attention directly to God because He, as your Source, is linked to everything you do, and to every good that you want to happen to you. He is linked to you as a person, as a family, to your concerns, your hopes and dreams, your real problems. He's linked in the most real way to that small business you're having such a hard time with and particularly to the $300 note you can't pay!" Next I said, "You've got to . . .

GIVE AWAY FROM YOURSELF

There are two reasons why God wants you to do this and then He will help you out of your troubles.

First, God is your Source of total supply. Second, when you give away from yourself, you're actually giving to Him AND HE IS AT THE POINT OF YOUR NEED."

They wrote back that it was hard for them to grasp the idea of Seed-Faith, that in your problem you *give away from yourself.* What they wanted was to pay attention to themselves, instead of *giving away* from themselves. They wanted something to be given *to* them.

They had missed the end result of giving away from themselves. We are giving away from ourselves but we are giving to the one who is at the point of our need, and who is THE SOURCE of meeting that need!

"Well," they wrote, "we're going to lose our entire little business, yet you say for us to give the last $30 we have. That will leave us minus the $30 plus owing $300 — or a loss of $330. Besides do we give all the $30 or a part, and if so, who to?"

I replied that they didn't have to give to our ministry, for we are not the only ones doing God's work, but to give where they felt led, and give according to their "depth." That any part of the $30 they could feel a joy in giving, a purpose, to just go ahead and give it — and then watch and see what God would do. I said, "Don't take my word for it, take God's word in the Scriptures; for when you give, then the Scriptures will happen to you — it will take place. In Luke 6:38 Jesus says:

> *Give, and it shall be given unto you; good measure, pressed down, and shaken together, and running over, shall men give into your bosom . . .*

Finally, I gave them the very best I had — and I put it into my letter as a seed of my own for a need I faced. I concluded by saying, "The giving away from yourself out of your own need, it's to God your Source, and your Source is at the point of your need . . . SO

If you do it as I tell you, and do it in faith
God will multiply the seed and cause man to give to you, when right now it seems all men have forgotten you even exist."

Now that was strong medicine but I believe the Scriptures and I know Seed-Faith works both on God our Source, and upon men whom God uses as instruments.

Intellectually, that's hard to understand so you have to get down into your spirit, your inner self where the Holy Spirit can make it clear to your heart AND your intellect, or mind. In Seed-Faith you get it into your inner perception before you get it into your mind, your understanding.

I could just hear this couple talking as they read over my letter: "Oral Roberts talks to us about Source, giving away from ourselves, and that God is at the point of our need; therefore, when we give to Him we're giving to the one who will cause men to give to us—how can all this be?"

Real soon I got a letter back. It started off:

Dear Brother Roberts.
THE LIGHT HAS DAWNED!

They said that God shone the light upon them when they remembered a farmer always sows his seed away from himself, he puts it into the soil, then he waits for the miracle of reproduction which is always more than he planted.

Then they said, "We had only seven days left to pay the $300. It was pretty bleak. The light dawned and in Seed-Faith we started giving of our last $30. Cautiously at first, then joyously. There we were without the $30 and facing the note of $300—it all looked so impossible. But a strange thing happened. A deal came our way from some man. Our profit was exactly $300. The note is paid, and we're moving ahead again in our business."

I had to stop and wipe my eyes. This had happened to so many that I knew about, but it never ceases to break me up. God is so real, so interested, so true in what He says He will do when we do what He says.

The postscript on their letter though was the best of all. It said, "The most important thing about all this is we're learning through Seed-Faith we have God and God has it all."

HOW A GOLF PROFESSIONAL
AFTER LOSING HIS JOB
FACED HIS LOSS WITH HIS SEED-FAITH

One of the ways I can relax is to get in a few holes of golf. Five holes, or nine, or eighteen, it really doesn't matter. I can get my mind to sort of unwind while striking at that little white ball. Best of all, after studying the Bible I can while playing golf study God's "other book"—the green earth.

Well, I rushed up as usual and started to the starting tee when I met the head professional who is a friend of mine. I helped him receive the baptism in the Holy Spirit, and at a point of need in his life gave him my book, MIRACLE OF SEED-FAITH, and he really absorbed it, making it a way of life.

He's a quiet kind of fellow, very efficient, friendly and always helpful. He has often told me, "The Holy Spirit has changed my life. Before, I dreaded starting the day; now I can't wait to get to my job."

Several times he shared Seed-Faith answers to his prayers.

This time, however, he didn't say, "Hello, Oral, how are you?" He didn't say, "Have a good game."

What he said was, "Oral, I have lost my job."

I said, "What?"

He said, "After 12 years, I've lost my job. Yes, I've been here 12 years."

For a moment a flicker of dismay crossed his face. I could see he was hurt, deeply hurt. Then I saw a light come into his eyes that lighted his whole face. It was amazing. I've seen people crumple under the loss of their position—in my own losses there have been times I couldn't smile, I could hardly stand up.

He said, "The strange thing is that these people like me and I like them. They say I've done a good job and I know I have and I just think the world of them. Another strange thing is that I feel no bitterness of any kind. These people said they felt they needed a change and they've come and told me. You're the first one I've told."

I said, "Let's see what you have lost. You've lost an important position you've held for 12 years. It's gone. It's over with."

He said, "Yes."

I said, "Let's see what you've *not* lost. You've not lost your Source."

He replied, "No, sir, I've not lost Him, He's still everything to me and to my family."

I said, "You've planted a lot of seed."

He answered, "Well, I've sure tried and I'm sure I have. And you know I've enjoyed every moment of it. As you know I got into Seed-Faith about three years ago and I think it's great."

"Even now?" I asked.

"Yes, sir, even now because God is still my Source."

"All right. On one hand, you've lost your position; on the other hand, you've not lost your Source and your seed-planting."

He nodded.

"OK, let me ask you a question when it's the toughest for you. Have you lost your expectation for miracles?"

He said, "No, I haven't. That's one thing I've learned in Seed-Faith. There's a miracle I can expect for every seed I put in."

Then he said, "Look, don't let me hold you up, go on and tee off."

Several days later I returned and was batting a few balls to warm up. He saw me and came over. I had been praying for him, so I looked up to what I would see.

With a big smile he said, "I have a few months left on my contract and they want me to stay and help them out until they get a replacement."

"Isn't that wonderful," I said. "Now God has put you in a position to really practice Seed-Faith and that is to give of your love to these people as if you hadn't lost your job, to do the very best job you have ever done, and to let no bitterness step into your heart, continuing to look to God as your only Source.

"And remember this," I said, "and I speak from experience; as you do all this, keep in mind God has a **due season** for this seed sown. That means at the proper time and place God will open a door to a position better suited to you and you to it. You'll fit like a hand in a glove. When you look back you will see that God let this loss happen that you might gain Christ in a new dimension of trust in a job where you'll be able to do more good."

"Oh," he said, "I would like that."

He grabbed my hand and looked full into my face, "Seed-Faith worked for me these past three years, it's still working since I lost my job. I'm so happy in my soul. I just can't wait to see where God is going to take me next. I just can't wait."

You see, Seed-Faith doesn't keep you from suffering losses, for this is no perfect world we live in. Seed-Faith does, however, give us a stability in our losses, a mighty Source to look to—to trust—and to know that God has placed within every seed of faith planted the potential for a miracle greater than any loss Satan can cause us to suffer.

In the nitty-gritty of life, it gets serious about God being your Source. Because every one of us has losses.

I remember a loss I had that completely baffled me. I was just getting into Seed-Faith and didn't quite have the experience with it I have now. It was the loss of the friendship of some people very dear to me. We really loved each other. They didn't even know why they ceased liking me and turned against me. I couldn't explain it for I had done only good to them.

But it got me to Tulsa and into this ministry and when I look back I see that God was thinking of my welfare all the time.

When you suffer a loss that completely baffles you, *here's* what to do: Think about the *resurrection* of Christ—and the LIFE-GIVING and multiplying *power* in it.

Remember:

God is WITH you.

God is WORKING TO MEET YOUR NEEDS.

God is INDIVIDUALIZING YOU.

God is INDIVIDUALIZING your needs.

God is INDIVIDUALIZING His supply for your needs.

———◆◆◆———

Giving *AWAY* from yourself out of your need (or sacrificially) is giving *TO GOD*, your Source, whose resurrection power multiplies and multiplies and multiplies back to you—at the point of your need!

YOUR GOD-GIVEN KEY FOR TODAY

Now say again and again:

"I Will Plant Seed Away From Myself To Learn To Rely On My Source."

SECOND WEEK

SUNDAY   GOD'S WAY WILL BE MY WAY

MONDAY   GOD IS MY SOURCE

TUESDAY   I WILL PLANT SEED AND GOD WILL MOVE MY MOUNTAINS

WEDNESDAY   GOD IS THE MULTIPLIER OF MY SEED SOWN

THURSDAY   IT IS MORE PRODUCTIVE TO GIVE THAN TO RECEIVE

FRIDAY   I WILL HAVE A SEED-FAITH PROJECT

SATURDAY   I WILL PLANT SEED AWAY FROM MYSELF TO LEARN TO RELY ON MY SOURCE

THIRD WEEK

I Discovered The Source That Never Fails And
I Can Bring Him Alive In Your Life

SUNDAY Key:
GOD IS MY SOURCE OF TOTAL SUPPLY

or

How I Walked Out Of A Situation Of Doubt And
Into Faith That God Is My Source Of Total Supply

EARLY in this ministry I was answering my mail in our dining room. The mail kept increasing until we had to make the garage into an office, and then the entire house.

We moved to another house and settled down, not dreaming the mail would continue to increase until an office would have to be secured.

Soon I was looking for a larger building to rent. When nothing suitable was available I had the feeling that God wanted us to build one. My problem was this: I had no money to construct the building. I realized loans would have to be obtained. But how?

First, I saw a piece of ground that impressed me. As I stepped it off, something seemed to say, "This is your lot." The price was reasonable, but I didn't have the full purchase price and they would sell for cash only.

A man who had been blessed through the Blessing-Pact principle came to my mind. I called him and told him about the ministry's growth and the urgent need for larger quarters to serve the people. He asked me the price of the lot. I told him. He said, "How much do you need?"

I said, "I have half of it; I need the other half which I can repay over a period of time."

He said, "I'll pray about it."

In the mail came his check for the whole amount. I called him back. "You made a mistake. I only need half this amount."

He said, "You can use it, can't you?"

I said, "Yes, I can apply it toward the construction."

He said, "Just give me your word that you'll pay it back over a period of time."

I did. Then I woke up to the fact that a miracle had happened.

I hadn't asked this man for the entire loan. I only needed one-half of the purchase price of the lot. He sent the full price.

In those days the Blessing-Pact principle was just coming into my thinking. But I had not learned the first key principle — to look to God *alone* as my Source. So I allowed the ease with which the purchase money for the lot had come to give me a false confidence in getting a loan to construct the building.

With the deed to the lot in hand, I paid a visit to the bank where I had secured my first small loan. I had paid this back on time and had a good relationship with the bank.

COME BACK IN FIVE YEARS

To my surprise, when I applied for a building loan the banker said, "Come back in about five years after you've had experience and we'll let you have the money."

I couldn't understand it. I went back a second time and got another refusal. I knew no one else in the whole world to whom I could turn. Naturally, I had turned to the ones I knew. The first helped me, the other one had refused.

For days I prayed and meditated over this. Gradually I began to learn things. I discovered I no longer liked this banker. His refusal had canceled from my mind the appreciation of his first loan to me. I asked myself, "Why did he make the first loan? I was not nearly as good a financial risk then as I am now."

The banker had said, "Mr. Roberts, you are a sincere young man. We believe you are doing a good work. But you are in religious work. Therefore, from a business standpoint we have no guarantee you can repay the bank."

I said, "I paid off the first loan."

He said, "Yes, your record is good so far. But what if you died? What if the people stop supporting your work? You are asking for several thousand dollars. It's too risky for the bank. Now after you have operated for five years, you will have established yourself and . . ."

That's when I left.

"GOD IS MY SOURCE"

One day while in prayer, I was asking God to make this banker open up to us. As I did, I felt a check in my spirit. I remembered Philippians 4:19, "But my *God* shall supply all your need according to his riches in glory by Christ Jesus."

I thought, this banker is not God. He doesn't control all the money I need; God does. However, God's riches are in heaven and that's a mighty long way off. That's when it hit me. God didn't say He would supply my needs with His riches in heaven BUT ACCORDING TO HIS RICHES IN HEAVEN BY CHRIST JESUS. God was telling me that He is not poor. He was saying that it's all on deposit in heaven but payable in the coin of the realm down here IF I WOULD LOOK TO HIM AS MY SOURCE.

I never felt better in my life. With God as THE Source, and with my needs being supplied *according* to the amount of riches there in heaven, I would find the loan; the building would be constructed, and I would be able to serve the people.

My inner man was now standing up instead of lying down. When I thought of the banker I no longer disliked him, for he was only doing his job according to standard banking rules. I even prayed for God to bless him for the first loan he had made to help me get started. Then I found myself praying for God to supply this loan I needed.

I had discovered a principle that was to serve me in the future when many other loans, all of them larger, would be needed. **I had discovered the one infallible Source: God is the Source of supply for all my needs.** There would be times when I would forget this principle or neglect to apply it, but ultimately I would stake all my future supply on it and it would never let me down (that's still true today).

Evelyn knew something had happened to me. The brooding I had been going around with was gone. She said, "Honey, you must have gotten the loan."

I said, "No, but I will soon."

She said, "From the bank?"

I said, "Apparently not, but it's coming."

She said, "From where?"

I said, "From God."

Then I explained the new understanding I had found in God's Word. I said, "If our banker doesn't help us, God has somebody who will."

I dismissed the banker from my mind. However, it was not long until he found himself changing his mind. Men who run lending institutions may think they are in control, but when they are dealing with a man who has begun to look to God as THE Source of his supply, they find that God will move heaven and earth, if necessary, to meet his needs.

A NEW FRIEND CROSSES MY PATH

Meanwhile, a man had flown to one of our crusades to observe. While there he saw the largest number of people converted in a single service that he had ever seen. He saw some miracles that astonished him. One was a boy who had stammered all his life and after the healing prayer he could speak perfectly. Another was an alcoholic who was freed and restored to his family. A third was a commander in the United States Navy who had entered the prayer line for the healing of an incurable illness. He had returned at the end of the crusade to tell how the Navy doctors had X-rayed him and pronounced him totally free from the disease.

The man who had flown to the meeting observed all this. He talked with several of the people who had been helped. Then we met. His name was Lee Braxton, a banker and mayor in his city in North Carolina.

At our next crusade he was present with his family. He was also at the following crusade. Finally, he flew to Tulsa to investigate our standing in our home city. He talked to people we did business with, the newspapers, and many others. He liked what he heard and saw.

Then he came to the house where we were struggling to answer our mail. He saw me laying out the page proofs of our monthly magazine on the floor. There was literally no room elsewhere in the house.

He said, "Oral, this ministry has in it the seed of a worldwide spiritual renewal. It's going to grow and touch millions of lives. You've got to build an office and do this work in a businesslike way instead of piecemeal like you're having to do here."

I knew very little about business but I understood that what he said was right. I told him of the refusal of the bank and that I didn't know any other place to go. I said, "However, since the bank's refusal I have come into a new understanding of God's supplying our needs. God is going to work it out for the office to be built."

This knowledge had been revealed to me through God's Word as I studied it and I knew it couldn't fail. Outwardly, nothing was changed. But inside, I was different. I had the knowing inside that God was in the center of my thoughts concerning this need for an office.

Some people think you're crazy or something when you talk like this. For them everything must fit into their own little plan and reasoning. If it doesn't, they are apt to go to pieces or get bitter and resentful. Sometimes they end up saying, "Why has God let this happen to me?"

Maybe God lets this happen to us to show us who our Source of supply really is, and how futile our own way is.

By this time, Lee Braxton himself had been helped through this ministry. He had received a healing, also his son had been healed. In addition, Lee's faith had been increased to the possibility of greater miracles in his life. He was an experienced businessman; I had asked scores of questions and he had answered them. We were now on familiar terms.

Lee said, "Oral, what are you going to do about your new office?"

I replied, "Leave it to God." Now, I had my thoughts on the Lord where they should have been all the time.

I COUNTED MY ASSETS

He said, "Why don't you go back to your banker, and let me go with you this time."

I said, "Fine, but he's already told me I don't have enough assets or experience."

Lee said, "Come on, I'll go with you."

As we went I counted up my assets:

I knew God was at the center of my life.

I knew God is a good God.

I had demonstrated that God answers prayer and even performs miracles of healing.

I believed in what I was doing.

I had been giving generously to God's work.

I had SEED-FAITH working, although I didn't call it that at the time.

People were getting help and the number being helped was increasing with every crusade.

I was sincere, honest, a hard worker, and had faith.

I was expecting help from God and knew it would come sooner or later.

Those assets looked and felt mighty good to me. They were evidence on which I could release my faith.

The banker, I knew, was impressed with me as a person, as a man who paid his bills, as one interested in helping people. These were assets but not the kind the bank examiners would look at if they saw a good sized loan on the books of their institution.

My work had been incorporated as a nonprofit organization. Its financial assets were few. But its future was bright. From a cold, logical point of view, this was not enough. But God, I knew now, was enough.

When we entered the bank Lee said, "Wait a minute, Oral. Here's what I want you to tell the banker: Tell him that Lee Braxton is president of the First National Bank in his city back in North Carolina; he's been here, likes what he sees, and his bank will lend you the money you need to construct the new office."

I replied, "But, Lee, if your bank is going to do that why should I even see this banker?"

Lee said, "Just do as I tell you."

We went into the office of the president. I introduced Lee and blurted out what Lee had told me to say.

The president turned to Lee and said, "Mr. Braxton, you tell your bank to keep its money in North Carolina. We'll take care of our friend, Oral Roberts, here."

THE SOURCE THAT NEVER FAILS

You could have knocked me over with a feather. I didn't have any faith that this man would change his mind. Yet suddenly I had a loan of several thousand dollars from the same bank that had refused me twice before. I was the same man, my assets hadn't changed, still I was looking at a miracle. I realized I was looking at something else too —the Source that never fails: God.

"Thank you very much," I said. "I'll accept the loan." The papers were signed and in less than an hour we were on our way home.

When I returned a few weeks later to get the first installment on the loan, the president smiled and said, "Reverend Roberts, I should have my head examined. I just don't know what possessed me to make this loan."

I smiled right back and said, "I know."

"Yes, I guess you do," the banker replied.

This incident in my life was large at the time. It has helped me in much larger ones since, for through the growth of this ministry I've had to become not only an evangelist, but a businessman.

The Apostle Paul had to learn to be a businessman too, as well as being called of God to preach the gospel. He carried his business with him—tentmaking. I know he faced many of the same problems I have had to face. But he found God was sufficient in the same way I have come to see Him. It was Paul who said, "But my God shall supply ALL your need according to his riches in glory by Christ Jesus" (Philippians 4:19). Paul had tested this mighty Source and found Him never failing.

———◆◆◆———

"God is my Source of *total* supply." Remember, this is not a mere pleasant reassurance. Dare to take God literally. Think about the needs you are facing right now:

Are you physically sick?

Is your marriage breaking up?

Are your children breaking your heart?

Do you need spiritual help?

Don't forget this principle or neglect to apply it. Think about it constantly.

God controls *ALL* the sources of supply. Your Source will never let you down!

YOUR GOD-GIVEN KEY FOR TODAY

Say again and again:

"God Is My Source Of Total Supply."

MONDAY Key: I WILL NOT LIMIT GOD—EVER!

or
Learning The Difference Between Source And Instrument Took Away My Resentment For My Limited Income

While I was growing up we lived close to an uncle who made his living from his big orchard. In his later life it was my privilege to lead him to Christ. We spent many happy moments together. It was he who inadvertently first helped me to see the difference between *source* and *instrument.*

He raised apples, peaches, apricots, cherries, pears, grapes, berries, and other kinds of fruit. His pride and joy was the big luscious Elberta peach. People came from miles around to buy this peach.

When I entered the ministry I moved away; it was several years before I visited my uncle again. I was shocked when I saw the orchard, or what remained of it. Gone were most of the beautiful fruit-growing trees. Only one or two trees of the prized Elberta peach remained. They were stubby and produced only a few small peaches.

"What happened?" I asked my uncle. "Did you have a storm? Was there an invasion of insects? Where is the orchard—the peaches, and the other fruit?"

He said, "Oral, they're gone. But it wasn't a storm; it wasn't insects. It was me."

I said, "What did you do that caused this to happen?"

Sadly he replied, "I'll tell you what I did. As long as the fruit came each fall, I was satisfied to leave the trees alone. They bore fruit and I thought my source was the fruit. The fruit fed my family. We sold thousands of bushels and used the money. The fruit became everything to me. It was my business. I depended on it. Everything I did I judged according to how it related to the fruit. Then one year the crop was not so good. The next year it was less. That was when I stopped thinking about the fruit and started looking to the trees. Before, I had paid little attention to the trees. I cut the weeds and did a little plowing down each row. Then I woke up and realized that the peaches and the other fruit were just what they were—fruit of the tree. The supply was the tree. If I took care of the tree, the fruit would grow. Through poor understanding and haphazard care of the trees, I have only these few poor trees left. There's not enough fruit to pick anymore."

Then his eyes lighted up. He said, "But I'm putting in a young orchard. I've gone to the agricultural experts and learned how to take care of the tree first. So I'm starting over. This time I'll take care of my source."

Immediately I saw how I had been doing the same thing. I had looked to results as my source rather than to God who had sent them.

I had failed to see that the various people who had helped me, and the places where I drew an income, were instruments, results — not my Source at all. A source is where it all comes from. An instrument can be anything that is useful at a given time.

WHY LIMIT GOD?

When I was pastoring in Enid, Oklahoma, before I entered this ministry in 1947, the board of the church where I was pastoring set my salary. It was so small I couldn't pay the tuition at the university where I was studying. My family didn't have proper clothes; our car needed repairing. Sometimes Evelyn would go to the grocery store and fill up her cart, only to have to unload part of it at the cash register stand because she didn't have enough money to pay for it. It was getting us down.

There I was up before the people, trying to tell them about God. I knew they had needs too. I could triumphantly share God's love for their spiritual welfare and they understood it. When I attempted to apply the Word of God to the healing of their bodies and for the supplying of their material needs, the words would often stick in my throat.

I told how God met people's needs in Bible times, how He was concerned for the total person, but there was very little demonstration in my life or the lives of those to whom I ministered.

Then one day I told the board I had figured up the absolute minimum required for me and my family to exist. I included groceries, car care, clothes, even a haircut twice a month. I figured it almost to the penny. It came to $55 a week. They granted my request to the letter.

For the next several weeks we squeezed by until I realized I was limiting God by looking to the board for my supply. I discovered resentment in my heart. Why didn't they raise me? Why didn't they see the needs of my family? With the exception of the hours I spent each week in class, my whole life was engaged with the people of this church. I was on call day and night for sick calls, etc.

One day I saw that the board was not my source; God was. God wanted to meet my needs. I should take the lid off my faith. I should stop praying for the board to give me a raise. I should start looking to God who promised to supply all my needs according to His riches, not the meager resources of that little church. I should start looking to this group only as an *instrument* or *means* God could use.

When I faced needs, I should look to God in a direct way and trust Him to help me through any means He chose.

Gone was my resentment. I knew God could make a way. I knew He controlled all the means of supply, both expected and unexpected.

Sharing this with Evelyn was a great delight. She has always been practical about money matters, knowing it takes money to raise a family. I could tell the idea of looking to God as our Source inspired her.

We have learned that looking to people is the sure road to disillusionment. The same is often true if they look only to us. When we think that our friend, or our employer, or an employee is the source of our supply, we are dealing with *means* and not *Source*.

ONE SOURCE, MANY INSTRUMENTS

I'll never forget when I was in Israel the first time—in the early fifties. I traveled to the source of the Jordan River, in that portion of Israel that is called after one of the twelve sons of Israel, Dan. There I found water springing up from the earth and flowing into a tiny stream southward, getting bigger, wider, deeper and stronger as it went. I followed it for several miles where it flowed into an area called the sea of Galilee, a section of our earth below sea level. But it didn't stop, it flowed on through the blue waters of Galilee, coming out on the other side, still flowing on as the Jordan, and continued to flow southward but now a much bigger stream. Many miles farther down I saw it flow into the Dead Sea, whose bottom is the lowest point on earth, and there the Dead Sea received it and wouldn't let it through. So the waters of the Jordan die at the Dead Sea—the waters are dead containing no sea life of any kind.

From the moment the Jordan begins its journey important things happen, besides watering and enriching land on both sides and forming two lakes—Galilee and the Dead Sea—the really important thing is its source. Should that small spring dry up and cease to flow, the Jordan River would cease to be, the land it now waters would dry up, and its two seas would fail. It would mean failure, futility, lost hope for the nations of people who benefit from it.

The Jordan can say, "The Springs of Dan are my source. According to the waters flowing from Dan's Springs I become a stream, a river, large bodies of water, life to the desert and to the people. Without my source I no longer exist—I become a nothing."

I can say the same thing. Without God and His concern for me, without His power to meet all my needs, without His presence with me and in me, I no longer exist as a *full human* being; I merely exist as a part of a man, my need reducing my life to drabness, emptiness, failure, futility, fear, panic, loss of faith, loss of the will to live, a restlessness and a worry to myself and others.

I know. I have been there. I've gone through it. I failed because I had no Source for my life. Instruments, yes. People I believe in, yes. Things I trusted in, yes. Plans I made, yes. Dreams, yes. Efforts to succeed, yes. None of these things, however, was a source to me, but instruments only. Each failed me and I got exactly what I deserved.

I WILL NOT LIMIT GOD — *EVER*

FOR NO MAN, NO GROUP OF PEOPLE, NO EARTHLY INSTRUMENT OF ANY KIND, IS DESIGNED TO BE, OR EVER CAN BE, THE SOURCE OF MY TOTAL SUPPLY. ONLY GOD CAN BE MY SOURCE . . . YOUR SOURCE.

YOUR GOD-GIVEN KEY FOR TODAY

Say: **"I Will Not Limit God—Ever!"**

TUESDAY Key: AM I DOING ALL I CAN DO?

or
The Difference Between A Winner And A Loser
And What This Means To You

Over the years a two-part pattern has formed in which I have seen God work miracles. The first part of the pattern is that weeks or months after I've prayed and seeded for a miracle (and continued to look to my Source for it to happen), then suddenly there is my miracle right before my eyes.

The second part of the pattern is that sometimes miracles happen very quickly. It almost stuns me, it's so quick. But to be perfectly frank, most of my miracles do not happen quickly. Sometimes I'm tempted to actually believe God has forgotten me, or doesn't care. Sometimes I find myself saying:

"God, WHY? WHY is this happening to me?

What have I done to deserve it?"

Then I try to remember that questions like these are the signs of a loser. A winner doesn't dwell on, "Why has this happened to me? What have I done to deserve this?" A winner starts with different kinds of questions. He asks:

"Am I failing to do what God says in the Bible for me to do to come out of this?"

"Who am I making my source of total supply—man or God?"

"Have I been seeding for a miracle," as God says, *"cheerfully?"*

"Am I demanding that God send my miracle in my own way and time, OR AM I TRUSTING HIM AS MY SOURCE TO SEND IT IN HIS OWN TIME AND WAY?"

As I remember the difference between a loser and a winner, then I can try to do something about my situation. It helps me take action in a positive direction—God's. I try not to sit (or lie) there asking negative question after negative question, eating my heart out, increasing my misery. Taking action like this has been a great help to me. It has helped me receive many miracles that people had told me were impossible.

I'm learning a fierce, tenacious expectation for my miracle to happen . . . and at the same time . . . to really trust God my Source to make my miracle happen in *His* own *way* and *time*. It's not always easy to do this—I have to consciously and prayerfully work at it.

———————

Are you a loser or a winner?

A LOSER ASKS: "WHY HAS THIS HAPPENED TO ME?"
A WINNER ASKS: "AM I DOING ALL THAT GOD HAS TOLD ME TO DO? AM I GIVING AS A SEED I PLANT? HAVE I MADE GOD MY SOURCE? AM I EXPECTING A MIRACLE?"

YOUR GOD-GIVEN KEY FOR TODAY

Ask yourself:

"Am I Doing All I Can Do?"

WEDNESDAY Key: I REALLY KNOW GOD WILL HELP ME

or
Why I Know Your Needs Exist To Be Met

Jesus said, "I am come that they (you) might have . . ."

How different this is from what a person ordinarily associates with coming from God. Written into building contracts are such clauses as: Not responsible for acts of God such as earthquakes, storms, etc.

A man horribly misshapen, desperately poor, says, "Look, this is what God did to me,"

When disaster strikes, people are hurt or killed, there are those who say, "This is the will of God."

Not so with Jesus. "I am come," He declared, "that they might have life, and that they might have it more abundantly" (John 10:10).

When His own disciples wanted to incite a riot and have a certain city burned to the ground, Jesus replied, "The Son of man is not come to destroy men's lives, but to save them" (Luke 9:56).

The Bible says, "Every good gift and every perfect gift is from above, and cometh down from the Father of lights, with whom is no variableness, neither shadow of turning" (James 1:17).

And to the children of God: "Beloved, I wish above all things that thou mayest prosper and be in health, even as thy soul prospereth" (3 John 2).

The father of the prodigal son said to the elder brother, who was mad because the father had received the wayward brother back and given him new clothes and a feast with his friends, "Son, all that I have is yours."

The elder brother didn't really know his own father. He had to be reminded that all his father possessed was his at any time he asked for it (Luke 15:31).

The Bible says, "My God shall supply all your need according to his riches in glory by Christ Jesus" (Philippians 4:19).

Jesus demonstrated abundant life to all He met. He thought in terms of their needs being met, their sicknesses being healed, things they had been denied being restored to them, torments they had brought on themselves being relieved, and the curse of sin over them being removed. He came in the form of their needs.

Jesus looked on a need differently. Most people today see their needs and become negative. Often they say, "Why? Why has this happened to me? What have I done to deserve it?"

Jesus looks on a need in the most positive way. To Him . . .

A NEED EXISTS TO BE MET

To Jesus, a need in your life is not something to discourage and make you negative. It is a legitimate claim you have upon His limitless resources to be met in full!

This is what God's Word says, "God shall supply all your need." Now SHALL is a strong word. In other words, **the moment your need faces you, God's SHALL-SUPPLY PROMISE goes into effect.**

This is something you need to know and get positive about. No need should intimidate or bully you. If Christ is first in your life, and you are giving to Him, you are in connection! You are plugged in. God will answer! You should be expecting. What a difference this makes in your attitude!

Say this Scripture over and over again to yourself until you FEEL it deep down inside:

*But my God shall supply all your need according to his riches
in glory by Christ Jesus* (Philippians 4:19).

ALL! ALL! ALL! *ALL!*
Praise God! HE AIN'T POOR NO MORE!

Say: **YOUR GOD-GIVEN KEY FOR TODAY**

                              <u>**"I Really Know God Will Help Me."**</u>

THURSDAY Key: JESUS IS ALWAYS IN THE NOW OF MY NEED

or
How I Learned A Most Important Lesson—
God Is Always In The Now Of My Need . . . And Your Need

In 1947 I came to the crossroads of my life. As a young pastor and
college student, I had to have some answers that neither my church
nor my college was giving me. I began a study of the Bible as I never
had before. My Bible was usually open to one of the four Gospels or
the book of Acts in the New Testament. Often I studied these Scriptures on my knees. As I read the Gospels and the Acts . . .

> I saw how Jesus cared for people and had compassion and
> healed them.
> I saw that Jesus had come in the likeness of man and in the
> likeness of God—Son of God, Son of man. My mind
> couldn't understand it but my spirit could.
> I saw that Jesus had come to show us what God is like . . .
> that God is not against people—God is for people!
> I saw that **Jesus came to deliver and heal the people** . . . to
> set them free . . . to give them abundant LIFE in the NOW
> of their existence!
> I saw that Jesus is always IN THE NOW—the same yester-
> day, today, and forever.
> I saw that He is in the now of my generation, and He wants to
> continue to give men life more abundantly, to really be
> the Source of their lives and to supply all their needs.
> I saw that He actually sat where we sit, He feels what we feel,
> and He is at the point of need of each human being.
> I saw that it is at the point of your need where you look for
> Him and where you will find Him.

This thrilled and excited me; I felt I would burst inside if I didn't share it. Strangely enough, this brought a deep dissatisfaction in my life.

On the one hand, I was studying in the university, supposedly studying truth, learning how to ask questions. On the other hand, I was a Christian—a young pastor preaching the Word of God. I saw the gap between what I understood Jesus Christ to be in the NOW and what people's understanding of Him is. I saw what Jesus had done 2,000 years ago and is present to do in my generation, and what scant knowledge we have that He will actually do the same things, only greater, if we see Him as He is, and will believe.

I began to ask questions:

Why aren't we more like Jesus?

Why don't we heal the people as He did?

Why are we not concerned about the total man—his soul, mind, body, all of his needs—the whole of his existence, as well as his future in eternity?

Why aren't we concerned about the individual as he lives on earth facing life as it really is?

I shared these thoughts with some people but got no answers. I was shut up in the silence of my own heart, trying to understand this man Jesus of Nazareth.

GOD GAVE ME A DREAM

One night I had a dream. In that dream God let me see people, much as He SEES them . . . and HEARS them . . . and FEELS them. I saw that EVERYBODY HAS A NEED. EVERYBODY IS SICK IN SOME WAY. I saw that sickness is disharmony:

If something is wrong in the soul, to that extent the man is sick.

If something is wrong in the mind, to that extent the man is sick.

If something is wrong in the body, to that extent the man is sick.

If something is wrong in his family that touches his own life a man is often thrown out of rhythm and balance with his own life, and to that extent the man is sick.

If something is wrong financially, to that extent the man is sick.

If something is wrong in any way, in any part of his existence, to that extent he is sick.

In this way, I SAW THE SICKNESS OF PEOPLE AND . . . OH . . . IT TURNED ME ON TO WHAT JESUS CHRIST IS ALL ABOUT . . .

JESUS IS IN THE WORLD TO TOUCH
PEOPLE AT THE POINT OF THEIR NEED

And I was in the world with His message of His healing power.

Evelyn, my wife, said, "Oral, you've been getting up at night and walking the floor. What's wrong?"

"God has been giving me a dream," I said. "It has been the same dream night after night and it devastates me."

"What is the dream, Oral?"

"I dreamed that God showed me mankind as He sees them and as He hears them. What I see and hear takes my breath away."

"Well, what do they look like?" she asked.

"Have you ever gone into a hospital and heard the moans and groans of people really ill? Have you ever seen a person so sick with his problems and torments that he is beside himself? Have you ever seen a human being so down in his spirit it's like life is over for him? That is how I'm seeing people now. I did not know it before but everybody is sick in some way. They must have healing from God . . ."

I could say no more for my dream had become too real as I retold it. Evelyn took me into her arms and we cried together.

That night I began to grow up to the work God had made for me. I was 29½ years old.

But I was a man. I was finally ready to answer the calling of God. I knew WHAT God wanted me to do but I didn't know HOW. But the HOW would never have been answered if I had not had this deep feeling inside . . .

NOW WAS GOD'S TIME FOR ME TO BEGIN

I looked at Evelyn and said, "Honey, I have this knowing inside me that God wants me to follow Jesus the way He really is . . . to have His compassion for people . . . to try to bring His healing power to the people . . . but I don't know *how*."

Slowly and thoughtfully she said, "Oral, I've had a feeling from the very beginning of our marriage that God has had His hand on you—and I believe you know what you have to do . . ."

God was speaking through her and I felt it. I felt God directing me to enter into a fast and to spend time in meditation and prayer. It wouldn't be easy because I was carrying 16 hours in college, pastoring a church, and taking care of my young family. However, there was a drive in my soul which I could not explain.

It burned in me like a fire;
    it blew through me like a wind;
        it pounded me like a hammer;
            it roared in my mind night and day.

I could not get away from it.

One day I went to my little church study and opened my Bible to the book of Acts. I read about the miracles until the possibility of this happening in the now literally caused me to fall to the floor. There on my face before God I began talking to Him, saying things like this: "God, You spoke to people in the Bible. You had to speak to the people in the Bible or they couldn't have written it. You've spoken to men and women throughout the ages. You spoke to me 12 years ago that You were going to heal me and that I was to take Your healing power to my generation. Now, will You speak to me again? Will You tell me what I am . . . who I am . . . what I'm to do with my life . . . how I am to carry out the calling that You have given me?"

It seemed like I was a tiny speck in the universe. I was reaching up to God. I didn't even know if I was being heard but my heart was pounding and saying, "Speak to me, Lord." And He did speak! Later I felt these words deep within me:

> **"From this hour you will have My power to heal the sick, to detect the presence of demons, to know their number and their name and to have My power to cast them out!"**

I didn't understand those words completely, but I knew that I had heard from GOD and that if I ever did any of these things it would be by His power.

I drove home and told Evelyn to cook a meal for me. As we ate, we laughed and cried and talked and rejoiced. We knew it was a new day!!

Then I said, "Evelyn, we've got to be sure. It's easy to say that God is directing but it has to work in the practical realities of everyday life."

I was thinking of Jesus' words, "Thy will be done in earth, as it is in heaven" (Matthew 6:10).

So I decided to prove to myself that God had truly spoken to me here *on this earth*. I secured the use of an auditorium in downtown Enid, Oklahoma, for 2 p.m. the following Sunday and announced a service and invited the people to come for my message and prayer. I said, "God, if I really heard Your voice and I'm to do what You've asked me to do, then . . .

1. Give me an audience of at least 1,000 people (I had been preaching to a congregation of less than 200).
2. Supply the financial costs in an honorable way.
3. Heal the people by divine power so conclusively that they, as well as I, will know I am called of God to carry on this ministry of Your healing power!!"

I promised God, "If You will grant these three things I will resign my pastorate and enter immediately into evangelistic crusades; I will go to the people at the point of their needs."

But I was scared when the day arrived. I was so scared that I couldn't eat. It was Sunday. Some of the church people joined me. At 2 o'clock we went downtown to the auditorium.

The custodian met me at the door and said, "Mr. Roberts, there are 1,200 people here."

"Thank God," I said to myself, "condition number one is settled…"

Later we received the offering to pay the rent on the building, which was $160. This was a big amount in those days to a young preacher. When it was counted the offering was $163.03 — $3.03 over.

After I preached and began to pray for the people God began to bring His healing power to the needs of the people.

The first person I prayed for was a German woman. She had a bent and crippled hand which had been like that for 38 years. She spoke in broken English and when God healed her hand she cried at the top of her voice, "I'm healed!!! I'm healed!!!" People saw her and were broken up by it.

That afternoon I prayed for the unsaved and for the sick from about 3 until 6 o'clock. Soon there wasn't a dry thread of clothing on my body. But when I walked out of that building that evening . . .

I knew that Jesus Christ had come forth from the Gospels and the Acts of the Apostles like a hurricane into a young man's heart.

I saw a world that was hurting and I wanted to go to it.

I wanted to hug people — to touch them. I wanted to love them and tell them that Jesus of Nazareth loved them.

A knowing welled up within me that day — a knowing of God's NOWNESS.

a knowing of God's will and purpose for my life.

a knowing I was called of God to minister His miracle power to my generation.

a knowing that . . .

Jesus is in the now . . .
He is at the point of your need . . . and my needs!

God is in the NOW or He's never been.

God is here or He's nowhere.

God loves you or He doesn't love anybody.

God is concerned about your existence, or He's never been concerned about the existence of anyone (Hebrews 13:8).

YOUR GOD-GIVEN KEY FOR TODAY

Say again and again today:

"Jesus Is Always In The Now Of My Need!"

Key:

FRIDAY WHEN I DO ALL I CAN DO, I CAN LEAVE THE REST TO GOD

or

The Day My Son Said, "Dad, Get Off My Back"

Nowhere is there a greater need for the healing of relationships today than in our homes. You probably can count on your fingers the number of families in our country who don't have problems with their children. Or children who don't have problems with their parents. It seems like it is that kind of age, and a minister's family is no exception.

A Scripture that I have tried to live by, and that has the Three Keys in it, is Matthew 6:33:

> But seek ye first the kingdom of God . . . and all these things shall be added unto you.

I have tried to put God first in my life, to come under God's authority, to do what He has called me to do by putting in the seed, then trusting that He would take care of my family, that my children would become Christians and serve God, and that they would make something of their lives. In this way, I have expected miracles to happen to each of them.

Having been called into this ministry, I have had to travel throughout the world and be gone from home much of the time. Really, Evelyn raised our four children. When I was home, I was with the children a lot. I played with them and I taught them the Scriptures. But I was gone so much. Sometimes Evelyn would go with me because I would get so lonesome, especially when I was overseas for several weeks at a time.

We had babysitters to stay with our children; sometimes it worked out and sometimes it didn't. I remember when we went to Australia, I said, "Honey, go with me if you can. I will be over there a long time . . . maybe we can get someone to stay with the children."

Richard was just a little boy at that time. When we came home from Australia I went into his bedroom and discovered that someone had chopped off the bedpost. I said, "What happened?"

The lady who had stayed with the children said, "Well, Richard was upset because you and his mother were gone so he took his little hatchet and cut off the bedpost."

I wanted to "wear him out" but I couldn't, to save my life.

As Richard grew up a gap grew between us. He began to sing for coffeehouses and to lean toward show business. The more I wanted him to sing for me in the ministry, the less he wanted to. One Sunday morning I asked him to sing for one of our seminars at ORU and he said, "No, Dad, I don't want to sing for you."

It shouldn't have hurt me, but it did. It really got down inside. When children are little they step on your toes, but when they are older they step on your heart.

Then Richard went off to a state university. I could understand his not particularly wanting to attend ORU when his father was president. He was away from home for the first time on his own, and doing his own thing. I was back home, still traveling, still thinking about him, and praying and wondering about his gifted voice which was being developed more fully all the time.

Then one day he came home. He said, "Dad, let's go out and play a game of golf." We went out on the golf course and he was hitting the ball "a mile." He is a tremendous golfer. (I'm a pretty good golfer myself once in a while but I couldn't hit the ball that day because I was all bound up inside. My mind was not on the game.) As I talked to Richard I could see he was turning me off. Finally, I said, "OK, Richard, let's just go home." So we picked up our clubs right in the midst of the game and headed for the car. We sat there and just glared at each other. And I will remember his words as long as I live. He said, "Dad, get off my back—AND GET OUT OF MY LIFE!!"

Then it came to me that maybe I was on his back; maybe I was trying to save him. I was not trusting in my Source to do it. I thought about it a moment. I calmed down and I began to silently pray in the Spirit. Confidentially, I didn't know what to say to God with my own understanding (1 Corinthians 14:15).

Then I said, "OK, Richard, give me your hand." With his hand in mine, I said, "From this moment I am off your back. I am going to put you in the hands of God."

I felt then it was God's battle and not mine. The one who is my Source of total supply had him. A relief came over me. Richard went back to the university. Outwardly nothing had changed, but I had put the Three Miracle Keys of Seed-Faith to work and I was expecting a miracle.

Then one day his mother received a phone call and Richard said, "Mother, do you suppose that ORU would accept me for next year?"

She asked me and I said, "I don't know, Evelyn." Richard had taken up a bad habit or two and later, when he came to me, I told him he couldn't do the things he was doing and be a student on the ORU campus. I told him God had told me to build it on His authority, and that required definite rules and regulations.

He said, "I can quit the bad habits; I can discipline myself."

I said, "That will be up to you."

There is a point in dealing with your children when it has to be at arm's length. You are no longer emotionally involved. They are released to God and you can act without fear. The Holy Spirit operating in your life takes the gift of faith and drops it into your heart so that you can look upon your problems from the vantage point of God himself and believe as God believes. You can expect miracles.

Richard enrolled at ORU, and he followed the rules of the campus. But we were still having problems. Then he fell in love with Patti, an ORU student from Portland, Oregon, the young woman who is now his wife. Shortly before their wedding date something happened to their line of communication, particularly in spiritual matters. Although Patti was very much in love with Richard, she knew they didn't have a chance if they got bogged down there. She told him, "Richard, there's a special kind of communication between Christians—and a very special kind between a Christian man and woman who plan to be married. They are of one mind and their utmost goal is to serve the Lord and to live the way He wants them to live. I feel that somehow we are missing each other on this. If our communication breaks down here, it will break down in other areas of our lives. This frightens me. I know you are a Christian and if you die you will go to heaven, but of what earthly good are you to God? I know our plans are all finalized but unless something changes, I'll have to call off the wedding."

She later told me, "I was searching for an inner commitment in Richard that said, 'Lord, if You call me to the wilds of Africa, or to Brazil, or wherever, I will go because I love You.'"

During this time, Evelyn was with me in California. She said, "Oral, I feel impressed to go home." When she has these feelings I never oppose her. She got on a plane and was home within a few hours.

Richard was living in the dorm on campus at the time. His mother hadn't been home but a short time when he walked into the house. He said, "Mother, I'm so glad you are home. I've got to talk to you."

Evelyn said, "What is the trouble, Richard?"

"Well, something has happened to Patti. She can't seem to understand that I love her, and I really do."

Then he said, "Mother, she is going to call the wedding off."

Evelyn said, "Well, Richard, when you committed your life to the Lord recently, did you say, 'Lord, I will live for You if You will give me Patti?' You can't compromise with God—He doesn't want your commitment conditionally. God wants all of you, or nothing. Now He may, or may not give you Patti. You can live without Patti but you can't live without the Lord. The Lord wants all of you without reservations."

Then he got down on his knees and put his head in his mother's lap like he used to when he was a little boy, and they really prayed. And something happened inside Richard. He looked up, smiling through his tears, and he said, "It is all right, Mother. It is all right. I don't want to give up Patti, but if that is the way the Lord wants it, I must serve God regardless."

Then he picked up the phone and called me in California. He said, "Dad, everything is OK now."

I knew what he meant. "Dad, you are not on my back anymore."

The next morning Richard saw Patti and he started to tell her what had happened. But he didn't have to tell her. She said, "I was praying last night too. And suddenly that heaviness lifted. I knew something had happened. I didn't know what, exactly, but I wasn't worried anymore. Richard, I am ready to marry you."

They were married in November 1968. It has been a joy to Evelyn and me to see them putting God first in their total lives—their home, their time, their giving, and especially their talents. Richard is now deeply involved in this ministry with me. Although they now have two beautiful little girls, they still take time to minister and they are touching the hearts of thousands with their consecrated singing talents as they minister with us on our television programs and hour-long TV specials, as well as on tour with the ORU World Action Singers.

On one of our TV programs I asked, "Richard, do you still think I'm on your back?"

He smiled and said, "No, Dad. You're no longer on my back but I'm by your side."

Well, this Scripture is really true:

> Seek ye first the kingdom of God . . . and all these things shall be added unto you (Matthew 6:33).

You have been tested and you will be tested again . . . but if you put Him first—

if you make God the Source . . .

if you open up and put in the seed of your INNER SELF and expect a miracle . . .

if you are expecting God to take a hand in the situation...

wonderful things will happen in your inner man and with your relationships with your family and with people.

———◆———

Now, leave it to God.

YOUR GOD-GIVEN KEY FOR TODAY

"When I Do All I Can Do, I Can Leave The Rest To God."

SATURDAY
Key:
GOD WILL WORK FOR ME THROUGH MY NEED

or

Why Your Greatest Source Of Supply And Sense Of Security Is In The Things You Lack . . . Not In The Things You Have

There is a feeling that can come into a person's heart where he feels he has it made·. . . that no matter what happens, he's OK. He feels so secure that he can even command his soul and say, "Soul, take your ease. Eat, drink, and be merry." Our Lord told a parable about a man like this in Luke 12. He said:

The ground of a certain rich man brought forth plentifully: And he thought within himself, saying, What shall I do, because I have no room where to bestow my fruits? And he said, This will I do: I will pull down my barns, and build greater; and there will I bestow all my fruits and my goods. And I will say to my soul, Soul, thou hast much goods laid up for many years; take thine ease, eat, drink, and be merry. But God said unto him, Thou fool, this night thy soul shall be required of thee: then whose shall those things be, which thou hast provided? So is he that layeth up treasure for himself, and is not rich toward God (Luke 12:16-21).

Now here is a man who felt no sense of need. Certainly, he didn't feel any need of God. As a matter of fact, he thought that he controlled his own life, that he could even speak to his soul and order it around. He really believed that he could take the things of this world and with them satisfy the deepest longings of his inner self, his eternal soul. He thought that. He thought that so much it became a way of life, a pattern of his existence. It was in his heart so much so that he was going to carry that thought into death and the judgment. And that is when God judged him. God said, "Thou fool, this night thy soul is required of thee. And whose shall all these things be that you have provided . . . that you are leaning on and resting your life on?"

Then Jesus said a word to you and to me in the NOW:

Consider the lilies how they grow: they toil not, they spin not; and yet I say unto you, that Solomon in all his glory was not arrayed like one of these. If then God so clothe the grass, which is to day in the field, and to morrow is cast into the oven; how much more will he clothe you, O ye of little faith? (Luke 12:27,28).

Or in other words, Jesus said, "So is he that leans and depends on things and is not dependent upon God as his Source. If God can take care of the lilies of the field, certainly He can take care of you, O ye of little faith."

I dealt with a man not long ago who wanted to be employed by our ministry. He had much to offer and believed very much in what we were doing, but when we came down to it he said, "I don't think I can handle it."

I wanted to know why because I felt he was eminently able and qualified.

He said, "It would require work depending upon God as sort of an unknown Source. Where I am, I know how much I earn. No matter what goes, I'm taken care of. I've got security. At my age I've got to think about security for my family."

THE MOST DANGEROUS TIME IN OUR LIVES IS
WHEN WE DO NOT HAVE TO HAVE FAITH . . .
WHEN EVERYTHING IS TAKEN CARE OF

I thanked him for considering us and wished him Godspeed. I wish I could have talked with him more because I think he's in one of the most dangerous periods of his life. I think most people are in a dangerous period of their life when they feel that they have to stay at a place where there's no risk to be taken . . . where they don't have to cast out in faith upon God . . . where they feel that everything is going to be provided for them through good and bad . . . where they don't have to have faith. We are in a dangerous period when this is the position in which we live, when that feeling is in our hearts.

Your greatest source of supply and sense of security is in the things you lack . . . not in the things you have. For the things you have, if you are not careful, can become a god to you and you will lean on them.

When we lean on instruments only—on our job, the money we have in the bank, etc.,—we lose something too. Maybe we don't lose our souls today but we lose something in the inner man. We lose the sense of trust in God. The Three Miracle Keys of Seed-Faith have no place in our lives. And miracles cease to happen, or even to be expected.

THE GREATEST SOURCE OF SUPPLY YOU CAN
HAVE AND THE GREATEST SECURITY YOU CAN
FEEL IS WHEN YOU DON'T HAVE ANYTHING BECAUSE
THEN YOU ARE GOING TO HAVE TO LEARN TO BE LEAN
AND HUNGRY AND TO TRUST IN GOD

God put you here on this earth to till it and to plant seed for Him so He could use it and to multiply it back to meet your needs. God didn't put you here to have everything provided that you need and suddenly make that a false god. God put you here to trust in Him — hour-by-hour, day-by-day.

If you lack ability, that can be a great source of supply to you if you turn to God and call upon Him to help you.

If you don't have enough money, that can be a great source of security if you will turn to God and say, "God, I don't have enough money. I'm working as hard as I know how but I need Your help."

God has never permitted me to have any money when I start a project. Time after time He has said in my heart, "I'm going to let you start with the same ingredient I used when I made the earth — nothing."

I started this ministry with none of the world's goods, only a little faith.

I started the tent crusades without a dime promised me for support.

I started Oral Roberts University with no land, no buildings, no faculty, no students, no operations money.

I started our present nationwide television series with nothing but the belief in my own heart that "now is the time." And I live this way every day. At the time, I don't like it like this. Everything in me cries out against it.

I want security. I want to know where all the money is coming from, how, and when.

I want to quit struggling, from starting everything from point zero.

I want . . . I want . . . I want . . . But God says a big NO!

He says you develop through struggle — you advance through just enough faith to start and let Him increase it as you use it day-by-day. You get to the goal by reaching down deep inside and pulling up those extra resources of your spirit. You get down to the pain level — when you hurt and reach and strive and sow that extra seed.

This is my way for successful living, and through obedience you will reach it. If I've learned anything, anything at all in this ministry, it is to t-r-u-s-t in God and make Him the only Source of my life.

The most dangerous time in your life is when you think you do not have to have faith . . . when everything seems to be taken care of. These are only things . . . and they will fail you. On the other hand, your greatest source of supply and greatest security is when you don't have anything because then you are going to learn to trust in GOD — *your only true Source!*

You are going to learn to struggle,
    to press your way,
        to pull up your inner resources,
           to plant seeds of faith,
                and keep on planting...planting...planting...

Ask yourself: "Am I depending on things?" or . . .
    "Am I trusting in God my Source?"

Write your answer here:

_____

YOUR GOD-GIVEN KEY FOR TODAY

Say:

"God Will Work For Me Through My Need!"

THIRD WEEK

SUNDAY	GOD IS MY SOURCE OF TOTAL SUPPLY
MONDAY	I WILL NOT LIMIT GOD—*EVER!*
TUESDAY	AM I DOING ALL I CAN DO?
WEDNESDAY	I REALLY KNOW GOD WILL HELP ME
THURSDAY	JESUS IS ALWAYS IN THE NOW OF MY NEED
FRIDAY	WHEN I DO ALL I CAN DO, I CAN LEAVE THE REST TO GOD
SATURDAY	GOD WILL WORK FOR ME THROUGH MY NEED

FOURTH WEEK

How I Discovered The Fantastic Joy Of Giving As A Seed I Sow Rather Than As A Debt I Owe

SUNDAY

Key:
I WILL GIVE OFF THE TOP FOR A DESIRED RESULT

or

Giving Off The Top Will Bring Miracles Into Your Life

IF YOU'RE like me, you just don't like to pick up the paper anymore and read the headlines. The murders and burglaries and the hijackings . . . the food shortages . . . the government not knowing what to do . . . people's faith being shattered. It's a dark hour. But I bless God that we can see His light better when it's the darkest. The fact is . . . most of us won't take time to look up until it gets dark.

GOD GAVE FIRST

At the darkest hour in the history of humanity God *gave* that He might get *a desired result.*

> *For God so loved the world, that he gave his only begotten Son, that whosoever believeth in him should not perish, but have everlasting life* (John 3:16).

For God so loved. He didn't wait until men loved Him. He loved first. For God so loved that He gave. His love became a gift. Giving. Giving is what love is. You can't say you have love if you are not giving. Neither can I. Love has to become an act.

I want to tell you a story about Mary Martin, the great actress. She was in a Broadway production and evidently things were not going as they should, when one night she received a note from Oscar Hammerstein, the great songwriter who at that time was dying with cancer. She received this note just before she went onstage and it said:

> *A bell is not a bell till you ring it.*
> *A song is not a song till you sing it.*
> *Love in your heart is not put there to stay.*
> *Love is not love till you give it away.*

Well, she went ahead and performed and afterward the people rushed backstage and hugged her and said, "Oh, Mary, you did something to us tonight. What did you do that was so different?"

Opening the piece of paper she read it to them. And brushing the tears from her eyes, she said, "Tonight I gave my love away."

For God so loved that He gave—and He gave His what?

His only Son.

God gave His best. Listen, GOD GAVE OFF THE TOP. He gave of the cream, not the skimmed milk. He gave off the top, not off the bottom. *God didn't take one of millions of angels or something He could easily spare. But He spared not. He gave His only Son. He gave off the top.* God loved people who didn't love Him back, and most of whom would never love Him back. God so loved that He gave His only begotten Son, and He gave for a purpose.

GOD GAVE FOR A DESIRED RESULT

Let's read John 3:16 again:

> *For God so loved the world, that he gave his only begotten*
> *Son, that whosoever believeth in him should not perish . . .*

This is God's desired result: God gave that you should not be without life (desired result) . . . that you shouldn't be without your needs being supplied (desired result), that you should have life, eternal life (desired result).

God so loved, therefore, I must love. Oral Roberts must so love that he gives and he gives off the top. He gives his best.

SEED CORN IS THE BEST

When I was a little boy I grew up on a farm. My father who was a preacher was also a farmer. He would farm during the week and preach on the weekends. We children grew up on the farm and had to help him in the fields. The hardest part was the gathering up of the corn.

In those days we used wagons pulled by mules or horses. When we'd bring a wagonload of the corn back to the barn, Papa would have my brother Vaden and me pitch the corn into the barn. We would be throwing it in right and left and at one another sometimes, when suddenly he would stop us and say, "Boys—Vaden, Oral—be very careful with that corn. Take the big ears, the good ears, and put them in a special pile over here."

We were just little boys and didn't know the difference and he said, "Boys, those big good ears are my *seed corn*. That's what we'll plant next year so we'll have a better crop. We don't want to plant corn from those little ears; we want to plant the best."

He was concerned about his *seed corn* being the top quality because he knew whatever he planted, that's what he would get back.

God approaches giving entirely different than most people do. God so loved that He gave, and He gave first.

He gave off the top.

God gave of the cream.

And He gave for a desired result. He gave that He might receive. Now you think on that a moment and I hope you'll think on it every day. I say to myself every day, "Oral, give off the top."

This is tremendously important to you to understand what I'm going to say now because most Christians have never grasped it. The Christians who understand it have come into a whole new dimension and they are the ones who are going to go through their dark hours and come out ON TOP.

From the beginning, in the Bible God taught the people when they went out to gather in their grain that they were to give the very first they gathered to God. That's where it all started. They were to give God the firstfruits.

THE FIRSTFRUITS

In Pontotoc County, Oklahoma, where I grew up, the farmer who had the first bale of cotton got a premium price. So each farmer would watch his crop closely. He'd watch for the first stalks to appear that had the most bolls of cotton—those that were opening white and fleecy. Then he'd rush out into the field (every farmer would) and pick it and load it into a wagon and take it to the cotton gin. The man who got there first with the *firstfruits* would get about three times as much money for the first bale as anybody else would get the rest of the cotton season. That's the firstfruits.

THE CREAM IS AT THE TOP

Did you ever churn butter? Do you remember the old churn? I can tell you, I do. When I was growing up I had to help milk the cows. But that wasn't all. After we'd milked, Mamma would put the milk up and she'd let the cream rise to the top. She would not let us drink the cream. We'd sneak in there—my brother Vaden and I—and we'd get a little of that cream. Oh, it was so good. And Mamma would say, "Now, boys, you just get away from there. I'm saving that cream to make butter." What she meant was, "I'm going to put you boys on that handle and you are going to be churning pretty soon." Vaden and I could hardly wait to get our mouths on that thick, yellow butter with hot biscuits and jelly—I can almost taste it now. But you see, all that good stuff came from the cream on the top.

Why does Jesus say to give off the top? Because that's where the cream is. And what you give Him is what He multiplies back. How would you like to give Him the skimmed milk and have Him multiply it back? I'd rather give Him the cream and have the cream multiplied back into butter!

Now we are getting to the point of Christianity. This is where you are going to get out of the Law of Moses and get into Christianity . . . and start following the New Testament. It's a new contract . . . a new covenant. That's what it means. It's NEW. It isn't the OLD. Jesus fulfilled the old. He didn't do away with it. He just said, "We've done it. We've fulfilled it. Now we are going to do it a new way." So you give off the top, which is the cream, that can be multiplied back in many ways.

LEARN TO FOCUS YOUR GIVING FOR A DESIRED RESULT

In other words, when you know that your giving is a seed you sow and you know you've given off the top (of the cream) and that's exactly what God's going to use to multiply back to you, you can get excited about it. You are giving for a *desired result*. You are *focusing* your giving and you know God will give to you.

ONLY WHAT YOU GIVE CAN GOD MULTIPLY BACK

The last few verses of St. Mark 12 tell about Jesus Christ being in the temple watching the people in their giving. The rich are contributing, and the very poor are contributing, because everybody had to contribute. And the rich gave first. The last one that Christ saw was a widow who had only two mites to give, which would equal a couple of pennies today.

But the little widow got Christ's attention. He said to His disciples, "I want you to look at her. She has given more than all of the others put together, including the rich men."

Now that's obviously a mathematical impossibility. Because the rich people give out of their surplus and quite a large sum of money has been given, equal to maybe several hundred dollars in our money. But this little woman has given a couple of pennies. Now how in the world can you explain that mathematically?

Because God computes differently.

Then Jesus explained it. He said, "They gave out of their surplus, but she gave out of her *want* . . . out of her need."

Jesus did not condemn the rich for giving of their surplus, He just gave the praise to the woman who shows us how we are to give. We are to give out of our need . . . out of our want . . . with a purpose in our heart. We are to give for God's desired results to come into our lives.

DOES GOD EVER HAVE A NEED?

Does God ever have a need? Certainly He has needs. His greatest need was that man would share His life. And God so loved us that He gave. He gave out of His want. The widow gave out of her want. What was her want? Well, she needed money. She needed it desperately. So when she put in her two pennies, now God had something to multiply back because she gave off the top. She gave the cream. And Jesus was excited about it.

SEED FOR YOUR NEED

This is the Second Miracle Key of Seed-Faith: Seeding for your miracle (Luke 6:38). Jesus said in Matthew 17:20:

> *If ye have faith as a grain of mustard seed* (which is a very tiny seed), *ye shall say unto this mountain, Remove hence to yonder place; and it shall remove.*

Now break that down. Here He says when you have a problem, which the *mountain* represents, that's what you start thinking about. I know that's what I usually do. But He said, "Don't start with the mountain; don't start with the problem. Start with planting the seed." Then you speak to that problem because now you know the money you gave will be multiplied back. It will come back. The Bible gives three measures of multiplication, THIRTY, SIXTY, AND ONE HUNDRED TIMES (Matthew 13:8).

The Bible says:

> *Give, and it shall be given unto you; good measure, pressed down, and shaken together, and running over, shall men give into your bosom. For with the same measure that ye mete withal it shall be measured to you again* (Luke 6:38).

"GIVE." Say it out loud. Say it until it permeates your being. *Give* . . . because you are God's.

I am either God's property, or I have to admit I'm the devil's property. Which way are you going? Whose property are you? God's? Then you don't wait around until people start giving to you and then you take a little of it and give it back.

Luke 6:38 is so much a part of me, it's like every breath I breathe. "Give," it says. And whether you believe it or not, I practice giving. I think I do it at least ninety percent of the time and I'm working on that other ten percent.

I've got to give according to the way I'm led of God, and so must you. And I'd like to make that clear.

Your giving has to be directed from down in your heart. It's got to be something you feel deeply about, so you know it's a seed you have planted.

ALL OUR GIVING HAS TO BE OUR HEART'S LOVE TALKING

I remember once my mother really got me. She had a need and I came in and gave her a few dollars and said, "Well, I've got to go."

And she said, "Honey, I need the money, but you know what I need most? For you to sit down right there and talk to me and love me."

She was saying, "I need your money. That will feed my body and clothe my body and pay my rent, but money in itself won't help my inner self, my heart. Son, I thank you for your financial help; just love me too."

I KNOW THE WAY OUT OF TROUBLE

There are people all over the country who are down in their spirits. You yourself may be facing financial troubles that you don't even want to think about. But I tell you, there is a way out! Not only for NOW . . . but for the rest of your life. You *can* get your needs met.

OK. Now what I'm saying to you is this:

The way to get off the bottom of trouble—financial worries, marriage problems, and all those things that press you down—is wrapped up in this thought, "I will give off the top for a desired result," and these three Scriptures:

> *Give, and it shall be given unto you; good measure, pressed down, and shaken together, and running over, shall men give into your bosom. For with the same measure that ye mete withal it shall be measured to you again* (Luke 6:38).

> *But my God shall supply all your need according to His riches in glory by Christ Jesus* (Philippians 4:19).

> *For verily I say unto you, That whosoever shall say unto this mountain, Be thou removed, and be thou cast into the sea; and shall not doubt in his heart, but shall believe that those things which he saith shall come to pass; he shall have whatsoever he saith* (Mark 11:23).

Jesus said to *give* off the top . . . and you will RECEIVE. Your needs will be met—not half of them but ALL your need. But you've got to believe that. God will supply ALL your need!

It'll do you good to write this on a card and look at it every chance you get—I will GIVE OFF THE TOP. That is, give God my best, then ask Him for His best.

——————◆◆◆——————

YOUR GOD-GIVEN KEY FOR TODAY

Say again and again:

"I Will Give Off The Top For A Desired Result."

MONDAY Key:
GOD LOVES MY CHEERFUL GIVING

or
The Importance Of Giving As You PURPOSE In Your Heart . . .

In 2 Corinthians 9:7 the Apostle Paul makes a statement that's absolutely stunning. It's so different and yet if you and I could actually put it into practice—and we do sometimes—we would come into a measure of joy and cheer and blessing that would show us life is worth living!! Paul said:

> *Every man according as he purposeth in his heart, so let him give; not grudgingly, or of necessity: for God loveth a cheerful giver.*

In other words, Paul says, "Let every man give in a way that his *heart* is in it. Not an outward form of giving. Not giving because somebody demands it . . . giving grudgingly because someone talks us into it . . . saying, 'I'll do it but I don't really want to.'" When we do this, then afterwards we usually feel, "Well, I gave but I wish I hadn't. I shouldn't have let them talk me into it." Instead, Paul says, "When you give, give from the purpose of your heart. Give because you have purposed to do it."

In Luke 8 Jesus told the parable of the sower which illustrates what happens when we give. He said:

> *A sower went out to sow his seed: and as he sowed, some fell by the way side; and it was trodden down, and the fowls of the air devoured it. And some fell upon a rock; and as soon as it was sprung up, it withered away, because it lacked moisture. And some fell among thorns; and the thorns sprang up with it, and choked it. And other fell on good ground, and sprang up, and bare fruit an hundredfold* (Luke 8:5-8).

The seed the sower used was good seed but how and where he sowed it determined the amount of harvest. First, consider the seed sowed by the wayside. This was "uncultivated soil." He paid attention only to the seed. It bore no fruit.

Next, the seed carelessly sowed on rocky soil had no depth, nor could it hold moisture. No fruit.

The next seed was sowed among thorns and weeds which already had their growth and thus smothered the seed. No fruit.

Finally, the sower learned his lesson. He sowed only in soil he had carefully prepared and continued to cultivate. *There was one hundredfold harvest.*

"Are you saying," a man asked, "that what I give can result in nothing?"

"Yes, that's what I'm saying," I replied. "I've seen it happen."

I often think a mental sign, HANDLE WITH CARE, or *HANDLE WITH PRAYER,* would help you when you start to give.

The spirit in which you give is the most important part of giving. It is very important how you give. You see, if your gift is money, the gift is inanimate. It is a medium of exchange only. It is neither good nor bad except as you are. You clothe it in your spirit; it reflects you in your total self.

There's nothing you can do with the gift once you've given it. But there is everything you can do with your attitude and spirit of expectancy.

YOU MUST BOTH PLANT THE SEED AND CULTIVATE THE SOIL

The SEED is giving. The SOIL is your personal relationship with Christ. Without this personal relationship your giving will profit you nothing.

The many lessons I've learned the hard way along these lines are more than I care to mention, but there is one thing certain:

**If you and I are going to know joy in receiving
we must first experience joy in our giving.
And we can!**

Here's how you can check yourself to see if you are giving in joy:

1. Is my life in the right relationship with Christ?
   Yes_____ No_____
2. If you can check "yes" everything will work for your good as you give joyfully.
3. If you have to check "no" go to WEEK SIX and read it until you know Jesus Christ in a personal way.

YOUR GOD-GIVEN KEY FOR TODAY

Say to yourself again and again:

"God Loves My Cheerful Giving!"

TUESDAY

Key:
I WILL GIVE GOD MY VERY BEST AND ASK HIM FOR HIS BEST

or

The Greatest Day . . . When I Learned The Possibility Of Giving God My Best Then Asking Him For His Best

I was sitting in church one Sunday morning and a problem was on my mind. Several people had applied for a certain position on my staff, but each time when a decision was to be made something always happened. We were at the deadline and we were no nearer a solution.

I don't know of a better place to take your problems than to the house of God. One part of me was listening to the beautiful hymns and the other part was praying for God to send us His man. Instead of trying to settle on one, I endeavored to keep my mind open to God as the Source for the right person, the key one. Sitting there, I became aware that the offering trays were being passed. What happened next almost caused me to miss applying Seed-Faith in the one area I had, so far, not done in order to completely release my faith. Automatically, I guess, I took my wallet out and selected a bill. The church I was in was not my home church and although I always love to give something anywhere I worship, I ordinarily give a larger amount at my local church.

Suddenly, a feeling came over me: *Give your largest bill.* I found myself reacting, "I should write a check so we can secure a tax deduction. If I give a larger amount in cash, they probably will disallow it on our tax return."

Sounds foolish, doesn't it, for me to be sitting in God's house carrying on a conversation with myself like that? Well, I did.

For some reason the ushers were delayed in reaching our section. While debating on what I should do, another thought came: *Give God your largest bill, then ask Him for the best man for this position and expect the answer soon.*

A KNOWING CAME INTO MY HEART

That settled the matter. I realized God was showing me how to get this need met by first planting the seed. I knew I was moving with God. I selected my largest bill and folded it so the ushers could not tell what it was and dropped it into the offering. I felt a knowing come into my heart. I knew. It was faith. And mine was being released.

When the service was over I left there feeling mighty good. Through my gift I had invested SEED-FAITH for God to multiply back. I was able to move with confidence and soon we had our man.

I didn't know as I sat there deciding between my smallest and largest bill that the man we felt was right for the job and who felt right about it himself, had gone to bed the previous night deciding not to come.

The next morning while I was sitting in church, he and his family were watching our TV program. As he related this to me several weeks later, it dawned on me that I was giving my largest bill and he was watching the TV program at approximately the same time! He said, "After the program was over I turned to my wife and said, 'Honey, we're going.' She said, 'Fine.' My two children spoke up, 'Dad, we're so glad. We wanted to go all the time.'"

He said, "Although it meant a move of nearly a thousand miles, the entire family felt real good about it, and I did too."

———————

Give God your best—then ask Him for His best.

You have to decide yourself what is your best. Have you decided? It can be money, time, friendship, talent, a prayer—whatever is the very best in you.

Now that you've decided, write it here:

_____

_____

Then ask God to help you throughout the day to let this become as much a part of you as the very breath you breathe.

YOUR GOD-GIVEN KEY FOR TODAY

Say today: **"I Will Give God My Very Best And**

Ask Him For His Best!"

WEDNESDAY

Key:
I HAVE TO PUT SOMETHING IN
IF I WANT TO GET SOMETHING OUT

or
The Best "Cat-Seller" I Ever Had And Why You Can't
Get Something For Nothing

Most of us are like a certain antique dealer who tried to pick up antiques for a fraction of their value and sell them for a large amount. Wherever he went he looked for bargains in antiques. One day while in another town he visited a secondhand store. While he was looking around he noticed a cat in the middle of the floor drinking milk from a bowl. As he watched the cat, suddenly his practiced eyes saw that the bowl was no ordinary bowl. It was an antique and worth a lot of money. He thought to himself, this old boy doesn't know what that bowl is worth. I'll get that for little or nothing. So he walked up and said, "Mister, that's a beautiful cat. I've been needing a cat. I wonder if you would sell me that cat."

The man said, "I'll sell anything I've got. Give me $25 and that cat is yours."

He paid him, picked up the cat, and stroked him. Then he said, "What a beautiful cat. By the way I notice he's been drinking milk from this old bowl. He is used to it, so I believe I'll just take it with me."

The merchant said, "You put that bowl down. That's the best cat-seller I ever had."

I have to watch constantly to keep from falling into this kind of trap . . . for there seems to be something in each of us that wants to get something for nothing, but this isn't the way God works. Most of us want to get, but God says to *give*.

I remember a rich man who gave me a secret which is founded upon the Word of God. This man said to me, "I am 76 years old. I am worth millions of dollars. Oral Roberts, there is one thing I have learned and learned well."

I said, "What have you learned?"

He said, "I have learned there is a law that Almighty God put here. YOU MUST PUT SOMETHING IN, IF YOU WANT TO GET SOMETHING OUT."

I said, "Sir, would you say that again?"

He said, "I have learned there is a law that Almighty God has put here. You must put something in, if you want to get something out."

Now we want success — big success — but about all we do to get success is to wish for it and envy others who have it. We want the peace of God. We want forgiveness for our sins. We want release from tension. But, do we put something in? No. We do everything but the right thing. If we want the peace of God, we must stop seeking to get and we must start putting something in.

What is the *something* we put in?

We put our hearts into it. We put our sincerity into it. We come to God in a sincere, humble, earnest manner, and say, "O Lord, I repent of my sins. I repent of the way I've been living. I'm sincerely sorry for the criticisms I have made and the ugly accusations against others. Forgive me for the envy, the strife, the hatred in my heart. Give me Your peace." You see:

You must put something in
if you want to get something out.

What are you putting into the service of God, friend? The Bible says:

"Give, and it shall be given unto you."

Have you given?

Are you giving?

Have you given your service?

Have you given your talent?

Have you given some of your time?

Are you giving some of your money?

"Give, and it shall be given unto you . . ." This is the Second Miracle Key to Seed-Faith living and getting your needs met.

———◆———

STOP TRYING TO GET AND BEGIN GIVING—
PUT SOMETHING IN IF YOU WANT TO GET
SOMETHING OUT.

YOUR GOD-GIVEN KEY FOR TODAY

Say it now until you can't forget it:

"I Have To Put Something In If I Want

To Get Something Out!"

THURSDAY

Key:
WHEN ONE DOOR CLOSES, GOD WILL ALWAYS OPEN ANOTHER ONE FOR ME!

or

The Secret Of Planting Seed With A Spirit Of Thankfulness Even In The Face Of Great Loss

Thankfulness! I know at times this may be the hardest word for anybody to accept. When people like you and me are going through some pretty terrible experiences . . . when there's loss on every side and we don't know whether we are going to get through a situation or not, we get so disillusioned. But let me share with you a verse from 1 Corinthians 15. Here Paul was surrounded by death, loss, and suffering, but he looked around and found his moorings. Then he made a statement that's absolutely fabulous for you and me in the things we face in the now. Paul said:

But thanks be to God, which giveth us the victory through our Lord Jesus Christ . . . therefore . . . your labour is not in vain in the Lord (1 Corinthians 15:57).

It's pretty hard to look at a paycheck that's been cut in half and say, "Thanks be to God for the victory." It's pretty hard to thank God when a storm comes sweeping across the plains and almost blows your house away. I know . . . it happened to us.

In June of 1974, a tornado came across the campus of Oral Roberts University. It struck first our office building where we receive your letters and answer them. Then it cut across the road to a brand-new building we had finished the day before—our new Aerobics Building. We have an aerobics program here founded on the program of Dr. Kenneth Cooper of Dallas. All of us, our students and faculty, are involved in building up our bodies and taking care of this wonderful temple of our body that God has given us. But the day after the Aerobics Building was finished this tornado swept across the hill and took hold of that new building, with over 100,000 square feet in it, and exploded it, twisting those steel girders into worthless wreckage. The building was almost totaled.

That night Evelyn and I stood at the glass door in our home and watched those black clouds coming toward us, not knowing what was going to happen. The power was cut off in various parts of Tulsa and we didn't know what was going on down at the campus. (Fortunately, we had ended the spring semester and the students had gone home for the summer.) Then pretty soon some of my men came up the hill, barefooted, sloshing through the rain and mud, and told us what had happened.

They said the storm had ripped into these buildings and there was a terrible loss. I put on my tennis shoes and waded with them through the water over to the office building. The water was almost up to my knees. We went through the darkened rubble from office to office and seeing the wreckage, I asked, "Has anybody been hurt?"

And they said, "No, miraculously everybody has escaped."

And I said, "What about the mail? What about the letters?"

And they said, "Well, we don't know where they all are but we are searching for them."

Then we went across the street to the Aerobics Building and saw the twisted steel beams and that magnificent building half torn away.

I can't tell you how I felt.

Sure, I knew we had insurance but we had the deductible kind. You can't get a hundred percent coverage because of the deductible clause.

We went back up the hill to our house and finally Evelyn and I were by ourselves. Our very blood and entire life's savings have been poured into this University. We don't own anything personally anymore. It was a thrill, of course, to give out of our earnings to build ORU, but when you see what you have built through God virtually wiped out, you feel so down. You feel so lonely. You forget about the other buildings that were not touched by the storm. You forget about all the good things that God has done in your life and you think about the loss.

Evelyn and I got down on our knees and opened our Bible and began to pray. Out of it God spoke to my heart and reminded me of the Seed-Faith that I preach — that you can give, and give as a seed you plant. You can plant a seed for every need you have. I turned to Evelyn and I said, "Honey, we've been giving, but I feel that we should find a way to give more seed."

And she said, "How?" (We were already giving to our full capacity, we thought.)

And I said, "Let's sit down tonight and I'll handwrite a letter to the pastor of our church. Let's just say, 'Pastor, we are not giving this just because the church needs it. We are giving it because we've had a great loss.' Honey, you remember the Bible teaches that in your loss you can plant a seed of an equal benefit and it will wipe out the loss."

THE ONLY WAY TO HANDLE YOUR LOSSES IS TO PLANT A SEED OF FAITH

I said, "We are going to send this letter off and we are going to send the few extra dollars we can, and that will be our seed of faith. We'll tell the pastor this." (We got a beautiful letter back from him of thankfulness and his prayers.)

That was Saturday night and Monday at noon some miracles began to show up. First of all, not one letter from our friends and partners had been lost. Some of them were watersoaked but we could read the letter and could read the address. We never lost a letter.

The next thing was that the spouses, the husbands and wives of our staff and their teen-agers, donated their time to work all day and all night to help move everything — the typewriters and things like that, the various supplies — over across the street to the Student Union Building on campus. This building was vacant at this time. By Monday noon, 36 hours after the tornado struck, we were back at work full speed answering those letters.

The insurance company was very nice but they couldn't take care of the deductible clause. But out of the blue came some gifts — gifts that we never asked anybody for, never even mentioned the need, and God took care of it. By the time the fall term began, those buildings were 100 percent repaired and actually looked better. And were better.

NOW HERE'S WHAT I WANT YOU TO LEARN THAT WILL
HELP YOU:

>   Don't get so down in your losses that you
>   forget to give thanks to God . . .
>   That you forget God is your SOURCE . . .
>   That you forget you can plant a NEW seed.
>   AND IN THAT NEWLY PLANTED SEED GOD WILL WIPE
>   THAT LOSS OUT!

>   I BELIEVE IT.
>   I KNOW IT.
>   I STAKE MY LIFE ON IT.
>   IT WORKS FOR ME.

Repeat this phrase:

>   "When one door closes, God will open another one for me."

Say it, eat it, sleep it. BELIEVE IT. And it will work for you.

YOUR GOD-GIVEN KEY FOR TODAY

Here it is again:

"When One Door Closes, God Will Always
Open Another One For Me."

FRIDAY Key: I MUST GIVE GOD SOMETHING TO WORK WITH
or
The Secret Of Tapping God's Miracle Supply

We all face needs from time to time . . . and sometimes those
needs are so great that we don't see any way out. Some time ago I got
a letter from some partners of mine in Colorado. They told me how they
had turned on the TV one Sunday morning and heard me say, "Expect
a miracle!" Now this was entirely new to them, even though they were
church members and attended regularly. They were inspired by this
because they had really been struggling. But at last they had both
secured jobs and had just begun to climb out of debt. Things were beginning to look up for them when suddenly the bottom dropped out.

Did you ever have this happen to you? You thought everything
was going fine and suddenly LIFE happened!

Well, this is what happened to my friends:

First, the wife became seriously ill and had to undergo emergency surgery. She came through that OK but was told she could not work for at least six months . . . and she hadn't been working long enough for her hospitalization to be in effect.

Second, the day she came home from the hospital her husband lost his job.

There they were.

It was the middle of winter. Snow was on the ground and jobs were hard to find . . . especially for men over 40, like he was, with a history of poor health. Well, he tramped the streets day after day looking for work, but he didn't find any. He'd come home at night to find his dear wife red-eyed from crying all day, worrying about where their next meal was coming from and how they were going to pay the rent. It wasn't long before their meager savings were gone. Things really looked bleak.

They had heard me talk about the Three Miracle Keys but somehow the concept hadn't gotten through. They sent for my book, MIRACLE OF SEED-FAITH, and as they read it they found the answer. They weren't giving FIRST so they could RECEIVE BACK from God. They weren't EXPECTING God to do anything for them.

They had never read Luke 6:38 before . . . they didn't even know it was in the Bible. But they got out their Bible and there it was: "Give, and it shall be given unto you."

Well, they had only $5 left to their name . . . and no job . . . no groceries . . . no one to turn to. But this lady said to her husband:

"Honey, do you think we should take this $5 and give it as Seed-Faith? *If God's going to help us we've got to give Him something to work with!*" That is a terrific thought!

He thought about it for a minute and he said to himself, well, if she is willing to take this risk of faith . . . perhaps even go hungry . . . so am I. And he said, "Yes."

When they gave that Seed-Faith offering, something happened inside them. There was a positiveness, a realization that God would give them a miracle, that they would be taken care of. The idea of EXPECTING A MIRACLE IN THE NOW began to get down deep inside.

Within a few days he got the best job he had ever had. A short time later her hospital bill was paid in full in a totally unexpected way. You talk about two happy people—they were happy—and they still are. Yes, they still have needs, for when one need is met another takes its place. But they have discovered the secret of tapping God's miracle supply: They have learned *to give God something to work with.* And I have used that particular expression to help others get into Seed-Faith living.

THE SECRET OF TAPPING GOD'S MIRACLE SUPPLY
IS . . . GIVING GOD SOMETHING TO WORK WITH

It's beginning with our faith and making it into something. Jesus said:

If ye have faith as a grain of mustard seed . . . (Matthew 17:20). Now Jesus didn't say to "have faith" *only.* He said to have FAITH AS A GRAIN OF SEED YOU PLANT. That is, make your faith something you DO . . . something you give FIRST.

This is Seed-Faith. This is the message of the gospel. It is the GOOD NEWS!!

———————

Here's how you do it:

YOU PUT SOMETHING OF YOURSELF IN AS SEED . . .
> no matter how small you feel,
> or how big your need is,
> or how difficult your problem is,
> or how severe the shortages are in your life . . .

YOU START GIVING OF YOUR TOTAL SELF AND GOD'S LAW OF THE HARVEST DOES THE REST. IT REPRODUCES A MIRACULOUS HARVEST IN YOUR LIFE.

This is mountain-moving faith!!
It never fails!!

What a slogan! "Mountain-moving faith!"
Make it yours.

YOUR GOD-GIVEN KEY FOR TODAY

Now say repeatedly:

"I Must Give God Something To Work With!"

SATURDAY

Key: I CAN EXPECT GREAT MIRACLES WITH A LITTLE MEASURE OF FAITH

or

How You Can Use Your Little Faith To Receive A Great Miracle From God

Don't ever feel condemned when you hear the verse in the Bible where Jesus says:

O ye of little faith (Luke 12:28).

Now I know these words have a tendency to make you feel bad . . . as if Jesus is putting you down. Well, He isn't. Jesus is really complimenting you. He is saying to you:

> "Little faith is not so bad. You can do great things with your little faith. If you will learn to use your faith as a seed you plant, you can receive great miracles from God."

Remember, Jesus mentioned "great faith" only twice. In all the thousands of people Jesus dealt with, only *two* of them were said to have "great faith." Most of the people had *little* faith. In fact, not even *one* of the twelve disciples had "great faith." They had *little* faith. On several occasions they were the ones to whom Jesus said, "O ye of little faith." Yet Jesus performed some of His great miracles through people who had little faith.

The Apostle Paul said in Romans 12:3:

God hath dealt to every man the measure of faith.

This means . . .

GOD HAS GIVEN EVERY HUMAN BEING A PART OF HIS OWN GREAT FAITH . . .

Each of us has a little faith. Maybe you feel like your faith isn't great . . . or big . . . or powerful. Maybe you are wondering how the faith you have could possibly help you to receive a miracle from God. But God is trying to get you to see that the amount of faith you have is not as important as the fact that your faith is given to you by God.

> **The important thing is not the size of your faith—**
> **it is the one behind your faith—God himself.**

He is the one you depend on. He is the Source of your total supply. He is the one who returns the harvest to us.

The Apostle Paul says in 2 Corinthians 9:10:

> *He* (God) *that ministereth seed to the sower both minister bread for your food, and multiply your seed sown.*

So it's really not the seed of faith that is as important as *God* who gives us the faith.

**The real power is not our faith: It
is the object of our faith—God.**

The real power is God. And however small your faith is . . . even if it is only a tiny seed of faith that you put in, something you give, something you do to show your love and concern . . . the real power, the one you do it unto, is God. The power is in *God* who multiplies your giving.

HOW I USED MY LITTLE FAITH IN ANSWERING
A LETTER FROM A DESPERATE WOMAN AND
SHE RECEIVED A GREAT MIRACLE FROM GOD

As I talk to you about little faith many thoughts come to my mind. One of them goes all the way back to 1947 when the Lord's call came to me to bring this ministry of healing to my generation. I'd begun to pray for people to be saved and to be healed. I'd begun to preach, "God is a good God." Somehow the news spread out across America and I got a letter from out of state. In fact, the first week eight people wrote me and most of them were from outside Oklahoma.

But, anyway, I remember that first letter. Evelyn and I opened it and read it. It was from a woman who was very ill—not only ill in her body but also she had all kinds of problems. She poured out her heart to me. Well, not ever having received a letter like that and not having been asked to help someone with such dreadful needs, I almost wilted. I said to Evelyn, "What do you think I should do? How can I help someone who is as desperate as she is?"

Evelyn said, "Well, Oral, why don't you just write her back and tell her how you feel?"

I said, "I'll tell you how I feel. I feel God can help her."

"Well, why don't you tell her that?"

"I feel like praying for her," I added.

Evelyn said, "Why don't you pray and tell her you have prayed for her?"

Now that's all the faith I had. So I sat down and wrote her right back that I was praying for her and I believed God could heal her.

She turned right around and wrote me back another letter. I remember that letter because of a certain thing she said in it:

> *Oh, Mr. Roberts, when I got your letter and read it, it suddenly dawned on me that you are the first man who ever told*

*me that he was praying for me. You are the first one who ever
said God could heal me.*

Then she went on to tell how something had come over her, a warmth,
and that since she got the letter she had begun to improve. Things were
getting better.

The thought to me was, at least I had a little faith—enough to
write and tell her I was praying for her and to tell her that God could
do all these things.

O ye of little faith. Hold on to your little faith because that faith
is in the God of miracles. AND NOBODY OR NOTHING IS AS
STRONG OR AS RELIABLE AS GOD IS.

God gives you a measure of faith . . . a *little* faith . . . so you can
use this faith to get needs met in your life . . . so you can make your
faith as a seed you plant. God wants you to be in a continuous state of
expecting Him to supply your needs.

When you feel you are just about out of faith, say this:

**"I will never doubt the
power of my 'little'
faith. Never! Never! Never! . . .
Thank you, God, for even my little faith."**

And NOTHING, OR NOBODY, IS AS STRONG OR AS RELIABLE
AS GOD IS. Never . . . never . . . never doubt the power of your
"little" faith!!

Now say:

**YOUR GOD-GIVEN KEY FOR TODAY
"I Can Expect Great Miracles With A

'Little' Measure Of Faith."**

FOURTH WEEK

SUNDAY	I WILL GIVE OFF THE TOP FOR A DESIRED RESULT
MONDAY	GOD LOVES MY CHEERFUL GIVING
TUESDAY	I WILL GIVE GOD MY VERY BEST AND ASK HIM FOR HIS BEST
WEDNESDAY	I HAVE TO PUT SOMETHING IN IF I WANT TO GET SOMETHING OUT
THURSDAY	WHEN ONE DOOR CLOSES, GOD WILL ALWAYS OPEN ANOTHER ONE FOR ME!
FRIDAY	I MUST GIVE GOD SOMETHING TO WORK WITH
SATURDAY	I CAN EXPECT GREAT MIRACLES WITH A LITTLE MEASURE OF FAITH

FIFTH WEEK

The Greatest Thing You Can Ever Learn Is . . .
How To Expect A Miracle!

SUNDAY Key:
I CAN EXPECT A NEW MIRACLE EVERY DAY
or
God's Message To Me: Tell Your Friends And Partners To
Expect A Miracle . . . Every Day!

ONE of the most exciting periods of my life occurred January 4 and 5, 1963, during our Miami, Florida Crusade. For a period of 18 hours, God dealt with me almost as if we were face-to-face. My entire being was quickened by His presence as deep inside me I heard Him say several different things to me.

During the past months I had lived under the shadow of severe persecution. In the Miami Crusade an atheistic group had made threats through press, radio, and television that they would break up our crusade on the pretext that laying hands on the sick and praying for God to heal people constituted practicing medicine without a license. Although they knew it would not stand up in court, they felt that if they succeeded in having me arrested it would put this ministry in a bad light and elevate them in the public eye. As this harassment soared to a climax, God began to prepare me to be willing to suffer this or any other persecution for His cause. So for several days I had been "on the tiptoe of expectation."

God, in speaking to me over the years, has always spoken like a commander addressing a soldier—in clear, crisp terms. As I write, I still remember the tingling in my flesh as He said to me, "DO NOT FEAR THESE MEN. IF YOU WERE PUT IN JAIL IT WOULD NOT HURT YOUR MINISTRY. I HAVE GIVEN YOU A STRONG AND SOLID MINISTRY, AND I MYSELF AM WITH YOU."

I thought my soul would burst with joy as I heard these blessed words. I felt lifted up. Later that evening, while preaching and facing the enemy's last desperate effort to stop me from praying for the sick, I felt as if God's hand was folded around my hand; and as I reached out to the people I felt the tide turn for victory.

The people too had sensed that evil was trying to destroy this ministry. Now, in a moment, the atmosphere was electric with the power of the Holy Spirit. Hundreds came down the aisles to accept Christ as their Savior.

As I began to pray for the sick, the Lord spoke to me again. I told the people this: "The Holy Spirit is flooding up in me so strong tonight I feel as if I will burst. God wants to heal you and He has sent me to pray for you."

I had scarcely gotten the words out of my mouth when a man standing within 20 feet of me began to shout and jump up and down. He had been dying with a heart disease. Now he began to cry, "I am healed! I am healed!"

The power of God to heal swept over the audience in wave after wave. As I started praying for the people one by one, with the laying on of hands, I asked those who were suffering with a disease similar to that for which I was praying at that moment, to stand in the aisle and release their faith for healing.

The ministers on the platform were crying and rejoicing as God's healing power fell upon the audience. When the service concluded, I felt that every man, woman, and child in that great audience knew that God had sent me, and that this ministry would never be put down by the power of man. During the remainder of the crusade we witnessed some of the most powerful conversions and healings of our entire ministry. Also, those who made threats to prosecute me were unsuccessful.

During this time Jesus said something to me that has revolutionized my thinking, as well as those to whom I've ministered. He said:

> **"Expect a miracle every day. Tell your friends and partners to expect a miracle every day."**

I had always thought that miracles could happen rather frequently if we had faith for them, but it had never occurred to me that they could happen *daily*. I said, "Lord, is this possible?"

He said, "IF IT WERE NOT POSSIBLE, I WOULD NOT HAVE TOLD YOU TO EXPECT IT."

Never before have I stood in such awe, nor been filled with such joy, as I did when He said this to me. Think of it, you and I are to expect a new miracle to happen to us every day!

Then God showed me we are to expect daily miracles in · · ·
   our physical bodies
   our mortal minds
   our spiritual lives
   our finances
   and our person-to-person relationships.

He reminded me of: "Give us this day our DAILY bread," and of the "SIGNS" AND WONDERS that will follow them that believe. It came to me that what He was saying could become a part of my life. I thought, *it can happen to me every day if I expect and believe for it. It can happen to my body, to my mind and soul, to my finances, and to my friends and partners, and in our relationships with other people.*

You may say, "How can it happen to me?" Let me tell you of one of the members of my staff who asked me if I thought it was possible to have a miracle every day. When I told him how God had explained it to me, he said, "Then it *can* happen."

A few days later I saw him and he said, "Brother Roberts, I had my miracle today."

I said, "What was it?"

He said, "Did you read in the papers about the plane crashing in Kansas City?"

I said, "Yes."

He said, "I was scheduled to be on that plane. It is a miracle that I was not on it. Because of that, I am alive today."

When you get this idea, "EXPECT A MIRACLE," into your mind, body, and soul, your life can be REVOLUTIONIZED. It can change your circumstances and the very atmosphere in which you live!

Why?

Because it is from God. Say it:

EXPECT A MIRACLE!

Ladies: Write on a card and put it over the window, wall, or mirror in the kitchen and read it—let it sink in as you do the dishes.

Men: Write it on a card and put in on the visor in your car, or on your desk calendar, or in your billfold.

Students: Make it a poster on your wall or write for my little plaque that says:

EXPECT A MIRACLE.

I will send it to you free and postpaid.

YOUR GOD-GIVEN KEY FOR TODAY

Say it again:

"I Can Expect A New Miracle Every Day!"

MONDAY Key:
MY MIRACLE WILL SETTLE THE ISSUE
or
The Very Secret Of Life Is In Expecting Miracles

There is a God-implanted urge in every human being for miracles. God made you for miracles, and He made miracles for you. Therefore—

THE VERY SECRET OF LIFE IS IN EXPECTING MIRACLES—MIRACLES

I know there are people today who say they don't believe in miracles. They don't feel the need of miracles. Well, as I said to a group in a talk recently, it's been my experience that nobody believes in miracles until he needs one. It's when you need one that you start thinking about it.

The key is the need . . . and *feeling* the need. That's because, intuitively, we feel something about miracles.

Miracles settle the issue.

Miracles get the job done.

Let me tell you how I learned this.

At one time in my life I personally couldn't believe Jesus had lived, much less that He lives in the now. I lived as if He didn't exist. I had faith but I didn't put it in Jesus Christ. I put it in myself and in other people. I put it in taking my life into my own hands, in doing things my way.

The Bible was like a blur to me—its words meaningless as far as I was concerned. I didn't consciously pray. It didn't enter my mind to deliberately turn my life over to God, to have faith in Him as my personal Lord and Savior, or to be filled with the Holy Spirit, or to use my faith as a seed I plant.

As for expecting miracles, I felt I could make my own and I made some, at least they appeared to be. I did a lot of things that excited me. Then one day—I ran out of life.

I'll never forget, as a young man far from home, when this happened to me. Like a car out of gas—I couldn't go any further. Life had stalled for me.

With bleeding lungs and hemorrhaging almost daily, I simply RAN OUT OF LIFE. WHERE WAS MY OWN POWER TO MAKE MIRACLES? TO CONTROL MY LIFE? TO REACH THE HEIGHTS? TO DO IT ALL MYSELF?

NO MAN CAN EVER MAKE HIS OWN MIRACLES . . .

One day I woke up on the *inside*. It dawned on me and I understood it for the first time—*God had permitted me to try to make my own miracle and was showing me that I had failed.* Although I was young, I began to understand no man can ever make his own miracle. Somewhere—sometime—he *must* come to the end of himself and establish a personal relationship with God, the Source of all miracles.

When I received Christ as my personal Savior and Lord, a transformation began in me. I could feel it. Vibrations of His presence surged through me. I TURNED ON TO MIRACLES. A miracle of healing opened my lungs and loosed my stammering tongue. LIFE flowed up within my inner being. I experienced joy. Enthusiasm for life. Love for people. It never runs dry. It's there all the time. Day and night. I wanted to give to others the secret I had learned.

The only failures I've had have come because of my faults, my shortcomings, *or my failure to keep looking to God as the Source of my total supply,* or to give first and then to expect miracles. As long as I maintain a commitment of my life to Jesus Christ—as long as I follow my Lord in the Three Miracle Keys of Seed-Faith—I have miracle after miracle. Sometimes I get so elated I find myself looking around the corner to see what miracle God is going to give me next!

A MIRACLE IS NOT ALWAYS THE SAME TO ALL PEOPLE

A miracle to one person might not be a miracle to another. To most of us, a miracle is something happening that we can't explain but that makes a profound change for the better in our lives.

I have known many miracles, both of a completely extraordinary nature and of a nature that I alone might appreciate. We know that a miracle is a supernatural effect in the physical world; it is beyond the power of nature; it is incredible, wonderful, unaccountable, astonishing, mysterious.

To me there are many different types of miracles. One is a miracle that might happen to you or to me that we have been expecting. There can also be miracles that are unexpected. And there are miracles that are unseen or unknown to anyone but you. In such a miracle, you know that something has happened of an unusual nature, and you are thankful. The successful Christian life is partially made up of such miracles. Take, for an example, an accident that is averted, and you whisper in awe, "That was a miracle." Such a miracle often puts a person in the right frame of mind to make changes in his life. A year before I began this ministry of healing, I was involved in an automobile accident in which I narrowly escaped injury. When I related my escape to a group of men, one of them came up to me, put his hand on my shoulder, looked at me, and said, "Young man, God is not ready for you to die yet. He just gave you a miracle."

When things are going wrong in your work, you can pray and oftentimes there is such a change that it is a miracle. Tension is lifted, attitudes are improved, friendships are formed, apologies are made, things are straightened out and almost instantly you are aware that everything is all right.

It is so much easier to be efficient in your work when such miracles occur.

In the home a miracle can change the attitude of the members of the family toward each other.

I have known of children who believed that miracles would happen to their parents, and these miracles did happen. I have known of parents who believed for miracles in their wayward, delinquent children.

A minister whom I love very dearly was almost washed up because of the delinquency of his two sons, and particularly that of the older. This boy was eventually put into the state penitentiary. Every time this minister stood up to preach, his "failure" with his sons was almost like a physical blow. The fact was that he had taught these boys right. He had been a good example to them. He loved them very dearly, but for some unaccountable reason they went away from his teachings. Later, he said to me, "Oral, I believed every day that they would come back. Every morning when I arose, I would say, 'Today may be the day.'"

Both of those sons today are respected ministers of the gospel. One is a successful pastor, the other a successful evangelist. The expectant spirit of the father's faith for a miracle in his sons' lives brought this to pass. Again I say *THE SECRET OF LIFE* is in expecting miracles from our risen Lord.

THE PRESUMPTUOUSNESS OF LIFE is in expecting a miracle when there's no possible way to get one, because if we do not put the seed in we do not give God anything to work with.

––◆––

THE BIG QUESTION IS: ARE YOU SEEDING FOR A MIRACLE??
Or, are you living a *presumptuous* life? Are you *presuming* that God is going to do something in your life when you are *not* cooperating with Him, when you are *not* opening up your heart and giving—and giving first?

Learn the Three Miracle Keys of Seed-Faith.

Start practicing them today! Just one word characterizes each one.

TRUSTING!
SEEDING!
EXPECTING!

Now when you've got the revolutionary thought exploding in your being, you can shout it with everything you have.

YOUR GOD-GIVEN KEY FOR TODAY
"My Miracle Will Settle The Issue!"

TUESDAY Key:
GOD HAS A TIME AND A WAY FOR ME

or
Casting Your Bread Upon The Waters Is Giving In Order To Receive

A miracle is not something for nothing—you must seed for your miracle. You must GIVE *first*... before you can expect to receive.

Solomon, the wisest man who ever lived, said:

> *Cast thy bread upon the waters: for thou shalt find it after many days* (Ecclesiastes 11:1).

Casting your bread upon the waters is giving. It is putting in the seed of faith FIRST. Giving is sowing in joy. Giving is opening up your inner self and following Jesus in the NOW.

Your bread means your existence, your money, your time, your talent, your love, your faith, your life, your very being.

And when you give yourself, always give it as *unto* the Lord. In other words, although your giving may be to some person, or group, *you're really giving it to God your Source.*

What you give represents you—your heart, your love, your concern. You may give an offering of money. You may give time and concern. You may pray for someone. You may give friendship. Or you may give something else. Or it may be a combination or part of all of these by-products of your heart. Whatever you give, it's an act of your love and faith. It is a seed sown.

Upon the waters. In the Bible "waters" often stands for troubled humanity. Read Revelation 13:1 about the sea, the waters, speaking of the mass of troubled humanity . . .

And remember this about casting your bread upon the waters:

First, God says you will find it after many days. You *shall* find it.

When you cast your bread upon the waters, you may feel like it's gone. You may say, "I put it in and nobody cares, nobody thanks me." But the Bible says, "You SHALL find it." God will multiply it and return it. It may take a few days, a week, or He may wait longer. It may be *many days.* But IT *SHALL* RETURN to you after many days. *It shall return!!* This is the promise of God.

Second, the wave you cast your bread upon may not be the wave God will return it on. It may be another wave.

What this means to you is, God will return your giving—through your giving you will receive from God—BUT (and this is important to you) GOD WILL RETURN IT IN HIS OWN WAY AND AT HIS OWN TIME. I call this God's supply from an unexpected instrument. From someone you didn't expect would help you, or in a way you hadn't thought about.

The fact is that most of the important returns from casting my bread upon the waters came in almost totally unexpected ways or times or from those I least expected from. But always I knew my Source, the Lord, did it! It is Him I look to, not those other ways or times or people. Although I am grateful for these instruments, I give the glory to God.

———◄◆►———

Today when you finish reading this—start thinking about SOMEONE YOU KNOW IN TROUBLE.

Start thinking about someone you can give to today.

In other words, ask the Lord to help you decide who you can help and how.

Now when you have decided, write their name or names:

_____

_____

_____

_____

Call this person, or send them a note full of love . . .

Go offer a prayer . . .

DO whatever you are directed to do.

Cast out into the sea of troubled humanity—do it NOW.

And remember, don't look for the return to come back on the same wave you cast it upon.

YOUR GOD-GIVEN KEY FOR TODAY

"God Has A Time And A Way For Me!"

WEDNESDAY

Key:
GOD'S DUE SEASON WILL NOT BE TOO EARLY OR TOO LATE FOR MY NEED

or
The Businessman Who Learned God Has A "Due Season"— Not Too Late Or Too Early

I have a friend who is 70 years old. He is a wonderful giver. But something had happened in his life and he broke down and cried. He said, "Oral, I have put the seed in. For years I've practiced Seed-Faith just like you said. I've made a pattern of giving. I give of my money. I give of my time. I'm concerned about people."

The tears were running down his cheeks. As he cried, I cried too. I knew it was the truth. Yet this thing was so bad that he couldn't handle it. It was a mountain he could not remove from his life. In a way, I was embarrassed because I'd influenced his life and now it looked like what I had preached was false. All I could say to him was, "Dear, dear friend, what I've told you is the truth. What you've done is right. You have practiced the eternal law of our Lord. God is going to help you."

He said, "Well, He hasn't."

I said, "Have you ever thought of the Scripture that says:

> Let us not be weary in well doing: for in due season we shall reap, if we faint not (Galatians 6:9).

This means you will reap if you don't get discouraged!"

He said, "No, I hadn't thought of that."

I said, "Let me give you an example. There is a due season when you harvest. If you plant wheat or corn you don't go out to gather in the harvest until the due season. Another example: If you agree with a man to work for him for two weeks and then you will be paid . . . there is a due season for your pay. You work the two weeks first THEN you get paid. That is your due season."

"Well," he said, "when is my due season?"

I said, "I cannot tell you. Only God, our Source, knows. I wish I could tell you." We were like two children sitting there crying. He hurt and I hurt. It looked like everything I had preached was false. I said, "All I can tell you is: one, keep on sowing the seed; and two, know in your heart there's going to be a due season. Expect a miracle."

"Oh," he said, "I've expected the miracle."

But I said, "Keep on expecting the miracle. Don't give up . . . don't get weary in well-doing . . . don't throw it all away . . . don't stop now."

I didn't know if I had any effect on him in that moment because he sounded quite disappointed, even bitter. I could understand that because I've been bitter too. I've almost said, "God, You don't even know who I am. You don't care whether I live or die." But one thing is true, God is going to do what He says but He's going to do it at His time. And He's going to do it in His way. That's why you've got to learn His way.

Several months later I talked to my friend John again. He was so excited and thrilled. I said, "What's happened?"

To sum it all up, what he really said was, "My due season is beginning to come. Oral, what I needed in my own body is starting to happen." He was excited and in essence he said, "Man, am I going to keep on planting seed in the future!" He saw the value of staying a plant-ER.

I tell you, when you sow seed—seed of your concern, seed of your money, seed of your time—there's going to be a due season for it to be returned to you. You've got to expect it. Look for it. But if you get too discouraged you won't recognize the harvest when it comes. Discouraged people don't see miracles coming. You've got to look up to see them. LOOK UP!

In due season we shall reap. You see, there's a due season in God. There is a due season for you if you plant some seed. In due season you shall reap, you shall have a harvest. It will come back, multiplied . . . again . . . and again . . . and again.

This Scripture hits me right in the face because I'm a NOW fellow. As one farmer said, *I want a hybrid harvest in incubator time.* I knew what he meant for I want everything done yesterday. But I have discovered that God has His own timetables. God says, "If you don't get discouraged, if you keep looking to God for the miracle, you will get it." So what do you do when you don't get the miracle?

You keep on believing and expecting a miracle in the NOW . . .
You just KEEP ON, KEEPING ON until the miracle comes.

Listen, you and I have at least a hundred miracles that are on the way, that we have not received, for we have already seeded for them. I get excited when I think about that, don't you?

If you won't get discouraged, if you won't get weary—just keep seeding and keep on expecting the miracle—you shall reap if you faint not, if you don't give up.

THE QUICK RETURN VS. THE SLOW RETURN

In the long run I think you are better off with a slow return. There are exceptions, of course, times when you have to have a quick return. You have no choice. But a quick return is easily forgotten, whereas a slow return holds you steady. You have to focus more on your Source.

Now I love a quick return but I'm telling you I'm getting less and less quick returns. I'm getting more and more long-standing ones. Yet I'm seeing that God is doing something in me while I'm waiting . . . and trusting . . . and expecting. It holds me steady in the trial because I know God is going to do it. I'm no longer floundering . . . or vague . . . or lost . . . I know God is going to give me the miracle I need in His due season. I know without question that if I will hold steady, it will happen.

KEEP EXPECTING YOUR MIRACLE—
YOUR DUE SEASON WILL COME.

NOW CROWD CLOSE TO GOD AND W-A-I-T. I know it's the hardest part, but God is doing something for you while you are—

WAITING . . .
TRUSTING . . .
EXPECTING . . .

YOUR GOD-GIVEN KEY FOR TODAY

Say it out loud to yourself:

**"God's Due Season Will Not Be Too Early
Or Too Late For My Need."**

THURSDAY

**Key:
GOD'S STOREHOUSE OF
MIRACLES WILL NEVER FAIL ME**

**or
Miracles Don't Come "Out Of The Blue"—They Come
From Your Seed-Faith Storehouse**

Did you ever have anything come to you that just seemed to come OUT OF THE BLUE? I mean, you couldn't explain it? Well, I believe that what seemed to come out of the blue was really the harvest from seed that you had planted sometime before. In other words, your due season had arrived. God had just given you the harvest of your seed-sowing in a different way from what you had been expecting.

God has His own time . . . and His own way . . . to give you the harvest from the seed you plant. Did you know that you seldom get anything from God exactly the way you thought you wanted it? His ways are not our ways (Isaiah 55:8). I know that God seldom gives me exactly what I ask for. Seldom does He give it to me WHEN I want it because that would have been yesterday. Friend, if you don't think I can diagram it out for God, you ought to be around me sometime. I can tell Him exactly how to run matters—but am I glad He sticks to His method rather than mine! Because His way and time of doing it are always better than mine.

I want to encourage you to keep putting the seed in. Try to think about the seed and not the mountain. TRY! I know it's hard. Try to have the courage to put a seed in, rather than just begging God to move the mountain.

Honestly, friend, if you get the seed of faith in, God's going to work through that seed and then you can speak to the mountain in your way. If your problems are going to be solved you are going to have to put in the seed and let God do the solving. And He's not necessarily going to use your method. It may just come out of the blue. I don't mean to overemphasize that, but I can't think of another statement that fits so well. Because even though we say it came out of the blue, that's not what we mean. We mean that Somebody out there was thinking about us. We mean God remembered us.

I know that my God is so concerned about you. I know He wants to supply your needs. Perhaps you don't know what Seed-Faith is. You may give a little here and a little there but you haven't formed a pattern of giving as a seed.

Now one thing I have tried to do, and I recommend it to you, is to form a pattern of giving and make it the forward thrust of your life. To get into the rhythm of it.

Before I ask for anything from God, I give something. When we decided to build Oral Roberts University, Evelyn and I gave our entire savings, with the exception that any royalties from any books I wrote would go into a trust for our children, or directly to the University. The money we gave alone couldn't build the school but it was a seed and we put it in. I'm on a salary and I'm not bragging about it or complaining. I'm just telling the truth. We put some seed in and God gave the harvest.

Now sometimes I get busy or worried about something and forget who my Source is. Every time I forget who my Source is, I fail. Every time I fail to put a seed in and I expect God to give me a miracle, it never, never, never, never comes. Every time after I put the seed in and I demand to receive the harvest right now, nine times out of ten God doesn't give it then. He makes me wait. WAIT ON THE LORD (Proverbs 20:22).

Here's the nice thing about that. The nice thing about becoming a SOW-ER, or to translate that—to become a follower of Christ, not only to put in a few seeds once in a while but to constantly put seed in— is that the harvest becomes cumulative . . . CUMULATIVE! That is:

GOD BUILDS A PERSONAL STOREHOUSE FOR THE GIVER IN
WHICH HE STORES UP THE MIRACLES THAT WE WILL NEED IN
EACH OF OUR DUE SEASONS . . . THAT IS THE CUMULATIVE EFFECT!

I believe God has a personal storehouse in which He stores all of Oral Roberts' miracles, and all of your miracles—God holds our miracles for His due season. So those moments when I need a miracle . . . when you need a miracle . . . it seems to come to us out of the blue. It seems that our miracle has our name on it.

So when you give:

Think of your Seed-Faith as grain going into the storehouse God has for you.

Think of the grain going into the ground before it becomes a harvest.

Think of the harvest you are going to receive later.

When I give—and this is the truth—I think of it going into God's storehouse where it accumulates. I may have a hundred or more gifts that I've made to God that are in His storehouse. Every one of them has my name on it: "Oral Roberts put this seed here." On every seed I have given, there is God's handwriting saying, "I will multiply this seed sown by Oral Roberts. And if he'll expect it he'll recognize it when I multiply it back, and will reach out and receive it."

WHEN WE SAY A MIRACLE CAME OUT OF THE BLUE WE MEAN SOMEBODY—GOD—REMEMBERED US!

———◆◆◆———

God doesn't NEED what you give so He keeps what you plant in His storehouse to multiply back to you when you have a need.

So what you give accumulates—GOD KEEPS BOOKS FOR YOU AND HE'S NEVER IN THE RED!

Isn't that great!

Visualize, if you can, God's great big storehouse and when you have this faith image in your mind—even in the face of an "empty meal barrel"—repeat over and over:

YOUR GOD-GIVEN KEY FOR TODAY

"God's Storehouse Of Miracles
Will Never Fail Me!"

FRIDAY Key:
MY FAITH IS SOMETHING I AM DOING

or
The Golden Rule Is Something You Do To
Bring Miracles Into Your Life

God provided a way that our needs can be met but THERE IS SOMETHING WE MUST DO to bring these good things into our lives. Jesus said:

> *ASK, and it shall be given you;*
> *SEEK, and ye shall find;*
> *KNOCK, and it shall be opened unto you: For every one that asketh receiveth; and he that seeketh findeth; and to him that knocketh it shall be opened. Or what man is there of you, whom if his son ASK bread, will he give him a stone? Or if he ask a fish, will he give him a serpent? If ye then, being evil, know how to give good gifts unto your children, how much more shall your Father which is in heaven give good things to them that ask him?* (Matthew 7:7-11).

Notice Jesus is talking about *things*. Jesus went on to say in the next verse:

> *Therefore all THINGS whatsoever ye would that men should do to you, do ye even so to them* (Matthew 7:12).

This verse is often called:

THE GOLDEN RULE . . .
I BELIEVE IT IS THE LAW AND THE PROMISE

Now the Golden Rule is talked about a lot. But it isn't practiced much. The trouble is, we want the other person to practice the Golden Rule first. We say, "If this person would be nice to me, just look how nice I could be to him." You are insisting on doing things your own way . . . of trying to have your own will done . . . and you are lost to yourself and to God.

So many people try to figure out how to get a thing done, and when it doesn't work out they give up. Or they get frustrated. Sometimes they even give up and shoot themselves.

All right, here is a new twist to the Golden Rule: Jesus says, "Whatsoever you want done to you, you do it, and you do it *first*." This is the most dependable law in the universe.

THE GOLDEN RULE IS SOMETHING YOU DO!!

Jesus was talking about *things* in Matthew 7 when He gave us the Golden Rule. Most people take this Golden Rule and make it merely an ethical code of conduct. I certainly would say it is an ethical code of conduct, but Jesus did not stop there. Jesus said something else. You see . . .

Jesus was talking about asking and receiving, about knocking on doors and getting the doors opened.

You know how many doors you knock on to get opened and sometimes they don't open at all. Jesus said, "Ask, and ye shall receive." He also said, "If a son asks his parents for bread, they won't give him a stone. If he asks for fish, they won't give him a serpent. And if you, being evil, know how to give your children such good gifts, how much more will God give good gifts and good things to them—to them who will do first unto others what they want done back for themselves."

Figure out what your needs are—just exactly like a farmer does. The farmer says, "I need so many thousands of bushels of wheat, so I'm going to go out into the field and I'm going to sow a certain amount of seed wheat." Or, "I'm going to sow a certain amount of seed corn. I'm going to do what it takes to get the harvest I need."

FIGURE OUT WHAT YOUR NEEDS ARE AND THEN START GIVING SOME OF THAT . . . DOING THAT

In other words, what do you want someone else to do for you? You go do that either for him or for someone else. And what you are going to find is that now you are dealing with God and His eternal law. What you are going to discover further is that you are not dealing with things or people at all. You are dealing with God. As a matter of fact, you may *think* you are dealing with things and with people but you are not. You are actually dealing with God. Because only God is responsible to make His eternal law work!

The eternal law of sowing and reaping is: If you give, it will be given back.

The eternal law is: If you do good to someone, good will come back to you.

This is God's eternal law. You cannot expect the person you help always to do good back to you because that person is not responsible to operate God's law. He is not capable of operating his own eternal law. Don't you see that? God is the one who multiplies your giving back to you in the form of your need.

———◆ ◆ ◆———

.THE GOLDEN RULE IS FAR MORE THAN AN ETHICAL CODE
OF CONDUCT. IT IS THE ETERNAL LAW OF GOD TO MEET
EVERY NEED YOU HAVE ON THIS EARTH . . .
IT IS YOUR SEED-FAITH IN ACTION!
IT IS SOMETHING YOU DO!

In the Golden Rule Jesus is talking about
          asking and
          receiving . . .
          knocking on doors and
          getting doors opened!

Sometimes we wouldn't recognize an open door if we were standing in
it. But this is where "doing" comes in. While you are going about your
everyday duties and "doing" and "giving out," God will show you your
door and maybe even give you a little push through!

YOUR GOD-GIVEN KEY FOR TODAY

"My Faith Is Something I Am Doing."

SATURDAY
Key:
**MY MIRACLE BASKET IS ABOUT
TO TOUCH THE GROUND**

or
**You May Be Nearer To Your Miracle Than You Know,
So Keep On . . . Holding The Rope!**

Soon after the resurrection of Christ, thousands of people received
Him as their Savior, and became Christians. Then there came a very
serious movement against them, a serious persecution, which caused
many of them to be put into prison or put to death. The ringleader of
the persecutors was a young man by the name of Saul of Tarsus, who
received authority to persecute them not only in Jerusalem, but in
distant cities as far away as Damascus.

While this fierce, cruel, bitter young man was on his way to
Damascus he had a personal confrontation with Jesus Christ who came
to him in a brilliant light and whose voice rose up within him and called
him by name, "Saul, Saul, why persecutest thou me?"

In this experience Saul (later known as the Apostle Paul) found
Christ to be real, to be alive, in his life.

So when Saul got into Damascus, his life was completely transformed. This man who hated Christ now loved Him. The man who

had hunted the Christians to put them to death was looking for them as brothers. It wasn't long after that until the people with whom he had been in league to kill the Christians turned against him. Now the hunter became the hunted. The persecutor became the persecuted. His enemies watched the gates. They were everywhere to see that he didn't escape with his life. The Bible says that the Christians in Damascus, the ones he came to kill, took him by night and let him down by the wall in a basket (Acts 9). If you had been in Damascus that night, you would have seen several men, possibly four, crossing the city. As they walked over the old cobblestone pavements one of them carried a rope, another a basket, and they were whispering encouragement to each other in the night. Soon they came to the wall surrounding the city. They climbed it. They tied the rope to the basket, helped young Saul inside, and let him down over the side to the ground. Saul of Tarsus slipped away from Damascus under the cover of night. His life was spared.

The men who held the rope that night for Saul of Tarsus did not know that Saul of Tarsus would become Paul the great apostle—perhaps the greatest Christian of all time. All they knew was he was a man who had hated them and now loved them . . . who had had a great new change in his life and was about to be killed. So they held the rope for him.

For a few moments I want to share with you what it means in the NOW to "hold the rope."

FIRST, THEY HELD THE ROPE AT NIGHT
AT A GREAT PERSONAL RISK AND DANGER TO THEMSELVES

You know, the nights that you're tossing on the bed, when the problems are weighing down upon you, when you don't know if you're going to get to sleep, or if you do and wake up, if you'll ever make it through the day. When things are going bad all around you, it's a good time for God to thrust a rope into your hand.

This didn't have much meaning for me until I became a teen-ager. As a rebellious youth, I turned against my parents, I'm sorry to say. I turned away from the church and the idea of God. I left my family and ran away. I was gone nearly a year and I didn't come home until I collapsed with tuberculosis. When my coach picked me up from the basketball floor, put me in his car and said, "Oral, I'm taking you home," I was at the end of my way. When I finally arrived home my parents put me to bed. Mamma and Papa stood there . . . Mamma buried her face in her apron a moment and then she looked down at me and she said, "Oral, every night that you were gone I would awaken and get out of bed. I'd walk the floor and I'd call your name to God. I'd say, 'God, bring him home at any cost.' But I didn't know the cost would be so great."

It was in that experience that I found Christ as my Savior. I received a great healing of my body, and a call to preach the gospel that is as real to me now as it was then. My mother and father held the rope for me.

SECOND, THESE MEN HELD THE ROPE
AND DID NOT TURN LOOSE OF IT

They were tempted to turn loose. They were startled by every sound in the night. They knew if they were caught, not only would Saul be put to death but they themselves would be killed. But they did not turn loose.

You may say, "Oral Roberts, I can't hold on to the rope any longer." But let me give you two reasons why you cannot afford to turn loose of that rope.

One, you may be the only one God has holding that particular rope.

Second, your miracle basket may be about to touch the ground.

You may be a minister of the gospel, struggling with your church and trying to help the people and keep the gospel going, and things aren't going too well. But remember, you may be the only one who cares whether those people go to heaven or go to hell. So hold on to the rope . . . your basket may be about to touch the ground.

You may be a medical doctor, a surgeon. When things don't go right and you have to get up in the night and go back to the hospital to see if your patient is all right, to see if he's going to live through the night, and the terror clutches your own heart — hold on to that rope. Your basket may be about to touch the ground for that patient.

You may be a businessman in this inflationary society. It's tough to run a business and you may feel like quitting. But I tell you to hold on to that rope. There're a lot of people depending upon you as a businessman. I know business people have been maligned a lot, but without business people our country can't run. Hold on to the rope, your basket may be about to touch the ground.

You may be a worker, you may have lost your job, or you may not know where you're going to turn for a job. You may be worried about inflation, your finances. You may be in debt or you may be facing bankruptcy or you may have already gone there. Hold on to the rope. Your prosperity basket may be about to touch the ground.

You may be ill. You may have received the verdict that something is wrong, and they've worked at it, but it's still there. It may be a loved one or it may be a child who is at the point of death. Hold on to the rope for that person. You may be the only one God has holding that rope and that healing basket may be about to touch the ground. You may be near the greatest miracle you've ever had in your life.

THIRD, THESE MEN DID NOT KNOW HOW GREAT A MAN THEY HAD ON THE END OF THE ROPE

They did not know that Saul of Tarsus would become Paul the apostle. They didn't know that some day he would write half of our New Testament. They didn't know that he would be a great evangelist and apostle and preacher and stir the world and lay the foundation for the New Testament to be written as it is. They didn't know that. He was just someone who needed help. So they planted seeds of faith and held the rope.

I want to tell you a true story, something that actually happened. In the hills of eastern Tennessee in a little country church, a young boy stood up on Sunday morning to preach his first sermon. Well, the sanctuary was filled with his loved ones and friends and the pastor proudly presented him. The young fellow stood up, opened his Bible and read some Scripture. He bowed his head and prayed a brief prayer and then raised his head and started to preach. He looked around and became stage-frightened and forgot his sermon. He stood there a moment like someone blind and then he stumbled backward and fell into the seat.

Everybody was caught unawares and the pastor didn't know what to do. He got up and tried to smooth things over. He finished the service as best he could and everyone left. All but the boy, who sat up there with his head in his hands. All of a sudden he felt a hand on his shoulder. It was Mose, the janitor of the church, and Mose began to encourage him and the boy said, "Mose, if God will forgive me, I will never try to preach another sermon."

Mose said, "Son, now you can't feel like that. There'll be another time and you'll make it."

"No, I'll never preach again."

And Mose said, "Now, son, I'll tell you what you do. My wife is cooking a good meal. I want you to go home with me. We'll eat and we'll sit down and talk about the Lord and pray and everything will work out."

So he persuaded the boy. When they had finished eating they took two old cane bottom chairs, leaned them up against the side of the house, and they talked about the Lord.

It came time for the boy to leave and old Mose said, "Son, would you kneel down." Then he put his hand on his head and prayed a prayer like this, "O Lord, take this young boy, and send him around the world to bless the people."

Well, years passed and the little country church outgrew its quarters and built a new sanctuary. They called the bishop to come down and dedicate it to God. He came and preached the sermon. Then he told the story that I'm relating to you and said, "I was that boy. I remember the meal I ate that day and I would like to go home with somebody here today and have Sunday dinner with you and talk about the Lord. Who will invite me?"

Lots of hands went up.

Then he said, "Thank you, but no."

Then he looked up in the balcony, and there sat old Mose, now whitehaired. He said, "Mose, would you come down, please?" Mose made the long walk and the bishop put his arm around him and said, "Mose, I'd like to go home with you and have dinner again, then take those two old cane bottom chairs, lean them up against the side of the house and talk about the Lord. And I'd like to have you put your hand on my head and pray for me that God will use me." So they walked out of the sanctuary arm in arm, old Mose and the bishop.

Old Mose did not know those years before, that lonely Sunday morning, how great a man he had on the end of his rope. And I say to you, Mother—Dad, you don't know how great a person is on the end of your rope. As you lift up that son or that daughter, that loved one in prayer, you don't know how great a man, how great a woman, is on the end of that rope.

———◆———

My friend, hold on to that rope. Remember, you may be the only one God has on the end of that rope.

Hold on to your rope!

Heaven is bending low . . .

Your miracle is on the way!!

Second, hold on because your basket of miracles may be about to touch the ground. I won't promise you that you won't get a "rope burn," —you may and you may not. But I'm telling you there's a "balm" like no earthly salve. And you'll not only come through ON TOP, you'll be better than new. Remember this and remember it well, and say it: "MY MIRACLE BASKET IS ABOUT TO TOUCH THE GROUND!" And you know how good it is to get on your feet again—especially when God does it for you.

YOUR GOD-GIVEN KEY FOR TODAY

Say it once again:

"My Miracle Basket Is About To Touch The Ground!"

FIFTH WEEK

SUNDAY	I CAN EXPECT A NEW MIRACLE EVERY DAY
MONDAY	MY MIRACLE WILL SETTLE THE ISSUE
TUESDAY	GOD HAS A TIME AND A WAY FOR ME
WEDNESDAY	GOD'S DUE SEASON WILL NOT BE TOO EARLY OR TOO LATE FOR MY NEED
THURSDAY	GOD'S STOREHOUSE OF MIRACLES WILL NEVER FAIL ME
FRIDAY	MY FAITH IS SOMETHING I AM DOING
SATURDAY	MY MIRACLE BASKET IS ABOUT TO TOUCH THE GROUND

SIXTH WEEK
God's Greatest Miracle Is Your Personal Salvation

SUNDAY

Key:
I KNOW GOD AND I AM IN HIM AND HE IS IN ME

or

In This World It's Possible For You To Personally Know God

IN this world it's possible for you to know God . . . to know that He's real . . . to know that He's working in the now and to know that He means something to you.

In 1 John 1:1,3, St. John is saying these immortal words:

> *That which was from the beginning, which we have heard, which we have seen with our eyes, which we have looked upon, and our hands have handled, of the Word of life . . . That which we have seen and heard declare we unto you.*

And then St. John said in the very next chapter:

> *We do know that we know him* (1 John 2:3).

Then he said:

> *I know him* (1 John 2:4).

Then he added:

> *Know we that we are in him* (1 John 2:5).

John was one of the twelve apostles. He was alive and walked with Jesus and he said he heard Him. He saw Him. He touched Him. He knew Him personally.

John is now the oldest of the apostles. Most of them had been killed by this time—possibly all of them except John. He's 80 years old or past. Now he's looking back. He looks back to the other side of the cross, back there when he knew Christ. And now on this side of the Resurrection he writes and he says:

> "That which was from the beginning, which we've heard, and seen, and felt, and handled, with our own hands, Him we declare unto you. We know Him . . . I know Him . . . and we know that we are in Him."

You see, it means a lot for St. John to look back to Christ and then to look at the end of his own life which won't be very far away, and to be able to say, "I know, I know!"

THERE'S A GREAT POWER IN KNOWING

Many years ago in Yale University there was a very brilliant, but eccentric, professor of mathematics. And one day he assigned a problem to his students to solve and bring back the answer the next morning. Well, of course the students spent a lot of time on it that night. One of them in particular spent nearly all the night because he had a feeling this was an important assignment.

The next morning the professor said to various ones, "Would you go to the board and give us the solution to the problem I assigned you?"

Each time the professor said, "I'm sorry, that's wrong; would you please be seated."

And then he asked another young man who went to the board and put down the right answer.

But the professor said, "You are wrong, that's not the correct answer; please sit down."

The next was the young man who had studied throughout the night. So he raised his hand and the professor said, "Go to the board and give us the solution."

And he went up and wrote down the same solution the other young man did who had been refused.

And the professor said, "That's wrong, didn't you hear me tell this other young man that his solution was wrong and you've written the same one?"

The young man said, "Professor, it's correct."

The professor said, "Are you trying to put me down?"

And he said, "No, sir, I'm not. I respect you very highly, but that is the correct answer."

The professor said, "Are you sure?"

He said, "I'm sure."

He said, "Are you absolutely sure?"

And the young man said, "I am absolutely sure."

The professor smiled and said, "You are correct; it's the right answer."

There was a wave of protest from the student body but the professor said, "Now wait a minute, students. I'll tell you why I did what I did. I know that soon you'll be out in the world and people will be demanding answers and solutions to problems. They will want not only the correct answer, they will want to know that the person who gives the solution has confidence in his answer. And this young person has demonstrated to me and to you that he knows the solution. He *knows* that he knows! That's the way life is. You've got to have not only the answer, but you must have confidence in your answer."

And that's the spirit that St. John gave us in these great words, "We know . . . we know because we saw Him. We saw the Lord Jesus Christ. We heard His voice . . . we handled Him . . . we embraced Him . . . and we put our hands in the nailprints and our hand in the spear-riven side. We saw Him. We saw Him after the Resurrection alive for-evermore . . . **we know Him.**"

In the New Testament we are told of one of the great miracles of Christ and the healing of a man who had been born blind. And one day Christ restored his sight. It was amazing. Some were glad but many, strangely enough, were angry because they didn't believe in our Lord. And then they jumped on the man who had been healed of blindness. They tried to argue him out of it. And then the theologians got hold of him. They didn't believe in the blind man's healing and they made it hard for him. Finally the young man just stopped them cold with these words, "You ask me all kinds of questions. Well, I'll just tell you one thing: Whereas I was once blind, now I see."

He not only saw, but he knew that he was able to see. He knew it because he had the evidence.

Oh, Jesus Christ shows us how we can know Him. We can know His power, His love, His compassion. We can know Him in every moment of our existence.

THE DIFFERENCE IN HEAD-KNOWING AND HEART-KNOWING

I think one of the most dramatic stories that I've ever heard was about a great Hollywood actor. He was also a dramatist and traveled throughout America drawing great crowds, giving readings from the great writers like Shakespeare. But he would always end his performances with something special—a dramatic reading from the Bible. Usually it was the 23rd Psalm. And on this particular occasion he gave it with great power, with the ability to cause his voice to rise and fall at just the proper moment, and to carry you with him as he gave the 23rd Psalm.

When he had finished, the crowd began to applaud and he bowed, very thrilled with the reception. Then they looked over to the right and very slowly an old gentleman was rising. They recognized him as an old retired preacher. He walked over, stood in front of the crowd, turned to the actor and said, "Sir, how beautiful that was; would you let me recite the 23rd Psalm too?"

The actor graciously said, "Of course."

And the old man with a voice that wasn't quite so strong anymore, who didn't know all the ways to bring forth the nuances that are proper when one gives such a reading, began: "The Lord is my shepherd; I shall not want . . ." He went on through until he got to the close, "Surely goodness and mercy shall follow me all the days of my life: and I will dwell in the house of the Lord for ever."

There wasn't a sound. Nobody moved. Over on one side a woman began to wipe the tears away. A man nearby pulled his handkerchief out. There was no applause but it was obvious that the entire audience was deeply moved. Finally the great dramatist could not stand it any longer. He walked over to the old minister and said, "Sir, when I gave the 23rd Psalm there was great applause. But here you gave it, not in the way I did. You didn't have the proper intonation and inflection, but people are crying. I feel like crying myself. What's the difference in the way I gave it and the way you gave it?"

And the old pastor said, "Well, sir, you gave it better than I did. But the difference is this: You know the Psalm but I know the Shepherd. I know Him as the Lord of my life, who has walked with me since I was a child, who has been in my heart through these years, been with me in the deep waters, in my sorrows. He's been with me on the mountaintops of my joys and in sickness and health. And now as I take my last steps and will soon be with Him, you see He's everything. He's my Shepherd. I *know* the Shepherd."

John says, "We know Him." And then he said, "*I* know Him." And I tell you with all my heart today, based on the authority of the Bible and the experiences of millions who've gone before us and millions who are living now who know it, *you* can know. **You can know God.**

———————

Maybe you have never been told that YOU CAN KNOW GOD PERSONALLY. If this is so, lean into these truths that I have been telling you—LEAN HARD, because *it is so.*

Here are just some of the ways you can know God:

You can know Him in the might of His healing power.

You can know Him in the joy of salvation.

You can know Him in the solving of your financial problems.

You can know Him by getting closer to your children.

You can know . . . YOU CAN KNOW HIM!

YOU CAN KNOW HIM IN THESE WAYS AND IN EVERY AREA OF YOUR LIFE IF YOU INVITE HIM INTO YOUR LIFE AND ASK FOR HIS HELP. HE IS MORE WILLING TO HELP THAN YOU COULD EVER IMAGINE.

God is in you—this is why you are capable of doing good, of loving, of giving, of being compassionate—of doing anything that is good. Because God is a good God.

NOW . . . GET OUT OF ALL THIS "HEAD-KNOWING" AND LET
THE LORD GET INSIDE YOU—THAT'S THE DIFFERENCE BE-
TWEEN "HEAD-KNOWING" AND "HEART-KNOWING."

YOUR GOD-GIVEN KEY FOR TODAY

Now say it:

"I Know God And I Am In Him . . . And He Is In Me!"

MONDAY Key: JESUS IS GIVING ME PERFECT PEACE
or
How You Can Be At Peace With Yourself Over Personal Guilt

In a recent issue of *The Tulsa Tribune*, which is owned and edited
by my good friend, Jenkin Lloyd Jones, also a nationally known syndi-
cated writer, he wrote an article entitled "The Fading Alibi." In it he
quoted Dr. Karl Menninger, the famous psychiatrist who has just published a new book, *Whatever Became of Sin*. Mr. Jones says:

> The concept of sin has been out of fashion too long. We have
> been deep in the business of inventing tortured alibis for human
> misbehavior and the result has been a growing chaos in our society
> and a danger to our citizens.

> "There is sin," writes Dr. Menninger, "which cannot be sub-
> sumed under verbal artifacts such as disease, deliquency, deviancy.
> There is immorality. There is unethical behavior. There is wrong-
> doing."

> That's why a . . . man must have a sense of sin. He must be
> uncomfortable with his tendencies toward evil and irresponsi-
> bility . . . It has been a long time since Billy Sunday ordered his
> weeping tent congregations to "hit the sawdust trail." It was a
> pretty corny . . . way to salvation. But recently we have been on a
> six-lane, limited access, superhighway to hell.

> And for our own personal happiness and peace of mind, the
> eminent Dr. Menninger suggests we get off at the next exit.

I think that's one of the most powerful statements said in the now
to you and me of our generation.

In Paul's writing is the statement about our Lord Jesus:

> *This is a faithful saying, and worthy of all acceptation, that
> Christ Jesus came into the world to save sinners; of whom I
> am chief* (1 Timothy 1:15).

Jesus Christ always told the truth. When He began His public ministry, He talked about the good news of the gospel. He went around opening doors for people and showing them the better life. But as He neared the end of His life, the last five or six months, He began to talk about the consequences of rejecting God, the consequences of sin, and what's going to happen to a person who remains a sin-NER. Jesus taught . . .

FIRST, ALL SIN WILL BE PUNISHED

All sin will be punished unless it's repented of and forgiven of God. Now the lines are drawn for that not only in the published laws of the Bible, the Word of God, but in the moral and physical laws of this universe. It's an accepted scientific fact that nature will rise up and punish you if you break its laws. Even in your everyday life, if you run a red light you may get by the first time or the second or even the third time. But if you keep running red lights you are going to hurt someone, or get hurt. You are going to kill somebody, or get killed.

Those who build the spaceships to the moon tell us that unless they obey the laws of nature in an exact way, the laws of nature will rise up and punish them. The spaceship will explode. If the astronaut tries to breathe on the moon without the proper oxygen equipment, it will destroy him because the moon has no atmosphere. So the laws of both the Bible and the universe tell us that all sin will be punished.

SECOND, THE PUNISHMENT FOR SIN WILL BE JUST

It will be just because of the Man (Jesus) who is the judge. There will be no bribery. There will be no political influence because He will go by the eternal laws of God.

Now consider who He is. Jesus Christ is the one who came down to earth and became a man. He was tempted in all points like you and I are (Hebrews 4:15).

If you've ever been tempted, and surely you are every day, just remember that Christ faced the same temptation, only more so because the devil wanted to destroy Him more than anyone else. If you've ever had the feeling of lust, remember that the devil tempted our Lord with lust even more so. If you've had the urge of anger to the extent of killing, remember that the devil brought that same temptation to our Lord. When it was all over, Jesus had faced every sin, every temptation. He had faced them as a mere human being, and He did it without yielding to one temptation. He showed us that it could be done. Then as God, He went to the cross to die and become the Savior. He said, "I went through it and overcame it." This is why it's so important to know Jesus and follow Him because He's the only one qualified to take you through life. He became our Savior, but at the judgment He is no longer our Savior. He becomes our Judge.

TODAY JESUS CHRIST IS YOUR SAVIOR
BUT TOMORROW HE WILL BE YOUR JUDGE

His judgment will be eminently fair and just. You will be judged and you will be found guilty because in your heart you've decided to sin forever; because in your heart you have formed a life pattern, a way of life that has a tendency toward sin, a direction toward wrong. You will carry this with you into death and into the judgment.

For example, the act of fornication between two unmarried people can be forgiven. Even two or three times. But after awhile that person becomes a fornicator. There's a difference in committing an act of fornication and becoming a fornicat-OR, so that it becomes a way of life. It becomes a sin that is a way of life—a fornicat-OR.

The Bible says in 1 Corinthians 6:9 that no fornicator or adulterer or liar shall have any part in the kingdom of God. It also says:

> All liars shall have their part in the lake which burneth with fire . . . (Revelation 21:8).

One can tell a lie and be forgiven but if he becomes a liar, that is, if it becomes a way of life, a life-style, he becomes a sin-NER.

Friend, I'm not saying that. The Bible says that whatsoever you sow (for bad or for good) it will be multiplied back to you (Galatians 6:7). This is why Seed-Faith living is so important. Seed-Faith is the eternal answer. When you make God your Source and you're always giving and sowing *good* seed, then you can expect to reap God's goodness and mercy. God's eternal law of sowing and reaping is infallible. It's the eternal law. It will never fail. Anyplace . . . anytime . . . anywhere . . . it'll work for any human being. But we must say, on the other hand, the seeds of sin are the same. They work the same . . . but with the opposite results.

One man, an intellectual, had difficulty believing that a good God would ever send a man to judgment and ultimately to hell. He went to a great Christian theologian to discuss it. Patiently the Christian minister took him through the Bible and showed him the published moral law of God. Then he led him through the paths of the universal laws of nature and showed him that punishment is always sure and just. Reluctantly the great man accepted the fact that there is punishment for sin, that there is a hell. He said with great anguish of spirit to the minister, "I would give everything I have if I could change it."

The minister's face lighted up and he said, "That's just the point God has already done just that. He gave His Son Jesus Christ to die on the cross, to break the chains, to forgive the sins that are repented of to change your life-style, to break the pattern, to forgive and to say 'Go, and sin no more.'"

Friend, after you have repented and been forgiven you may stumble again, but through Christ your life-style is changed. The direction of your life now is toward God. Remember what the Bible says:

> This is a faithful saying . . . that Christ Jesus came into the world to save sinners . . . (1 Timothy 1:15).

I believe that you can be saved through Christ — not only saved in the NOW, but SAVED FOREVER.

HERE, IN FOUR STEPS, IS
HOW YOU MAY BE SAVED

1. Come

Jesus himself extends the invitation:

> Come unto me, all ye that labour and are heavy laden, and I will give you rest (Matthew 11:28).

He also said:

> Him that cometh to me I will in no wise cast out (John 6:37).

Many people put off coming to Jesus with the thought, I am not good enough — I cannot live a good life.

All of life is a result of the marriage of opposite laws. For instance, in the laws of electricity it takes the negative wire and the positive wire to produce light. In the kingdom of God, it takes the negative and the positive — opposites — coming together to produce life.

This means it is impossible for us to meet Jesus in our own righteousness. You cannot become "good enough" to meet Him because in God's eyes "all our righteousnesses are as filthy rags" (Isaiah 64:6). We can't have our righteousness and His too. You have to recognize your sins before you can get His righteousness.

Jesus said, "The Son of man is come to seek and to save that which was lost" (Luke 19:10). Again He said, "They that are whole have no need of the physician, but they that are sick: I came not to call the righteous, but sinners to repentance" (Mark 2:17). So we come to Jesus just as we are — in our need.

You come. You come as you are . . . with all your sins and needs and frustrations — you bring yourself to Him.

2. Repent

The next step is to repent of your sins. The basic meaning of "repentance" is simply to change your mind. However, it is far more than intellectual choice because it involves the heart and the deepest convictions of the soul. Repentance is made up of three things: (1) change of mind, (2) change of heart, and (3) change of living (Romans 12:2; Ezekiel 18:31; Philippians 2:13). The Bible says:

> Godly sorrow worketh repentance to salvation not to be repented of . . . (2 Corinthians 7:10).

You must be sorry for your sins. Many people repent who do not get saved. They are sorry for what they have done because they are having to reap the results of sin. But they don't repent because of godly sorrow. They repent because they have been caught, or because they are suddenly confronted with their wrong and they are terribly embarrassed by it.

Jesus taught us the attitude in which we are to come to God when He pictured two men who went into the temple to pray (Luke 18:10-14). One man said, "Lord, I am a righteous man. I do this and I do that." However, the other man in humility stood afar off, smote his chest and would not so much as lift up his head. "God, be merciful to me a sinner," he prayed. Although we are taught to approach the throne of grace "boldly," we do not come in a proud, boastful, self-sufficient way. We come to God humbly, confessing our need of forgiveness. We have His promise that "if we confess our sins, he is faithful and just to forgive us our sins, and to cleanse us from all unrighteousness" (1 John 1:9). God will accept your repentance.

3. Believe

Too often we try by our own efforts to answer the sin question. But it cannot be done. Salvation is found in a Person—in the Man Jesus Christ. He is the Savior. The church is not the Savior; water baptism is not the Savior; philosophy is not the Savior; reformation is not the Savior. Jesus is the Savior. Whosoever believes on Him and His transforming power can be saved. The Bible says:

> As many as received him, to them gave he power to become the sons of God, even to them that believe on his name (John 1:12).

A father tells of his little girl's conversion. After attending a children's revival one day, she ran into the house, put her arms around her father's neck and said, "Daddy, I'm a Christian!"

"Honey, I'm so glad to hear that," said the father. "When did you become a Christian?"

"This morning," she replied happily.

He asked her to tell him what had happened.

"Well," she said, "the evangelist said that Jesus Christ was there in the room, and that if we would let Him come into our hearts He would receive us. I received Him, and Jesus took me in."

Wanting to make sure she understood the experience of salvation the father dared to press another question, "Honey, how do you know that Jesus took you in?"

The father says he will never forget the look on his little girl's face as she drew herself up and said, "Why, Daddy, because He said He would!"

Take God at His Word. It is just that simple. Believe that He will do what His Word says He will do.

4. Confess

Acknowledging Christ as your Savior is a vital part of your salvation. The Bible says, "If thou shalt confess with thy mouth the Lord Jesus, and shalt believe in thine heart that God hath raised him from the dead, thou shalt be saved. For with the heart man believeth unto righteousness; and with the mouth confession is made unto salvation" (Romans 10:9,10).

So you see that confessing the Lord publicly with your mouth is important. It is just as important as believing Him with your heart. Both are necessary.

Jesus said:

> Whosoever therefore shall confess me before men, him will I confess also before my Father which is in heaven. But whosoever shall deny me before men, him will I also deny before my Father which is in heaven (Matthew 10:32,33).

I believe in a "personal experience" religion—one in which Jesus Christ knows you and you know Him, where you walk hand in hand together in personal companionship and where you speak to one another with familiarity and understanding.

Now follow through . . .

Although you are now converted *it will require* a LIFETIME to become a disciple. We are to grow in wisdom. A fruit tree may be perfect in its first year of growth, but it has not attained its maturity. It has to grow, mature, and produce fruit. It is the same way in your Christian life.

Let's just review the four simple steps to being *saved*—or if you'd rather, call this experience "receiving Christ as Savior and Lord of your life."

1. Come (Matthew 11:28).
2. Repent (2 Corinthians 7:10).
3. Believe (John 1:12).
4. Confess (Matthew 10:32, 33).

Jesus made the way to heaven so clear that "the wayfaring men, though fools, shall not err therein" (Isaiah 35:8). Even a little child can understand this—and they seem inclined to do it so much more readily than adults.

If you have any doubt that Christ is your personal Savior, now is the time to remove that doubt. Pray this prayer with me and let God give you a new life this very moment:

> Dear Jesus, have mercy on my lost soul and forgive my sins. Take away this heavy load, this awful burden, from my heart and set me free. Deliver me from every wrong desire and

> *every bad habit that binds my life. And, dear Lord, give me*
> *Your peace for my soul and Your power to make me Your*
> *child right now. Dear Lord, I receive You into my heart this*
> *very moment as my Lord and Savior. I will serve You from this*
> *hour all the days of my life. This I will do by the help of God*
> *and in the name of Jesus Christ. Amen.*

NOW NAIL THIS TRUTH ON THE WALLS OF YOUR SOUL: **Because
I have confessed my sins and believed in Jesus Christ ...**

YOUR GOD-GIVEN KEY FOR TODAY
"Jesus Is Giving Me Perfect Peace . . . !"

TUESDAY
Key:
GOD LOVES ME AND HE NEVER GIVES UP ON ME

or
How God Can Make Your Broken Life New Again

Have you ever felt that you had so miserably failed that there was
no way to start over, no place to begin again, your friends and loved
ones had deserted you and there was just nothing to live for? And even
worse, it seemed that God was dead or didn't care about you. The
fact is you had just made such a mess of things and caused so much
grief for those around you that you seriously considered taking your
own life? Well, don't feel like you're alone, friend. I get letters from
people every day who feel just like this. But I've got good news for you
... GOD IS NOT THROUGH WITH YOU ... HE NEVER GIVES UP
... HE LOVES YOU ... HE LOVES YOU ... HE LOVES YOU ...
YES! YOU, JUST LIKE YOU ARE.

There was a man in the Old Testament who was a prophet of
Israel. His name was Jeremiah. He was called "the weeping prophet,"
because he wept so much over the spiritual condition of the children
of Israel. In one place in the Bible he said:

> *Oh that my head were waters, and mine eyes a fountain of*
> *tears, that I might weep day and night for . . . my people . . .*
> *(Jeremiah 9:1).*

But one day he discovered that crying about the problem and feeling
sorry for people wasn't going to get the job done. Just about the time he
thought God was through worrying with man, the Lord just jerked him
up short and said, "Jeremiah, go down to the potter's house . . ."

Well, it's a good thing that Jeremiah was sensitive to the voice of God. He didn't ask any questions. He just went.

When he walked in he saw the wheel spinning and the clay on it and the potter's hands skillfully working. And Jeremiah said, "Mr. Potter, what are you doing?"

He said, "I'm making a beautiful vessel."

And Jeremiah said, "With that little bit of shapeless clay on the wheel?"

He said, "Yes."

"Well, how do you know it's going to be a beautiful vessel?"

"Because I have a plan and a dream for this bit of clay—I have a design for it."

As Jeremiah watched it there came a new appreciation for man in his heart and for God's great design for every human being. He began to realize that every human being is unique and irreplaceable, that he's a person of great worth.

As the potter was shaping the mass of clay according to his own design and trying to make of it a beautiful vessel, suddenly his face clouded up and he stopped.

Jeremiah said, "Potter, why are you stopping?"

He said, "I've just discovered a defect, a flaw, in my clay. It's marred. There's something wrong."

GOD IS NOT GOING TO QUIT

Jeremiah began to realize why God had sent him down to the potter's house, because he too realized something was wrong with man. Man was doing all those wrong things because something is wrong inside him. There is a flaw, a defect. He's marred. And all of his terrible behavior is because there is a flaw in him.

As Jeremiah watched, the potter began to reshape the clay. He realized that the potter was not going to give up. And it came to him that GOD IS NOT GOING TO QUIT. God has not given up on man. God has not given up on you! And God won't quit! As long as you have a breath in your nostrils, God won't quit.

What did the potter do next? It was an amazing thing. He pulled the clay off the wheel and with his hands he began to break it. He mashed it and began to knead it again. And Jeremiah said, "Mr. Potter, what are you doing now?"

He said, "I'm breaking the clay in order to remake it." So he crushed it and kneaded it and worked at it until it was pliable again and he worked out the flaw. He put it back on the wheel and began to spin the wheel, and with his skillful hands he began to reshape it according to his design and his plan.

Jeremiah looked up with a smile on his face and he knew that he had a message of hope to take back to the children of Israel. And that message is:

> God's skillful hands are upon you . . . just a bit of clay . . .
> BECAUSE HE HAS A DESIGN FOR YOUR LIFE. He has a plan for you. No matter how your life is marred—regardless of the flaws, He has something wonderful for you. He's going to make a beautiful vessel of you yet.

And, friend, I believe that with all my heart.

I can almost hear you saying:

> "BUT YOU DON'T KNOW HOW BAD THE FLAW IS . . ."

I may not know how bad *your* flaw is, but . . .

> I KNOW THE POWER OF THE "FLAW REMOVER"!

God made you and He can make you brand-new all over again.

> GOD WON'T QUIT.
>> HE LOVES YOU.
>>> HE HAS A PLAN FOR YOUR LIFE . . . YES, YOURS!

REMEMBER, GOD SPECIALIZES IN CLAY VESSELS—all you have to do is let yourself become pliable in His great big hands!

YOUR GOD-GIVEN KEY FOR TODAY

And . . . remembering . . . say:

"God Loves Me . . Me . . . Me . . . And
He Never Gives Up On Me!"

WEDNESDAY Key: I CAN WALK WITH JESUS EVERY DAY

or
How To Make Your Christian Experience Work As Well On This Earth As In Heaven

It's so easy when things go wrong for someone to say to you, "Trust in God." But people are always saying to me, "Oral Roberts, HOW? How do I trust in God?"

This is especially true of new Christians. They have accepted Christ and now the problems start coming. And they begin to wonder.

They want to trust God as their Source to see them through these problems but they wonder HOW?

I want to share with you from the Word of God how you can learn to trust in God. The Apostle Peter tells us:

> Casting all your care upon him (God); for he careth for you (1 Peter 5:7).

God is concerned about *you* . . . the person. He is concerned about your loved ones . . . He is concerned about every situation in your life. You can TRUST God. You can trust Him because God is the Source of your supply (Philippians 4:19).

God lays the riches of His glory end to end in heaven and says, "According to these I will supply your need."

Now man cannot say that, earth cannot give such an abundance of supply, but God is the Source of *total* supply. Not only *can* God, but God *is*. God is our Supply.

TRUST

Trust is *commitment*. Commitment is like sitting down in a chair. But it's more than sitting in the chair, it's resting your full weight upon the chair—it's relaxing.

One of the most powerful and dramatic examples of how to commit your whole weight upon God is found in Matthew 14. Here the story is told of how Peter attempted to walk on the water. Now Peter had been raised on the water, but he had never walked on it. But during the storm when the disciples were out there in a boat and they were about to lose their lives, Jesus came to them walking on the water. They looked up and saw Jesus out there perfectly balanced on the water. It was a liquid pavement beneath His feet. But there they were over there in the boat which was shaking to pieces. It looked like it was going under any minute.

Well, it doesn't take a very smart man to know that he ought to get out of a sinking boat and get over there where Jesus is. And Peter said, "Lord, if it is really You, bid me come to You on the water."

And Jesus said, "Come . . . Come on out of that shaking, tossing boat." That is, "Come on out here to Me where it is safe."

Peter leaped out and with his eyes on the Lord, his Source, he began to walk on the water. He began to walk above that problem that was about to take his very life. Then in his ear he heard the winds blow and he looked around and saw those huge waves. He no longer was looking at God his Source, or trusting in Him, and he began to sink.

There's another part of that story that is seldom told and it's absolutely fascinating. Peter began to sink and he cried, "Lord, save me. I perish." Very short prayer but if he'd prayed any longer prayer he would have drowned. I know one thing, it's not the long prayer that gets the job done; it's how you are reaching out on the inside.

Well, I can just see this old boy as he starts going under. He goes under once and comes back up and he says, "Jesus."

He goes under the second time and he comes back up and says, "Jesus, Jesus, I perish." By this time he's not trusting in the waves nor in anything else. By this time he has his eyes back on his Source. Each time he came up he saw Christ. He'd put his eyes on Him—Jesus.

Jesus reached out His hand and took Peter's hand in His. That's one thing you can feel. You can feel when He has His hand on you, and when He doesn't. There's a big difference when He is reaching out His hand to you and when He's not. Jesus took Peter by the hand and lifted him up and he stood there beside Jesus.

I can see them now as Jesus takes Peter by the hand and they go arm in arm, walking back to the boat. They *walk* on the water back to the boat. Peter did walk on the water but he didn't walk on it by himself. And God never asks you to do anything by yourself. You don't have to feel alone because God is closer to you than your breath.

You know, it's all very simple when you get right down to it. I said *simple*, but I know it isn't *easy*. To keep your trust in God your Source, you've got to keep your eyes on Him . . . and Him alone. Just as soon as you start looking to someone or something else to meet your need, you'll begin, like Peter, to sink beneath the problem. And before you know it, the problem will be on top of you. I know because this happens to me all the time. But I also know that just as soon as I get my eyes back on my Source, when I remember who my Source is—GOD—I begin to climb up out of the problem and get on top of it. Then I can sit back and relax. I can TRUST my Source because I know He has never failed me . . . and He won't.

USE YOUR INNER RESOURCES OF PRAYER AND FAITH

Christ said, "Men ought always to pray, and not to faint" (Luke 18:1). The feeling you get when you enter a rushing stream is to go with the current instead of against it. That's the human, the natural, feeling. Jesus says you should not do that. You ought not to faint. You ought not to give way and go with the current. You should pray. You should have faith.

Now faith is centering your believing upon God as a Being. Believing that His power is superior to all other forms of power. You put your mind upon God rather than upon something negative. As a matter of fact, the Christian who knows God's way does this. He makes Christ the center of his life. The Bible says:

> Looking unto Jesus the author and finisher of our faith (Hebrews 12:2).

Have you ever thought about your faith having an origin? Faith having a beginning? Faith actually starting? Yes, perhaps you have, but have you thought about its ending? Christ is the Author and the FINISHER of your faith. The faith that He began in you, He can and will and desires to finish. In order to have faith, one must look to God. In order for that faith to be finished, to be consummated, to become a fact, one must continue to look to God. Looking to Christ, the Author and Finisher of your faith.

Now who is your supply? Who is the real supplier of life? Who is it who intervenes in your behalf? Who is it who takes people and things and moves them into proper place so that they touch your life exactly right?

GOD.

The Apostle Paul said, "GOD shall supply all your need." Not someone else, not something else, but God.

What I've been trying to say is . . .

GOD IS THE ONE WHO MAKES OUR
CHRISTIAN EXPERIENCE WORK

Prayer and faith help us reach God. Expectancy keeps our minds tuned in to God so that we look to Him for all our needs to be met, and all our lives to be used for His glory. This will cause God to release His power in us so that our faith will be completed.

SATURATE YOUR MIND WITH THE WORD OF GOD

As a young boy I used to watch my father read the Bible. He loved to sit in a chair leaning against the house in the cool of the day and read for hours. Frequently he would pause to mark a passage. He would become so absorbed that he would be completely oblivious to his surroundings. We children could run and play and shout but he would not be disturbed. Sometimes he would look up and I would see tears in his eyes.

"Papa, why do you cry when you read the Bible?" I would ask.

Brushing away the tears and closing the Bible for a minute, he would smile and say, "Son, someday when the Lord Jesus is real to you as a person—when you feel Him standing by your side, when you know He is closer to you than your breath—you will know and understand."

I was a teen-ager before I accepted Christ and the first thing I did was get out the Bible my parents had given to me and begin to read it for myself.

You see, when I accepted Christ into my heart, I did not just embrace an idea or a philosophy, I embraced a person—Jesus Christ. Today Jesus is the most real person I know . . . and I know Him better than anyone else on this earth. And I came to know Him best by reading the four Gospels and Acts. Through the Word I followed Him down the dusty roads of Galilee, into the sick rooms, as He ministered to those with deep problems . . . and I began to find the answer to my own problems.

But I didn't stop with the Gospels and Acts, I read through the entire Bible—many times—and each time I read a verse (although most of it is familiar to me now) I found something new and exciting that helps me in my walk with Jesus.

So I suggest to you, if you do not have a Bible, get one. One that will be yours—and yours alone. One that has print large enough to read easily and that is a comfortable size for you to carry . . . and be sure there is room in the margin to write. Yes. It's all right to write in your Bible. Pretty soon it will be like an old friend to you and it will help and comfort you in your time of need or despair. So as you read, underscore those verses that seem to leap out at you. Make a note in the margin, now and then, as God speaks to your heart.

In times of discouragement or loneliness or confusion read your Bible often.

It always helps to read the Bible. It helps more when you are in need of strength or courage or stronger faith. At a time when you are tired, even the touch of the Bible is wonderful. On rare occasions I take it to bed with me and sleep with it cradled in my arm. The feel of it gives me confidence for I know it is true and eternal. Things may be going to pieces all around, but the Word of God is sure and steadfast. It is an anchor to the soul.

The passage I read over and over *when I feel weak* is Luke 10:19:
Behold, I give unto you power . . . over all the power of the enemy: and nothing shall by any means hurt you.
This always reads well when you are accosted by the enemy and have feelings of inadequacy.

When I feel bad in body or mind or spirit, and the devil would have me believe God is making me feel that way, I turn to Luke 9:56 and read it until Satan no longer can keep me from believing that:
The Son of man is not come to destroy men's lives, but to save them.
Anything that would destroy me, such as sickness, oppression or fear, is not sent by God. He came to save, not destroy.

And when I still need help along this line, John 10:10 supplies it fully. "The thief (Satan) cometh not, but for to steal, and to kill, and to destroy: I am come that they might have life, and that they might have it more abundantly."

God wants us to be happy, normal, and to enjoy life more abundantly.

When I can't pay my bills, or acquire financial security, 3 John 2 always helps me: "Beloved, I wish above all things that thou mayest prosper . . ." This is a verse I often read a dozen times without stopping. God is interested in our material needs and gives us His promise. "My God shall supply all your need according to his riches in glory by Christ Jesus" (Philippians 4:19).

Psalms 1, 23, 37, 91 are especially inspiring to me *when I need strength and confidence,* and I read them often.

Matthew 8 is another chapter I frequently read, especially in times of *personal sickness* or when I need healing faith for others.

All of us come up against things we should have, but which appear hopeless to us. Mark 9:23 is my verse for this. "If thou canst believe, all things are possible to him that believeth."

Reading the Bible like this, and having it near me all the time, helps me to think and believe in a positive manner. It strengthens my determination and increases my faith.

GO OFTEN TO THE HOUSE OF GOD AND HEAR A
GOOD ANOINTED SERMON

The Bible says, "Faith cometh by hearing, and hearing by the word of God" (Romans 10:17). In a sense, you "hear the Word of God" as you read it. Nothing, however, can take the place of "hearing."

When the preacher is anointed by the Spirit of God he handles the Word very skillfully. He seems to say just the right thing to help you believe and release your faith. He puts you in a better attitude, a faith attitude. When you leave God's house for your home or job, you carry a new strength, an inner light, a deeper knowledge, a stronger determination, and a greater faith. I especially love the services of the church, and have found no substitute for the blessings of strength and help they bring to me.

CONNECT YOURSELF WITH A CAUSE
THAT IS GREATER

After my salvation and healing, I began to give myself completely to God. Many times I have quoted the poem that best illustrates how I feel about this:

I had walked life's way with an easy tread,
 Had followed where comforts and pleasures led,
 Until one day in a quiet place,
 I met the Master face-to-face.
With station and rank and wealth for my goal,
 Much thought for my body but none for my soul,
 I had entered to win in life's mad race,
 When I met the Master face-to-face.

I met him and knew him and blushed to see,
That his eyes full of sorrow were fixed on me.
And I faltered and fell at his feet that day,
While my castles melted and vanished away.
Melted and vanished and in their place,
Naught else could see, but my Master's face.
And I cried aloud, O, make me meet
To follow the steps of thy wounded feet.
My thought is now for the souls of men.
I've lost my life to find it again.
E'er since that day in a quiet place,
I met the Master face-to-face.

Now let's get down to the business of everyday Christian living. Some people call it "walking with Christ." You may want to put your own handle on it, but what it really amounts to is this:

JOY AND PEACE BEGIN IN YOUR HEART WHEN YOU
RECEIVE CHRIST INTO YOUR LIFE. BUT THEY COME TO
HARVEST AS YOU FOLLOW THROUGH AND LIVE OUT IN
YOUR EVERYDAY LIFE THE *REALITY* OF CHRIST WHO
DWELLS WITHIN YOU.

Christ saved you . . .
Christ keeps you saved . . .
Now you must build your life around your Savior,
JESUS CHRIST.

YOUR GOD-GIVEN KEY FOR TODAY

Say this until it is as natural as breathing out and breathing in:

"I Can Walk With Jesus Every Day . . ."

And what a walk!

THURSDAY

Key:
**JESUS HAS WALKED THIS ROAD
BEFORE ME ... ALL I NEED TO
DO IS FOLLOW**

or

Something That Will Really Help You ... Knowing The Difference Between Conversion And Discipleship

I was converted to Christ at 17 in a single, heartfelt, heartwarming act of repenting of my sins and believing on Christ to save my soul. It was a struggle for me at first to reach the point at which I felt I needed to repent and where I wanted to believe that Jesus Christ is the Son of God, that He died for me, and was willing and able to give me salvation. But the struggle came to an end and there was that moment an instantaneous conversion in which all at once I knew Christ had become and was *my personal Savior.*

But listen! That was when I was 17.

Now it's nearly 41 years later and I am almost 58. Through God I have more good years ahead for I fully expect to live all my days as He has planned. The point is this:

It is one thing to come to the act of receiving Christ as your personal Savior.

It is entirely another to become a *disciple* or follower of Jesus Christ.

Your conversion and your becoming a disciple are two different things: Your conversion is what Christ does for you. Your becoming a disciple is what you do for Christ in the days or years of the rest of your life.

The act of your conversion was probably like mine—a struggle for you to get yourself to repent and believe on Jesus so He could do for you what no one else can—save you from your sins and give you salvation.

HOW YOU BECOME A DISCIPLE

Becoming a disciple is not a single act, it is something you *do* as a way of life the rest of your life. Jesus explains it:

If any man will come after me (be my disciple), *let him deny himself, and take up his cross daily, and follow me* (Luke 9:23).

The key word here is D-A-I-L-Y. Not one act . . . in one day . . . of turning your life over to Christ but more, much more than that. It is being willing *daily* to follow Christ and become His disciple. It is a continuous daily action of *becoming* more than what you have been doing. It is going from your start as a baby, born into the kingdom of God (John 3:1, 2), growing into an adult in Christ, into Christian maturity in which the living Christ is being daily formed in you (Galatians 4:19).

It means you take on Jesus' own life and life-style and discover daily His way of doing things and do them joyfully, continuously. Every day is a new day. Every day you try to *give God your best then ask Him for His best* which is what Seed-Faith really is.

Oh, you look back at the act of your conversion which was your spiritual birth and your starting time with Christ, but you go on daily letting Christ take over your thoughts and deeds, your very life. It is taking up *your* cross. And what is the cross?

The cross to Jesus was the giving of himself in sincere acts of love and concern, in doing good to people, giving of His time and talent and efforts, giving of His resources until one day it would all be *given.* For you see, the cross of Calvary was actually the *last* of Jesus' giving of himself. He had been doing it from the beginning (Acts 10:38). I think this is very important for you and me to know.

Seed-Faith giving as a way of life is taking up your cross daily. Why is it a cross? Because you and I, as human beings, have been taught to *get,* not to give. And we don't like to give because we feel we are losing something. And when we give to God we are taught by people not to expect anything back from God.

That's the way people lived when Jesus came but He opened up a "new and living way" (Hebrews 10:20). The way of giving, and giving first. Of giving cheerfully and finding God's love coming back to us in the form of our need (2 Corinthians 9:7). Of giving, not as a debt owed but as a seed sown. Of giving with the expectation of a harvest that would come back to *us!* Of giving for a desired result.

Discipleship, as Jesus teaches us, is to take up your cross daily and *gladly* follow Him. Learn of Him and His ways and F-O-L-L-O-W. This is Seed-Faith which will move you into a new life of expecting and receiving your most-needed miracles.

AN EASY FORMULA FOR DISCIPLESHIP — (walking with Christ daily)

Make an acrostic:

> F — Follow Christ daily.
> O — Obey Jesus' Word.
> L — Love Him.
> L — Lean on Him.
> O — Open up and start giving.
> W — Walk daily with Him.

YOUR GOD-GIVEN KEY FOR TODAY

Now, no matter how rough it gets, keep saying:

"Jesus Has Walked This Road Before Me . . .

All I Need To Do Is Follow."

FRIDAY

Key:
ONE OF THE GREATEST SEEDS I'LL EVER PLANT IS FORGIVENESS

or
The Greatest Word Christ Ever Used . . ."Forgiven!"

Jesus gave us two impossibles . . . maybe more . . . but two in particular. First, He said:

It is impossible, but that offences will come (Matthew 18:7).

He meant by that we're going to offend somebody and somebody is going to offend us . . . that it is going to happen. It's impossible for it not to happen in the stresses and strain of living.

The second *impossible* Jesus mentioned is . . .

Unless we forgive we cannot be forgiven (Matthew 6:14, 15).

This means unless I forgive someone else for what they've done to me, I cannot be forgiven for what I have done to them or . . . to someone else—two impossibles.

There's something about offending someone or living in the strain of that offense and being unforgiven that is evidently too heavy for a human being to bear. It throws us off balance.

MY GRANDDAUGHTER BRENDA

I remember once when my oldest granddaughter, little Brenda Nash, came to spend the night with Evelyn and me. She was just 10 at the time. Now our grandchildren love to come to our house and spend as many nights as their mothers and fathers will let them. Evelyn and I love to have them. But this time when little Brenda came in, you could tell that everything was not all right. The usual joy of coming to see us was not there. Her little shoulders were slumped. She looked uptight. She sat down and sort of piddled around. Soon the phone rang and she said to Evelyn, "Muna, I'll get it." So Brenda stepped over to the phone and pretty soon we heard Brenda say, "Mommy, I'm sorry too."

A little more talk and we heard her say, "Well, Mommy, I want you to forgive me too."

Then finally she said, "Mommy, I forgive you."

Apparently Rebecca, her mother, and little Brenda had had a dispute. Everything hadn't gone too well and the load of it was upon her little frail shoulders and her heart couldn't bear it. So Brenda was eager to get to the phone when her mother telephoned and get that thing straight.

Later we learned that Rebecca, the mother of three children, had felt uptight too, and she needed to apologize as much as Brenda did. She needed also to say, "I'm sorry." And she had that same release that Brenda did.

Because Brenda was no longer uptight we had that marvelous time we always have with our grandchildren.

Now isn't that like you and me? But isn't it like the Lord to show us a way out? And there isn't any other way out.

> Forgive and you shall be forgiven. But unless you forgive, you will not be forgiven by your Father in heaven (Matthew 6:14).

Sometimes we don't seem to care whether someone else forgives us or not or maybe we have offended someone and we say, "Well, so what!" But remember, there is someone else we deal with and that is God. God has so constructed us that we cannot live successfully having committed offenses and not having made them right.

JESUS IS IN TUNE WITH PEOPLE WITH PROBLEMS

In the Bible is the story of a paralyzed man. Four good friends brought him on a long journey to where Jesus was because they felt that Jesus could heal him. When they arrived the crowd was surrounding the house where Jesus was preaching so they climbed the roof, lifted their friend up, tore off the tiling of the roof, and let their friend down in the midst of the crowd. There he lay right in the presence of Jesus.

When you're sick or afflicted or bowed down in anyway, Jesus is in tune with you. When He looked at this man, Jesus saw him paralyzed and something went out of Jesus toward him. Apparently the man was not only paralyzed in his body, but in his speech, because he was evidently unable to even speak to Jesus. The important thing was that he had wanted to come. His friends had brought him and now he was in the presence of Jesus in his paralyzed state and unable to speak.

Jesus knew what he was thinking. He knew that there was another kind of sickness, a sickness other than paralysis and it gripped the man's inner self. It was troubling him and it was a terrible weight. Our Lord knew that he was sorry, so he said to the paralyzed man, "Son, thy sins are forgiven thee! You are forgiven all of the bitterness you've built up over your affliction . . . all of that striking back at people . . . and striking back at whatever it was that caused you to be ill . . . all of what you've held inside you, you are forgiven!"

How difficult it is to be sick and not be bitter. How hard it is not to strike at the very ones you love and who love you. I remember when I was ill with tuberculosis. My loving parents waited upon me hand

and foot. I would lose patience and raise my voice and say things to Mamma and to Papa that I should not have said. There they were, not responsible for my illness, but waiting on me. But if they didn't wait on me like I wanted, or if they didn't come when I called, I would lash out at them. It's so easy to do that. It's so easy to strike at people until we build up something wrong in us, but Jesus said, "You are forgiven."

FORGIVEN!

How many of us are forgiven? Are you forgiven? Am I forgiven?

Jesus said, "Son . . . thy sins are forgiven thee . . . take up thy bed, and go unto thine house" (Matthew 9:2-6). Notice that Jesus dealt with a man's soul first. He dealt with the pile of unforgiven sins, then Jesus followed it by a dramatic physical healing, "Take up thy bed and walk!"

And the man was able to do it.

You see, apparently when we are unforgiven, it paralyzes our inner man and it's lying there unable to function. It's so difficult then for medicine or for prayer to work upon our outward bodies. But according to our Lord, the healing of our bodies works better when there's been a healing of our inner spirit. When we're free—actually *free*—we are forgiven!

We are affected by forgiveness—whether we have it or we don't have it. Here's what I think you and I should do and that is to plant a seed of faith. That seed of faith can be no better than a seed of forgiveness. I think it is the greatest word that Christ ever used—FORGIVENESS.

Whether anyone ever forgives you or not . . . you forgive . . . for that's what Christ did on the cross. He said:

Father, forgive them; for they know not what they do (Luke 23:34).

You see, Christ could have ruined it all there on the cross by striking back at the people who had hurt and now were killing Him. But He reached down into the innermost part of His being and said:

Father, forgive . . .

Many of them never responded, but the important thing was that He responded . . . He forgave . . . and a great wave of forgiveness came washing over their lives.

I love Jesus Christ today because He forgave me and He keeps on forgiving me. He is teaching me to forgive and to keep on forgiving. I want to learn better how to forgive. Maybe you do too. Maybe you feel something in your heart that should be brought up. Maybe you have an urgency to say something to your wife, or husband, or child, or parents, or to a stranger or a friend. I tell you this, it will be one of the greatest seeds of faith you've ever planted and God will multiply it back to you . . . and through forgiving, you also will be forgiven.

Friend, this is a tough one. Maybe this is why *forgiven* is the greatest word Christ ever said. It's tough to forgive, especially when you feel like the other guy is the one who should ask forgiveness. Well, maybe I can help you. Here's what I do. NO MATTER HOW I HAVE BEEN WRONGED, I JUST SAY: "Lord, I FORGIVE that person, as a seed I plant." Then the burden of the whole thing is no longer mine to bear. Because when I FORGIVE as a seed I plant, I KNOW GOD WILL STRAIGHTEN EVERYTHING OUT BETTER THAN I COULD EVER HAVE THOUGHT OF.

So remember this, and say it:

> "ONE OF THE GREATEST SEEDS I'LL
> EVER PLANT IS FORGIVENESS."

Now if you really mean that, write down on a piece of paper the biggest wrong someone has dealt you. You can put down their name if you want to, but you don't have to, God knows.

Now throw it away—just like you were planting a seed in the ground . . . and watch for the harvest.

YOUR GOD-GIVEN KEY FOR TODAY

Say it again so you'll remember:

"One Of The Greatest Seeds I'll

Ever Plant Is Forgiveness."

SATURDAY

Key:
I AM OBEYING GOD AND HE
KEEPS BLESSING ME

or

The Greatest Advice I Ever Received

My mother, who is now with the Lord, gave me the greatest advice I ever received. She said:

"Son, stay little in your own eyes and God will bless the world through you."

I'm sure she gave me that advice because she knew that would be a difficult assignment for me. Then she gave me a second piece of advice. She said:

"Oral, always obey God."

Now Mamma didn't say that to me one or two or three times. She said it to me constantly over a great many years. And just a few hours before she slipped away, she said those same words to me again. She said this because she knew the importance of humility to God so one can learn obedience.

WE MUST ALL LEARN OBEDIENCE . . . ONE WAY OR ANOTHER

I'm reminded of a story that Reverend Tommy Tyson, our first chaplain at Oral Roberts University, tells of the remarkable training process of the Arabian horse in the Middle East. As you know, only recently has a mechanized form of travel been available in the Middle East, in the Arabian deserts. There are hundreds of miles of trackless deserts in those countries and in the past the Arabian horse was the way many people traveled. In many instances, they still travel that way today.

Tommy said in order for the Arabian horse to become a highly regarded horse, a horse of great quality and of great price, it had to go through a very special schooling. He said the trainer would put the horses through all types of tests, but there was one test that was the most severe. When it came near the time for the graduation of the horse, the trainer would withhold water from it. He would have the horses do without water as long as they could without dying of thirst. You can imagine what those horses were enduring in the 130-degree heat of those deserts, going for days without a drink of water. All the while, the trainer is leading these horses to water. Of course as they drew near the water they could smell it. As they drew near they broke loose, and with the last strength they had they ran to the water to plunge in. Just as they got there, the trainer blew his whistle. The horses that stopped without drinking and turned around and trotted back to the trainer, graduated. They were perfectly obedient horses.

Now why is such a test . . . such an obedience . . . necessary? Because the life of the man on that horse is entrusted to the horse. Imagine yourself out on the trackless desert on the back of a disobedient horse, a horse that will not obey the signals you give him. You could both die.

Christianity is tough. It's not easy. It was not intended to be easy, because man has to learn obedience. If he does not learn to obey God, he will obey man or he will obey the devil. He will learn some kind of discipline whether he wants to or not. He may have to learn it by the law, and there are many men behind prison walls today who are being subjected to the learning of discipline. Whether they willingly obey or not, they obey.

Each one of us has to learn for himself the meaning of Christ's words:
If any man will come after me (be my disciple), *let him deny himself, and take up his cross daily, and follow me* (Luke 9:23).

FOLLOW ME. We must become sensitive to the promptings of the Holy Spirit, open-minded to whatever the Lord would have us do. We must be willing to OBEY.

ARE YOU LIVING IN OBEDIENCE?
ARE YOU UNDER THE AUTHORITY OF GOD?

I can relate to any person today who wants to be a law to himself, or seeks to be an island, or wants to have his own way—to rebel against his parents, society, God, the church, or anything else. I can relate because—I'm ashamed to say—that's what I did. But it only brought me heartache and almost destroyed my being.

But I came under the authority of God—that is, I *began* to come under the authority of God. I don't obey all the time as I should. Sometimes I think I have and then I realize I haven't, because I slip back into that disobedient spirit. I rebel and I don't want anyone to say anything to me. I don't want to listen to God. That's the way we humans are in our own natural state, without God's grace. But I know this:

THE ONLY WAY TO LIVE A SUCCESSFUL CHRISTIAN LIFE
IS TO COME UNDER THE AUTHORITY OF GOD . . .
TO BE IN OBEDIENCE TO HIM

So I ask you, "Are you living in obedience to God?" Have you accepted God's authority to the extent that you are willing to give up your way and take God's way, to give up your will and take God's will?"

Even Jesus had to say:

Not my will, but thine be done (Luke 22:42).

The Bible tells us:

Though he (Jesus) *were a Son, yet LEARNED he obedience by the things which he suffered* (Hebrews 5:8).

Can we understand that Jesus, the Man, had to learn obedience to God exactly like you and I do? The writer of Hebrews spoke of His learning obedience, I mean having to LEARN it like I have to learn it—like you have to learn it.

Eventually Jesus had to face the thing that God wanted Him to do. For . . .

He (Jesus) *had offered up prayers and supplications with strong crying and tears unto him that was able to save him from death* (Hebrews 5:7).

Jesus didn't want to go to the cross. He didn't want nails driven into His hands. Can you imagine how that would hurt? Imagine having the flesh and bones of your hands crunched by nails being driven through them and then having nails driven through your feet.

But that was not the worst of it. Imagine being stripped and hung there before the crowd, derided and cast out. Jesus didn't look forward to that. He wanted men to understand that He came to the world to save them, but they did not. And He cried for God to grant Him some other way, but there was no other way granted, because . . .

YOU MUST PUT A SEED IN IF YOU WANT IT TO BE MULTIPLIED . . . YOU MUST GIVE IN ORDER TO RECEIVE

That's the law of God. That's the law of nature and so Jesus had to give. He had to obey God. The human part of Him didn't want to do it any more than we do. But Jesus is our example in giving up own own way and taking God's. We can say, "Not my will, but God's be done." And how glorious it is when we go through it and endure the pain of it and come out with a resurrection, come out with a seed multiplied, come out with the joy of the Lord flowing in our hearts, and with our needs met.

I ASK AGAIN:

Are you putting yourself under God's authority?

Are you living in obedience . . . disciplining yourself, as Jesus did, to take God's will for yourself?

If you are, God is going to bless you. Maybe you are not in perfect obedience. That's all right . . . this is something we GROW into. The important thing is, are you trying to be obedient? After all, we as Christians are not perfect—just forgiven and walking toward perfection.

There are all kinds of stories in the Bible where God's people wanted to do something besides obey—obedience is tough. But if you'll start by verbalizing it, that's a start.

YOUR GOD-GIVEN KEY FOR TODAY
"I Am Obeying God And He Keeps Blessing Me."

SIXTH WEEK

SUNDAY	I KNOW GOD AND I AM IN HIM AND HE IS IN ME
MONDAY	JESUS IS GIVING ME PERFECT PEACE
TUESDAY	GOD LOVES ME AND HE NEVER GIVES UP ON ME
WEDNESDAY	I CAN WALK WITH JESUS EVERY DAY
THURSDAY	JESUS HAS WALKED THIS ROAD BEFORE ME . . . ALL I NEED TO DO IS FOLLOW
FRIDAY	ONE OF THE GREATEST SEEDS I'LL EVER PLANT IS FORGIVENESS
SATURDAY	I AM OBEYING GOD AND HE KEEPS BLESSING ME

SEVENTH WEEK

How I Overcame The Question: Have Miracles Ceased? And How Miracles Can Open Up To You

SUNDAY Key:
MIRACLES BELONG IN MY DAY TODAY

or
An Answer God Gave Me That Helped Settle The Question: Should We Pray For Miracles Today?

SEVERAL years ago I was invited by Billy Graham to participate in the World Conference on Evangelism in Berlin. While I was there a minister from India approached me between sessions and said, "Are you Oral Roberts?"

I said, "Yes."

He said, "I've been wanting to meet you. One of the reasons I came was to meet you."

I told him I was flattered to hear that, and asked what I could do for him.

He said, "I have a very difficult problem. I've never understood or believed in miracles or that God healed the sick, although I've preached for many years. Here is my problem. Two of my members rushed into the church one day with their child who was dying. The doctors had just given him up. The parents thrust their little child into my hands and said, 'Pastor, pray for God to heal him.'

"I was in a dilemma. They'd asked me to do what I didn't believe could happen . . . to ask God to heal. Before I realized, though, I did pray for him and to my utter amazement God healed him."

I said, "Well, what's your problem?"

And he said, "My problem is very serious. Did I do right? Did I do right in praying for the little boy?"

My intellect started to respond instantly and cry, "Of course you did right." You know I wanted to say, "Of course you should have prayed for him. And God healed him. Give God the thanks." That's my mind, but the Holy Spirit checked me. I knew instantly that was not the answer to give to this man. Up out of me came a phrase and it was a word of wisdom (1 Corinthians 12:8). I heard it inside me and I knew if I would speak it, it would be a word of wisdom and it was this: "You want to ask me if you did right in praying for the little boy and God healed him?"

And he said, "Yes."

I said, "Why don't you ask the little boy?"

He said, "Oh, oh. Why don't I ask the little boy? Yes, why don't I ask the little boy? Oh, I see what you mean. You have given me the answer and I'm going back to India and have a healing ministry."

"ASK THE LITTLE BOY"

All I said was, "Why don't you ask the little boy?" It wasn't something coming out of my intellect. It was by the Holy Spirit, and planted in my mind, then I spoke it. "Why don't you ask the little boy?"—became the sounding phrase all over the Congress. Everywhere I went people would stop me and say, "Are you the man that said, 'Why don't you ask the little boy?'"

And I said, "Yes. I'm the man."

It became a great blessing and as Billy Graham later told me, "Oral, we had no idea when we invited you that you would have such a chance to witness for the healing power of our Lord."

I didn't go there to do anything special but just to be a guest and a delegate and to sit there, which is what I did, but these things just came.

You see, anybody that has been sick and received a miracle from God has no question in his mind about the rightness of believing God for a miracle . . . or whether God still heals today. He knows!!

The fact is, my friend, you can spend hours, days, even weeks in arguing whether or not miracles still happen today and get nowhere. If you really want to know, find someone who has experienced a miracle. Ask them what they think! Or better still, ask God to give you a miracle. Once you, or someone close to you, has experienced a miracle, there will be no question in your mind.

———————

THE MOST IMPORTANT THING IN YOUR LIFE IS A MIRACLE... ESPECIALLY WHEN YOU NEED ONE!

Why? Because you have a seven-day-a-week life . . .

seven-day-a-week needs . . .

seven-day-a-week faith . . .

Friend, I believe GOD MADE MIRACLES FOR YOU—AND YOU FOR MIRACLES.

YOUR GOD-GIVEN KEY FOR TODAY

"Miracles Belong In My Day Today!!"

And they will happen!

MONDAY Key: I WILL NOT TAKE NO FOR AN ANSWER!

or
The Five "I Wills" Of Jesus And Their Importance To Your Life

I have a terrific excitement, a joyous excitement to share with you about what the Lord spoke to my heart recently. HE HAS SPOKEN TO ME TWELVE TIMES DURING MY MINISTRY, and each time it's an electric moment when deep within me I hear His voice speaking to me positively in regard to His love and healing power for my generation.

I was just getting ready for bed one night when His words came so forcibly into my heart. He said:

"I WANT YOU TO EMPHASIZE HEALING MORE. I WANT YOU TO TELL THE PEOPLE THAT I WANT TO HEAL THEM. I *WILL* TO HEAL THEM. TELL THEM NOT TO TAKE NO FOR AN ANSWER, FOR HEALING IS THEIR HERITAGE. TELL THEM TO RISE UP AND DEMAND IT, FOR I *WILL* TO HEAL THE PEOPLE."

I had just lain down when His words came into my heart. And when He had finished talking to me, I picked up my Bible and it fell open to the eighth chapter of St. Matthew. That's the great healing chapter. I began to study and I discovered in that chapter FIVE great healings and outstanding miracles of our Lord in which He said (or demonstrated by His actions):

"I WILL . . .
I WILL HEAL . . .
I WILL DELIVER . . .
I WILL . . .
I WILL . . ."

It was totally in harmony with what He had just spoken so forcibly in my heart:

"TELL THE PEOPLE I WANT TO HEAL THEM . . .
I *WILL* TO HEAL THEM . . ."

So I want to share with you here these five tremendous "I WILLS" of our Lord for they apply directly to your life in the NOW.

JESUS AND THE LEPER

In the first one, Jesus has just come down from the mountain where He has just finished His great "Sermon on the Mount" when a leper came and fell at His feet and worshiped Him and said:

"Lord, if thou wilt, thou canst make me clean . . ." (Matthew 8:2).

Can you imagine the audacity of this leper. In those days lepers were considered unclean and forbidden by the law to mingle with the rest of the people. A leper was supposed to stand afar off and cry, "Unclean . . . !" But this leper, no doubt, saw the love and compassion in the eyes of Jesus and knew that it is His WILL to heal the people.

"If you will . . ." cried the leper and suddenly he heard Jesus say:

> *I will; be thou clean* (Matthew 8:3).

And the Bible says:

> *Immediately his leprosy was cleansed* (Matthew 8:3).

"I WILL . . ." I've often wondered what could have happened if Jesus had said, "I won't." What if He had not been involved with human beings and their needs? What if He'd just made a garden and sculptured the mountains and made it a dress parade for His creation to see? What if He had said no? But He said, "YES, I WILL." He *is* involved.

JESUS AND A ROMAN WAR LORD

The next incident in the eighth chapter of Matthew is about a Roman army captain coming to Christ and kneeling there in the dusty road saying:

> *Lord, my servant lieth at home sick of the palsy grievously tormented* (Matthew 8:6).

And Christ said these words:

> *I will come and heal him* (Matthew 8:7).

I will . . . You see He could have said to this Roman who was an overlord there in Palestine, who had been abusing the people, who had bowed to no man but Caesar:

> "Look, you rough, rude, uncultured, paganistic, brutal soldier, if you think you have any part in My kingdom, you are wrong. And I don't have any time for you. Why don't you take your soldiers and get back to Rome?"

But Jesus didn't. Instead, He was involved with the need and desperation of the man for his servant. Jesus was concerned when the Roman centurion said, "My servant is lying at home grievously tormented."

And our Lord said:

> *I WILL come and heal him . . . I WILL . . .*

And I want you to know, friend, there's nobody outside the pale of Christ's human and divine love—you, nor no one else is outside—you are inside. Jesus is concerned about you.

CHRIST'S CONCERN FOR A MOTHER-IN-LAW

The next "I will," in this eighth chapter is when Jesus Christ had gone home with Peter. When they arrived at his house to eat, they found Peter's wife's mother was in the bedroom very ill with a hot, burning fever. And so when they told Him, Jesus (by His actions) said:

"I will heal her."

He went in, took her by the hand, rebuked the fever, and raised her up. The Bible says she came in and ministered unto them.

What if Jesus had said no? It would have meant an unconcern for me, for you, for our loved ones. Speaking of loved ones, I have been quite touched and concerned and impressed the past few weeks as I've read my mail. I made a survey, actually, while I was in the Prayer Tower with my partners' prayer requests. And do you know the number one request we are now receiving? It is this:

Pray for my loved ones, for my mother, my daddy, my son, my daughter, my sister, my brother, my relative, my dear one. Something has happened to him, to her. Oral Roberts, pray for my loved ones . . .

I think it's wonderful that Jesus Christ would heal Peter's wife's mother. There are so many jokes about mothers-in-law today, but here Jesus Christ was as much concerned about the mother-in-law as He was His own mother, or anybody's mother. Christ is concerned about every human need.

JESUS STILLS THE STORM

The next incident in this same eighth chapter of Matthew happened as the disciples were on a journey across the sea of Galilee in a boat.

Jesus was asleep on a pillow in the back part of the boat when a great storm rushed down upon them and suddenly they were confronted with death. The disciples rushed back and awakened Jesus and cried:

Lord, save us: we perish (Matthew 8:25).

And Jesus looked up and heard the roar of the storm and saw the dashing of the waves and felt the rocking and jarring of the boat and He said:

"I will still this storm."

Jesus walked to the bow of the ship and there as the wind was blowing His clothes around Him, He raised His hand and said:

Peace, be still (Mark 4:39).

He hushed the sea to sleep. And the disciples' personal safety was insured.

Most of us are concerned about our personal safety. Planes are being hijacked, bombs being thrown, people being killed without reason on every hand—there's violence as we've never known it in the history of our country and other countries as well. People are afraid—afraid to go anywhere at certain times and particularly certain places. But Jesus is saying to us that His WILL to heal us has a lot to do with our personal safety—to keep us from harm.

JESUS DELIVERS A MAN FROM DEMONS

The last "I will" of Jesus in this chapter had to do with a wretched, tormented man filled with demons (See also Mark 5:1-19 and Luke 8:26-33). He was antisocial and so filled with suicidal tendencies that he left his town and lived among the tombs where he cut his body with sharp rocks and screamed out in the night. He was completely untamable—even breaking great chains that the people had tried to chain him with. Today we would probably call him a psychopath. And when Christ came on the scene, the demons in the man cried:

"Art thou come to torment us before the time?" And the man in whom those demons dwelled, was crying out for.help and Jesus said:

"I will command those demons to come out of you . . . I will set you free."

He spoke the word of power. And the demons came out. Then the man got dressed and came and sat at the feet of Jesus. And the Bible describes him as now being in his right mind and saying:

"Lord, I want to go with You wherever You go . . ."

JESUS WILLS TO HEAL YOU NOW

Now you see, the position of Christ is a very positive one toward you. "I will come and heal . . ."

Your position must be just as powerful and positive toward Him.

"Yes, Lord, I *will* to be healed. I will not take no for an answer. Healing is my heritage. I will not give up . . ."

You've got to hold on—don't give up.

DOWN TO ONE STRING

There is a story about a great concert violinist who was playing his heart out to a tremendous crowd of music lovers. Suddenly something happened that all violinists dread—a string broke. Well, the violinist usually carried extra strings but this time he had none. So he just calmly removed the broken string and continued playing on three strings, when, would you believe it, immediately a second string broke . . . then a third string went. There he stood.

Well, the crowd gasped and sat up on the edge of their seats wondering what he would do. They felt for him. Sweat popped out on his brow. He could handle one broken string, but now *three* strings were gone. And so with trembling hand he just removed the second and third strings. Holding up his violin to the audience he said, "One string."

And he began to play and finished that great masterpiece of music on one string. By that time the people were crying and cheering. Later this man said, "I was determined I would not give up."

Now listen, friend, my Lord said to me:
YOU TELL THE PEOPLE I WANT TO HEAL THEM. I *WILL* TO
HEAL THEM...TELL THEM NOT TO TAKE NO FOR AN ANSWER
... Don't give up—Jesus is saying, "Don't give up." Your attitude toward
Him can be just as positive as His is toward you. *Your* will is important.
Determine—"I WILL BE HEALED BY MY LORD!"

Oh! how much power we can release toward Him and how much He
can release toward us—toward me, toward you.

Rise up! Assert yourself! Take command . . . say to the whole world
and especially to the devil . . .

YOUR GOD-GIVEN KEY FOR TODAY

"I Will Not Take No For An Answer!"

TUESDAY Key: GOD'S WORK MEANS A MIRACLE TO ME

or
Jesus Tells Us A Miracle Is A "Work of God"

Only about once did Jesus refer to miracles and that is found in
John 6:26. The rest of the time He referred to miracles as the WORKS
OF GOD or the WORKS OF THE FATHER. Now Matthew, Mark,
Luke, and John continually said Christ performed miracles but Jesus
called them the WORKS OF GOD. For example:

> *For the works which the Father hath given me to finish, the
> same works that I do, bear witness of me, that the Father hath
> sent me* (John 5:36).

In other words, Jesus said, "I do the *works* of my Father." Jesus is
talking about doing the works of God. WORKS OF GOD. In John 10:37,
38, Jesus said:

> *If I do not the works of my Father, believe me not. But if I do,
> though ye believe not me, believe the works . . .*

Jesus was saying, "If you cannot believe that I am the Son of God, believe these works—these works of God."

Jesus indicates a miracle is not a sometime or onetime thing. It is
not some sort of magic. He places a miracle in the category of the *works
of God.* Now the moment you stop calling them miracles and put them
into the area of the works of God, then you see that Jesus Christ has
only come to do what God has been doing all through the centuries and

will do forever. Jesus came to do the *works* of the Father. He is carrying out the essential nature of His Father which is to bring His works of LIFE to the world. He explains here that the Spirit of God is upon Him and He's come to do these mighty works of the Father.

Acts 10:38 says:

> *God anointed Jesus of Nazareth with the Holy Ghost* (Spirit) *and with power: who went about doing good, and healing all that were oppressed of the devil; for God was with him.*

First, Jesus was anointed with the Holy Spirit. Then He went about doing good and healing all that were oppressed of the devil, for God was with Him. He was doing the WORKS OF GOD. If you're turned off by the word *miracles*, don't worry that they were miracles, but remember He emphasized that these miracles were really the works of God.

Jesus is still talking about the works of God in Luke 4:18 when He says:

> *The Spirit of the Lord is upon me, because he hath anointed me to preach the gospel to the poor.*

He was really saying, "God has sent me with good news to the poor— YOU DON'T HAVE TO BE POOR ANYMORE."

> *He hath sent me to heal the brokenhearted, to preach deliverance to the captives, and recovering of sight to the blind, to set at liberty them that are bruised, To preach the acceptable year of the Lord* (Luke 4:18).

These are the WORKS Jesus is doing. These are the works of the Father. These are what the Gospel writers call miracles (or wonders).

In 1 Corinthians 12:10, we learn that one of the nine gifts of the Spirit is the working of miracles. The *working* of them. Here again are WORKS. The works of our Father.

In John 14:12, we read:

> *Greater works than these shall* (ye) *do; because I go unto my Father.*

Greater WORKS shall ye do.

In Acts 3 the story is told of how the apostles brought healing to the lame man who was carried daily and placed at the gate of the Temple in Jerusalem. Peter and John came by one day and by faith the man was healed. Because of this healing they were persecuted.

> *And they called them, and commanded them not to speak at all nor teach in the name of Jesus. But Peter and John answered and said unto them, Whether it be right in the sight of God to hearken unto you more than unto God, judge ye. For we cannot but speak the things which we have seen and heard. So*

> *when they had further threatened them, they let them go,*
> *finding nothing how they might punish them, because of the*
> *people* (Acts 4:18-21).

The apostles returned unto their own company. And they prayed:

> *And now, Lord, behold their threatenings: and grant unto*
> *thy servants, that with all boldness they may speak thy word,*
> *by stretching forth thine hand to heal: and that signs and*
> *wonders may be done by the name of thy holy child Jesus*
> (Acts 4:29,30).

This is after the ascension of Christ. Christ is no longer on the earth in His flesh. He's been crucified and resurrected. He has now ascended back to His Father as the glorified Christ. His disciples are still doing the same works, even greater works. They are being persecuted for it. They've returned to pray and they call upon the Lord *not* to deliver them from persecution but to grant that they may speak His words with boldness by stretching forth His hand to heal . . . *by letting them continue to do the works of God.*

What I'm saying is this: This beginning of miracles, or *this beginning of the WORKS OF GOD, did our Lord* (John 2). It was not an *ending* of the works of God but a *beginning* of the works of God. These WORKS OF GOD carried over into the lives of His followers. And they are in the lives of His followers today if we'll only accept them.

E. Stanley Jones, who is now with our Lord, was a famous Methodist missionary in India for some 50 years. He wrote many books. *The Christ of the Indian Road* is one of them. You may be familiar with his books. I'm told that sometime before his homegoing, when he was in his 80's, he had a stroke of paralysis. The doctors were able to help him in a Boston, Massachusetts hospital, but not enough to make him walk.

He asked his family to let him go back to India. There in India he called in many of the people whom he had led to Christ, who now were strong in the Lord. He said to them, "Open the Bible to the book of Acts, Chapter 3, where Peter and John said to the lame man, 'In the name of Jesus Christ, rise up and walk.' Now each morning I want you to come into my room before daylight, before I awaken, and whisper in my ear, 'In the name of Jesus Christ, rise up and walk.' "

They did as he asked. Then one day E. Stanley Jones felt a stirring in his body. He took the first step. Then other steps. Someone told him it was Columbus Day. Columbus Day celebrates the discovery of America by Christopher Columbus in 1492. On this particular day E. Stanley Jones felt God in a new way. He said, "I'm going to walk. In the name of Christ, I'm going to walk." And he walked. He counted his steps — *1492 steps.* E. Stanley Jones in his 80's, just prior to his going to be with the Lord, found the WORKS of God were still worked in him.

God doing His thing in life may be considered extraordinary by people—or a miracle—but it is ordinary to God. It is not something big God is doing—it is simply God being himself, extending and expressing His love and concern for human beings, coming to them at the point of their needs, coming to them where a miracle has to happen or they will be destroyed in some way.

———•———•———

When you have insurmountable needs, needs that are so baffling and so terrible that they require something beyond the natural, beyond the ordinary, you have recourse to God and His wonderful WORKS.

GOD CAN . . .

AND HE WILL . . .

COME TO YOU IN THE NOW IN HIS WONDERFUL WORKS!

HE WILL COME TO YOU IN A MIRACLE!

IF YOU ARE STILL TRYING TO FIND GOD . . .

LOOK FOR HIM IN A MIRACLE—

THAT'S HIS THING AND THAT'S

WHERE YOU'LL ALWAYS FIND HIM.

YOUR GOD-GIVEN KEY FOR TODAY

Now say:

"God's Works Mean A Miracle To Me."

Key:

WEDNESDAY

I CAN CLAIM MY DEAREST LOVED ONE TO BE GOD'S PROPERTY—NOW!

or

How I Used The Seed Of Commanding The Devil To Take His Hands Off God's Property—For My Son Ronnie

Several years ago our oldest son Ronald David was inducted into the United States Army. He had had mononucleosis at one time and after he had recovered he went back to college. After he was inducted into the Army he was sent to Fort Ord, in California, where there was an infectious hepatitis outbreak. It struck Ronald David's body. I think it struck him a little harder because he had just barely overcome a lesser form of it.

The doctors isolated Ronnie and he was all alone. Then they sent word to Evelyn and me that if it were possible, for us to come by because our son was seriously ill. When we got there the doctor was kind enough to allow us to be alone with our son.

When Ronnie got off the cot and stood up, we had to grab him to keep him from falling because he was just skin and bones. I'll never forget how his body shook and trembled—he weighed so little and was so terribly ill.

Those Army doctors had worked with him and all the other hundreds who had been taken down with hepatitis, but Ronnie apparently had a worse case than any of the others.

I don't think it is possible for anybody to feel the same about other people as he does his own family. He may get near to it and if we get enough anointing from God, maybe we can. But there's something about your own family that can tear you up.

We stood there, Evelyn and I, and it broke us up. I don't know . . . I felt personally affronted. There I was believing in the power of prayer and there was my own son, just skin and bones. I believe in medical science. Those fine Army doctors had done everything they knew to do and were kind enough to ask us to come in. I knew they didn't ask us to come in to pass the time of day. I knew by the fact they had asked us to come that they needed something that we represented.

We took our son in our arms and began to pray, but we felt we were not getting anywhere. Later Evelyn told me that I began to shake this disease out of Ronnie's body. What she meant was, I took hold of Ronnie with my two hands and I began to address the devil. I began to say, "In the name of Jesus, devil, take your hands off God's property. This boy belongs to God. When he was born we laid our hands on him and gave him to God and, devil, you shall not have him."

I suppose while I had hold of him I was shaking him. So my wife later said that I shook the devil loose. Anyway, I was doing that and my wife was backing me up. We prayed until we felt that this oppression of sickness had to go—the hold of it had been broken.

When we finished Evelyn looked at Ronald David and she spoke like she can speak sometimes. She said, "Ronald David, the doctors have told us that it will be a minimum of four months before you can get off your back, but I want to tell you that it doesn't have to be four months. Not only do we have medical science on your case but God himself is on your case. We have commanded the devil to take his hands off God's property, and we've done it not in our name but we've done it in the name of Jesus. Ronald David, it doesn't have to be four months."

Ronnie was so sick he could hardly reply. He just nodded and said, "Yes, Mother." And we left.

In four weeks' time that boy was as well as any human can be. Sixteen weeks had been shortened to four weeks and twelve weeks of suffering had been blotted out. Ronnie had received a miracle of healing because Evelyn and I, along with what the doctors had done, had planted the seed to claim him as God's property—and so can you, for yourself and your loved ones.

When you say, "I AM GOD'S PROPERTY," you are really saying something. You are saying, "THE DEVIL HAS NO PART OF ME!" This goes for your loved ones too.

YOUR GOD-GIVEN KEY FOR TODAY

Seal off the devil and his demons by affirming:

"I Can Claim My Dearest Loved One To Be God's Property—Now!"

Write the name of that loved one with a need here and be vicious with the devil. Through God, he is a defeated foe!

THURSDAY

Key:
WHEN I PRAY FOR ANOTHER PERSON I HAVE AN OPPORTUNITY FOR GOD TO HEAL ME

or
The Miraculous Method Of Bringing Health To Yourself Through A New Idea

A few years ago one of our faculty members at Oral Roberts' University, Mrs. Marie Fischer, discovered that she had cancer in the advanced stage. She underwent surgery and miraculously recovered. That is, she recovered physically. In her spirit she was haunted by some research material she had read—that only one out of three people who had cancer as advanced as she did, lives. The fear of recurring cancer preyed on her mind with the appearance of every little physical symptom.

The following summer she became ill again. Her blood pressure soared far beyond a safe level; she was dizzy and continually nauseated. Her doctor was able to bring her blood pressure under control but could not seem to find the cause of the nausea or dizziness. It was only a few weeks before the fall term was to begin. Later she shared with me how God came to her in her hour of need. She said:

"Fear tormented me day and night. I was so sick and seemingly nothing could be done. So I thought, *I'll try praying for my healing* . . .

"I began . . .'Lord, I love You. You know that I've given my life to You, that it's my heart's desire to serve You, for I have served You these many years. I take care of my health. I eat the foods that are healthful for me. I do everything I am supposed to do . . .'

"On and on I went. Finally I stopped and the Lord spoke to my heart, 'If you'd be quiet long enough we could have a conversation.'

"I thought, that makes sense. After all, I do counsel the students to LISTEN in order to understand what the other person is feeling or attempting to say.

"So I listened. And the Lord seemed to say, 'Sure, Marie, you've given your life to Me. You've been saved a long time. But you haven't learned as much as I'd hoped you would.'

"'What should I do?'"

"And the Lord said, 'What is it that you want?'

"'I want healing.'

"He said, 'How about planting a seed of healing for someone else who is in need of healing?'

"OF COURSE, I thought! It was just as though a light came on. The truths of Seed-Faith living had worked in other areas of my life. Why not use these Seed-Faith principles to bring about my healing?

"Immediately I set about obtaining the names of people who had a need for healing: a man who was going to have brain surgery—another one who was to have heart surgery—a child who was seriously ill. I made the list complete with the person's name and his need. I got out of bed and I began to walk back and forth across the floor with the list in my hand.

"I asked myself, how would you feel if you were facing brain surgery? Get in there! *Feel* compassion. Put yourself in his shoes. Be with that person.

"And I did. I went down my list calling the name of every person and praying with real heartfelt compassion. And when I knew I had reached this point I said, 'Now, Lord, be with this person. Let him live and move and have his being in You . . . as You did for me.'

"For three days I prayed like this. It wasn't easy. The first two days I was weak and dizzy and nauseated. More than once I had to rush to the bathroom, nauseated. I had to hold on to the furniture to keep my balance. But I ignored myself. And the more I concentrated on these people and their needs, the less I thought of myself. Eventually I became relaxed in my praying. I really enjoyed this time of intercession. And by the end of three days of praying for others I found that I was perfectly healed.

"Now it was a week before school started at ORU. But I was refreshed, rejuvenated, and ready. I cleaned house and did all kinds of things that I hadn't had the energy to do for the past year. And I've felt just great ever since.

"School opened. And work! We worked like Trojans—but it was a joy.

"And my healing is still good today. Seed-Faith living is the abundant way of our Lord Jesus Christ to get needs met in my life . . . and I found that the three miracle keys of Seed-Faith work for healing in my body . . . and I thank God for it."

Marie Fischer and I have talked many times about her healing. I want to say that receiving a miracle of healing is a struggle. It's not something that happens just like snapping your fingers. You have to lay a foundation for it. There's preparation of your inner man. There's an opening up of your heart. You have to start by doing something first.

The Bible says:

> *Confess your faults one to another, and pray one for another, that ye may be healed* (James 5:16).

I was praying one day when I had a tremendous urge to write a letter to a man who had wronged me. The Holy Spirit was urging me to write and tell him how sorry I was and ask him to forgive me. My human reaction was:

> *Why should I ask HIM to forgive me? I didn't do him wrong. HE did me wrong.*

But the Spirit had searched deep within my inner self and found a resentment in me because this man had done me wrong. I had carried that resentment for about two years but I was not really aware of it. All I knew was that every time I thought about that man I got a sick feeling in the pit of my stomach.

The Holy Spirit revealed to me that was resentment. I saw my resentment was wrong, that the fact he had wronged me did not justify my resenting him. **I saw that I had to love him as though he had never wronged me.** Well, I've never found that easy to do. But I wrote him a letter and told him that I felt bad toward him and I wanted him to forgive me. When I mailed the letter I felt great.

It never occurred to me he would even answer me. But lo and behold! he wrote me a beautiful letter and said, *I am the one who needs to apologize* . . . Today we are great friends. But even if he had not replied, I still would have felt good. I had done what the Bible says and it caused me to feel released. There was a healing of my own spirit.

We all have faults, shortcomings, failures. There are places where none of us measure up like we ought. There are days when we can sing and rejoice and feel close to God. There are other days when we feel that God is a million miles away. It's hard on those days and maybe we will say things we shouldn't say and do things we ought not to do. And our Lord says, "Accept the fact that you have faults. Accept the fact that your brothers and your sisters have faults. But just go ahead and love one another. Accept one another—warts and all!"

Pray one for another, that ye may be healed (James 5:16).

The emphasis here is upon the ONE doing the praying. Often when I pray for someone I suggest a two-way prayer—I ask him to pray for me FIRST before I begin my prayer for him. This is to help the sick person plant the seed of concern for someone else, FIRST. The Master is saying:

"You pray for someone else to be healed so that YOU also may be healed." He is saying:

"Put the seed in first so I can have something from your heart to work with."

God is trying to get you and me opened up inside. Deep down, each of us is inhibited. We are tense. We don't often let the real person come out. We are taught from infancy not to reveal our inner heart because people might misunderstand or betray us. They might think less of us if we are totally frank. And it's true. People are not like God. They don't know how to be merciful or how to appreciate one another properly.

But when we need healing in any area of our lives, we are dealing directly with the Healer—God. And He's saying to us, "OPEN UP! OPEN UP! Pray one for another that ye may be healed." It is another way of saying, GIVE, AND IT SHALL BE GIVEN UNTO YOU (Luke 6:38)—another way of seeding for a miracle.

When you are so sick that you don't care whether you live or die—you're just too sick to pray for yourself (at least that's the way I feel), try this—try . . .

LISTENING TO GOD . . . LISTEN!

And from that time of introspection, or listening inside yourself, God just may say: *You may think you are hopeless but there's always someone worse off than you—PRAY FOR THAT PERSON!* And you know, it really works! You can always pray more *objectively* than you can *subjectively* because you know all the problems about yourself, and you have problems having faith. On the other hand, you don't know all the negative things about the person who is worse off than you, so you can really believe for that person's healing.

YOUR GOD-GIVEN KEY FOR TODAY

Make a note of *James 5:16* and keep saying to yourself:

"When I Pray For Another Person, I Have The Opportunity For God To Heal Me."

It will work because God keeps His Word.

FRIDAY

**Key:
NOTHING LESS THAN A MIRACLE
WILL DO FOR ME**

or

The Simplest But Greatest Miracle Of Healing I Ever Saw

Willie Phelps was healed in our Roanoke, Virginia Crusade in 1951. Recently we again contacted the Phelps family to inquire about Willie. We found that he works for a paint company in his city and is still — after 24 years — a living, breathing, walking testimony to a miracle. While we waited for Willie to come in from work, his mother told us what she recalls happening the night of Willie's miracle.

"I HAD A DEEP KNOWING INSIDE"

"As we stood in the semidarkness the snow began to fall. A chill swept through my body but the presence of God warmed my spirit. From all outward signs it looked hopeless, but I had a knowing deep down inside me that this was Willie's hour — God was going to heal him.

"We had already made two trips to Roanoke, only to be turned away with the hundreds of other latecomers. This was our third try, over a hundred miles round trip — that was a long way, back in those days. When we arrived it was the same as before. The crowds were so thick that you could scarcely find the entrance. But it wouldn't have done any good. No one could get in. The auditorium was packed to overflowing. Tonight was Saturday night — the last night of the crusade — and I was feeling desperate.

"I looked over at Willie — I can see him like it was yesterday. He was standing there in the snow leaning on those little crutches and one shoe built up 2 1/2 inches, his chubby little face full of expectancy, never doubting for one minute that this time we would get inside.

"I would have given up when they barred the doors, but when you're desperate you can't lose hope.

"As we stood shivering in the snow I silently prayed . . . and we walked. Pretty soon I heard someone say, 'They will be taking some ambulance cases into the invalid room pretty soon.' I didn't know what this meant but I thought this might be a chance for Willie to get in. So we pushed our way out of the crowd and around to the side, only to find another crowd. We waited there and prayed. Willie was the only one left in the crowd on crutches. Suddenly an usher stood in the door and said, 'The little boy on crutches — make way for him . . .' His daddy helped him through the crowd and they both went in. I was left outside. But I didn't care. Willie and his daddy were inside and I knew God could take care of the rest. Outside I praised the Lord in my heart, prayed . . . and waited. Pretty soon, the usher appeared at the door again and said:

"'The mother of the little crippled boy—let her in . . .' There was just room enough for the three of us to stand in the corner. As we listened to Brother Roberts' sermon over the loudspeaker my eyes swept across a roomful of suffering humanity—many seemingly more desperate than Willie. Yet, in spite of the stench of sickness and death, you could feel the atmosphere electric with hope.

"Then I looked at Willie leaning heavily on his crutches. His eyes sparkled and my mind went back four years before to the day he was injured. He had been as healthy and rowdy as any 6-year-old boy. But one day while playing and running through the house he accidentally fell on the andirons by the fireplace. I remember we didn't think much about it at the time. But in a few days he began to limp and complain about the pain in his hip. We took him to the doctor. He didn't find anything more than a bruise at the time and told us to bathe Willie three times a day, for an hour each time, in hot salt water.

WILLIE'S LEG HAD SHRUNK 2 1/2 INCHES

"When this failed to bring relief we took Willie to the hospital. His leg had shrunk 2 1/2 inches and he could not walk. The doctor at the hospital diagnosed his problem as Perthes' disease and said there was nothing that could be done for it . . . although they tried different means to relieve the pain.

"Willie was in the hospital for three weeks with a ten-pound weight attached to his leg. When this failed they placed him in a heavy cast up to his shoulders. This seemed to relieve the pain but when the cast was removed, one leg was still 2 1/2 inches shorter than the other and Willie could not walk.

"The specialists devised a built-up shoe for him and fitted him with crutches. The first time I saw him trying to hobble around on that ugly shoe and those heavy crutches I thought my heart would break into a million pieces. The doctors tried to comfort me by saying, 'Mrs. Phelps, Willie is lucky to be able to walk, even with crutches . . . nine out of ten children with this disease *never* walk again . . .'

"So we had tried everything we knew and the doctors had done everything they knew, but Willie was a cripple.

NOW, NOTHING LESS THAN A MIRACLE WOULD DO

"My thoughts were interrupted when suddenly the door opened and Brother Roberts came into the invalid room. But it seemed ages before he finally got to us. By this time everyone in the room had been prayed for. Many had been instantly healed and some were still laughing and crying and praising God. For a moment it looked like Brother Roberts had missed Willie—he passed him by. My heart sank. I couldn't

believe we had come this close, only to be overlooked. My heart broke.
Tears soaked my face. I was lost in my own grief when suddenly I heard
a voice weary with exhaustion, but full of compassion, say:

"'SON, WHAT ARE YOU DOING HERE?'

" 'I'm waiting for Oral Roberts.'

" 'What do you want with him?'

" 'I'm supposed to be healed tonight.'

" 'Son, I'm Oral Roberts.'

" 'You are?'

" 'Yes.'

" 'Well, I'm supposed to be healed tonight.'

"Then Brother Roberts looked down at Willie with a sort of tired
smile and said, 'Do you believe that Jesus can heal you?'

"Willie said, 'Uh, huh.'

"Then Brother Roberts touched Willie's head and said simply, 'BE
HEALED IN THE NAME OF JESUS.'

"And he left the room, never turning back. BUT IN THAT IN-
STANT OUR MIRACLE HAPPENED. (Brother Roberts didn't know
until 18 months later when he returned to Roanoke.)

"God's miracle power was working in that place that night. Willie
was full of childlike faith. And when Brother Roberts prayed that
simple prayer the divine healing power of God went through Willie's
body. He was seemingly stunned for a moment. Then he yelled, 'Mom!
I'M HEALED.' Quick as a wink he took off his shoe, threw his crutches
aside, and said, 'I'M GOING TO WALK!' But he didn't walk . . . HE
RAN! . . . and without the slightest limp. In an instant both legs became
the same length. Willie had his miracle. And talk about a time! We had
it — laughing and crying and hugging everybody and praising the Lord.

"God didn't move the mountains but He did something better —
He gave Willie a miracle so he could climb over them."

THE MOST IMPORTANT THING IN YOUR LIFE IS A MIRACLE . . .
ESPECIALLY WHEN YOU NEED ONE.

When you can learn to have faith like a little child, you can be emptied
of all doubt. I've always said that children can believe for miracles so
much easier than we can because they are so fresh out of heaven. So
when you need that special miracle, try to become as a little child in
your faith. Then hang on to this:

YOUR GOD-GIVEN KEY FOR TODAY
"Nothing Less Than A Miracle Will Do For Me!"

SATURDAY Key:
GOD IS HEALING ME

or
How I Learned From My Illnesses, Sickness Is An Inside Job

God has taught me that everyone is sick in some way, and that sickness is anything that throws any part of a person out of harmony with the rest of himself. Above all, God has taught me:

SICKNESS IS AN INSIDE JOB

The first thought that went through my mind when I was sick was that my tongue wouldn't speak normally and my lungs did not function normally. I didn't know I was sick.

Oh, they said, "Oral Roberts is sick." However, I thought it was my tongue and my lungs. The idea of the whole man being affected by sickness was many years away from my understanding and experience.

Jewel had said, "Oral, God is going to heal *you*." Somehow it ended up with my believing God would heal my *physical disorders* . . . that those physical disorders constituted my sickness. I was looking *outside*. But it was an *inside* job. Soon I came face-to-face with the fact that I had to look inside myself and find some meaning for my life. I had to get straight with God, to cooperate with Him in what He had planned my destiny to be. Then I could see the possibility of a cure for my physical disabilities.

The ill feeling I had toward the world—even the animosity I still held toward parents who loved me and held only the highest wishes for me, had to be faced. Above all, I had to believe my sister Jewel. I had to allow my brother Elmer to dress and pick me up and carry me to the car and drive me to a healing meeting. I had to put some meaning into God's words I had heard inside myself as we drove along. Finally, I had to believe the man who prayed for me was someone I was sent to and who was prepared by God to help me.

I had doubted. Doubted if God was real, who He was, or where He was. Really *ignored* is a better word, for I simply ignored Him. Now I faced Him in my sister, my brother, my parents, and the minister who prayed for me.

The fact was that as badly as my tongue was unable to express my thoughts, as frightfully as my diseased lungs hurt and angered me, they were only parts of the whole of me that was sick.

When I stuttered I was affected by it in a horribly negative way. I was severely restricted especially in nerves and throat. It threw my mind into panic. It destroyed my mechanism for believing I *could* talk.

At the same time my hurting, bleeding lungs knocked me off my feet, first in a championship high-school basketball game as I was making a driving layup, and second, in the bed from which I could not rise under my own strength for five long months. It destroyed my peace of mind, it blasted my hopes, it took me out of school, it ruined the taste of food, it made me curse and almost blaspheme.

I was unkind and rude to my doting parents, cross with people who visited me, resentful of preachers who came to say a kind word of prayer. I despised myself because I couldn't do anything about it. I nearly lost respect for doctors in their inability to bring healing through medicine. Religion was totally meaningless and irrelevant.

I was sick, not merely my tongue and lungs.

I needed healing, salvation — wholeness.

My body was me, I knew that much. But religion as I knew it separated it from my real self. The doctors treated my body, the preachers and Christians prayed for my soul. Lying there I was further split in two!

I had lost my health. Without it I was nothing.

It was precisely at this point of my need, my need of healing, that Jesus Christ came to me.

To my body, yes, but really to *me*. Jewel's seven words were, "Oral, God is going to heal you," not, "Oral, God is going to heal your tongue and your lungs." This put God squarely at the point of the greatest need I ever had — the need of Someone who cared, Someone who could do something that neither I nor any other could do.

It rings in my heart today . . .

GOD IS AT THE POINT OF MY NEED

And it's a song for you too. God is at the point of *your* need. There's where you look for Him. He's in the now . . . your now. He's always been in the now . . . your now.

God had been absent from my life . . . *I thought*. I had yearned for God but didn't know it. I had been hurt and hurt and hurt in the world, much of it my own doing but at last I took heart. It finally dawned on me that my illnesses were tied to my inside self, my entire being, and the way was to bring myself to God in repentance and ask for forgiveness and His saving grace.

When Christ came into the world He talked about men being made whole.

He talked about the spirit being renewed . . .

the body being healed . . .

the mind being transformed.

He talked about men being born again. He talked about people being made whole in spirit, soul, and body. He touched every phase of the individual's life and left nothing untouched, so that when He finished working with someone, that person could say, "I am a whole man," or "I am a whole woman." This is the glory of Jesus, that He lifted man into a new dimension of living that gave him purpose for his existence.

When Christ dealt with people He usually came to them with a question, "Will *you* be made whole?" He thought of them as a person to be made in a new way. He thought of them as people who should be changed. He always thought in terms of change. He never accepted the status quo. Everything He touched, He changed. Even plain water, He made into wine.

A blind eye, He made to see.
A crippled foot, He made straight.
Souls that were filled with sin,
He made clean.
JESUS CHANGED PEOPLE!

———◆———

JESUS CHRIST CAME TO MAKE ME WHOLE,
TO HEAL ME FROM MY HEAD TO MY FEET,
INSIDE AND OUTSIDE,
TO MAKE ME A NEW CREATURE.
HE CAME TO GIVE ME . . .
HEALING FOR THE WHOLE MAN

YOUR GOD-GIVEN KEY FOR TODAY

Now say:

"God Is Healing Me!"

SEVENTH WEEK

SUNDAY	MIRACLES BELONG IN MY DAY TODAY
MONDAY	I WILL NOT TAKE NO FOR AN ANSWER
TUESDAY	GOD'S WORK MEANS A MIRACLE TO ME
WEDNESDAY	I CAN CLAIM MY DEAREST LOVED ONE TO BE GOD'S PROPERTY—NOW!
THURSDAY	WHEN I PRAY FOR ANOTHER PERSON I HAVE AN OPPORTUNITY FOR GOD TO HEAL ME
FRIDAY	NOTHING LESS THAN A MIRACLE WILL DO FOR ME
SATURDAY	GOD IS HEALING ME

EIGHTH WEEK
The Infallible Way I Discovered Of Helping You To Release Your Faith To God

SUNDAY
Key: WHEN I ACT, MY FAITH BEGINS TO WORK

or

How I Discovered The Point Of Contact Which Was Used In Jesus' Ministry On Earth And Exactly How You Can Use It Today To Release Your Faith To God For Miracles In Your Life

I'M extremely happy to share with you something that you can use seven days a week for the rest of your mortal life . . .

THE POINT OF CONTACT

Now listen, all power has a point at which you make contact. In your automobile you turn on the key, or step on the starter, and the motor turns over. Or if you flip a light switch there is an instant contact with the powerhouse that causes the power to come singing through the wires to give you light. The point of contact is made with the power that causes the motor to come on.

There has to be a point of contact. The light switch, the accelerator in your car—any source of power you can name—must have a point by which you make contact with it. The important thing is not the point of contact. The important thing is that you release the power. The power is the thing that you want released. So we put the point of contact in its proper context of usefulness. It is not an end in itself but it's a very useful *instrument*.

SPEAKING THE WORD IS A POINT OF CONTACT

One of the best points of contact that I have used and still use is the one we read about in Matthew 8. A man, who was not a Jew, not what we call a religious man, a captain in the Roman army, had a very definite need of healing for his servant. Eventually he went beyond the emperor's physician, the army doctors, and came directly to Christ himself. (I mentioned this centurion very briefly in Seventh Week, Monday.)

Now it was a very, very great step of faith that the centurion took. The Romans were ruling over Palestine. They were the overlords and Jesus was a Jew. The Romans and the Jews did not fraternize or have anything to do with each other. As a matter of fact, the Romans laid heavy burdens upon the Jewish people. So it was a very unpopular thing among the Romans for one of their number to fraternize with a Jew, particularly from a religious standpoint. Caesar was believed to be a god by the Romans and they called him "Lord Caesar."

MIGHT BOWING TO MEEKNESS

But suddenly something takes place in the captain's life, where he called Jesus Christ "Lord." Now that was a dangerous thing to do. Because he's switching his allegiance from not only the commander in chief of the Roman armies under whom he had his appointment as a captain, but also from calling him lord, from bowing down to him as a divinity—to a lowly Nazarene, Jesus of Nazareth.

The captain did it because, first, he had this need that could not be met by any power that he knew about.

Second, the captain had come to see in Jesus the embodiment of life itself. So he came to Christ.

Then he bowed. He'd never bowed to any man before, except Caesar. And as he bows there in the open street, bowing before Jesus Christ, it's a really dramatic scene.

It is force bowing to meekness . . .

armed might before the unarmed . . .

the proud uniform of war before the seamless robe.

He's bowing before Jesus, calling Him Lord, and telling Him about his servant lying at home sick of the palsy and being deeply tormented by the disease.

Christ responded immediately and said, "I'll come and heal him."

Then the man said, "No, no, it's not necessary for You to come to my house where my servant lieth ill. It isn't necessary at all because, Lord, I'm a man under authority also. I know what authority is. You don't have to come. You just speak the word. I speak the word and men obey my voice. Caesar is in Rome and he speaks a word of authority and I obey it over here in Palestine. I, in turn, speak a word to a soldier and he does what I tell him. So You don't have to come over here. You just speak the word and my servant shall be healed."

And Jesus said, "I've not found faith like this even in the nation of Israel where it's supposed to be."

Jesus indicated that . . .

FAITH IS WHERE YOU FIND IT

Sometimes you find faith where you don't expect to find it. Also when you look for it in places where you expect to find it, faith isn't always there.

Then Jesus said to the man, "You go your way and as you have believed, it shall be done unto you."

Here's the commanding power of faith when it is released. The point of contact was to SPEAK THE WORD.

Why?

Because this is a man who recognized authority and power. Up till this hour he had thought Caesar represented the very zenith of authority and power. Now he recognizes that Jesus Christ has authority and power above that of Caesar or anybody else. So he says that God has the greatest authority and power. Therefore, for him his point of contact was a spoken word from the Lord . . . just A WORD FROM JESUS. He did not require Him to touch his servant, or to go over there in person. He just said, "Speak the word, Lord, let me hear You say it and I will believe."

That's why Christ said, "As you have *believed*, it shall be done." Remember Jesus did not say, "As I've *spoken the word*." He said, "As you have BELIEVED."

What happened when Jesus spoke the word?

It became the point of contact that the captain's faith had with God.

The Source of power for the healing of his servant was God, but the captain had to have a point of contact with that Source of power. He was unable to release his faith unless he had some point of contact.

THE POINT OF CONTACT HELPS YOU REALIZE
GOD AS THE SOURCE OF ALL POWER

What does the point of contact do? The first thing it does is to recognize God. It recognizes Him as the Source of all power. The second thing is . . .

THE POINT OF CONTACT SETS THE TIME FOR
THE RELEASING OF YOUR FAITH

The point of contact sets the time. Now how? If I were to say to you, "I'd like to meet you."

And you say, "Fine, Oral Roberts, when?"

And I said, "Oh, anytime."

And you said, "Where?"

And I said, "Oh, anywhere," you and I would never meet.

But if I said, "I will meet you."

And you said, "Where?"

And I said, "In front of the United States Post Office in downtown Tulsa."

And you said, "When?"

And I said, "Tomorrow at 3 p.m.," we would be setting the time and place so that all of our interaction would be used toward getting to that point at the appointed hour.

You see what I mean? It's very important to set the time for anything you do. So the point of contact sets the time for the *releasing* of your faith. But it is very important to remember . . .

THE POINT OF CONTACT DOESN'T NECESSARILY SET THE TIME FOR THE HEALING OR FOR THE MIRACLE TO HAPPEN . . . IT DOES SET THE TIME FOR THE RELEASING OF YOUR FAITH

Now you can do several things with your faith. One of them is to just keep your faith inside you.

One man said to me, "I have all the faith in the world."

"Well," I said, "that's your trouble."

He didn't understand. He said, "What do you mean?"

I said, "The trouble is you still *have* it."

He said, "What are you trying to say?"

"I'm trying to say to you that it isn't enough to have faith, you have to *release* it."

For example, a person can have all the money in the world and still starve to death. We read in the paper every now and then where a recluse starves to death and $50,000 or some other large sum of money is found stuffed in a mattress in the room. In the same way, what's the use of having faith unless you release it?

Someone says, "Well, how do I know I have faith?" Because the Bible says you do:

> God hath dealt to every man the measure of faith (Romans 12:3).

GOD HAS A CERTAIN MEASURE OF FAITH AND A PART OF IT IS GIVEN TO EVERY MAN. You have it but you might not use your faith. What Christ is seeking is for you to *release* your faith.

FAITH HAS TO BECOME AN ACT

What must faith become?

An ACT.

For example, in order for you to have faith in a chair you have to *act* on your faith and sit down in the chair. For your faith to be useful it has to become an act. You have to act on it. That is to say, you must release it.

The Roman army captain had faith in Jesus' authority and power so much so that he placed Christ's authority and power above Caesar's,

ut even that was not enough. He had to act on that. And for him to
ct on it, he used the point of contact of having Christ say the word.
The moment Christ said the word the man simply turned and went
ome. When he arrived he found the servant was healed. The point of
ontact did not heal the servant but the point of contact helped the
aptain release his faith. He set the time to release his faith. What
vas the time he set? The moment Jesus spoke the word, his point of
ontact released the power of God and his servant was healed.

> THE POINT OF CONTACT WORKS BEST FOR PEOPLE
> WHO BELIEVE IN THE AUTHORITY OF CHRIST, THAT
> HE'S NOT ONLY THEIR SAVIOR BUT HE'S THEIR LORD.
> HE'S THE LORD OF THEIR LIFE AND HE'S THE MAS-
> TER OVER EVERY SITUATION THAT THEY'LL EVER
> FACE.

This is a practical level of living daily under the mastership, the
ordship, of Christ where you see that everything of a negative nature
nust yield to Christ. You never say, "God can't do that." You never say,
That's impossible." You cut the word *impossible* out of your dictionary.
You come into a relationship with Christ till you believe that Christ is
Il in all and that Christ can do anything!

THE LAYING ON OF HANDS AS A POINT OF CONTACT

The second point of contact—the laying on of hands—was used
y Jairus, a ruler of the synagogue of the Jews. He may not have been
rabbi but he was a *leader* in the synagogue. He had a very responsible
osition. His little daughter became so ill that she was at the point
f death.

Now it was difficult for such a man to come to Christ just as much
s it was for the Roman army captain. The Jewish leaders never did
ully accept Jesus Christ as the Son of God. Some of them believed He
as a prophet or a teacher, but they did not accept Him as the Messiah.

The Jews believed in the personhood of God. That is to say, they
elieved that some day the Messiah would come, and they are still
oking for Him.

So here is a man who is making God a person. Jesus Christ repre-
ented to Jairus the personhood of God. His point of contact, therefore,
ad to do with Jesus' hands.

> THE LAYING ON OF HANDS IS BEST USED BY AN INDI-
> VIDUAL WHO IS MORE INFLUENCED BY A PERSON, WHO
> WANTS TO FEEL THE WARMTH OF ANOTHER PERSON,
> WHO WANTS THE INTIMACY OF HUMAN CONTACT.

Jairus said, "Come and lay thy hands on her, that she may be
ealed; and she shall live" (Mark 5:23).

Jesus responded. When Jesus arrived the little girl had apparently died, but because the point of contact was made prior to her death and the man held on to his point of contact—never giving it up—Jesus did lay His hands on the little girl and she revived.

This point of contact—the laying on of hands—set the time for Jairus to release his faith. While he and Jesus were on the way to the little girl's bedside, some people met them and said to Jairus, "She's already dead, why trouble the Master any further?"

And Jesus immediately said, "Fear not, only believe and she shall be healed."

That is, "Keep your point of contact! Don't turn loose of it. You want the laying on of hands and that's your point of contact. Hold on to it."

SPEAKING THE WORD WAS THE POINT OF CONTACT USED BY THE APOSTLES

Paul was preaching one day and there was a crippled man in the crowd and he looked out and saw him. Paul saw the faith that he had and cried, "Stand upright on thy feet" (Acts 14:10). That's all Paul said: "Stand on thy feet." That's the spoken word. He spoke the word and the crippled man responded to that type of point of contact. He leaped and walked.

Well, the same man—Paul—used the laying on of his hands while on the island of Melita and great healing came to masses of people there (Acts 28).

So various points of contact were used in the New Testament. The particular one used was usually in context with the background of the person who needed the healing power of Christ. In other words . .

> God loves you so much that in a sense He
> accommodates himself to the way you respond.

And the thing that will help you establish your point of contact is usually honored by God.

THE HOLY COMMUNION AS A POINT OF CONTACT

The third point of contact that I wish to discuss briefly with you is the Holy Communion discussed in 1 Corinthians 11. Our friends in the Episcopal and Catholic faiths call it the Mass or the Eucharist. The word "eucharist" is really a derivative of charisma, one of the gifts or graces of God. It really means great thanksgiving. It's a vertical thing from your heart, going up to God.

The Protestants call it Holy Communion, communion of the saints communing with one another. The Holy Communion is both a eucharist and a communion. It is both a vertical praise to God for His sacrifice upon the cross and it is a horizontal communion with one another. It is a faith in Christ and a love toward the brethren. So in a sense, both terms are beautiful and highly useful.

The Holy Communion has through faith not only great power to deal with your soul but also with your body. It is indicated in 1 Corinthians 11 that some of the Corinthians who were taking the cup and the bread were taking it unworthily. That is, they were not grasping the meaning of our Lord's Body. They were just eating and drinking without faith and they were missing what it was all about . . .

The sicknesses they had were not being healed.

Some of them were dying before their time. They were not taking advantage, through faith, of the bread and the cup.

First, they were not grasping the meaning of the Body of Christ in that they were not looking up to Him in great thanksgiving.

Second, they were not grasping the meaning of His Body in their relationships with one another.

In other words, there was bickering. There was division. There was quarreling and fussing and fighting among the brethren in Corinth.

When they took the Communion the faith they had in their heart was not being released. Because it was not released this great healing of our Lord was not rushing into them. It was like they were being cut off, like they were dying of thirst. And Paul was saying to them, "When you eat of the bread and drink of the cup, *do it in faith, do it in love, and do it in expectation.*"

The greatest miracle I've ever seen with the Holy Communion being used as a point of contact happened at ORU in one of our lay seminars. A woman was in a wheelchair. She had received the healing prayer through laying on of hands and various things, and nothing had happened. She had used the best of medical science and nothing had happened. There she was. I was teaching on the Holy Communion in that particular seminar, urging the people to go beyond and use it as a point of contact. I said, "Release your faith . . . do it the moment you take the cup to your lips or the bread to your lips. Release your faith. Let the Holy Communion be a point of contact."

When this lady took the bread and the cup, immediately her faith was released. She hadn't walked a step in three years but suddenly she got out of that wheelchair and came walking down the aisle toward me. I took her hand and said, "Ma'am, what happened?"

She said, "When I took the cup and I took the bread, I let all my faith go to God. And I felt the warmth of His love. I felt I could walk and here I am."

At the Oral Roberts University we serve the Holy Communion every noon and several nights during the week. Hundreds of our students and faculty partake of the Holy Communion every day. I love to take it. I love to take it often for many reasons, not the least of which is because it is my point of contact to let my faith go to God and my love go to my brethren to meet our needs. And I know that when we recognize how to discern the elements of Communion, great miracles of healing will come to us.

When you make anything you do toward God your point of contact, you are planting a seed of faith. And you can *always* depend on God to multiply the seed back to you in the form of the miracle you need.

THE POINT OF CONTACT is so important that I want to summarize it for you with *FIVE* specific points. And I promise you that if you will follow these step-by-step, you will see the difference in your PRAYER POWER! Now let's get to the issue and stamp it in your heart.

1. A POINT OF CONTACT IS SOMETHING YOU DO, AND WHEN YOU DO IT YOU RELEASE YOUR FAITH. Now faith is inside you. "God hath dealt to every man the measure of faith" (Romans 12:3). Faith is something you have . . . but until you release it, it is as though you have none. Faith has to come out of you. It has to become an act . . . a single act of believing.

2. EVERY POWER MUST HAVE A POINT OF CONTACT TO RELEASE IT. With electricity, for example, you flip the light switch to release the power to the bulb which in turn lights the room. In the same way your point of contact releases your faith to God which releases His power back into your life.

3. A POINT OF CONTACT HELPS YOU TO RECOGNIZE YOUR SOURCE—GOD.

4. A POINT OF CONTACT SETS THE TIME FOR THE RELEASING OF YOUR FAITH. It does not set the time for your healing—it sets the time for the *releasing* of your faith for miracles to meet your needs.

5. THE POINT OF CONTACT MAY BE MANY THINGS. It may be..
   A. The spoken word
   B. The laying on of hands
   C. The Holy Communion
   D. My letter to you or your letter to me
   E. The prayer time during our telecasts when I stretch forth my hands to pray for you
   F. Anything that helps you to turn loose of all doubt and release your faith to God

YOUR GOD-GIVEN KEY FOR TODAY

Now say:

"When I Act, My Faith Begins To Work."

MONDAY

Key:
JESUS IS UNLIMITED . . . HE'S WITH ME NOW

or

Why I Say: There Is No Distance In Prayer

The first understanding I had of this great truth was in the '50s. I received a letter from a woman in Baltimore, Maryland. At the time, I was conducting a crusade in Oakland, California, so the letter went from the East Coast to the West Coast. It read like this:

Dear Brother Roberts:

I am very ill. I wanted to come to your Oakland Crusade and have you lay your hands upon me and pray for me, but I do not have the money to travel. So I am writing you this letter instead and asking you to pray for me. I realize there is no distance in prayer . . .

A shock of comprehension swept through my being. It was an electrifying current of understanding. There I was some 2,000 or more miles from this woman and she believed in me and she believed in my prayers. But suddenly she transcended me. She went above and beyond me. She was no longer limited by me. She caught hold of a tremendous truth . . . THERE IS NO DISTANCE IN PRAYER. She went on to say:

You pray there and I'll pray here, and God will heal me . . .

Well, I prayed for her and wrote her back. In a short time I received another letter back from her, praising God for her healing.

This glorious truth came home to me again in a crusade in South Carolina. This was one of the largest crusades we had ever had. It imposed burdens upon me and upon the people because so many wanted to come through the prayer line at the same time and have me lay my hands upon them and pray. The larger the crowd grew, the more impossible it became for one man to do this. The crowds grew to 30,000 people in one day.

One night a young girl, 12 or 13 years old, was in the audience. She had been born with crooked legs. I mean, they were so bowed she wore her dresses nearly to her ankles because she was embarrassed for people to see the shape of her legs. Many times the children at school would laugh at her. Her mother and father had been born with misshapen limbs and evidently this condition was passed on to her. That night she was sitting in the back. I didn't know she was there. I didn't know she existed.

In that service I shared the letter from the woman in Baltimore who said, "There is no distance in prayer." From time to time I would ask the entire audience to stand and touch each other or hold the back of their chair as a *point of contact*. Then I'd pray that the Lord would heal. I would try to see Jesus' hands touching them where they were.

As the audience was getting ready to do as I said, this little girl was understanding something. She was saying in herself, "I wish I could go up into the prayer line. I wish I could go there and have Brother Roberts pray for me. I believe I would be healed, but if I go for prayer people will see my legs." (I learned this later from her and her parents.)

Then she heard me say, "Why don't you just stand where you are and let me pray for you, for there is no distance in prayer." As the crowd stood up, she stood up. And as she stood up she said a warmth came into her legs and she felt something happening to them. She lifted her dress to her knees and she saw that her legs were perfectly straight. She grabbed her father and mother and said, "Look at my legs." The father found their pastor and told him. He immediately rushed to the platform and said, "Brother Roberts, let me bring a little girl from my church to the platform. A miracle has happened."

He brought her up and she stood there, no longer ashamed, and lifted that long dress to her knees and showed us how straight her legs were. I stood there so moved I was crying like a baby. I had not touched her. I'd not even prayed for her as an individual. She was just there in that crowd doing business with the King of kings and Lord of lords. I patted her hand and talked to her. I tried to get her to explain it to me but all she could say was, "You said Jesus could do it anywhere and He did."

That's about the best answer anybody can give. You can try to explain a miracle all you want to, but God either did it or He didn't. You either have a miracle or you don't. The more you try to explain a miracle, the harder it is. When it happens it really is simple—it is the *work of the Father*.

———◆◆◆———

If I could put my arm around your shoulder and talk to you, this is what I would say to you:

> DON'T BE AFRAID OF THE WORD *PRAYER*—IT'S JUST TALKING TO GOD LIKE YOU WOULD TALK TO YOUR DEAREST FRIEND—THE ONLY DIFFERENCE IS WHEN YOU TALK TO GOD, *THINGS HAPPEN!* HE'S NOT A WHITE FLEECY BLOB AWAY OFF SOMEWHERE IN THE SKY—HE'S RIGHT INSIDE YOU. THIS IS WHY *THERE IS NO DISTANCE IN PRAYER!*

YOUR GOD-GIVEN KEY FOR TODAY

So when you pray, keep in the very top of your mind:

"Jesus Is Unlimited. He's With Me Now."

And, friend, He'll listen, and when you talk to Him, then miracles will happen.

TUESDAY Key: GOD IS TURNED ON TO ME

or

A Letter Became A Point Of Contact For This Woman And She Received A Miracle Of Healing

I often say when I write a letter to someone who has asked for prayer:

> *This letter is anointed. Lay it upon your body as a point of contact to release your faith to God for your healing.*

I especially remember one woman who did this. She had been prayed for many times and had received the laying on of hands but still she was not healed. Then one day she sat down and wrote me a letter. It was just a few lines telling me of her disappointment. She wanted me to read her letter, to offer a prayer for her, and to write her back telling her that I had done so. She said:

> *I've come to the place I am no longer looking to you or to any other person, just the Lord.*

(She had evidently learned Miracle Key No. 1 of Seed-Faith: Look to God, the Source of your total supply, because GOD is the Source of ALL healing.)

Of course I read her letter. I prayed, and I wrote her back. In my letter to her I said:

> *As I pray I feel God's power going through me; therefore, this letter is anointed. Lay it on your body as a point of contact, let your faith go to God, AND BE HEALED IN JESUS' NAME.*

In just a short time there came back a three-page letter full of praises to God. She told me how she had read my letter, and as she held the letter in her hand she said to the Lord:

> *Your Spirit is in Oral Roberts; I feel it in this letter. As I place this letter on my body I am expecting You to give me a miracle of healing.*

Then she said:

> *Something that felt like a warm liquid started flowing through my entire being. I felt strength, well-being, joy. I knew from that moment that God was healing me . . . and He did.*

I thought, Lord, what this woman did, others can do if they will just look to YOU, the Source of all healing power. I believe this with all my heart.

THE POINT OF CONTACT IS SOMETHING YOU DO

Oh, I want to stress that. It's something YOU do. It is simply like going over to the light switch. Now the light switch is connected to the powerhouse but you are not going to turn the powerhouse on. You are going to turn the switch on . . . and the switch is the point of contact. You flip on the light switch and things begin to happen. The current is released from the powerhouse and it begins to flow down the line and the lights come on. Well, now, God is the Source of all healing. But we're not going to turn God on.

GOD IS ALREADY TURNED ON TOWARD US.

We are turned on to lots of things in this world, but are we turned on to God? That's the big question. The Bible says:

> *I am the Lord that healeth thee* (Exodus 15:26).

Get turned on to God. Flip that switch of faith to bring God's healing power into your life. *DO* SOMETHING!

YOUR GOD-GIVEN KEY FOR TODAY

And when you make a move toward God, say:

"God Is Turned On To Me!"

WEDNESDAY

Key:
I AM FOCUSING MY FAITH ON JESUS

or

The Miracle My Associate Received When He Learned The Great Secret Of Focusing His Faith On God

Several years ago one of my associates, Collins Steele, had an accident and hurt his back. It got so bad that he couldn't stand the pain. No matter what shots the doctor gave him the pain was still there

Evelyn and I went over to his home one day. I sat down on the edge of his bed and I said, "Collins, where do you hurt?"

"Well," he said, "Rev (he has always called me Rev), right here in my back."

I took his hand to shake it and he said, "Oh, don't shake my hand too roughly—I can feel it here in my back."

I knew he was really hurting because he has never been one to complain. I said, "Collins, I'm going to pray for you."

He said, "Good."

I said, "Look at my hands a moment. My hands have no healing power but the hands of Jesus have healing power. When I touch you, don't think about my hands. But just try to picture Christ coming into this house, coming into your bedroom. Collins, if Jesus Christ walked into your bedroom, right where you are on the bed today, what do you think would happen?"

He said, "He'd heal me."

"Well," I said, "Jesus said, 'I am with you always, even unto the end of the world' (Matthew 28:20). So just focus your faith on Him; think now of our Lord coming in and putting His hands on you." I touched him and prayed and I could feel the Spirit of God. You know, when you're praying and making contact with God you can feel it. People say, "What do you feel?" I don't know how to explain it except you can feel it. I looked at him and said, "What's happening?"

Big tears rolled down his cheeks and he said, "Rev, I feel a warmth going into my back."

I said, "Do you think you can sit up on the side of the bed?"

He said, "I think so."

He sat up on the side of the bed and said, "Just give me your hand . . ."

I lifted him up, and when he stood to his feet his whole body rose free and strong. He was healed from his head to his feet by the power of faith in the living Christ.

You know, it seems so easy when you do it. It only seems hard when you don't do it. Once you get into the stream of faith and you're putting your mind upon Christ, you're seeing Him coming to you—it makes all the difference in the world.

Maybe the easiest way for you to think of this idea is to think of a camera. You know how you have to look through the view finder—and unless your lens is RIGHT ON TARGET the image is fuzzy. You then have to adjust the lens until the image comes into FOCUS.

All right now, picture in your mind God coming to you in His Son, Jesus. The image is *fuzzy* at first, but as you think on it, it'll become easier.

———————

Picture Christ coming to you at the point of your need.
FOCUS YOUR FAITH ON HIM!
A MIRACLE COMES THROUGH FAITH IN GOD . . .
A MIRACLE COMES WHEN WE ACT UPON OUR FAITH . . .
WHEN WE *DO* SOMETHING.

YOUR GOD-GIVEN KEY FOR TODAY

As you work at this, say to yourself, and say it out loud:

"I Am Focusing My Faith On Jesus."

THURSDAY
Key:
I WILL 'TOUCH AND AGREE'
FOR MY NEED TO BE MET

or
How I Learned You Can Touch And Agree For A Miracle
Even Though Separated By A Great Distance

Some time ago Richard and I were on the Mike Douglas Show. As we came to the end of the interview, Mike said, "I have one more question, Oral. I can understand your praying for people face-to-face and their responding and receiving help. What I cannot understand is how you do it on television. That camera there, I . . ."

I said, "Wait a minute, Mike. To me, that camera is a person. In fact, when I stand before that camera, I feel so close to the viewer that I feel like I can just reach out and touch him. And I think people feel that."

"How?" he said.

And I said, "By our closeness, by thinking about what Christ can do." Jesus said:

> *If two of you shall agree on earth as touching any* (one) *thing . . . it shall be done for them of my Father which is in heaven* (Matthew 18:19).

For years people focused on my hands and many were able to make them their point of contact. Then almost overnight this method was not nearly so effective.

When I returned to television with a new format in 1969, my guidance was to stretch forth my hands toward the people in need of healing BUT TO ASK THEM TO TOUCH ONE ANOTHER . . . to touch and agree!

Although I expected God to work through this new method (because He gave it to me), I am astounded sometimes at the miracle of it being so right for the NOW. Perhaps people have changed, perhaps there is a deep inner desire people feel to reach out and touch one another. I know I feel it. As we touch and agree, our Father will work His wonders.

The same thing is true of a letter. When a person writes me, and I write back, we join in faith and *touch and agree!* It is the same when I reach forth my hands on TV or radio and people touch in their homes —TOUCHING AND AGREEING—it is God doing the healing.

There's a Spiritual excitement about our television programs. I can scarcely wait to get to that camera for, you see, when I'm talking into that television camera I feel an extreme closeness to the individual person and his need. There's no traveling or waiting—the person watching and I can come together there in the quietness of his own home. I can share God's Word; I can reach forth my hands and pray for him ACCORDING TO HIS NEED. I can *touch and agree* with him through the Spirit. We can become one in faith and love. This has become the most effective means God has given me to help people find God and get their needs met.

— • —

Actually, this is another form of THE POINT OF CONTACT. Even if you are alone and have no one to TOUCH AND AGREE with, it is just as effective to touch yourself and pray for your needs to be met.

As I mentioned earlier, the Bible says:

> If two of you shall agree . . . as touching any (one) thing . . . it shall be done (Matthew 18:19).

All right now, when you are watching me on television, or using my letter to you as your point of contact, I am ONE—and you are TWO—and *you* and *me* and GOD together make a MAJORITY.

YOUR GOD-GIVEN KEY FOR TODAY

So when you pray, say:

<u>"I Will Touch And Agree For My Need To Be Met!"</u>

And then expect a miracle to happen.

FRIDAY

Key:
I WILL PLANT SEEDS OF FAITH, HOPE,
AND LOVE EVERY DAY

or
How A Friend Got His Dream Job Through Applying The Three Miracle Keys Of Seed-Faith

A friend of mine had a job that required him to drive 120 miles round trip daily. Within walking distance of his home was a large plant which paid good wages and offered good working conditions. Besides saving wear and tear on his car and himself, if he worked there he could come home each day for lunch. For several years he had applied regularly for a job there but was turned down each time. During this period the company hired hundreds of new employees. He couldn't understand this and finally gave up.

One day he heard me speak on the key principles of the Blessing-Pact. I explained and gave examples of its three key principles:

First, look to God as the Source of your supply.

Second, give as seed-giving and it will become SEED-FAITH for God to multiply back in the form of your need.

Third, by looking to God as your Source, and giving as SEED-FAITH, this is evidence on which your faith can act—so expect a miracle of God's supply.

In my message I made a statement that turned this man and his wife around. Or, as they said later, "It turned us on."

The statement was this: **A rejected opportunity to give is a lost opportunity to receive.**

This statement is in harmony with Jesus' statement in Luke 6:38, "Give, and it shall be given unto you; good measure, pressed down, and shaken together, and running over, shall men give into your bosom. For with the same measure that ye mete withal it shall be measured to you again."

RECEIVING FOLLOWS GIVING

They saw that receiving follows giving. A miracle follows believing. Breathing in follows breathing out. The harvest follows seed-sowing and soil-tending.

In 2 Corinthians 9:10 we read, "Now he that ministereth seed to the sower both minister bread for your food, and multiply your seed sown, and increase the fruits of your righteousness." In other words, *God who gives you seed to sow is the one who multiplies the seed sown!*

God gives you an opportunity to give which, if you accept it, turns into an opportunity for you to receive.

Well, this man and his wife accepted the Blessing-Pact Covenant and put in seed-money that very day to help in our ministry. Regularly, each month, they send a Seed-Faith gift. Meanwhile they were learning to look to God as their Source and to put Him first in their lives.

I think it was four months later that I had occasion to chat with them. An amazing story unfolded.

He thought no more about applying at the plant, as he had done several times before. He told me, "But one morning at breakfast I felt something drawing me to apply again." He looked at his wife. She seemed to be experiencing the same feeling. "Oh, it's no use," he told her, "they'll just say no, like before."

I said, "You were still in the old pattern, expecting nothing after being refused so many times. You still had your mind set that there was no further hope."

He said, "I had been working on my thoughts, to put them on God and to trust Him to open doors for me. It didn't come easy. Gradually, my Blessing-Pact became real to me. God had become my *Source*. I was giving as Jesus told me to, and I knew God would start multiplying it back. How? I didn't know. But I knew He would do it in His own time and way. I knew He would open the door to a different and better job — I was expecting it. But when I felt this urge to apply again at the plant near us, I was a little surprised. I hadn't expected God to work in that direction. I told my wife that I just couldn't go ask again, and dismissed it from my mind."

Then his wife remembered: A rejected opportunity to give is a lost opportunity to receive. She thought, we've made a Blessing-Pact Covenant with God as the Source of our supply, and for our guidance. We have been giving seed into His kingdom by helping His servant do God's work. We have both been expecting a miracle. Then she said, "Well, why not?"

He said, "Well, why not what?"

She answered, "You've been wearing yourself and the car out driving 120 miles a day, just to hold down a job. God has something better for us. Our Blessing-Pact is up-to-date. That feeling we have is God starting to multiply our SEED-FAITH back to us."

Growing more excited, she said, "I think you should go down there in the morning and go to work."

He said, "You know, her face shone. The Blessing-Pact was shining through. I felt the same way she did but her conviction about this encouraged me. So I told her I'd drive the 120 miles one more day, then I'd apply. If that door doesn't open, I know God will open another."

FIRST CLASS

Now I like to talk to people who are standing up on the inside. Something reaches out and grips me. I know they mean business with God. They have finished accepting second or third best when God has only one class—FIRST CLASS.

I like to hear people say, "Well, why not? God is alive. He's here at the point of my need. I've given Him my best and I'm going to expect His best."

The way some people are going they are never going to get anywhere. They are like the woman who said, "I always feel the worst when I feel the best, because I know how bad I'm going to feel when I start feeling bad again."

Others are going to get up on the inside and start doing what God told them in His Word. They are going to change from looking to self or to men and start looking to God to move in on the scene. God is going to become their SOURCE, all other sources will be instruments only. If one instrument fails, they will keep their mind on Him and expect Him to help through another instrument.

I admit I get excited about applying the principles of Seed-Faith.

My friend rose the next morning feeling as if he owned the world. He bowed his head at breakfast, gave thanks, ate, told his wife to keep looking up and strode off to the employment office of this plant near his home. Pretty soon he was back. Bounding through the door, he said, "Honey, I got the job!"

She said, "How? Tell me all about it."

He said, "When I walked in I told them my name and that I had come to go to work. The man actually acted as if he had been waiting for me. He told me they would be ready for me as soon as I could come. Then he signed me up and told me to hurry back and report to work."

My friend said, "This is my dream come true. The thing I like best is that I can walk to work and walk home for lunch if I like. Each day I give thanks to God, for truly He sent this miracle to us."

Call this a coincidence . . .

Call it positive thinking . . .

Call it an accident.

I call it the Blessing-Pact, as SEED-FAITH in action! It proves God is where the need is, and when SEED-FAITH is sown God multiplies it back in the form of that need.

If you have been faithfully practicing Seed-Faith and putting the Three Miracle Keys to work, it's time for your miracle. You can say, just like the man and his wife in this story, "WELL, WHY NOT?"

———— ◆ ◆ ————

Whatever your lifelong dream may be, it looks like it's time for your miracle—"WHY NOT?" Because . . . and say it . . . "I have planted seeds". . .

YOUR GOD-GIVEN KEY FOR TODAY

"I Will Plant Seeds Of Faith, Hope, And Love Every Day!"

SATURDAY
Key:
SEED I HAVE PLANTED IS READY TO BE HARVESTED BACK IN MIRACLES FOR ME

or
How The First $100 Of Seed-Faith A Man Gave Me Was Multiplied To $1,400 In One Week

In 1954 when we were striving to go on television, God gave me a plan which I called the Blessing-Pact which I mentioned briefly in the Second Week of this book, and in more detail in the Twelfth Week. This was a plan whereby we asked our partners to enter into a pact with us and pledge one hundred dollars to help film the crusades. And I promised them if God did not return their money within one year from an unexpected source, we would return their pledge. That is how certain I was that the plan was from God.

The late Dr. Myrᴵ ᴵ Sackett, who was at that time director of our outreach to the Jews, was the first to enter into a Blessing-Pact pledge with us. He said, "I do not want the money back."

And I said, "Then we cannot enter into the pact, because these are my directions from the Lord."

Doc said, "All right, I will do as you say."

This was during a crusade in Baltimore. During that week Doc came to me and he said, "A woman whom I've never met handed me three one-hundred-dollar bills." Then he said, "I have already given you my Blessing-Pact pledge of a hundred dollars, so I am going to buy Hebrew Bibles with this $300."

Before the crusade was over he came to me again and said, "I was ready to mail this off for the Hebrew Bibles, but the Lord told me to give you the $300 for the Blessing-Pact."

I said, "Are you sure?"

He said, "Yes." So that made $400 he had given that week.

On the last day of the crusade he came to me again and said, "I've just met a man who gave me $1,000." (Now you had to know Doc to appreciate the way he said that.) And he said, "I'm going to send this check overseas and buy $1,000 worth of Hebrew Bibles."

And I said, "Yes, and we have $400 for our television outreach that we didn't have before . . ."

Then Doc said, "Just think, I gave $100 and it increased to $1,400 in one week."

Now this was Doc—the simplicity of a child, the faith of a child, but the boldness of a strong man.

By the way, out of the thousands who joined in the Blessing-Pact with me I recall only one who wrote and asked for his money back—which we gladly returned. A few days later he sent it back again with the explanation: "I just wanted to see if you would keep your word . . ."

———◆———

Have you checked on your SEED-FAITH PROJECT today? It may be that your DUE SEASON, or harvest, is at your front door and you are overlooking it. I'm not saying that every seed you plant will be multiplied back to you this quickly, BUT IT WILL BE MULTIPLIED BACK TO YOU RIGHT ON TIME—and you can be sure of that. GOD IS NEVER LATE AND HE IS NEVER EARLY—HE'S RIGHT ON SCHEDULE.

YOUR GOD-GIVEN KEY FOR TODAY

So bear down on this today:

"Seed I Have Planted Is Ready To Be Harvested Back In Miracles For Me."

EIGHTH WEEK

SUNDAY	WHEN I ACT, MY FAITH BEGINS TO WORK
MONDAY	JESUS IS UNLIMITED . . . HE'S WITH ME NOW
TUESDAY	GOD IS TURNED ON TO ME
WEDNESDAY	I AM FOCUSING MY FAITH ON JESUS
THURSDAY	I WILL TOUCH AND AGREE FOR MY NEED TO BE MET
FRIDAY	I WILL PLANT SEEDS OF FAITH, HOPE, AND LOVE EVERY DAY
SATURDAY	SEED I HAVE PLANTED IS READY TO BE HARVESTED BACK IN MIRACLES FOR ME

NINTH WEEK

How You And I Can Talk To God
And He Can Talk To Us

SUNDAY
Key:
I TALK TO GOD AND HE TALKS TO ME

or
How You Can Pray And Know God Will Hear You

THERE was one thing about Jesus that stood out to His disciples and that was His prayer life. They noticed when Jesus prayed that something happened! Now it wasn't like that when they prayed—something might or might not happen. Doubtless some of them didn't even *like* to pray. There was something about Jesus' prayer that always turned people on. Deeply impressed by the way He prayed, the disciples eagerly came to Jesus and said:

Teach us to pray . . . (Luke 11:1).

And Jesus began by saying:

After this manner therefore pray ye . . . (Matthew 6:9).

After this manner. Now Jesus was not indicating that this was to be the disciples' sole prayer . . . or that those were to be the only words they were ever to say in prayer. It was not to be a substitute for their prayers. But Jesus meant that they were to pray after the FASHION of this particular prayer, which we today call "The Lord's Prayer."

> *Our Father which art in heaven, Hallowed be thy name. Thy kingdom come. Thy will be done in earth, as it is in heaven. Give us this day our daily bread. And forgive us our (trespasses), as we forgive (those who trespass against us). And lead us not into temptation, but deliver us from evil: For thine is the kingdom, and the power, and the glory, for ever. Amen (Matthew 6:9-13).*

Our Father . . .

Jesus began the prayer with "Our Father . . ." Now the word "Father" as it pertains to God was not used in a personal way by the people of the Old Testament, although God was sometimes referred to

225

as a father. It was first used in a personal way by our Lord Jesus Christ. The term *Father* signified the closeness they had together. It meant that He and God the Father were intimately and personally related. This was the new dimension that Christ brought out of the Old Testament into the New Testament and into the NOW. He tells us to call God *Father,* suggesting the closeness of our relationship with Him.

Many years ago I read a story about President Abraham Lincoln and his son Tad. One day Tad was outside the White House playing in the yard while his father was busy inside with the affairs of State. Little Tad apparently got into a fist fight and came out the loser. He ran into the White House with his lip cut, his nose bleeding, and his clothes torn. When he got to his father's outer office, there sat several members of the President's Cabinet waiting to see him. The little boy, sobbing, said, "I want to see my father . . . I want to see my father!"

The Secretary of the Treasury—in sort of a spirit of jest—spoke up and said, "You wish to see the President of the United States?"

And the little boy said, "I want to see my FATHER!"

"Well," he said, "I will take you in personally to see the Chief Executive Officer of the United States."

But the little boy again said, "I want to see my FATHER."

Then the Secretary of State spoke up and said, "Look, I'll take care of the lad . . . 'Son, I'll take you into the presence of the greatest diplomat in the whole world—the head of our nation'."

The little boy just kept on sobbing, "I want to see my FATHER."

Finally, the Secretary of War said, "Son, I'll take you in to see the Commander in Chief of the armed forces of the United States of America."

And the little boy said, "I just want to see my FATHER!"

Everything these men said about Lincoln was true, but to the little boy that head of state, the great diplomat, the Commander in Chief of the armed forces was his father. And he knew if he could just get in there to his dad—with his cut lip, bleeding nose, and torn clothes—that his father would put his arms around him, pull him up close, and things would be all right again.

Jesus indicated that this is the relationship we have with God in prayer. We are to think of Him as "Our FATHER . . ."

There was something about my own father that was so deeply a part of my life. I was always close to my mother but . . . oh . . . there was a relationship I had with my father that I cannot put into words. He stood for affection . . . for confidence . . . for protection . . . for love. He was especially near us children when we were ill . . . when we were in trouble.

PAPA! Jesus was saying to you and to me, "When you pray, say, *Our Father . . . Our Papa . . . Our Daddy.*"

Which art . . .

God is. Jesus said when you pray, pray to someone who IS . . . who never changes. The weather changes . . . people change . . . circumstances change . . . but God never changes. God exists . . . HE IS.

Listen, say to yourself over and over again, "God IS . . . God is in the NOW!"

Say, "If He is not here in the NOW, He has never been."

Say, "He is willing to help me!"

Say, "If He is not willing to help me, He has not been willing to help anybody. But He IS . . . and He WILL!"

GOD IS! God is . . . in your total life—physical, material, spiritual. You have a seven-day-a-week life . . . seven-day-a-week needs . . . and you have a seven-day-a-week God. God is with you every moment, every day, everywhere. GOD IS!

In heaven . . .

Now Jesus was not trying to locate God. He was using this term to express the ability and power of God to take care of us and our needs. On another occasion Jesus said:

I am come that they might have life, and that they might have it more abundantly (John 10:10).

When Jesus spoke those words the world was filled with impossibilities. All around Him, Jesus saw people hemmed in by circumstances, disease, discrimination, poverty, fear, and failure. And He knew that IN HEAVEN there were resources for man's needs—

water for his thirst . . .

food for his hunger . . .

strength for his weakness . . .

riches for his poverty . . .

a kiss for his sorrow . . .

gladness for his misery . . .

and love for his loneliness.

So Jesus reached up and took heaven and kissed the earth with it and opened it and gave to the children of men. He came with outstretched hands filled with God's blessing, *with an open heaven* behind Him. He came into people's lives at the point of their need, performing miracles and setting them free.

So Jesus tells you when you pray to remember that God your Father is IN HEAVEN. And IN HEAVEN there is no shortage of any good thing. God's riches are laid end-to-end across heaven waiting to be given to you.

Hallowed be thy name . . .

Jesus had a deep feeling about the name of God. He never used it irreverently . . . nor in vain . . . nor as an obscenity. In fact, Jesus never used an obscenity. He reverenced the name of the Father with great honor and love. And He said to you and to me, "When you pray, be sure that you have reverence for the name of God."

When I was in Moscow, Russia, a number of years ago I had an experience that gave me a new understanding of "reverence." Every day I saw a long line of people—perhaps two miles long—line up to visit the tomb of Lenin in Red Square. This was the man who brought Communism to Russia. He is entombed there exactly as he died. His right hand is upon his chest and it's not open into a hand but it is closed into a fist, indicative to me of the violence with which he associated himself during his lifetime.

Each day people walk by on either side of his coffin to see his body. Soldiers stand guard over the casket, about three feet apart. No one is allowed to stop. The lines just keep moving. I decided to go one day. I caught just a glimpse of the dead Lenin as I walked by.

The thing that stood out most to me was the reverence which these many, many communists gave to their long dead leader. I mean they reverenced him.

Not far away is the house in which Lenin died. In the room where he spent his last moments, everything has been left untouched. It is exactly like it was when Lenin died. There is the book that he was reading. You will be surprised to know it is a book about our Lord Jesus Christ—the one Lenin said he could not believe in. The book is open and it is lying there. However, because it is written in English, and most Russian people do not speak English, they look at the book, smile, and pass on. They don't know that it is a book about Christ. They reverence Lenin as the dead leader of Communism and on the other hand they pass by his book that is about the Christian faith.

Lenin died with his fist clenched in hatred.

Jesus died with His hand open in love and healing to every human being.

How much more we should reverence His name!

Many years ago in Tulsa there was a famous photographer who worked for our *Tulsa Daily World* newspaper. He was known from coast to coast. He also was a rather obscene man, according to his own testimony. He cursed, almost without realizing that he was cursing. It was a part of him. He had a habit of taking God's name in vain.

His wife became a Christian and she was very close to God. The name of Jesus was precious to her. She stood about all she could, then one day when he began to curse God she looked at him with the firmness that only a wife can have toward her husband and she said, "Lee, don't you ever do that again in my presence!"

He whirled around and said, "What do you mean?"

And she said, "Don't you ever curse the name of my Lord in my presence again. He changed my life—He gave me back my life. Although I love you, Lee, and I am your wife, Jesus of Nazareth means more to me and He has done more for me than anyone else."

A strange quietness came over Lee.

Years later when I got to know him he told me this story and he said, "Oral, when she said that, something went into my heart—not merely my mind but my HEART. The Holy Spirit convicted me of my sins. And I said to her, 'Honey, will you pray for me?' She did and I accepted Christ."

Later Lee gave up his photography and his position, and became an evangelist. You see, the name of God and the name of Jesus Christ meant something to Lee's wife. She didn't like to hear God's name used irreverently. His name was hallowed to her. And because she took a strong stand for the name of God, her husband came to know Christ.

Thy kingdom come . . .

Jesus was very concerned about the nations . . . the kingdoms . . . that existed on the earth. But He was even more concerned about another kingdom . . . a higher kingdom . . . God's kingdom. And He taught us to pray, ". . . thy kingdom come." A newspaper story I read in the '50s illustrates what Jesus meant when He said this.

A British team of mountain climbers were trying to scale the heights of Mt. Everest. While they were climbing, their leader—by the name of Mallory—slipped and plunged hundreds of feet below into the snow and disappeared.

This of course broke up that particular team and they went back to London to give their report. As they spoke to a packed audience there was a screen behind them showing pictures of Mt. Everest and the different levels where they had climbed and the exact spot where Mr. Mallory lost his life. They talked about their great leader, the hardships that they had undergone—the cold, the winds, the snow. Then the man who was doing the most talking straightened up, turned toward the picture of Mt. Everest on the screen, and began talking to it as if it were a living thing. He said:

"Mighty Mt. Everest, we tried to conquer you once and you beat us. We tried to conquer you the second time and you beat us. But we are going to conquer you because YOU CANNOT GET ANY BIGGER, BUT WE CAN!"

This is what Jesus is saying. We live in earthly kingdoms. These kingdoms are only going to be so powerful—they are limited. Jesus lived in the Roman Empire, a kingdom of men that had spread over the then-known world. It had conquered the nations and had control over all the people who lived in them. But Jesus said that these kingdoms of men are not going to fully conquer everybody . . . these earthly kingdoms are not going to get any bigger, but God's kingdom IS . . . and through Him you will get bigger too.

Thy will be done

in earth

as it is in heaven . . .

Every time you pray this, you are praying a revolutionary, radical prayer. You are praying for a new kind of kingdom to come into being. You are praying that what is IN HEAVEN will come to be . . . down here IN THE EARTH. And that starts with you (in earth, the substance from which our bodies are made), with your repentance and love. *The will of God starts in heaven but it must be lived out in this earthen vessel.* This affects you where you are and as you are.

One day a couple came to a pastor because they knew he was a man who preached a lot about Jesus and about love. They said, "We love each other but don't feel that it is necessary to be married — we just live together but we have a great love. Now you preach love, pastor, and love is in the Bible. So can you tell us what's wrong with our living together if we love each other as we do?"

The pastor said, "Well, first of all, you have missed the whole point. Our Lord said, 'Thy will be done in earth as it is in heaven.' It's the will of God that people marry. Fornication and adultery are inventions of men. Divorce was given because of the hardness of men's hearts (Matthew 19:8), but marriage is the creation of God. So you've missed the whole point. You've got to live according to the will of God. The will of God is that you marry and that you do not defile your earthen body — this earthen vessel of your body is the temple of the Holy Spirit and the Bible says:

> *If any man defile the temple of God, him shall God destroy, for the temple of God is holy, which temple ye are* (1 Corinthians 3:17).

So you are cancelling out this so-called loving because you are defiling your bodies and you are not living in the will of God."

I used to be afraid of the will of God. I thought if I did God's will that it would tie me in knots . . . it would restrict my life . . . that I'd never be able to do anything worthwhile. But . . . oh . . . when I began to do God's will, I really began to LIVE. You see . . .

THE WILL OF GOD IS FULL OF LOVE

It means love in marriage . . . love for little children . . . love that builds a stable home.

It means love that deals right with our brother and our sister in our family, and with other families and races.

It means loving ourselves and respecting ourselves too.

So the most important question we can ask ourselves is, "Am I doing God's will in earth as well as in heaven?"

Give us this day our daily bread . . .

I'm glad Jesus didn't leave the bread out. The hip folks today call money "bread." They say, "Do you have any bread?" which means, "Do you have any money?" When Jesus said, "Give us this day our daily bread," He meant, "Give us this day our material needs." Jesus knew all about physical necessities of life. He knew the worth of a widow's mite and what the loss of a coin meant to a housewife. He knew about clothes that needed mending and about not having a place to sleep at night.

Even after Jesus' resurrection He showed concern for His disciples' physical needs. The day He walked home with two of His friends He sat down at the table and broke bread with them. Several days later when the disciples had been out all night fishing, Jesus knew they would be hungry, so He prepared breakfast for them.

I'm glad Jesus didn't tell us to pray, "Sell us this day our daily bread," because we could never pay God. Instead Jesus said, "[God], give us this day . . ." You see, Jesus is saying that we can't get away from our Source. God is the Source of our total supply. We can never be very far away from our Source, who is God. The only true bread, the only true supply of our material needs, comes through God.

Jesus is talking about bread . . . about GOD'S BREAD. He's talking about a supply of our needs that really satisfies . . . about clothes that satisfy . . . about an automobile that works . . . about a house that becomes a home. He's talking about God meeting our needs.

God is concerned about your bread. He's concerned about money that you need . . . and the clothing you need . . . and the home you need. He's concerned about your physical health. He does not want you to die before your time. God wants you to have peace. He wants you to live out your days in health and happiness.

Forgive us our trespasses
as we forgive those who
trespass against us . . .

After Jesus concluded the Lord's Prayer He added these words:

> For if ye forgive men their trespasses, your heavenly Father will also forgive you: But if ye forgive not men their trespasses, neither will your Father forgive your trespasses (Matthew 6:14,15).

Jesus indicated that the human race is guilty of trespasses . . . we are debtors. Each of us is a trespasser.

We DO things we ought not to do . . .

We SAY things we should not say . . .

We THINK things we should not think . . .

We are trespassers and our forgiveness must come from God. There is one Forgiver—and that is God. Men may or may not forgive us, but God WILL forgive.

A man once said to John Wesley, "I'll never forgive."

Wesley replied, "Then pray that you will never sin."

In other words, the only way you are ever going to be forgiven by God of your own trespasses is to forgive the one who trespasses against you.

When we were in England a few years ago making a prime-time TV special, most of it was taped in the ruins of the Coventry Cathedral in Coventry. Coventry was one of the early sites to be bombed by Nazi Germany because it was an industrial city. They almost bombed it off the map and they didn't spare the churches. A bomb struck Coventry Cathedral—that tremendous edifice that was several hundred years old and beyond price—and destroyed it. Only a little of it was left standing.

When the war was over the people rebuilt the cathedral but they left the old, scarred, bombed-out part like it was. They picked up three hand-forged nails from the ruins, put them together in the form of a cross and wrote on them . . . "Father, forgive." How could they forgive the Nazis? How could they forgive a people who killed six million Jews? How could they forgive a people who burned up their city? Destroyed their church?

In their hearts they reached a place where they said, "Father, forgive . . ." You see, they might have harbored some trespasses also. They might have been hating back just as much as the Nazis hated them. So I believe it was a double prayer: "Father, forgive . . . (us and them)."

Lead us not into temptation
but deliver us from evil . . .

In other words, Jesus said when we pray we should say: "God, don't forsake us when the going gets rough. Don't let us get into situations that are bigger than we are. Don't let us get into water over our heads."

I'm going to tell you a funny story but it makes a point. A fellow was asked where he was going and he said, "I'm going to get drunk and, oh, how I dread it!" You see, he wasn't enjoying drinking . . . he wasn't enjoying doing these terrible things to himself, but they had a hold on him. He wanted God's help and that's what he was saying when he said, ". . . and, oh, how I dread it." It was a prayer. Now it may not sound like a prayer but a prayer can be just a sigh—or a groan. Or it may be a deluge of tears.

A man who came to me for prayer broke down and began to cry. As he tried to regain his composure he apologized, saying, "Mr. Roberts,

I'm sorry. I know a grown man shouldn't cry but I can't help it." I encouraged him to let his tears flow. I told him they were a release for his spirit and an expression of his prayer to God.

Tears are not a sign of weakness, nor do they show a lack of manliness. Christ was a man's Man, and the Bible speaks of occasions when He wept. In the Garden of Gethsemane He prayed with "strong crying and tears" (Hebrews 5:7).

In whatever way we express the sincere desire of our heart to God He will understand and He will help us.

> For thine is the kingdom,
> and the power,
> and the glory, forever.
> Amen.

When Jesus said these words He was living in an outpost of the Roman Empire. The Roman soldiers in their barbaric cruelty were everywhere putting their burdens on the people. They were acting like they were going to rule forever . . . that Rome would always be the master kingdom. But Jesus looked beyond Rome . . . beyond every other kingdom that would arise on the earth . . . and He said, ". . . THINE is the kingdom."

That is, Jesus was saying that there is something bigger and better and more stable than this or any other earthly kingdom . . . and that kingdom is ruled by the King of kings and the Lord of lords.

Jesus is saying to you:

"You are not alone. You are surrounded by the kingdom of God . . . an incomparable power that can set you free . . . a glory that can fill your breast. So why settle for the transient things of this world when you can have the permanent kingdom of God within you? You can have the limitlessness of the Spirit of God helping you to receive health again. You can have your soul saved . . . your material needs met . . . and this can start today."

Just for starters, you can think of the Lord's Prayer this way:

The opening, that says:

"OUR FATHER WHICH ART IN HEAVEN . . ."

Think of that opener as God's "front porch." When you get on the front porch, start knocking and asking and expecting. This is why you can say to yourself every day:

YOUR GOD-GIVEN KEY FOR TODAY
"I Talk To God And He Talks To Me."

MONDAY Key:
I WILL PLANT A SEED TO MATCH MY NEED

or
Why I Believe You Can Pray For Your Daily Needs And KNOW That God Will Give Them To You

In John 6 is the story of five thousand men, plus women and children, who were hungry to the point of fainting. They needed bread . . . and through a miracle Jesus gave it to them. When the multitude had finished eating they gathered up twelve basketsful of fragments. All this, and Jesus began with only a boy's lunch of five loaves and two fishes.

There's a very important point in this story. This is, Jesus Christ is concerned about people having bread. These people were out of bread. They followed Him so long and so far into the desert that their food ran out. The disciples suggested He send them away to buy bread but Jesus said, "If I do, they will faint by the wayside." Jesus immediately became concerned about these people and their *NOW* need for bread.

GOD IS CONCERNED ABOUT YOUR DAILY NEEDS

Bread represents the totality of man's needs. Everyone needs bread. We need bread for our bodies. We also need clothes for our bodies and houses and automobiles and money for our needs and things to take care of our family with. We need these things right down here on earth . . . and our Father knows we need them.

Jesus told us to pray, "Give us this day our daily bread . . ." Then He said, "for your heavenly Father knoweth that ye have need of all these *things*" (Matthew 6:11,32).

Things. Jesus says we are to pray and ask God for the *things* we need . . . He says that God is concerned!

Jesus was there in the midst of thousands of hungry people and He did something about it.

I appreciate God. I appreciate God because He's concerned about the body I live in. He is concerned about the mind I have to think through. He's concerned about my soul and my spirit. He's concerned about the house I live in, or am supposed to live in. He's concerned about my needs being met. He is God and I am a human being, yet He loves me. He loves *me*.

There's another very important statement here that we should not miss. This is:

JESUS HIMSELF KNEW WHAT HE WOULD DO

Right in the midst of those five thousand people being hungry, yet not having any bread, and not being able to send them away for fear they might faint by the wayside, the Bible says, Jesus knew himself what He would do. He had a plan. And it was a plan of Seed-Faith. Jesus needed someone to put in *a seed to match the need*. And that person turned out to be a little boy.

The Bible says:

> *Except ye be converted, and become as little children, ye shall not enter into the kingdom of heaven* (Matthew 18:3).

That is, become uninhibited. Just look up and ask and let God be what He is. That's what a little child is and does. He is so uninhibited about God; he believes God can do anything; he doesn't hesitate to pray for what he needs.

This little boy had a small lunch which he voluntarily gave to our Lord. And that little lunch became *a seed to match the need*.

Now you say, "That's crazy." Certainly, my mind says the same thing. My intellect says this is crazy! My mind asks *how* Jesus could take a boy's small lunch and multiply it to feed five thousand hungry men plus all those women and children that were there that day. (If that crowd was like most of our churches today, there were more women and children present than there were men. This would mean that there were more than ten thousand hungry mouths to feed that day.)

Now our minds just can't take that in. And there are some people who don't believe this miracle happened. But I've seen God take small things and multiply them in answer to prayer in my own life. I've seen it happen in other people's lives. Therefore, I believe.

I have just had an experience with a little black mother in Mississippi, whose older son prayed and put in some seed for her: *First,* that she would be healed or cured by open heart surgery. *Second,* that she would have a new brick home. (She had always lived in a small shack.) *Third,* he included himself that he might find a wife. And he put some seed in.

The day came for his mother to go into surgery. She had a growth in her heart the size of a golf ball. As she was praying that morning she had a vision. In the vision she saw Oral Roberts coming to her and she heard him saying, "Expect a miracle. God is at the point of your need. Expect a miracle." She said a warmth flooded through her.

When the doctor came in to examine her before surgery he could tell that something had happened, so he said, "Would you like to wait a few days?"

And she said, "I believe I would."

A few days later she was examined again and this time they discovered that the growth was gone and that surgery would not be necessary. You see, a miracle had happened.

The next thing that happened is that two of her sons decided to build her a new home and now it is finished.

The third miracle also happened. The mother met a beautiful young girl that she thought would fit her son and she said, "You are supposed to marry my son." Sure enough, they fell in love.

This all happened because her son put in a little seed to meet the need. The mother told me this story with tears streaming down her cheeks . . . how that she is healed . . . how she has her own new home . . . how her son has a lovely wife.

Do you think that's crazy? If you do, let's just go on being crazy like that. What do you say? Let's pray in faith . . . and believe God to meet our needs.

Let's go on planting seeds—and remember . . .

A PRAYER SEED IS ONE OF THE MOST POWERFUL SEEDS YOU CAN PLANT.

YOUR GOD-GIVEN KEY FOR TODAY

As you pray, say:

"I Will Plant A Seed To Match My Need . . ."

And I promise you, you'll grow miracles!

TUESDAY
**Key:
I WILL TELL GOD HOW IT IS WITH ME . . . HE'LL UNDERSTAND**

**or
When You Pray Tell God Like It Is In Your Life . . .**

Forget for the moment the Sunday-in-church-type-of-prayer where every word has to be just so-so. INSTEAD, TALK TO JESUS RIGHT OUT OF YOUR INSIDES. Exactly like you feel. Use whatever words that come to you.

A brother said to me, "But I don't know how to pray. I've never learned."

I said, "How do you feel?"

He said, "I feel terrible."

"Then tell God that." He looked at me in wonderment.

"Is that the way to pray?"

I said, "Try it."

"Now?"

"Yes."

He blurted out, "God, I just feel terrible."

"Go on." Then he really got down to business.

He said, "God, I feel bad all over. I've disobeyed You; I've sinned. Nothing is turning out good. God, I'm scared. I don't think I'm going to make it . . ."

Then he looked up and said, "Brother Roberts, what do I do now?"

I said, "All right, you've told God like it is with you. Now tell Him how you feel toward Him."

He said, "Like I feel?"

I nodded.

Suddenly, words came tumbling out of his mouth, "God, sometimes I don't like You. I don't like You at all. You let me feel so alone. DO YOU REALLY CARE ABOUT ME?"

Start telling God like it is . . .

Then a change started coming over him. I could feel it. He cried, "God, I'm sorry I feel like that. I know You care. I've felt You at times but didn't always know it was You. Please forgive my sins and help me."

By this time both of us had tears in our eyes. He shook my hand. "That's the first time I feel I've really prayed," he said. "And I feel God heard me."

Sounds simple? Well, great things are always simple. But you've got to tell God like it is. If you are at fault, say it. If you have failed to put God first, say it. If you are living in sin, say it by confessing it to God. Be brave about asking for another chance.

IF YOU'RE SCARED, IF YOU'RE ANXIOUS, DON'T BE LIKE PEOPLE WHO WON'T ADMIT IT—TELL GOD YOU'RE SCARED

A little boy was given a part in a church play; he had just one line to say. And it was the words of Jesus that He used when He was walking on the water: "It is I; be not afraid." So his mother called him in and said, "Now, honey, all you have to say in the church play is, 'It is I; be not afraid.'" And she carefully rehearsed him over and over.

On the night of the play the little boy walked out onto the stage and he looked at the bright lights. There was a big crowd and he got frightened and forgot his lines. So he just stood there, shifting from foot to foot. Pretty soon, from behind the curtain, the prompter said, "It is I; be not afraid."

The little boy just kept shifting from foot to foot.

Once again the voice said, "It is I; be not afraid."

And suddenly the little boy blurted out, "It's only me, and I'm scared to death."

We all get scared like that little boy. It's wrong to hide it and to harbor it in your heart until it eats you up. Tell God how you feel, how scared you are, how depressed and frustrated you are—tell God like it is. Then look to God as your Source,

> your Source for faith,
>> your Source for deliverance from fear,
>>> your Source for salvation from sin.

Don't worry about formulating just the right word. Can you remember how easily you could understand your little child when he first started to talk? It sounded like jabber to everyone else, *but you knew exactly what your child was saying to you.* So . . . YOU ARE GOD'S CHILD . . . start talking to Him in your own way—pretty soon, you won't be hung up on how to talk to God.

YOUR GOD-GIVEN KEY FOR TODAY

Say:

"I Will Tell God How It Is With Me . . .
He'll Understand."

WEDNESDAY

Key:
THE PRAYER I PRAY IS A
SEED I PLANT

or

How I Sowed A Seed Of Prayer And Bought My Family A House With Only $25 In My Pocket And Started In My Highest Calling

When I resigned the pastorate in Enid to begin this ministry, we moved to Tulsa. I chose Tulsa because it is centrally located in the United States, because of its excellent travel facilities, and also because —as a native Oklahoman—I wanted to set up my headquarters in my home state. I think Tulsa is the most beautiful city I have ever seen and a wonderful place to live.

Our main difficulty was that I had very little money with which to locate in Tulsa. Evelyn and I searched for a house to lease, but none was to be found within our ability to handle.

Rev. Oscar Moore, the man who had married us and who had been called by the Enid church to take my place, lived in Tulsa at this time and was trying to sell his house as well as to help us secure a place to live. Upon his invitation, we stayed overnight in his home.

The following day he told us that he had sold his house to a man who was coming that evening at six o'clock to close the deal. Suddenly, I had the feeling that this was our house. Then I thought how absurd this was since he had already sold it.

In a few minutes I went into the bedroom to pray, but it seemed that I was unable to pray through on this problem. I told Oscar that I wanted to drive through a certain section of the city again and that I would be back soon. A few minutes later I parked my car near one of the city parks and sat there trying to work things out in my mind. Things now were growing serious. I had given up the Enid pastorate with its security for my family, and launched upon a ministry that had many unknown quantities. The amount of money I had was very small — $25 to be exact. Still, I felt each step I had taken had been ordered by the Lord.

As I sat there behind the steering wheel, things looked pretty dark. I felt stranded. There was no human source to which I could turn for help. With an almost uncontrollable urge to cry out to God, I bowed my head over the steering wheel and told Him of the predicament I was in. I told Him of the needs of my family and of His call upon my life and that if I were to begin in this ministry, I must have help immediately.

When I had prayed myself out, I became quiet before God. It was then that I felt the Holy Spirit come upon me. The words of an old hymn, one I had known since early childhood, came into my mind:

> O the joy of sins forgiv'n!
> O the bliss the blood-washed know!
> O the peace akin to heav'n,
> Where the healing waters flow!

The thought came to me: Why am I worrying? My sins are forgiven; I am washed in the blood of Christ, and the peace akin to heaven is in my heart. I felt everything was going to be all right. I drove back and arrived in time for dinner.

The man who had agreed to buy Oscar's home did not arrive at the appointed time. He still had not appeared at 7:30 that evening. We had all planned to attend the revival meeting under Rev. Steve Pringle's big tent that night. Oscar urged us to go on and he would stay and wait for the man a little longer. It was that night at this service that Steve Pringle asked me to conduct my first Tulsa Crusade under his tent. I agreed to preach for one week.

The next morning as we sat around the breakfast table, Oscar said he would give his friend until 8 o'clock that morning to appear. A little after 8 o'clock a strange look came across his face; and turning to me, he said, "Oral, would you and Evelyn like to have this house?"

I smiled and said, "Oh, I don't know."

He said, "It's a nice house."

The serenity that I felt in that hour was indescribable.

Oscar said, "Oral, would you like to buy this house?"

I said, "Perhaps."

He told me how much he would take for it and I replied that it was too much. He asked me how much I would give and I told him. When he said he would accept my offer, I said, "Sold."

I looked over at Evelyn, who did not know of the prayer the day before or of the confidence I now possessed. She knew that the sum of money we had was too little for us to be thinking about buying a home.

While Oscar was gone to the bank to arrange for the papers, I told Evelyn that everything would work out all right.

Nothing had been said about a down payment. When Oscar returned he told me how much the down payment would be. The amount almost took my breath away, but I nodded my head.

While we were going through the papers, he paused and looked at me. I looked at him. And for a few moments we just sat there looking at each other. Abruptly, he said, "Oral, Anna and I really have no need for the down payment at this time. If it is agreeable, you and Evelyn can simply take up the monthly payments beginning the first of the month and you can give us the down payment later, say half in six months and the other half in twelve months."

I caught my breath and said, "Oh, just as you say."

Later, in our room, Evelyn and I shed tears of joy because we knew we had witnessed the loving hand of God intervening in our behalf.

Oscar did not know until a year later that I had bought his home with only $25 in my pocket.

———◆◆◆———

You've probably heard ministers or others say that prayer is like a "chain reaction." But I tell you that it is even better than that. **When you pray and tell God your needs, it is like splitting the atom—and God takes note of that!**

YOUR GOD-GIVEN KEY FOR TODAY

So think of this kind of power when you say:

"The Prayer I Pray Is A Seed I Plant."

THURSDAY

Key:
GOD LIKES THE PRAYERS I SEND
TO HIM BECAUSE HIS BUSINESS IS ME!

or

How You Can Send A Message To A Miracle-Working God

Corrie ten Boom, a very dear elderly lady who spent years in a German concentration camp, literally survived because she lived on her faith and sending messages to God. One time when she was really low in spirit, wondering if this would be the day they would come to put her in the gas chamber, she said, "I got down on my knees and spread my Bible out in front of me—and I still do this often because as I pray I point to God's Word and remind Him of His promises to His children . . ." And then Corrie smiled, as only she can, and said, "God likes that!"

Regardless of your method of sending a message to God—
　you can reach out and touch God . . .
　　　in the silences of your life . . .
　　　in your deepest emotions.
　You can touch Him
　　　when you are in a crowd . . .
　　　or if you are alone . . .
　　　if your bills are piling up and you can't pay them . . .
　　　if you are troubled . . .
　　　if you are young or old . . .
　　　if you are scared and frightened . . .
　God is there!
　"But God is so busy," someone says. Yes, He is busy . . .
　　but His business is YOU!

————◆————

Have you ever gotten too busy to listen to your own child? You may have, but usually your child is so insistent that you will finally stop and listen. And doesn't it always please you when your child takes you at your word? This is the finite area, but when you're talking about God and His Word and His time you're talking about the infinite. It's like someone said not long ago: "If God gets too busy and runs out of time, He'll just make some more . . . for after all, He made it in the first place."

YOUR GOD-GIVEN KEY FOR TODAY

"God Likes The Prayers I Send To Him Because
His Business Is Me."

FRIDAY Key: GOD IS IN CONTROL OF ALL MY LIFE!

or
The God Of The Sunsets Is Also The God Of The Storms

A woman recently wrote and shared this experience. She said, "One hot summer evening we were under a tornado alert. Lightning streaked the sky and thunder roared ominously. The wind began to blow wildly. I tried to pray but I was so terrified that I just walked the floor wringing my hands. Suddenly the lights went out and I was panic-stricken.

"My husband said, 'You've got the get yourself under control. Don't you remember?—when you see a rainbow or a beautiful sunset you always say you feel so close to the Lord. But every time it storms you are full of fear. *Is your faith in the God of the sunsets or in the God of the storms?*'

"His question startled me. 'How ridiculous,' I said to him, 'You know that I believe in one God.'

"He said, 'Then act like it.'"

The woman went on to say, "That statement changed my life. As I calmed down I realized I'd been so full of fear I'd lost sight of the fact that God controls the storms as well as the sunshine. So my prayers brought me no peace. But now I no longer go into panic when it storms or when problems arise. I simply pray and put my faith in God, confident that He is God of all storms."

———————

REMEMBER, GOD NEVER FADES FROM THE VISION OF
A PERSON UNTIL HE CEASES TO PRAY . . .
SO KEEP PRAYER *FRESH* IN YOUR LIFE EVERY DAY—AND
AFFIRM THIS GREAT TRUTH:

YOUR GOD-GIVEN KEY FOR TODAY

"God Is In Control Of All My Life."

SATURDAY

Key:
I'LL JUST PRAY EASY BECAUSE GOD DOES THE WORK!

or
Something You Should Know About Prayer That Leads To Miracles . . .

Recently when I was in the Prayer Tower reading letters from the people and praying over their great needs, my heart just involuntarily cried out to God. I found myself praying real hard for the people. As I was there praying the Lord began to speak to my heart and say:

"DON'T PRAY HARD, PRAY EASY . . .
PRAYER DOESN'T DO IT—GOD DOES!"

As I look back over this ministry and the outstanding miracles that have occurred, I realize that these miracles have not happened because of long, hard prayers. Often, it was a very short, simple prayer. You see, I pray for people the way the Holy Spirit directs me to pray for them because I am not the healer—GOD IS!

———————

LISTEN, FRIEND: This would make a great pocket reminder—just jot it down on a little card and keep it in your pocket or billfold:

YOUR GOD-GIVEN KEY FOR TODAY
"I'll Just Pray Easy Because God Does The Work."

NINTH WEEK

SUNDAY	I TALK TO GOD AND HE TALKS TO ME
MONDAY	I WILL PLANT A SEED TO MATCH MY NEED
TUESDAY	I WILL TELL GOD HOW IT IS WITH ME . . . HE WILL UNDERSTAND
WEDNESDAY	THE PRAYER I PRAY IS A SEED I PLANT
THURSDAY	GOD LIKES THE PRAYERS I SEND TO HIM BECAUSE HIS BUSINESS IS ME
FRIDAY	GOD IS IN CONTROL OF MY LIFE
SATURDAY	I'LL JUST PRAY EASY BECAUSE GOD DOES THE WORK

TENTH WEEK

How I Learned To Have A Knowing That God Will Make A Way Where There Is No Way

SUNDAY

Key:
I CAN COMMUNICATE DIRECTLY WITH GOD—HE HELPS ME

or

How You Can Pray In The Holy Spirit And With Your Understanding Also

IN 1947 when God let me know that my time had come to take His healing power to my generation, my first reaction was . . .

"I don't know how!"

I knew I had been healed myself. I knew that I believed in God's great healing power—both medical and divine healing. But I didn't know HOW God was going to use me because I did not consider myself a gifted person. I struggled with this day and night. During those days of heart-searching I would often say to God:

"Let me see Jesus Christ with my eyes like the disciples did . . . like Peter, James, and John did. Let me SEE Him. Let me have a vision of this Man *physically* as they did. Then I can go and pray for the people. I can go where they are. I can enter into their sufferings. Otherwise, I don't know HOW."

It was at this point that God spoke to me again. I heard His voice deep inside me. He said:

"Do you have the baptism in the Holy Spirit?" And I said:

"Yes." (I had received this charisma—this gift of the Spirit—shortly after my conversion. I had also spoken in tongues a few times since then.)

Then the Lord said to me:

"Do you know what you have?"

In all honesty I had to reply that I did not.

Then God said . . .

"You said you wanted to SEE Jesus. Well, having the baptism in the Holy Spirit gives you a sense of His physical being, as well as His spiritual being. When you have the baptism in the Holy Spirit, it's precisely as if Jesus is walking by your side in the flesh. Do you understand that?"

And of course I did not fully understand. No one had ever really explained it to me this way before. So I began a study of the Holy Spirit that was to continue until today . . . a study into . . .

WHAT IT MEANS TO BE BAPTIZED IN THE HOLY SPIRIT AND TO SPEAK IN TONGUES . . . WHICH I CALL THE PRAYER LANGUAGE OF THE SPIRIT.

(I use the terms synonymously—speaking in tongues, the prayer language of the Spirit, and praying in the Spirit—they mean the same thing.)

I read in the Bible where Jesus said:

> It is expedient for you that I go away: for if I go not away, the Comforter will not come unto you; but if I depart, I will send him unto you (John 16:7).

I looked in the Greek and found that in this Scripture the word "comforter" means PARACLETE. The word "paraclete" is translated *comforter* in the King James Version of the Bible. It means "one called alongside to help . . . one who warns, one who admonishes . . . one who helps us over our rough spots." So the divine Paraclete is one who gives us what we need at the time we need it.

Once when I was teaching on this, I called up a member of my class and illustrated it this way.

Roberts: Will you open your billfold a moment, please, and take out a dollar bill?

Student: Yes.

Roberts: OK. I'm going to take your dollar.

Student: I thought you would.

Roberts: But, I'm going to give you another dollar. Will you take it?

Student: Yes.

Roberts: Now that dollar is just as genuine as the one you gave me. It is also printed by Uncle Sam—it's a genuine dollar. Now do you have as much as you had before you gave me your dollar?

Student: Yes.

Roberts: I gave you another dollar. And that dollar has the identical buying power of the dollar you gave me?

Student: That's right.

I want you to notice that when the student gave me his dollar and I gave him back another dollar, he was just as well off as he had been before. In the same way, Jesus was saying to His disciples:

"If I go away I will send you another Paraclete . . . one called alongside to help. I have been by your side physically. I have been everything to you. Now you are distressed because I'm physically leaving the earth, but if I go back to My Father I will send you another Paraclete."

When Jesus physically left from the earth He said He would send us another Paraclete, one called alongside to help, and we would do better with our lives than if He (Jesus) had remained physically with us.

So back in Enid, Oklahoma, in 1947, these things were happening in my spirit and understanding. I began to realize—

> I DON'T HAVE TO SEE JESUS CHRIST AS A PHYSICAL MAN. JESUS HAS FILLED ME WITH THE HOLY SPIRIT. I HAVE THE COMFORTER, THE DIVINE PARACLETE, THE ONE CALLED ALONGSIDE TO HELP. IT'S AS IF JESUS CHRIST IS WALKING BY ME IN THE FLESH . . . EXCEPT THAT HE IS NOW IN HIS INVISIBLE UN-LIMITED FORM. HE IS IN ME; THEREFORE, HE CAN DO THESE THINGS THROUGH ME.

This was the key that opened the lock. This was the beginning of my understanding of the baptism in the Holy Spirit and the prayer language of the Spirit and what it means to have the Holy Spirit working in our lives.

THE PRAYER LANGUAGE IS A LANGUAGE OF THE SPIRIT—NOT OF THE INTELLECT

Your spirit communicates directly with God—without the aid of your mind—through "other tongues". . . another language that you have never learned . . . a language given you by the Holy Spirit. Your spirit talks to God out of the depths of your inner being. Your spirit is now able to talk to God freely because the Holy Spirit has come in and by the fusion of your spirit with the Holy Spirit (much like your two hands joining together) the "tongues," or the prayer language of the Spirit, is produced.

You see, through the fall of man his mind has become blurred. He no longer could see God clearly. As someone has said, man's mind now acts as a censor and too often it censors out what God says to him.

A censor just lets certain things go by. For example, if a prisoner writes a letter, that letter is intercepted by a censor and read; and portions of it may be deleted, so that the person who receives the letter may or may not receive the entire letter as it was written. In the same way, when Jesus was on the earth talking to His disciples they listened to Him, but their minds censored out parts of what He said. Their minds intercepted lots of things that Jesus said, and did not let them get down into their spirit. Therefore, they did not understand what Jesus was saying.

But on the Day of Pentecost when Jesus baptized them in the Holy Spirit and the Spirit got down into their spirit, they were able to speak in another language . . . a tongue that their minds had not learned and did not understand. This new tongue could not be censored by the mind because the mind did not understand what the spirit was saying. So once again man could communicate directly with God from his spirit *and mind,* as Adam first did.

THE PRAYER LANGUAGE OF THE SPIRIT RESTORES
OUR ABILITY TO COMMUNICATE DIRECTLY WITH GOD

As mortals, we cannot look upon God. We are not at ease with God. We cannot talk freely to God. Somehow our understanding, our ability to grasp God, to communicate with Him, to understand life as God intended us to, has been blurred. It has been submerged. Something negative has happened to it.

Adam—the first man—had perfect communication with God. But he lost that full communication with God.

You see, God made man a spiritual being. God made man's spirit to be supreme over his mind and his body.

God didn't make man physical, He just gave him a body.

God didn't make man mental, He just gave him a mind.

GOD MADE MAN SPIRITUAL!

God put everything in the spirit that had to do with the life of God. And the spirit then was to use 'the mind and the body as instruments (1 Corinthians 6:19, 20). Through his spirit man would talk and walk with God and subdue the earth and have his LIFE as a WHOLE person.

God loved man and put him together as a perfect being. But the devil sought to separate man and disintegrate his total personality so that he would lose contact with God and would depend only on his powers of reason. That way the devil could get in and influence man's life. The devil knew if he ever got man to die spiritually, if he was successful in disintegrating the inner part of man then he could cause the spiritual likeness of God to disappear from the spirit of man. Then . . .

Man would be left with a mind and a body, with the ashes of his spirit scattered around him.

He would be like a pale ghost walking through the world . . . not knowing where he was going . . . not knowing how to talk with God . . . running into problems and not knowing how to solve them . . . getting into darkness and not knowing how to create light.

Man would find all kinds of knowledge but would have little wisdom to use it.

Certainly we see in the world that is operated by the mind of man much knowledge but very little of the wisdom of God. As a result, things are getting worse and worse.

Adam and Eve saw that the tree of knowledge of good and evil had to do with their intellect; it had to do with their minds. God had told them that they had the power to say yes, but He also said, "The day that you eat of the tree you will die . . . your spirit will die . . . the real part of you will disintegrate. It will be dead." (When the Apostle Paul talks about being "dead in trespasses and sins" (Ephesians 2:1), this is what he means.)

When Adam and Eve ate of the tree, the Bible says: "They knew . . ." THEY KNEW!

This is when the mind took ascendancy over the spirit. For the first time since God had created man out of nothing, the mind became boss. It was no longer a servant of the spirit of man. It now began to suppress the spirit, to put it down until it was like a ghost. It was without the life of God.

When Adam chose to eat of the tree of the knowledge of good and evil, he was saying to God, "I want to do what I want to do. I'm going to elevate my mind and make the pursuit of knowledge the main thing in my life" (Genesis 3).

The spirit of man died that day. His spirit was pushed down and his mind rose up and took charge. The mind became ascendant, or supreme, and from that moment on knowledge has been man's goal, his god.

But knowledge by itself is not an end. It cannot solve anything . . . it has to have something greater than it is . . . the wisdom of God. To have the wisdom of God you must be reawakened by the Holy Spirit and born again . . . until the spirit with which God made you, comes alive and you become a living soul again.

THE HOLY SPIRIT NOW LIVES WITH YOU!

When you are converted (saved, born again, accept Christ — these terms all mean the same thing) the Holy Spirit brings you to Christ. The Holy Spirit gives you a new birth. In the same way that the Holy Spirit conceived Jesus, you are born again. You are born the first time of the flesh of your parents but now you must be born the second time of the Holy Spirit. Why? Because that spirit of yours is not alive. Your spirit has to be born again — it has to come into existence a second time. Jesus said:

> Verily, verily, I say unto thee, Except a man be born again, he cannot see the kingdom of God (John 3:3).

How do we have this experience? The Bible says:

> *Repent, and be baptized every one of you in the name of Jesus Christ for the remission of sins, and ye shall receive the gift of the Holy Ghost* (Spirit) (Acts 2:38).

Repent. The word "repent" means "to change your mind." I want you to notice how this all goes back to the mind of man. What happened in the Garden of Eden back there was that man chose something, mentally. Man used his mind to choose knowledge. When God sent the Messiah, Christ, He was to bruise the head, or the mind, of the devil. So when the Bible tells us to repent, it literally means to change our MINDS.

God doesn't tell you to change your spirit because your spirit is dead. In order for God to get into your spirit you must open your mind and change it. HOW? By saying, "I am wrong." These are the three hardest words that you will ever say . . ."I am wrong." Repentance means "I am wrong," or "I have sinned."

Not only must you say, "I am wrong," as a first act to be born again, but you must also continue to say it the rest of your life. You must live in *a state of repentance* because you will be wrong again . . . and again . . . and again . . . and again! And so will I.

Repentance begins with the MIND. The Holy Spirit renews your mind!

> *Be not conformed to this world: but be ye transformed by the renewing of your mind* (Romans 12:2).

Jesus Christ became the Second Adam. His purpose was to liberate you and me, to bring us into a union with God . . . beginning with our spirit. Jesus came so that the mind which took dominance and supremacy over the spirit and the body and made knowledge its pursuit in life, could now resubmit itself to God. In this way, the spirit of man could become dominant and supreme again. Man could once again become a spiritual being.

He would be able to discern spiritually.

He would be able to understand spiritually.

He would be able to see that every problem he has begins in his spirit and every solution to that problem begins in his spirit.

Through the power of the Holy Spirit indwelling us we are discovering that no matter what the problem feels like, it originates in our spirit. It may seem to be a mental or physical or financial or marital or some other kind of problem, but it all begins in our spirit. But, thank God, that's where the answer also begins — in our spirit.

ONE OF THE WORKS OF THE HOLY SPIRIT IN YOUR LIFE IN THE NOW IS TO HELP YOU WITH THE THINGS YOU FACE AS A HUMAN BEING.

The Apostle Paul, who gave us most of the teaching that we have on the Holy Spirit, said:

> *Likewise the Spirit also helpeth our infirmities* (our weaknesses, our problems, our needs): *for we know not what we should pray for as we ought* (Romans 8:26).

(That is, we just don't know how to pray. Our mind, our intellect, doesn't have this power. The mind is not a creator. It is only an instrument of the spirit. The creative part of us is in our spirit.)

> *But the Spirit itself* (himself) *maketh intercession for us with groanings which cannot be uttered. And he that searcheth the hearts knoweth what is the mind of the Spirit, because he maketh intercession for the saints according to the will of God* (Romans 8:27).

When we reach the place that we just don't know how to pray . . . or the words to say . . . or even what to ask God for, we must not surrender. We must not give up and sit back and say, "It's hopeless." We must not say, "I can't do it." We must understand that within us is the Holy Spirit.

THE HOLY SPIRIT RESIDES DEEP DOWN INSIDE YOU

He is like a river of living water. And He's there flowing 24 hours of the day. Jesus said:

> *If any man thirst, let him come unto me, and drink. He that believeth on me, as the scripture hath said, out of his belly shall flow rivers of living water. (But this spake he of the Spirit, which they that believe on him should receive: for the Holy Ghost was not yet given; because that Jesus was not yet glorified)* (John 7:37-39).

Then Paul said, "He that searcheth the hearts knoweth what is the mind of the Spirit . . ." The Holy Spirit is a Person. As a Person, He talks. He has an intellect, and in the mind of the Holy Spirit is all knowledge. In the Holy Spirit's mind is the understanding of all languages. In the Holy Spirit's infinite mind is the ability to communicate with God. So the Holy Spirit searches our hearts and finds what it is that is troubling us.

THE HOLY SPIRIT'S GREATEST FUNCTION IS TO INTERCEDE FOR YOU THROUGH THE PRAYER LANGUAGE OF THE SPIRIT ACCORDING TO THE WILL OF GOD

He really wants to pray in your behalf and to enable you to *enter into His prayer for you.* The Holy Spirit is within you and He's down there searching your heart . . . searching out what the real problem is

. . . searching for that thing that you feel deep down inside on the "gut level" of life which Jesus called the belly, or the inner man.

    The Holy Spirit goes into the deepest level of your being . . .

        finding things that may have started when you were only 3, 6, or 10 years old . . .

        finding things that you were hung up on when you were in your teens . . .

        finding something way back in your marriage that hurt you . . .

        finding that problem that was so severe it looked like it would strangle you to death and crush you out of existence . . .

The thing is there and with all of your praying with your mind, your intellect, you've not been able to bring it up. You've not been able to locate that thing that is troubling you, and to pray according to the will of God for it. Now the mind of the Spirit finds that problem and gathers all that up and begins to pray, to intercede with God, according to the will of God for you.

    The Holy Spirit prays in your behalf according to God's will, in tongues—in words that your mind has not developed or created. Praying in the prayer language of the Spirit *first,* and then praying with *the understanding* also puts us at least partially on the level with Adam (1 Corinthians 14:14,15). Our spirit and mind are no longer strangers . . . they are brothers, they belong together. They are now one unit again. Now, through the power of the Holy Spirit, we can pray with the Spirit AND we can pray with the understanding. Now, we get on a level where we can communicate with God, where we lose our fear, where we can talk with Him and walk with Him in a different way than we ever have before. We can become truly creative. We can discover new knowledge combined with wisdom and understanding. We can come into a oneness with God and into a deeper love with one another. We can come into a renewing (or blossoming) of our minds by the Holy Spirit.

————◆————

THE PRAYER LANGUAGE OF THE SPIRIT . . . or TONGUES . . . may be the single hardest hurdle you will ever have to leap over. Because the battleground is your intellect. It wants to be supreme—it does not want to bow to the deepest longing of your heart or soul.

On the other hand, you may have already received this experience. If you have, that's great. Just keep on talking with God like this.

If you haven't—believe this: IT IS FOR YOU. And as you study this book along with your Bible, and pray, this experience may BURST upon you—or it might be like the gentle dawn breaking inside your soul. Whichever way it comes, remember this great gift of the Holy Spirit is given to help you. You can pray in your own language—sure.

But when you are so overcome with a problem that you just can't even formulate the words to express it to God, this is when the Holy Spirit—or "PARACLETE" (remember that word means "one called alongside to help") is there inside you to pray in the Spirit for you.

YOUR GOD-GIVEN KEY FOR TODAY

It will help you to say:

"I Can Communicate Directly With God . . . He Helps Me."

MONDAY

Key:
THE PRAYER LANGUAGE OF THE SPIRIT PUTS ME TOGETHER

or
How The Prayer Language Of The Spirit Will Enrich Your Life

The Holy Spirit was active throughout the Old Testament times. But when our Lord—the Second Adam—came, it seemed that only then was the Holy Spirit's personality fully revealed. And we are now faced with the glorious prospect that . . .

OUR ENTIRE PERSONALITY—SPIRIT, MIND, AND
BODY—CAN BE REINTEGRATED

What we have lost—the gift of language which originates in the spirit by which we can talk directly to God—can be restored. We can reach down into the inner recesses of our beings and with our spirit start using our speech organs and create a language which, according to Paul, is "unto God" (1 Corinthians 14:2). This language is "speaking in tongues" or *the prayer language of the Spirit.*

It's so difficult for our reason, our intellect, to understand that which is spiritual. In 1 Corinthians 2:14 we are told:

> *But the natural man receiveth not the things of the Spirit of God: for they are foolishness unto him: neither can he know them, because they are spiritually discerned.*

That is, one has to get down inside his spirit to understand the things of God. Now there is a difference between your spirit and your intellect, or mind. Even though they exist together, there are times they act almost independently of each other.

St. Paul said:

> *For if I pray in an unknown tongue, my spirit prayeth, but my understanding is unfruitful* (1 Corinthians 14:14).

I recall various times when I have held that verse before the Lord and tried to relate it to my own personal experience. Eventually, I was able to do so. I believe Paul is saying here that he actually is praying with his spirit, but his mind is not necessarily part of that prayer. That is, his mind is not *creating* the prayer. Paul even goes so far as to say that his mind doesn't even comprehend it at all. It is in an unfruitful or inactive state. It is as though his mind were an observer, but it's not comprehending the words or the sentences that the spirit is putting together. Because what is coming over the tongue, through the speech organs, is not originating in the intellect. It's coming from within, from the spirit. It is as though the mind has been suspended from its activity temporarily. For maybe 30 seconds or a minute, or even longer, it's standing there observing as the Spirit—which is within—takes over and uses the speech organs and is in direct communication with God.

This communication is as perfect as Adam and Eve could ever have spoken to God, in the will of God, when they were in their original perfect state. They had that marvelous gift of language with which they could talk to God.

This is not to say that if one doesn't pray in tongues he can't pray at all. We do pray with our minds. And we should. Many people have never prayed with *tongues*. And I'm the last one to say that they have not prayed, because many such people have had a marvelous prayer life. It remains to be seen what could happen to their prayer life if they went deeper into the Spirit and were able to understand that they could pray with their spirit independently of their minds.

As a matter of fact, Paul indicates in the very next verse:

> *What is it then? I will pray with the spirit, and I will pray with the understanding also: I will sing with the spirit, and I will sing with the understanding also* (1 Corinthians 14:15).

PAUL JOINS THE SPIRIT AND THE MIND

He indicates there is a separation of spirit and mind. Any person who would take time to think about it, knows Paul is accurately diagnosing the very key issue of life. Man has cultivated his intellect almost to the exclusion of his spiritual being. It's as though he doesn't have a soul.

Jesus asks us:

> *For what is a man profited, if he shall gain the whole world, and lose his own soul? or what shall a man give in exchange for his soul?* (Matthew 16:26).

Jesus was concerned about the problem of man's spiritual self being born again, being raised to newness of life, being redeemed and restored, being filled with the Holy Spirit . . . and living in the Spirit.

THE PRAYER LANGUAGE OF THE SPIRIT HELPS US TO
GIVE FULLER EXPRESSION OF OUR TOTAL SELVES

The ability to express ourselves to God both by the intellect and by our spirit—is exactly what God is trying to get us into. Because now we are going to give fuller expression of our total selves.

Your total self is seldom ever expressed. Even in your relationship with other people you scarcely ever reveal but a part of yourself. The seemingly most perfect marriage doesn't always have the fullest expression between the husband and wife. There is something about us that inhibits our opening up. Maybe it is because we are afraid of being betrayed. Or perhaps we have been betrayed before, we've been disappointed, and we've decided that we're not going to be hurt again.

I think our Lord is trying to say that we can pray *in the spirit* to God and never be disappointed. We never have to be afraid that God will not hear us. Or that God will not receive us. But we can talk to God for what He is . . . our Father. And He will talk back to us . . . as His children, as His son or His daughter. As co-heirs with His Son, Jesus Christ (Romans 8:17).

PRAYING IN THE SPIRIT IS PART OF
OUR SPIRITUAL ARMOR

In Ephesians 6, Paul speaks concerning our spiritual warfare:
> *Finally, my brethren, be strong in the Lord, and in the power of his might. Put on the whole armour of God, that ye may be able to stand against the wiles of the devil. For we wrestle not against flesh and blood, but against principalities, against powers, against the rulers of the darkness of this world, against spiritual wickedness in high places* (Ephesians 6: 10-12).

Notice that Paul says we are in a spiritual warfare. It is a warfare first with the devil, and then with the princes of the devil which could be translated demons—cohorts of the devil. You can't see the devil. You can't see these demons. They are fallen creatures. They are spiritual beings.

GOD WHO IS SPIRIT, AND THE DEVIL WHO IS SPIRIT,
AND THE HUMAN BEING WHO IS SPIRIT,
ARE LOCKED IN BATTLE

The battle is between God and the devil. It's not between you and me, or you and someone else. Back of every conflict that we face in life is not another human being . . . although a human being may be involved. Everything that comes against us from a destructive point of view originates in the devil. It originates in these evil spiritual forces.

So Paul is saying:

> "Because of this, you must be strong in the Lord. You must
> have the strength of God in you. And you must have the power
> of God in you. You must put on the armor of God that ye
> may be able to stand. Otherwise, you will not stand. You'll
> become discouraged and you will give up."

Paul likens the battle of life to a wrestling match. Have you ever
watched a wrestling match? Have you seen how the wrestlers grapple
with one another? How they turn and twist and lunge forward and
then draw back, trying to find the other's point of weakness? They
throw themselves to the mat or one picks up the other and throws him
as far as he can. Sometimes they get down on their knees and they
grapple with one another as if it were a matter of life and death. This
is the picture that Paul paints of our spiritual warfare with the devil.

It's a spiritual battle. Therefore, we need to take on the whole
armor of God. In Ephesians 6:13-18, Paul enumerates seven pieces of
that armor, all of which are terribly important:

> *Wherefore take unto you the whole armour of God, that ye*
> *may be able to withstand in the evil day, and having done all,*
> *to stand. Stand therefore, having*
>
> *(1) your loins girt about with truth,*
> *(2) and having on the breastplate of righteousness;*
> *(3) And your feet shod with the preparation of the gospel*
> *of peace;*
> *(4) Above all, taking the shield of faith, wherewith ye shall*
> *be able to quench all the fiery darts of the wicked.*
> *(5) And take the helmet of salvation,*
> *(6) and the sword of the Spirit, which is the word of God:*
> *(7) Praying always with all prayer and supplication in the*
> *Spirit . . .*

Here Paul likens the spiritual armor to the armor used by the
soldiers of that day. He speaks of the breastplate. This covers the entire
chest area so that an arrow could not penetrate and pierce the heart.
He mentioned also the shield of faith. This shield covered the entire
body. It was held on the arm and was used to ward off the arrows of
the enemy. By moving it around, the soldier could protect his entire
body. Paul called this the shield of faith. He says we are to be so full
of faith that we can repulse the attacks of Satan.

The seventh piece of armor Paul mentions is "praying always with
all prayer and supplication *in the Spirit.*"

Praying always. Thessalonians 5:17 says:

> *Pray without ceasing.*

How do we fight a spiritual warfare? We can't see the enemy. We
feel the enemy. We feel the attack of a human against us, either phy-

sically attacking us or mentally attacking us or lying to us or disappointing us. Or we are disappointing someone else. It works both ways.

How are we to fight this spiritual warfare? Paul says we are to pray without ceasing, and to pray always *in the Spirit*. The key words are "in the spirit . . ." We find these words repeated two other times:

> For he that speaketh in an unknown tongue speaketh not unto men, but unto God: for no man understandeth him; howbeit in the Spirit he speaketh mysteries (1 Corinthians 14:2. But ye, beloved, building up yourselves on your most holy faith, praying in the Holy Ghost (Spirit) (Jude 20).

There is something about the Spirit taking charge of the vocal chords, or the speech organs, and bringing up what is down inside us—bringing it up over our tongue to God in another language—that is most important in winning our spiritual battles.

THROUGH THE PRAYER LANGUAGE OF THE
SPIRIT WE CAN PRAY WITHOUT CEASING

Praying always and praying without ceasing. I used to wonder how in the world anyone could pray without ceasing. I thought if one prayed without ceasing, he'd never get anything else done. He'd just go around praying all the time. My idea of prayer then was that when you prayed you had to pray out loud. You had to pray with so many words. It didn't take me long to exhaust all the prayer words I knew. I was left dangling because I couldn't pray very long.

Not until the prayer language of the Spirit was released within me did I begin to understand what Jesus meant and what it means to pray without ceasing and to pray in the Spirit. For with the prayer language, it could just be coming up all the time. As a matter of fact, Jesus indicated this would happen:

> He that believeth on me, as the scripture hath said, out of his belly shall flow rivers of living water (John 7:38).

In other words, Jesus says here that the Holy Spirit would be like a river within us. Now think about a river for a moment. A river has to start somewhere. So the prayer language, this river of the Holy Spirit, has to start—and it starts within you.

Then a river has to flow. In the same way as you continually use the prayer language, it gets bigger and wider and deeper and stronger —that is, more natural and more useful.

A river enriches whatever it touches. That's why the most fertile land is down by the riverside. And as the prayer language is continuously used, it enriches every part of our lives. It's described in Jude 20 as "building up yourself . . . praying in the Holy Ghost." In 1 Corinthians 14:4 Paul says:

> He that speaketh in an unknown tongue edifieth himself . . .

When we pray in the prayer language of the Spirit we build up our inner man. We get stronger and deeper and the flow increases. We are enriching our own life.

THROUGH THE PRAYER LANGUAGE OF
THE SPIRIT, GOD RESPONDS TO US

The ultimate purpose of the prayer language of the Spirit is that it goes to God. Then God has the prayer that originates in our spirit and that is carried to Him by the power of the Holy Spirit. It's a prayer that was prayed in the will of God. It's a prayer that was prayed without the inhibitions of the intellect. The mind was in a completely unfruitful state. It's a prayer that originates in our spirit BY THE HOLY SPIRIT.

This is why God responds . . . always!!

How does God respond? How does this take place? Paul makes it clear:

> *Let him that speaketh in an unknown tongue pray that he may interpret* (1 Corinthians 14:13).

After you pray in tongues . . . or in the spirit . . . just stop a moment and ask God to give you the interpretation . . . to speak back in your own understanding. Then begin praying again in English or your own language. For in the process of praying in the spirit, the Holy Spirit has enriched your mind and you will find God's response comes back in the mind. I have discovered that what I have said with my spirit now becomes what I say with my intellect—and so I am able to pray with the understanding.

When I pray I start in my spirit, or in tongues (the prayer language of the Spirit), then I immediately go to my own tongue, my own language. I pray back and forth in tongues and then with my understanding until it's like they're one. It puts me together again. It reintegrates my entire personality . . . and yours.

THE PRAYER LANGUAGE OF THE SPIRIT BRINGS US CLOSER TO
THE WHOLE MAN GOD CREATED US TO BE

The final point is this. I feel the nearness to being a whole man—to the extent that I can think more properly, I can make decisions more decisively and wisely, I can reach the highest degree of what I'm to be on this earth—when I pray with the spirit AND with the understanding also. Through this experience I really am in my journey with Jesus in discipleship. From the point I started as a born-again Christian —just like the river starts as a little spring coming up out of the earth— the Holy Spirit began flowing. As I follow on after Christ I get stronger and deeper. My life is enriched constantly. Ultimately, I will end in God.

There are two points to that.

One, is that the prayer language of the Spirit ends up in God.

Two, my life—my human life—will ultimately come to an end. But my real life ends up in God when my body dies. My body will be resurrected when our Lord returns. I will become as man once was when God first made him . . . perfect and immortal and eternal.

So I feel the greatest degree of wholeness, of being a whole person, when my prayer life is right, when I am able *to pray with my spirit and with my understanding.* I then am conscious of my inner gifts and capabilities in a greater way. I have a much deeper assurance of life. I seem to develop a "knowing" of what I am to do. In spite of the fact that I still make mistakes, there's always that upward moving of my life overcoming those mistakes, not letting them destroy me. My movement is upward.

—————◆———◆—————

I have shared with you, as honestly as I know how, the value of the prayer language of the Spirit as it fits into the total Christian life.

Again I say, as I've said many times, this gift is not anything in itself. Just like your hand apart from your arm is nothing. Your hand is valuable only when it's properly attached to your arm and your body and in proper use.

When properly used, as a natural part of the expression of your deeper self to God, THE PRAYER LANGUAGE OF THE SPIRIT is so valuable and helpful that I cannot overemphasize its importance.

TO UNDERSTAND THE TRUE IMPORTANCE OF THE PRAYER LANGUAGE OF THE SPIRIT, KNOW THIS: IT IS TO BE IMMEDIATELY FOLLOWED BY YOUR PRAYER WITH YOUR UNDERSTANDING.

PRAYING WITH YOUR SPIRIT AND WITH YOUR UNDERSTANDING PUTS YOU TOGETHER AGAIN!

This is the essence of Paul's teaching and his own personal prayer life— and it certainly is mine:

YOUR GOD-GIVEN KEY FOR TODAY

"The Prayer Language Of The Spirit Puts Me Together."

TUESDAY
Key:
THROUGH THE HOLY SPIRIT
I OPEN UP TO JESUS

or
How I Personally Received The Baptism In The Holy Spirit
And The Prayer Language Of The Spirit

When I was a child I remember times when my parents would be having family prayer with us children and my mother would suddenly use the prayer language of the Spirit. I can even recall some of the strange words she used during those brief moments, and how a glow would come on her countenance, and sometimes a cry of joy that would make us know something wondrous was happening within her.

My father used the prayer language of the Spirit, too. He talked a lot about the Holy Spirit as a Person and urged people to receive the gift of the Holy Spirit. But it was my mother who would help them receive and start using the prayer language of the Spirit.

I am convinced in my talks with her over the last years of her life that all my mother knew about the prayer language of the Spirit was that it gave a tremendous inner lift—it let something up and out over the tongue and always left the Christian feeling better, especially more confident, and feeling closer to God.

As my mother helped seekers—and I observed this many times while growing up—she would not stop praying with them until they ceased speaking momentarily in their own language and started speaking in a language they had never learned. They too would do what I had seen my mother do, have a glow on their countenance, say some strange-sounding words, and look like they were filled with a satisfaction that was worth more to them than all the money in the world.

However, there was a disquieting thing about this, at least to my childish mind. It took me a long time to begin to feel I understood, at least partially, why it happened as it did. It seemed such a physical struggle for many of those people to receive or enter into this ability to speak the new words, new in the sense they had not learned them by their minds.

Sometimes they would fall to the floor and turn and twist in what appeared to be agony. Some would shake rather violently, often pleading or begging God to give them the gift of the Holy Spirit. Others would receive the baptism in the Holy Spirit very gently and without any physical gyrations. Still others would become boisterous and loud—but in every case, they all ended up joyous.

The end result was very impressive.

I remember I used to think, if you have to go through all that seeking and apparently some form of suffering just to feel better inside, I don't believe I'm interested. But my parents were interested and urged others to be. They never urged it on us children, but it was clear they believed it was there for us.

As a teen-ager I began to seek this gift. Many times I prayed hard to receive the baptism in the Holy Spirit and to have this new language that made one feel so good and so close to God, but it just about wore me out.

Then one night I dreamed I spoke in this new language. It was all so easy . . . so natural. The words were clear, not to my intellectual understanding but to my inner self. In the dream, I simply started talking to God and in place of words I had learned there were words I hadn't learned. When I awakened it was an experience so real it was as though I had actually done it, rather than dreamed it.

I told my parents and they encouraged me to stay open to God.

Well, two or three days later it happened again, only this time it was not a dream. I was sitting and meditating on God and I felt these words coming up. They seemed to be coming up from the deepest levels of my being. I simply opened my mouth and spoke them. Only a few words. The moment I spoke them I felt good, a warm glow inside. Immediately I wanted to speak them again, and I did. Again—that good, warm feeling inside.

From that moment on, I knew I had received the baptism in the Holy Spirit. I immediately thought back to the night I was converted and remembered how this same sensation of joy swelled up from my inner self. Had I known then, or had someone instructed me from the Scriptures, I realized I could have spoken to God in the words of this new language at my conversion. But no one told me, not even my beloved parents who used the prayer language of the Spirit themselves.

The reason?

They had the gift of the Spirit but didn't know it was subject to the will and could be used as needed simply by doing what St. Paul said he did:

> I will pray with the spirit, and I will pray with the understanding also (1 Corinthians 14:15).

If they had known the Greek word for "I will," as used here by St. Paul, they would have known it means, "I am determined or I determined." Paul was DETERMINED by *an act of his will* to pray "with the spirit . . . and . . . with his understanding also." I thought it was a spiritual thing happening inside me and over my tongue as I spoke the words of this new language. I thought it was to make me feel good and warm and electric inside. *That something meaningful was happening to my intellect and understanding as a result of speaking this new language, never occurred to me, nor did anybody instruct me.*

Clearly this experience was in the Bible. St. Paul talked about a language of prayer and praise (1 Corinthians 14). He said it was talking to God . . . that when you do it you are speaking with both your spirit and the Holy Spirit. He said when you use the new language you can interpret it back to yourself, and not only will it edify you, but it will have a wholesome effect on your *understanding.*

I know all those things now. When I pray with the spirit or praise God with the spirit, I ALWAYS PAUSE AND ASK GOD FOR THE INTERPRETATION. I feel I receive the interpretation almost every time. For I notice after using the prayer language of the Spirit if I pause and ask God for the interpretation, all I have to do to get it is to start praying in my own language. What usually happens is I receive an almost uncanny awareness in my mind, an opening up of my understanding, and a much greater ease to pray in English. I find I'm saying words in my own tongue that *feel* exactly like what I *felt* when I was praying with the spirit. I am convinced this is what is happening. The results prove it to me.

Not that the problem always disappears. Or the need. Often it is still there, still pressing me. But I feel differently about it. Or I see it in a different light. My perspective is now more like God's than my own, or of someone else.

Also, I feel loosened up. I'm bolder, more positive.

And *in time* I get more knowledge, more wisdom. It's like my brain works better, or like I'm being handed inside information. Sometimes it's like my comprehension of the problem gets so sharp I look around to see if Jesus has walked up and taken over.

My *understanding* may not clear up *all* the way, for St. Paul reminds us that . . .

"We see through a glass, darkly" (1 Corinthians 13:12).

The prayer language of the Spirit is prayer from within you, from the living Spirit of Christ who lives in you. It is G-O-D as the Holy Spirit doing what needs to be done to help you pray, to talk to Him as naturally as you breathe, and knowing that you are getting through.

———◆———

Now I have related to you how I experienced the baptism in the Holy Spirit. *By all means, don't make this the norm or the pattern for you or anyone else to receive this experience.* You may or may not receive it in this way. But *I BELIEVE GOD, THE HOLY SPIRIT, ACCOMMODATES HIMSELF TO WORK IN YOU IN A WAY THAT WILL JUST SUIT YOU.*

YOUR GOD-GIVEN KEY FOR TODAY

So you can truly say:

"Through The Holy Spirit I Open Up To Jesus."

WEDNESDAY

**Key:
THROUGH THE PRAYER LANGUAGE
OF THE SPIRIT I CAN KNOW GOD'S
BEST WAY FOR ME**

or

A Personal Example Of How I Prayed In The Prayer Language Of The Spirit And Found The Understanding And Courage To Obey God And Build Oral Roberts University

When I began to build Oral Roberts University back in the early '60s I was confronted with two or three limitations: One, my own inability. I didn't know how to build it but God told me to build it. Now how are you going to do something that God tells you to do when you don't know HOW?

Secondly, God told me to build the University out of the same ingredient He used when He made the world—and He made it out of NOTHING. So He told me to build Him a university and to build it out of nothing. This may sound funny to you. But believe me, it wasn't funny to me.

Just after I was healed and converted, at the age of 17, God said to me:

> **"Some day you are to build Me a university.**
> **You are to build it on My authority**
> **and on the Holy Spirit."**

At age 17, I didn't even know the meaning of those words. Me! Oral Roberts, who never finished his senior year in college, was to build God a university—on His authority and on the Holy Spirit.

So in 1947 God thrust me into a healing ministry that spread all over the world. He gave me a concern for people, a feeling for them. Then in the early '60s God told me the time had come to build the University. "How do I build a university?" I asked. "I'm in the healing ministry. My ministry is even put down by the educators. I'm at the lowest rung on the ladder. I have kept up my studies. I finished three years but I never graduated. And now I'm going to build a university and I don't even know what one really is. I'm just a reasonably intelligent man and I have a gift of God in my life to win souls, to pray for the healing of sick humanity, and that's all I have."

But God said, "Your time has come. Build Me a university. Build it on My authority and on the Holy Spirit."

Nobody understood me when I said I was to do this and nobody believed I could do it.

In my heart, God was saying:

"Build Me a university and build it on the authority of God and
on the Holy Spirit."

My heart was saying:

"Yes, yes."

And my mind was saying:

"No, no."

Now have you ever had this experience of your heart saying to God,
"Yes, yes" — but your mind saying, "No, no"?

You see, we had no land, no campus, no building, no students, no
faculty, no money, and a man who felt very unqualified . . . and he's
going to build a university!! No wonder the skeptics had a field day. Even
my own intellect was saying, "You dumb-dumb!!"

But thank God for the baptism in the Holy Spirit and the prayer
language of the Spirit. By this time I had learned — like Paul — to pray with
my spirit and to pray with my understanding also (1 Corinthians
14:14,15). I would first pray in tongues, then I would pause and interpret back to my mind, or with my understanding.

One day I was walking across a piece of pasture land at the edge of
Tulsa which hopefully would some day be the campus of Oral Roberts
University. I was praying with my understanding — that is, in my own
language, and getting nowhere. My mind was saying:

"NO! NO! NO! NO! NO! . . . YOU CAN'T DO THIS!!!"

Then I shifted — by my will — and began to pray in tongues and my
heart began saying:

"YES! YES! YES! YES! YES!"

"You can!"

"You will!"

"You can!"

"You will!"

Then this *knowing* was transferred to my understanding. It came
out of my belly — my inner man — it came up like a river. It came up
into my mind AND I SAW IT. My mind began to blossom, to sharpen,
to come alive to what God was saying to me.

All at once — believe me, friend, when I say this — I understood
enough to build a university. I didn't understand all the details but I
understood the basics. I saw that this healing ministry had been born
for a purpose . . . including praying for people's bodies and souls . . .
but much more . . . it was a ministry to the TOTALITY OF MAN'S
NEEDS.

I saw that God could reintegrate the total personality of man.

I saw that we would create a higher education for your sons and
daughters and mine through which they would be educated in the

spirit, in the mind, and in the body. They would get a TOTAL EDUCA-
TION—for the whole man.

I SAW IT!

I KNEW IT!

Today Oral Roberts University is a reality and growing all the time,
including its graduate schools, and fully accredited.

And the dream for it has only begun. Schools of medicine, dentis-
try, and law are on the drawing boards to open by 1978.

These schools with the undergraduate school, the school of business and the school of theology, will round out the original dream God
gave me for the University.

It is all a wonder to me: its 500-acre campus, its 18 major buildings, its carefully selected students from all 50 states and 40 countries,
its highly qualified faculty filled with the Holy Spirit, its continual cross-
fertilization of all its dimensions—both in the undergraduate and
graduate dimensions—above all, the Holy Spirit working His will and
way with us.

The wonder of ORU goes far beyond me as a man—or any other—
it is at the heart of God's call to take His healing power to this generation and those to come.

"Raise up your students to hear My voice," He said to me, "to go
where My light is dim, My voice is not heard, My power is unknown,
even to the uttermost bounds of the earth. Their work will exceed
yours and in this I am well pleased."

With my life already God's property, it may seem strange that the
prayer language of the Spirit coming to new life in me in the founding
days of ORU could have that much effect upon my spirit and my understanding, but the results of ORU speak for themselves. I thank Him
from the bottom of my heart. I continue daily to pray with both the
spirit and the understanding, undergirded by the power of the Spirit in
my life, and I continue to expect many miracles.

———◆—◆———

It's not likely God will call you to build a university. But God does have
a will and a way and a purpose for everyone's life. And when you pray
in the prayer language of the Spirit, you can be one hundred percent
sure that . . .

YOUR GOD-GIVEN KEY FOR TODAY

**"Through The Prayer Language Of The
Spirit I Can Know God's Best Way For Me."**

THURSDAY
Key:
LORD, I RECEIVE
YOUR HOLY SPIRIT NOW!

or

How You Can Receive The Baptism In The Holy Spirit And Your Prayer Language

People often say to me, "Well, when God is ready He can give me the Holy Spirit."

My reply is, "The baptism in the Holy Spirit has to be RECEIVED."

Anything received involves action on *your* part. Receiving is something YOU do. I can offer you a gift, but in order for it to be yours you have to receive it . . . you have to reach out and take it.

Let's consider the word "receive." John 1:12 says:

> But as many as received him, to them gave he power to become the sons of God, even to them that believe on his name.

When you believe on Christ you receive power. The Greek word for power used here means "legal right," or the legal right to become a child of God.

Now read Acts 1:8 and notice that Christ is talking about RECEIVING in a deeper dimension of power. He says:

> But ye shall receive power, after that the Holy Ghost is come upon you: and ye shall be witnesses unto me both in Jerusalem, and in all Judaea, and in Samaria, and unto the uttermost part of the earth.

The Greek word used here for power is "dunamis" and in our language it means "the explosive power of dynamite." This is the kind of power that Jesus said we would receive when we receive the gift of the Holy Spirit.

RECEIVING IS AN ACT—THERE IS SOMETHING YOU MUST DO
IN ORDER TO RECEIVE THE BAPTISM IN THE HOLY SPIRIT
AND THE PRAYER LANGUAGE OF THE SPIRIT

I think it is natural to feel that such a high experience as receiving the gift of the baptism in the Holy Spirit would be rather complex. I also think it is a natural reaction to think, who am I that God would give me this gift?

It's my own deep conviction that Jesus is absolutely right when He said that if you thirst (that is, if you come to Him; and if you believe on Him) out of your belly (your inner man) will flow rivers of living water, which is the Holy Spirit. (See John 7:37-39.)

It's my conviction that when you believe on our Lord, the Holy Spirit—the Person of the Holy Spirit—is there. He is *in* you.

Now there is also a sense in which this indwelling Christ will suffuse you, or *baptize* you. He will just suffuse you in the Spirit, and the Spirit will flow up. But the flowing is from within you.

I've often said if you can just shut your mind down for a few moments and open your mouth, you will release the Holy Spirit within you. If you could pray with someone who prays in the Spirit, and just sort of start, then the Holy Spirit will take you right into your own prayer language. I've never seen this fail.

What I'm saying is very simple so I hope you don't stumble over it. Yet, at the same time, I would say this is not the only way you can receive, because you can't box God in.

In the New Testament we find that people received this gift in different ways. In Samaria the people received the laying on of hands before they received the gift of the Spirit (Acts 8). At Pentecost the one hundred and twenty were sitting and praying (Acts 2). At the house of Cornelius, in Acts 10, they received while Peter was preaching.

It's apparent that the Holy Spirit is so near you that there is simply a receiving to do.

A RECEIVING

For example, if I were to give you a Bible, you would have to reach out and actually take it in your hand before it would be yours. Peter told the crowd on the day of Pentecost:

> *Repent, and be baptized every one of you in the name of Jesus Christ for the remission of sins, and ye shall receive the gift of the Holy Ghost* (Acts 2:38).

The *receiving* is so important.

I have dealt with hundreds and hundreds of people and I've never seen it fail. All a person has to do is to open up, because the Holy Spirit already dwells *in* the Christian. He is there! *If a person will let the Holy Spirit have his tongue, just like he lets the mind have his tongue, he can receive.* Just like your mind takes your tongue to speak through it, let your spirit take your tongue and through the power of the Holy Spirit speak through it.

The tongues are in the spirit, not in the mind. The tongues of the Holy Spirit are in your spirit by the Holy Spirit. They're there, so your mind has to stop and let your spirit take control of your tongue. The Spirit takes authority over your tongue and uses it as an instrument.

All right, now our spirit has to do that. In order to speak in tongues, my spirit has to take my tongue and speak through it without the aid of my mind. But that's not impossible because the Holy Spirit is there within me.

The prayer language is a natural part of the infilling of the Holy Spirit. It's a *natural part!* Remember that Christ said, "He that believeth on me . . . out of his belly (innermost being) shall flow rivers of living water . . ."

Have you ever felt the Spirit of God coming up within you?

I've never talked to a Christian yet who said that it had not happened to him. I don't mean that he used the language that I'm using because each one of us says it in his own way. But each of us is conscious of something coming up inside, something good. We who understand it—at least who understand it to some extent—know it is the Spirit of God like rivers flooding up. And in that river is the prayer language of the Holy Spirit. This is the Holy Spirit coming up, trying to speak through you, but . . . YOU HAVE TO OPEN YOUR MOUTH.

God is not going to pump it into you and *make* you speak in tongues. Therefore, you have no right to say, "When God is ready, I'm ready," because you are 2,000 years late. In order for this baptism in the Holy Spirit to be released within you, you have to stop your own speech momentarily and open your mouth and start to speak . . .

AS THE SPIRIT GIVES YOU UTTERANCE

The Holy Spirit gives us utterance; He gives His own language. And what is that language?

First of all, you don't understand.

Then what good is it? you might ask.

The good of it is that it gets beyond your understanding, down where your spirit is, where the deepest part of you lives. Through that language coming out, you are saying what you wish you could say through your mind but you don't know how. The end result is that you edify yourself.

He that speaketh in an unknown tongue, edifieth himself (1 Corinthians 14:4).

It's a very personal subjective experience. It is for prayer in your own personal life. The prayer language—speaking in tongues—comes through the baptism in the Holy Spirit. As far as I'm concerned—and as I understand the Bible—this experience is for everyone.

Notice I want to point out the variety of methods that God uses. You cannot simply say, "This is the way God does it and there is no other way." God uses many methods.

I keep saying to people, "Quit worrying about HOW, just do. Just come into the experience." We're not worrying about how this denomination emphasizes it, or that denomination emphasizes it, or does not emphasize it. We are concerned about individuals receiving the gift of the Holy Spirit. God will direct you. God will lead you.

First of all, you must believe in the Lord Jesus Christ, repent of your sins, and from that moment on you can receive the gift of the Holy Spirit. The very moment that you accept Jesus Christ is the best time to receive. There's no doubt about that. But if you don't have the knowledge, if you don't stop talking in your own tongue for a moment and open your mouth, it probably will not happen.

You know, that's a real tragedy. How willing we are to open our mouths on other good things and yet we keep it shut when it comes to speaking in the Spirit and using the prayer language. Is it because we are frightened that if we relinquish the intellect for a moment and get down here into the real us, the real spirit of ourselves, that something bad will happen to us? Is it that we're afraid the stored up language in the inner man is something that we should never express to God? Or is the real reason just simply a lack of proper teaching?

People always ask me, "Why haven't we been taught this?"

Well, I wish I could answer that. I wish they could have been taught earlier but they have not been. I wish I had been taught it earlier.

When you accept Christ you receive the Holy Spirit and you can very scripturally and honestly say, "Yes, I'm a Christian. I have the Holy Spirit." You do have the Holy Spirit but you may not have the dimension of the baptism in the Holy Spirit that our Lord is talking about and that is talked about in the book of Acts . . . this experience by which you can open up the inner man and the Spirit gives you utterance and prayer and praise that comes out of your inner man.

As you exercise your *will,* using common sense and courtesy, you will find that you can pray "in the Spirit" as often each day as you need to, and then you can pray much more satisfyingly with your "understanding." Literally, you can pray without ceasing since your spirit and your intellect are one again and are in a constant state of response to God.

While it is not a cure-all, I can tell you personally that the baptism in the Holy Spirit is one of the most soul-satisfying experiences I have ever known. Until you receive it, you will not be able to fully understand what I am saying. Yet the moment you receive the experience you will understand what I am talking about.

You will edify yourself.

You will strengthen yourself in the inner man.

You will empty out many of the things in your inner man which, through the intellect, are not being emptied out.

You will feel a freedom within . . . and you will find a blossoming of your intellect.

I feel my own need of it more and more as I face problems with myself and with others. It is a gift of God I would not want to be without — ever!

In faith say this, and ask God to help you yield to the Holy Spirit.

YOUR GOD-GIVEN KEY FOR TODAY
"Lord, I Receive Your Holy Spirit Now!"

FRIDAY

Key:
THROUGH THE HOLY SPIRIT I CAN PRAY AS I OUGHT!

or

How The Prayer Language Of The Spirit Gave Me Insight When I Dealt With A Woman Whose Marriage Was About To End In Divorce

I dealt with a couple of women some time ago in New York whom my wife and I have known for a long time. They were staying in the same hotel and happened to see me in the lobby. They asked if they could say a word to me and one of them, the mother of six children and wife of quite an important businessman for 18 years, was almost the picture of death. I said to her, calling her by her first name, "What's wrong?"

And she said, "My husband and I are about to get a divorce."

And I said, "Oh, no! Oh, no!"

One reason I said it like that was because about six or seven years ago they were converted in one of the great evangelistic meetings in this country. They gave their testimony on national television of how they were brought back together in a beautiful relationship. The love that they had had was restored. But now—maybe in the past two years—deterioration had set in. Here were two born-again people, two Christian people with six children, who now had come to the point that they could not endure each other. Never mind what the Bible teaches about marriage—they just simply couldn't endure each other.

She indicated that she had walked out and told her husband that he could go . . . he knew where. She said, "I'm terribly ashamed of what I said, but it's the way I felt. What shall I do?"

I said, "Have you tried prayer?"

She said, "Yes. But I don't know what to pray for as I ought."

She had inadvertently quoted a Scripture in the Bible so I said, "Do you know where that verse is?"

She said, "I think so."

But she didn't quite know so I said, "It's Romans 8:26,27."

> *Likewise the Spirit also helpeth our infirmities: for we know not what we should pray for as we ought: but the Spirit itself maketh intercession for us with groanings which cannot be uttered. And he that searcheth the hearts knoweth what is the mind of the Spirit, because he maketh intercession for the saints according to the will of God.*

I said, "What happened is that you have not gone on into the Holy Spirit so that you could respond to life first through your spirit (I knew they were charismatic Christians). You are responding through your intellect. *You are mad in your mind.*"

She said, "I sure am."

(This was not a funny scene; this was terribly serious.) I said, "How about deep down inside you?"

She said, "I have to admit I still love him."

I said, "You love him in your heart but up here in your mind you can't stand him. I want to share with you some of the things I've been sharing in the Holy Spirit course at ORU about the way God made you. God made you a spiritual being. He made you a spirit. You have a mind to use and you have a body to use, but you are neither mind nor body. You are a spirit and you have to get back in your spirit."

"Well, what about him—my husband?"

I said, "The same is true of him. It's not impossible. It's not hopeless, but let's start with you . . . let's have a prayer together now."

She said, "Right here in this hotel?"

I said, "It's not the place, it's the attitude that's important."

"Oh," she said, "not here!"

"Well," I said, "How serious is the problem?"

She said, "So serious that I think when I get there, I'll have no home."

Then she said, "Well, do say a prayer for us." So the three of us took hands and prayed a little prayer together. Then she said, "I've never really understood praying in the Spirit."

We were surrounded now by quite a number of people, not listening to us but milling about. I said, "All right, I don't do this for exhibition, but because you need help I will pray in the Spirit very quietly and you listen. Then I'll pray in my own understanding." And I did. As I prayed in the prayer language of the Spirit the Holy Spirit spoke back to me what their real problem was, and so as I prayed in my own tongue, or understanding, I talked about the real problem of their marriage.

When I finished she said, "How did you know? I didn't tell you."

I said, "You've demonstrated the point. I did not know. Only the Holy Spirit knows. His communication is with us first of all in our spirit."

We laid the problem bare and she said, "For the first time I have some hope that I can go home and save my marriage."

━━━◆━◆━━━

YOU *CAN* PRAY AS YOU OUGHT!

This is the real practicality of the Holy Spirit in our lives. I tell you with all my heart . . .

Be filled with His Spirit,
        learn to pray in the prayer language, but don't stop there.

DON'T STOP THERE.

Go on into your intellect and pray now with understanding. You can pray in English with understanding. Instead of saying, "I don't know what to pray for as I ought," know that you can pray for the things as you should. You *can* pray as you ought. Know that you can get into a prayer that will lead you either to a solution of your problem, or give you an ability to live victoriously no matter what the outcome is.

So praying as you "ought" means being guided by the Holy Spirit to find the key to the problem. This is why you need to burn this truth into your very soul:

YOUR GOD-GIVEN KEY FOR TODAY

"Through The Holy Spirit

I Can Pray As I Ought."

SATURDAY

**Key:
THE HOLY SPIRIT IS GIVING ME
A NEW POWER FOR LIVING**

or

Evelyn And I Discuss Questions Frequently Asked About The Holy Spirit . . . And Speaking In Tongues

(Note: For several semesters I have been teaching a course on *The Holy Spirit In The NOW* at Oral Roberts University. This is the chair of the Holy Spirit established by J. Arthur Rank, better known as Lord Rank of London, whose estate funded the chair. Often at the close of my lecture I ask Evelyn to join me in a discussion. These questions and answers were taken from some of those discussions.)

EVELYN: I have often heard you say that according to John 7:37-39 and Acts 2:38, when a person repents of his sins and believes on Jesus that he receives the gift of the Holy Spirit. Is this the same as the baptism in the Holy Spirit?

ORAL: When you accept Christ as your personal Lord and Savior, of course you receive the Holy Spirit, for without the Holy Spirit himself you are none of His. But there is a baptism in which you are submerged in the Holy Spirit. It's an extra dimension. Jesus referred to it as the rivers of the Holy Spirit flowing up out of your belly—your innermost being (John 7:38,39). Of course the tongues, the new language of prayer and praise, are in that river as it flows up. They are in the baptism, the immersion of you, in the Holy Spirit.

EVELYN: What is the purpose of the baptism in the Holy Spirit?

ORAL: Before I answer this question I want to give some background. The Bible says that God made man in His image. That is, we are made in the likeness of God. God is not speaking of a physical shape. He was talking about His spiritual and moral likeness. God is pure, which is the way He made Adam and Eve. God is Love; God is Truth. That's how He made us. But by man's rejection of God and by our hurting one another, too often with malice, we have thrust God out of our lives. That is why we have to be born again by the Holy Spirit. God is trying to restore His moral and spiritual likeness, His truth, His life, His values to us, inside.

EVELYN: Does this mean, then, that our spirit inside will be remade in the image of God?

ORAL: When God saves us, we are made a new creation (2 Corinthians 5:17). This is the work of the Holy Spirit. But the baptism in the Holy Spirit has a different purpose altogether. Its purpose is *communication with God*. It is to open up the heart, the inner man, which is all too often closed up by hurts, lack of understanding, and our own intellect. Also we don't always know how to pray. The baptism in the Holy Spirit gives a person a new prayer language so he can communicate directly with God. He can edify or build himself up inside spiritually. His intellect blossoms and he can understand God better, also his own purpose in life better.

EVELYN: Often when I mention the baptism in the Holy Spirit and speaking in tongues people say, "But how can I reconcile 1 Corinthians 13:8-10 and speaking in tongues?"

ORAL: This is one of the most serious questions I have ever been asked. In 1 Corinthians 13 (the love chapter), verse 8, Paul said:

> Charity (love) *never faileth: but whether there be prophecies, they shall fail; whether there be tongues, they shall cease; whether there be knowledge, it shall vanish away. For we know in part, and we prophesy in part. But when that which is perfect is come, then that which is in part shall be done away.*

So the real question is, *have tongues ceased?* To be absolutely objective and take it like the Bible says, then we have to say no. If you say tongues have ceased, then objectively and honestly you have to say that prophecy has ceased, also all knowledge—and we know these have not ceased.

First, Paul said, "For we know in part." That is why we now pray in tongues. We don't know fully how to pray. We only know partly how to prophesy and we only know part of knowledge. Not even all of us compositely have all knowledge.

"But," Paul continues, "when that which is perfect is come, then that which is in part shall be done away." When our Lord comes—and that is what I think this means—He is the Truth, He is the Light, He is all wisdom, He is all knowledge. We will be face-to-face with Him. We will not need to speak in tongues.

EVELYN: Would you say that the Holy Spirit now illuminates our minds, but when Jesus comes we won't need to speak in tongues to get our minds illuminated?

ORAL: Yes, because He will be here face-to-face with us. For example, if Jesus Christ were sitting in your chair, do you think I would speak in tongues to Him?

EVELYN: No, you wouldn't need to. So, in other words, the Holy Spirit is to help us get through to Him while we are on this earth.

ORAL: Yes, this earth! This life! Before our Lord returns to this earth and before we get to heaven. The baptism in the Holy Spirit is for the NOW.

EVELYN: So many times people ask me, "Is speaking in tongues an evidence that you have the Holy Spirit?"

ORAL: This is a question a lot of people ask and they ask it honestly. They have a right to ask it, but I think it's the wrong *way* to ask the question. When you ask, "Is speaking in tongues an evidence that you have the baptism in the Holy Spirit?" you are limiting the Holy Spirit. So much so, if you are not careful, when you receive this experience you may only get tongues and not much to go with it. And that's a disaster. That's what turns a lot of people off, including me.

EVELYN: All right now, let's have a Scripture for what you are saying.

ORAL: Well, there is no Scripture that says tongues is the evidence.

EVELYN: But there is one in Acts that says what will happen to you when you receive the Holy Spirit.

ORAL: That's Acts 1:8, "Ye shall receive *power*, after that the Holy Ghost (Spirit) is come upon you." This actually means this experience puts you into the area of *the Holy Spirit's ministries and powers and gifts of the Holy Spirit.* There you have access constantly to them. This includes tongues or the prayer language of the Spirit which releases your inner self, which helps you pray with your understanding. To isolate tongues and to build everything around tongues is like taking a piece of your clothing and saying that little piece of clothing is evidence that you are dressed.

EVELYN: I'm glad you said that because I wanted to hear you say what else comes with the Holy Spirit besides the prayer language, because there is so much more.

ORAL: Speaking in tongues is not so much the evidence that you have something as it is the revelation of the Spirit's power within you. The beauty of the prayer language is that it opens up the person. It edifies him. That is, it releases the inner man and gives a warmth, a therapeutic or healing influence inside him. It's a tremendous help in dealing with alienation, loneliness, a feeling of isolation, a feeling of helplessness. When one prays in the Spirit, it opens him up. But it also opens up his understanding, or what we call the mind-intellect. And it puts him more into the circle where the other ministries and gifts of the Holy Spirit may operate through him.

I think the term "evidence" came about near the turn of the century, when the Holy Spirit baptism was rejected. When people received it they often were kicked out of their churches. So they had to form a new movement or denomination. Speaking in tongues became more or less THE distinguishing characteristic of their spiritual evidence. Although it was genuine and real, it should not have been put up so high that it was all people could hear or see. These people didn't mean it that way, don't misunderstand me. My parents became a part of that group and they didn't mean it the way people interpreted it. However, in their own way they contributed to it by not knowing a better phrase to use. But I think that we should grow. We should be better able to put tongues in proper perspective and find their most practical and expectative use. First, we have those people who suffered, people like my parents who paid the price to hold on to this experience. They never gave it up, even with the abuses of it. They held on to it, but now we have more light on the baptism in the Holy Spirit and speaking in tongues and we see it's the normal part of the Christian life. To me, it's like breathing. It's so much a part of my normal communication with God, but mostly in my private devotions.

I do hope that no one will take negatively what I said because it is meant to be a positive statement and not to put anybody down. We need to take speaking in tongues, or the prayer language of the Spirit, and put it in its place. Just like we put anything in its place. For example, the Lord's Supper, the Holy Communion, is not everything. But it is an integral, living, redeeming part of the Christian experience. It's a part of our Christian walk, but it's not everything. There's more. In the same way, the prayer language of the Spirit is not everything, but it has its valid and valuable place in the Christian's daily life. I believe every child of God has the prayer language of the Spirit stored up inside, whether he knows it or not. It's been there all the time. He doesn't have to seek it, it's there. What he has to do is release it, to learn to use it to release his deepest feelings to God—to receive back God's response to it in his own understanding SO THAT HE CAN BETTER PRAY AND PRAISE GOD WITH HIS UNDERSTANDING.

The prayer language of the Spirit is not an either/or. It's the originating point of the inner man of our prayer life leading directly into aiding our minds to pray with the fullest of our understanding. In actual practice, the primary function of tongues is to improve the mind's ability and capacity to express oneself *to* God and to receive *from* God and to *understand.* The edification that comes with it is the most refreshing, instructive, and releasing — bringing into us God's kind of release. And it's for the NOW.

EVELYN: Honey, I've never heard you express it in such detail before, but in my own experience and in the experience of many other Christians, I know it's true. And I praise God for it. Someone asked me if speaking in tongues is a result of emotion, or does it bring about emotion? I personally think it causes the emotion. Because when you speak in tongues you must exercise your will and know that you are talking to God, and there is a joy that hits you down inside . . . and joy is an emotion. What do you say?

ORAL: Sometimes it is not joy that hits you. Sometimes it is something else. For example, if you are going through a tremendous personal traumatic experience and you begin to pray in tongues, although you feel something inside, it isn't always joy. It's a struggle, strain, burden — sometimes deep sorrow. You may have lost a loved one. There may be a problem in the marriage in which the marriage is dissolving. Remember, we prayed with a dear person the other day whose marriage is dissolving. And she would reach way down where the Spirit of God is and take hold of that sorrow that was breaking her up — a marriage that she has had all these years and suddenly it is going. Later she felt joy when she had emptied herself out and the Spirit began to move in her. She felt joy in that God was with her and she knew God was going to help her. She may or may not solve that marriage problem. But something marvelous happened to her, Evelyn, and *is* happening to her. She has a sense that God is with her and God is going to help her. We don't know what the outcome will be, but we know God is going to help her.

EVELYN: Will the baptism in the Holy Spirit and speaking in tongues mean I will solve all my problems?

ORAL: No. The difference is that when you receive the baptism in the Holy Spirit and speak in tongues, your approach to problems will be different. You will have help in the form of an inner release. You will have help in your intellect if you know how to pause and wait for the interpretation. The problems will still be there but you will see them in a different light. You will have to fight them just exactly like you did before you received this gift, but you will have very special help in facing those problems.

EVELYN: I am a very practical person. To me, an experience has to be practical or it doesn't do me any good. I believe the infilling of the Holy Spirit can make you more effective in any area of life—He is sent to give you the abundant life in the NOW of your existence.

ORAL: I can say AMEN to that.

YOUR GOD-GIVEN KEY FOR TODAY
"The Holy Spirit Is Giving Me A New Power
For Living."

TENTH WEEK

SUNDAY	I CAN COMMUNICATE DIRECTLY WITH GOD—HE HELPS ME
MONDAY	THE PRAYER LANGUAGE OF THE SPIRIT PUTS ME TOGETHER
TUESDAY	THROUGH THE HOLY SPIRIT I OPEN UP TO JESUS
WEDNESDAY	THROUGH THE PRAYER LANGUAGE OF THE SPIRIT I CAN KNOW GOD'S BEST WAY FOR ME
THURSDAY	LORD, I RECEIVE YOUR HOLY SPIRIT NOW
FRIDAY	THROUGH THE HOLY SPIRIT I CAN PRAY AS I OUGHT
SATURDAY	THE HOLY SPIRIT IS GIVING ME A NEW POWER FOR LIVING

ELEVENTH WEEK

How You Can Stop Failing
And Start Succeeding

SUNDAY Key:
I WILL PLANT SEEDS OF LOVE AND NOT FEAR

or
How I Learned Not To Be Afraid Of Failure

MY greatest fear faced me a few days before I conducted my first healing service in downtown Enid, Oklahoma, in 1947. As I looked forward to this critical meeting . . .

I was suddenly faced with an overwhelming sense of failure.
I awakened one night in a cold sweat. I had been dreaming of standing before the people and having them pass by me to receive prayer. In my dream many outstanding miracles of healings were wrought by God. But I awakened with the realization that mere dreaming was not enough. I slept very little the rest of the night.

The next morning I began fasting and praying for I was conscious of the beginning of a gnawing pain inside myself. Later that morning I was sitting in my sociology class in the university when something made me ask myself this dreaded question:

"What if I fail?"

For the rest of that day and the next I wrestled with this awful question. It pounded in my breast. "What if I fail? What if I fail? What if I fail?"

I had no desire to eat, to talk with anyone, or to do anything. Yet I knew unless I overcame this tormenting fear I never would start. Everything hinged on my conquering the fear of failure.

My victory came almost like a flash. I was sitting in my office repeating over and over to myself, "What if I fail?" Finally I fell on my knees and prayed, "O God, what if I fail?" Then it hit me like a bombshell.

And again, deep inside me, God said, "Son, you have already done that."

Of course! What I had been doing was a failure. Now I had a chance to succeed if I could learn to really rely upon God, if I could truly make Him the Source of my total supply. I had no reason to be afraid of failure.

I had already failed;
now God was giving me the chance
to begin again.

I shall never forget the feeling of meekness that came over me. I had never felt so dependent upon God—or so SECURE.

I have learned since then that the fear of failure is responsible for more good things being left undone . . . more jobs not being asked for . . . more successful businesses never having been started . . . and more relationships never being restored . . . than any other factor.

So what do you do when you have failed? When things have collapsed around you . . . and you feel as if you are at the end of your life?

I've studied a lot about failure and where it comes from. A Scripture that is really full of Seed-Faith is St. Paul's statement, "For God hath not given us the spirit of fear; but of power, and of love, and of a sound mind" (2 Timothy 1:7).

First, fear does *not* come from God. God is the Source of faith, not fear. Paul says, further, fear is a spirit. As far as I'm concerned I believe fear is the devil's own spirit which he attempts to transfer to us.

Second, God gives us the spirit of power, and the spirit of a sound —balanced—mind. Therefore, when you think of any fear that is trying to hold you back, try to put your thoughts on God, your Source of POWER AND A STRONG, STRAIGHT-THINKING MIND. For that is what God stands ready to give you.

The Bible also says:

> There is no fear in love; but perfect love casteth out fear: because fear hath torment. He that feareth is not made perfect in love (1 John 4:18).

Love is giving, giving out of your heart, or a seed you plant. I know that when the fear of failure was tormenting me and I finally was able to get my mind on who my Source is, I plunged right into giving of myself to help people. I began to *do* something in the place of *fearing*. Love that you give away has great power, not only upon the one you give it to, but upon yourself. Loving God with all your heart and being, and loving other people as you love yourself, and really trusting God as your Source—that puts you in a frame of mind where fear CANNOT dominate you.

———◆◆◆———

When the question hits you, "What if I fail?" remember by not doing anything, you have already failed. You're at the bottom rung of the ladder and there is no place to go but up. This is what I love about God being the Source. He gives you another chance!

Make this affirmation from your heart and tack it over every failure:

"Fear is a *spirit* . . . faith is a *spirit*. And it's up to me to choose the one I want to follow. Therefore, to bring success, security, and miracles to my life—

"I WILL PLANT SEEDS OF *LOVE* AND NOT FEAR!"

YOUR GOD-GIVEN KEY FOR TODAY

Say it again:

"I Will Plant Seeds Of Love And Not Fear!"

MONDAY

**Key:
GOD IS ALIVE AND CONTINUOUSLY ACTIVE IN MY LIFE**

or

What The Bible Says—And What I Personally Learned—About Overcoming One Of Life's Greatest Problems . . . Discouragement

People sometimes say to me, "Oral Roberts, what do you do when you get discouraged? How do you handle it when you get depressed . . . when the bills are piling up and you can't pay them . . . when you do all that you know how to do and it still doesn't work . . . what do you do? Oral Roberts, tell us like it is!"

Now some people think I never get discouraged. But they are wrong. I know what it means to get discouraged . . . to really get low. I've been so discouraged that if I'd died they would have had to jack me up to bury me; I mean, I know what it is to get discouraged and feel I'm going under.

And to be real honest and frank with you, when I get discouraged I get scared. I get that sick feeling in the pit of my stomach. Then I get irritated and I get hard to live with. I find that my words are coming out sharp and hard. Even though I try to be kind, the discouragement in my spirit comes through. My darling wife Evelyn says, "Now, honey, remember people get more from your spirit than they get from what you say . . ." And I know what she says is the truth. So then I have to get myself by the collar and say, "Oral Roberts, what does God have to say about this?"

I love to read the Bible because it has a lot to say to us human beings . . . to us who are down here on this earth struggling to be successful. It has a lot to say about doing the best you can and still failing . . . and about becoming so discouraged you want to give up.

In Exodus 3 is the story of a man who had tried and failed . . . who found himself inadequate for the task and fled to the desert. His name was Moses.

You remember the story. Moses was born the son of Hebrew slaves. He was doomed to death—Pharaoh had decreed that all male Hebrew infants should be killed because the people were multiplying too quickly—but his parents hid him.

One day the daughter of Pharaoh found little Moses hidden in the bulrushes. She looked into the face of that little baby and she loved him. She could not destroy him so she adopted him. Moses grew up in the royal palaces of Egypt . . . the son of the Pharaoh's daughter. But his real mother nursed him and cared for him as a young child . . . and she instilled in him his heritage—the knowledge of who he really was.

As young Moses grew to manhood he became more and more disturbed by the treatment of the Hebrews. One day he came upon an Egyptian overseer beating a Hebrew slave. Suddenly all the anger against the unjust treatment of his people rose to the surface. Looking around to see if anyone were watching, Moses grabbed the whip. In fury, he began to beat the Egyptian until he killed him. Then Moses hid the Egyptian in the sand. But his act *was* seen. Now Moses thought even if a Hebrew saw what he did that he would be glad. But he was wrong. Word of his deed was carried to Pharaoh and finally Moses had to flee for his life from the land of Egypt.

Moses ended up in Midian . . . on the backside of the desert tending sheep for a living. Quite a comedown from the palaces of Egypt to a tent in the desert . . . from being honored as the son of Pharaoh's daughter to being a sheepherder. And all because Moses did what he *thought* was right. He had tried to help his people—and he failed.

So there he was on the vast desert . . . with its endless sand, rocks, and bushes. And for 40 long years Moses suffered disillusionment because of his failure. He was in a negative cycle of discouragement. Round and round he went . . .

day after day he watched the sheep . . .

he did the mundane tasks . . .

and he thought of his failure.

Does this sound familiar to you? Are you going around in a meaningless circle? Have you tried to bring your dream to pass and failed? Are you daily being devastated by this negative cycle?

If you are, friend, I tell you there is hope! you see . . .

God exists!

God is real!

God is concerned about you!

God cares about the cycle you are in!

God knows the feelings you are experiencing in the NOW . . . just as He did about Moses.

Well, God came to Moses out there in the desert. Isn't that a tremendous thought! GOD CAME TO HIM! And God will come to you . . . right at the point of your greatest need . . . right there where you are in that negative cycle . . . where you think nothing can ever change . . . suddenly, GOD WILL COME TO YOU.

Now God came to Moses in a way that awed him at first . . . a way Moses didn't understand. God appeared in a bush that caught on fire . . . it kept on burning but was not consumed. Naturally, Moses went out of his way to see this strange happening.

You see, first, God got Moses' attention. That's important. And God will get your attention and my attention. He didn't get my attention until I was lying on a bed, dying of tuberculosis and I suddenly learned that I could be healed by the goodness and love of God. Then God got my attention!

GOD IS GOING TO GET YOUR ATTENTION . . . ONE WAY OR THE OTHER!

When He does, it will be a great day in your life. It will be a great day for suddenly you will see that God your Source is the way out . . . He is the one who can break the cycle of bad things happening in your life. You will see that by trusting in Him, good things will begin to happen to you.

The fact that the burning bush was not consumed says something else to you and me. The burning bush speaks of the continuity of God. It says that . . .

GOD IS CONTINUOUSLY ALIVE
AND ACTIVE IN HUMAN AFFAIRS

It said to Moses that just as God was alive in the palaces of Egypt when Moses had been a prince, God is alive now among the rocks and sand and bushes of the desolate desert. He's as much alive out there where Moses is like a tiny speck lost in the universe as He was when Moses, robed in royalty, walked the halls of the palaces of Egypt. God was in Egypt. And God was there in the desert when Moses was alone.

Now that's a terrific idea . . . to know that . . .

Wherever you are,
and whatever condition you are in,
God is continuously alive and
active in your life.

God told Moses to take off his shoes for he was standing on holy ground. It is always holy ground when you become aware of God. The awareness of God gives you the feeling that you are standing on holy ground.

THE COMPASSIONATE CARING OF GOD

God spoke to Moses from the bush and said, "I have seen the affliction of My people in Egypt. I have heard their cry and I've come to send you to lead them out of bondage to a land of promise, a land flowing with milk and honey."

"I HAVE HEARD THEIR CRY . . ." This means that . . .

God cares when you are oppressed.

God cares when you are beat down.

God cares when you can't fling off the obstacles that are in your path.

God sees the afflictions, the torments, the needs, the problems of you . . . of me . . . of every human being in the world.

God cares! And He sees every teardrop that falls.

Then God said, "I am going to send you, Moses, to deliver My people."

Moses was so serious he was almost comical. It's so much like the way you and I would probably have acted if we had been there. Moses said, "You are going to send *me* back to Egypt, God?"

"Yes, I'm going to send you."

"Who am I, Lord? I've already tried it and failed," Moses said. "Lord, I blew it!"

And that's a word we use today. "I blew it."

The next thing Moses said was, "I don't even know Your name."

You know, Moses was down there in Egypt trying to do God's work and didn't even know who God was. A lot of people have never had an experience with God. They've never been truly saved by His grace or filled with His Holy Spirit, yet they are doing religious things . . . and it won't work. At least Moses was honest about it. He said, "I don't know Your name."

And God said, "My name is I AM. That will be My name forever. I AM. I am in the NOW. I am always. I am."

Well, Moses kept piling up his excuses. He said, "If I go down there they won't believe me. I'll stand up and tell them that You sent me and they won't believe that You sent me. What will I do then?"

God said, "You tell them that I AM sent you."

Well, that didn't convince Moses so God said, "What do you have in your hand?"

It was a rod Moses used with the sheep.

God said, "Throw it down."

It became a serpent.

God said, "Take it by the tail."

Moses did and it became a rod again. It was a miracle.

God said, "Listen, I'll go with you in MIRACLE POWER."

That's what Moses had not counted on. He had merely counted on his own strength. He had not counted on the miracles of God. Listen, there are miracles.

GOD IS A GOD OF MIRACLES

One miracle can do more in your life in five seconds than you can do in a lifetime.

Finally Moses said, "God, I stutter. I have a slow tongue and besides that, I'm not eloquent when I do get the words out."

God said, "I'll be your mouth."

Then Moses got into what we call today the miracle of Seed-Faith. He became willing to go because he understood now that he didn't have to go in his own strength, that he had a Source for his life. He had the great I AM—God—in his heart and by his side . . . going before him . . . and above him . . . and beneath him . . . and around him. Moses had a Source for his life.

Moses began to open himself up, to put himself into this affair, to give of his talent, his time, his life. It was a seed of faith that he planted that God could multiply back. Moses gave out of his own need of being delivered, his own need of freedom, his own need of having the miracles of God. Moses began to give for a desired result . . . and so can you!

And Moses began to expect miracles! He knew if he went down there to Pharaoh that he was no match for this monarch of the empire of Egypt. He knew he could not lead two million slaves out of Egyptian bondage. He knew he could not cross the Red Sea or bring water from the flinty rock or lead them to the land of promise. He knew he would have to have miracles and he began to expect mighty miracles.

The exodus of two million slaves from Egypt is one of the greatest miracles of all time and it happened through a lowly shepherd who had been in a 40-year negative cycle of discouragement . . . who finally opened himself up and despite his own shortcomings let God have a chance to work in his life.

It's my own story. I stuttered and stammered. I ran away from my problems and myself. When I came back to face God I didn't know who God was. I was sick and afflicted and lost, but, oh, how God tenderly dealt with me. I finally learned who my Source is . . . God. And I am continuing to learn how to put seeds of faith in, how to give, and how to expect miracles.

Can you see that Moses first got control of himself when he discovered God and learned He was the true Source of his life? Then when he began to open up, not in discouragement and bitterness but in GIVING of himself, he could really expect the mighty God to go *with* him back to the scene of his failure and right there start him on the road to success!

Think about that for a moment! The eternal principles of Seed-Faith have been in the Bible through the centuries, even in Moses' time. These Three Miracle Keys changed the direction of his life. God in the NOW became so real to Moses that nothing could stop him. And neither can anything stop you . . . when you grasp that Seed-Faith is real and workable in and through you.

———— ◆ ————

Now . . . to help you make Seed-Faith workable I want you to let this one dynamic thought come through to your heart as it did Moses':

"GOD IS ALIVE AND CONTINUOUSLY ACTIVE IN MY LIFE!" Latch on to that truth—just that one—and say it in the face of every discouragement:

YOUR GOD-GIVEN KEY FOR TODAY

"God Is Alive And Continuously Active In My Life!"

TUESDAY Key: NO WEAPON FORMED AGAINST ME WILL PROSPER IF I KEEP MY SPIRIT RIGHT!

or
How I Learned Criticism Was For My Good And Not To Destroy Me

I doubt if anyone will ever reach the place where criticism doesn't hurt when it first strikes. But I believe it is possible to create an attitude that will in due course of time take the sting completely away. I know because I have burned and seethed with resentment.

Then one day I made up my mind to overcome criticism—to learn the way out. This chapter was written out of one of my bitterest moments. I confess that the rules given here saved my life. I was fast reaching the point at which my resentment against my critics was turning into contempt and malice. I developed a double resentment; resentment against untrue criticism and resentment against myself for not knowing how to conquer my fear of what criticism would accomplish against me.

Rather than thinking of reasons for resenting my critics and what they had to say about me, I began seeking reasons why I should not be angry and resentful. The reasons came to me so fast that I sat down and wrote them just like they appear here. By the time I was through I had a rare experience. I was free of resentment and contempt. The criticism that had stung my very soul had lost its barbs to pierce my spirit. I felt friendly toward my critics. In fact, I felt light and free again. In a sense, I felt grateful to the people who had taken notice of my progress enough to criticize me.

RULE 1. WHEN YOU ARE CRITICIZED, ASK YOURSELF THIS QUESTION: IS IT TRUE?

Not, is it fair? Or was it given by a person who seeks to help you? But, is there a *basis* for this criticism? Have you given cause to be criticized? Is it true?

That is the only criterion.

By asking yourself, is it true? you can come to know the value of being criticized.

If your self-appointed critic has discovered a fault, a weakness, an error in your makeup or actions, you have no right to ignore it. In fact, you should be grateful. We can learn a lot from our critics. Often they are the only ones with enough courage to tell us when we are pursuing a wrong course. Many times they are only honest appraisers.

When we ask ourselves, is this criticism true? we are objectively facing life; any other course is to escape from reality.

Why should we act like a spoiled child who, when told of his bad manners, sticks out his tongue and blindly strikes at his correctors. How much better it is to say, "It is true and I will sincerely try to change."

By adopting this technique we make our critics the inspired watchmen of our souls.

RULE 2. WHEN THE CRITICISM IS NOT TRUE, MAKE A FAITH-IMAGE OF THE POWER OF TRUTH OVER ERROR

The only way to conquer an untruth is to take recourse in the changeless principle of the triumph of truth over error, right over wrong, righteousness over evil.

> *Truth crushed to earth will rise again,*
> *The eternal years of God are hers;*
> *But error wounded writhes in pain*
> *And lies amid her worshipers.*

Here is one thing to remember: If the criticism is not true, it is based on a lie. Neither the universe nor the human spirit is created to accommodate a lie. Truth is built in the very nature of things.

This is the way of faith. If you are right and know it, you can afford to wait and see your salvation.

Through the power of faith you know something your critic doesn't know: that you cannot be hurt by untrue criticism, that just as surely as light banishes darkness because it is the stronger power, so truth will conquer a lie.

Jesus was crucified on erroneous testimony, misquotations, and twisted meanings. But He just kept on loving God, giving of himself to people, and expecting miracles. It was in the spirit of Seed-Faith that He went to the cross. There He was crushed. *But crushed truth has in it the seeds of resurrection.* Death and defeat could keep Him in the grave only temporarily. The third day He arose, alive forevermore. It was the miracle of miracles. It was God reproducing the seed into the mightiest harvest of all . . . for Jesus' life and ours!

By holding Seed-Faith in your mind you can make a faith-image of eventual triumph. You will not try to hurry things up and try to prove that the critics are wrong. Only those who are bound by fear can be panicked into striking back on the spur of the moment; those who know their course is right are content to wait, to trust their Source, who is Truth. They know truth will triumph.

RULE 3. PRACTICE FORGIVENESS OF YOUR CRITICS, NOT RESENTMENT

You can neutralize your critic when you practice forgiveness toward him. Resentment causes more resentment but you can win through forgiveness.

Jesus accomplished a forgiveness even while on the cross. Not a thing His critics had said about Him was true. The passions of the people had been whipped into a flame by the untrue criticism given Him by those who were prejudiced against Him. In His darkest hour, when seemingly He was isolated forever from His friends, when His cause seemed to be eternally lost, He did an astounding thing—He forgave His critics! "Forgive them," He cried, "for they know not what they do."

In this prayer of forgiveness He pictured His critics as not knowing what they did. They were afraid and having no faith they struck at the One who was in the lead. Jesus knew they were driven by their fears, blinded by their terror, and had been prejudiced against the truth. They were playthings of fear, pushed this way and that by the fear of their own failure. Why should He despise and resent them? They did not know what they were doing.

Why don't you just forgive?

Some time ago a friend of mine was treated in a manner that was unjust and unfair. He was deeply hurt. The more he thought about it, the worse he felt. In a few days he found he was unable to think about anything except this wrong. He would go to bed thinking about it. He would say, "Did I deserve this?" He knew that he did not.

When he turned his attention to the person who was responsible for his hurt, he grew resentful of him. "Why did he do it?" he asked himself over and over. He even tried to straighten things out on his own initiative. Nothing came of it.

One morning he woke up with this thing on his mind. He decided something must be done or he would become frustrated. All day he tried to force it from his mind. It refused to go.

He knew if he did not succeed in winning the victory over being hurt that his resentment would influence his daily decisions in his business and he would be upset every time he remembered it.

"The next morning," he told me, "I woke up feeling like I had been up all night. My head hurt. My muscles were tense. I shook my head trying to clear my brain of this mental obstruction and this spiritual bondage. Then something happened and I have been a new man ever since."

I said, "What happened?"

"Well," he continued, "I dressed to go to my office. I drove off. Then all of a sudden it seemed like someone spoke to me, whether audibly I couldn't tell, but it was clear enough for me to understand."

He looked at me and smiled. I waited, anxious to know what the voice had said to him. He said these were the words he had heard, "Why don't you just forgive this person?"

"Well," he added seriously, "I said to myself, why not?"

"When I said that, I felt a tingle all through my body. Something was happening to me and it felt good. I had forgiven this fellow and it made me feel like shouting that I was free!"

My friend discovered the rule that never fails, and that is to practice forgiveness. By this method you are planting a seed that secures personal release and peace of mind again.

RULE 4. DON'T ALLOW YOURSELF TO BE DRAWN INTO THE WEB OF HATE

All too often we do not seek to overcome our resentments through forgiveness. We allow hate, like a spider, to spin its web around our souls.

Whenever an insect becomes entangled in the web, the spider immediately attacks the insect, filling its body with poison. Then the spider strengthens the web, preventing escape and making death sure.

Hate is like that. It fills the soul with hate sensations, setting off a chemical reaction in the body, poisoning the bloodstream, and upsetting the nervous system. Few people, once enmeshed in hate, ever escape.

Love is the only antidote for hate. The only way you can make love operative against hate is to remember that Christ died for your critic as well as He did for you. Your critic too is made in the image of God, carrying a divine imprint on his soul. For that reason you have no right to hate him, for in hating him you are also hating God.

Once love becomes active in your spirit it will tear down the web of hate as well as destroying the spider of hate itself, cleansing your entire being from the poison and making you free. "I shall never let anyone drag me down," Henry Ford once said, "by making me hate him."

RULE 5. REFUSE TO STRIKE BACK

When the critics of Jesus came to arrest Him one of the disciples, Peter, drew his sword and cut off the ear of the high priest's servant. Jesus healed and restored the man's ear, and turning to Peter He sharply rebuked him: "Put up again thy sword into his place for all they that take the sword shall perish with the sword."

This is an eternal principle: They who live by force shall perish by force.

To strike back at criticism is to meet force with force. This is the way of defeat and frustration. This way is motivated by fear. Fear makes one feel so on the defensive that unless he strikes back quickly he feels he will suffer loss.

In contrast, faith in God your Source never unsheathes the sword for it is a stronger power to hurl at criticism. Faith strengthens one's inner defenses by taking away the fear of what criticism can accomplish. Faith takes away tension and anxiety.

Jesus did not seek to strike back by justifying His own course of action; He took a way of greater power through forgiving his enemies and He won.

There is no successful way to justify yourself to your critics because they won't believe anything good about you. **Adverse criticism will not convert your friends and your defense will not convert your critics.** Your friends are the ones who already know the worst about you and like you in spite of it. Your critics despise your virtues and usually criticize you because of them.

In effect, Jesus said to Peter, "You can win by refusing to strike back. By a loving, forgiving spirit you can lift yourself from the lowest form of defense to the highest."

The Seed-Faith way lets you keep your self-respect. You have the knowledge that you could have licked your critic and you know that he knows it too. Yet you have dignified your own course by having confidence in its rightness and at the same time kept your self-respect. No one can continually strike back without losing respect not only for his critic but for himself as well.

He who has lost self-respect has lost his way in life.

RULE 6. REFUSE TO BECOME DISCOURAGED

When you allow yourself to get discouraged through criticism you are permitting your critic to dictate your course.

Discouragement is the most dangerous feeling you can get because failure and success are often separated by only the distance of that one word—discouragement.

According to an old fable the devil once held a sale and offered all the tools of his trade to anyone who would pay their price. They were spread out on the table, each one labeled: hatred, malice, envy, despair, sickness, sensuality—all the weapons that everyone knows so well.

But off to one side, apart from the rest, lay a harmless looking instrument marked "discouragement." It was old and worn looking, but it was priced far above all the rest. When asked the reason why, the devil replied:

"Because I can use this one so much more easily than the others. No one knows that it belongs to me, so with it I can open doors that are tight bolted against the others. Once I get inside I can use any tool that suits me best."

No one knows how small the margin is between failure and success, faith and fear. The tendency of most people is to become discouraged to the point of quitting when they are adversely criticized. All too often discouragement is the deciding factor in the defeat of some person who was on his way to making good.

I know how it feels to say, "Oh, what's the use, I might as well quit."

Many times I have felt like quitting. So many odds were stacked against me. Every move I made was criticized. Seemingly I was judged even before I made a move. Sometimes I have tried to make myself think my critics were not serious and soon they would stop. But I found wishful thinking will not turn the tide. A superior force is the only power that will conquer. That power is God working through your Seed-Faith.

RULE 7. USE THE POWER OF PRAYER

In dealing effectively and lastingly with the bruising effects of criticism you will discover there is one other principle that will liberate you after all others have failed. That is the power of prayer.

Here is the way to pray:

First, review the matter of your problem to God. Tell Him all about it. Talk to Him without shame or fear of condemnation. Tell Him what your critics have done and how the problem seems to be beyond your power to solve.

Second, freely acknowledge to Him that you have been wounded and hurt. Confide in Him all your resentments, your bitterness, your fears. Do not justify yourself or defend your own actions. Never, never let self-justification slip into your praying. Let God be the judge.

Third, confess your own weakness and inability to overcome your problems.

Fourth, ask God to personally intervene, to take a hand in the matter. Ask Him to take charge and work things out for the good of all concerned. Be sure to emphasize things being worked out for the good of *all* concerned. This is the unselfish way. God will bless you for your seed of unselfishness. By praying this way, you are planting a seed that God can use to give you a harvest of good . . . out of a situation that seems all bad.

These four steps in prayer take the whole problem out of your hands and place it in the hands of a higher power—a power that never fails . . . the Source of your total supply—God. You are assured that your Source shall be working for you around the clock every day.

The final thing in using the power of prayer is to put your faith to work to bring about the desired results you have asked for through prayer. With your faith you form an image of God, your Source, doing the very thing you have asked Him to do.

This is the guiding principle of believing prayer given by Jesus, who said:

> *What things soever ye desire, when ye pray, believe that ye re-ceive* (are receiving) *them, and ye shall have them* (Mark 11:24).

By this, Jesus means that as you believe you will begin receiving the things you have prayed for. By holding the image of these things before God and in your own thinking, your faith will release them to you.

This is an irrevocable fact. You can depend on it. So go to bed and sleep because you know God is awake all night long working in your behalf. This is what Paul meant when he wrote, "If God be for us, who can be against us?"

There is an infallible secret of success in any piece of work undertaken for the right. There is no one who can defeat us. If we fail, it is because we allow ourselves to become embittered or discouraged so that we eventually give up. Defeat comes from within, it is not an outside circumstance.

There is no way, however, to apply these rules without first secur-ing the consent of your mind that you are determined to meet criticism objectively and successfully. Once you *decide* to win this victory the pattern of success will become increasingly clearer.

If you do not wish to face criticism in a way to make it serve life's higher purposes, then giving mere lip-service to the seven rules given in this chapter will end in frustration. If you try to take matters into your own hands by resenting and striking back at your critics, God and your friends will let you fight your own battles. You will lose, your energies will be wasted. You will be let down into the bottomless pit of self-despair.

On the other hand you can be assured of victory. Know where you stand. Face each criticism squarely. Don't take yourself too seriously. Be able to smile at yourself. See some humorous element in the criticism. Consider the source, the content; accept the part you need, discard the rest. Relax. Your main job now *is* to go on with life and you do that best through your own Seed-Faith.

CHECK YOURSELF . . .
MAKE THE SEVEN-WAY TEST!

Rule 1. When you are criticized, ask yourself this question: Is it true? If it is, don't ignore it. Face yourself and make needed changes. Be grateful to your critic for being the unpaid watchman of your soul.

Rule 2. If the criticism is not true, form a faith-image of the power of truth over error. Don't forget the issue. Because you are right, you can afford to wait.

Rule 3. Practice forgiveness of your critics, not resentment. By accomplishing a forgiveness of your critic you will release yourself and find peace of mind again.

Rule 4. Don't allow yourself to be drawn into the web of hate. Hate will destroy you. You have no right to hate your fellowman for he too is made in the image of God. Only love is stronger than hate.

Rule 5. Refuse to strike back. Meekness is power. This is because meekness is based on faith, not fear.

Rule 6. Don't allow yourself to become discouraged. Discouragement is the most dangerous feeling you can get. Remember, if you never give way to discouragement you will never quit.

Rule 7. Use the power of sincere prayer. Prayer has cleansing and lifting power. It is turning to a higher power than yourself. Once you have prayed, form an image of the fact that God is working things out for you. Believe that is being done and it will be.

You've followed the rules . . . now cue in on this powerful thought. Let it sustain you. It does me.

YOUR GOD-GIVEN KEY FOR TODAY
"No Weapon Formed Against Me Will Prosper

If I Keep My Spirit Right!"

WEDNESDAY

Key:
I'LL KEEP ON TOP BY
LEARNING TO TRUST GOD'S
LAW OF AVERAGES

or
God's Law Of Averages Works For You If Only You Know It

Babe Ruth is renowned as the "Home-run King" in baseball because he hit 714 home runs during his great career. (Recently Hank Aaron broke Babe's record.) What is not known is that Babe was also the "Strike-out King." He struck out 1,330 times, far more than he hit home runs. However, the swish of the mighty bat sending the ball over the field and emptying the bases, seemed to make people forget that every two times he struck out, he was due a home run. It is said that Babe Ruth developed this law of averages in his own thinking so that he was never nonplussed when he was struck out. He always believed the home run would come.

The story is told about the last game of the season that would decide the pennant. The Yankees and the Athletics were fighting it out. Lefty Grove was pitching for Philadelphia and Babe Ruth had come to bat. It was the ninth inning with two out and the score was tied. They say this thought was going through Babe's mind. *Lefty Grove has struck me out three times.* (Lefty had struck him out three times in that game.) *I am now due my first home run.*

The crowd pleaded with Lefty Grove. "Just one more strikeout, Lefty."

They had booed Babe Ruth when he struck out. But every time he struck out, he would do the same things he did when he knocked a home run! When he hit a home run, trotted around the bases and stepped on home plate, he took his cap off, doffed it to the crowd and went to the dugout. When he struck out, he also turned to the crowd, doffed his cap and went to the dugout.

Now the tension was so high that everyone was silent as death as Babe got up to bat. Lefty bore down and threw Babe two strikes and three balls. They say that going through Babe's mind was this thought. *My law of averages is now going to help me. It's going to take just one swat and this game is over.*

Lefty bore down and threw the ball with such speed that few people saw it. There was a mighty swish and a crack and they all knew the ball was gone and it was over.

GOD'S LAW OF AVERAGES

I believe that God has a law of averages too for those who are doing His work and trying to live a sincere Christlike life. This belief in the law of averages has given me balance in many hard and difficult situations.

For example, one night in one of our North Carolina Crusades, I was in about the same situation in which Babe Ruth found himself. I was not at bat on a baseball diamond but I was at bat in the prayer line. The crowd was so large we could scarcely breathe. Many of the curious were there and I had the feeling some were saying, "Come on, preacher. Show us what you can do." I did not feel that *I* could do anything but I knew the Lord could . . . if we would all cooperate with Him and believe. So I summoned all my courage and determined to send my faith to God. It was difficult to preach, but a ray of sunshine filtered through when over 800 people came forward to accept Christ.

Then as the people came for prayer, it seemed that my prayers did not rise much above my head. This was strange, for my first large successful crusade was conducted in North Carolina back in June 1948, and every succeeding crusade had been larger and larger. The North Carolina people received me like their own son and I love them very dearly. However, in this particular service I was having a hard time. I felt as if the devil were making a fool of me and it seemed I should quit and go home. That night when person after person passed by seemingly not receiving the help I thought they should, I remembered God's law of averages. I knew if I would be faithful to pray earnestly for each one and not become discouraged, my time would come to knock a home run for the Lord.

Looking at the huge crowd that had come for prayer, I saw a mother bringing her little boy. He was hobbling along on crutches. Faith leaped in my heart and I whispered, "O Lord, this is the one."

When they stood before me I noticed one of the boy's feet was secured by a strap which was looped over his shoulder. I asked to hold him on my knee, and with my arm about him I prayed and sent my faith to God.

Suddenly the entire atmosphere became electric with expectation. The audience leaned forward and I heard prayers going up from many. The Spirit of the Lord flooded through me and I knew that the afflicted leg dangling from this boy's hip would be healed, and he would be able to run and play like other children. My prayer was not long but my heart was full of assurance. I said to little Douglas, "Son, what do you feel like doing now?"

He said, "Running."

I put him down. And at his mother's insistence, they took off the shoulder strap and let his foot touch the floor. The moment his foot touched the floor, the Spirit of God surged into that leg. Mrs. Sutton (his mother) was overcome.

I said, "Douglas, do you believe God can help you walk off this ramp?"

He said, "Oh, yes, sir."

I said, "Mrs. Sutton, what do you say?"

She was weeping and nodded her permission.

I told her to go to the end of the ramp, and if she wanted her boy to walk to tell him to come on.

So she said, "Come on, Douglas."

He took one step . . . then another . . . then he broke into a run. Someone picked up his crutches and handed them to him. He put them over his shoulder and ran up and down the aisles crying at the top of his voice.

In an instant that vast audience came to their feet. They forgot the seeming failures. Strong men cried like children and women shouted for joy. This went on for several minutes.

Finally, I said, "People, will you be seated?" It was like speaking to the ocean. When I saw they were not going to stop I said, "Help yourselves."

One of my team members later said to me, "Oral, this is the first time I ever saw you lose control of your crowd."

I said, "No one could have held those people that night. Their faith and my faith had knocked a home run and it was right that they should rejoice."

HOW DOES THIS APPLY TO ME?

Friend, while I've talked to you about God's law of averages, you may have said in your heart: Well, how does this apply to me? Simply in this way. You may have had some failures. As a matter of fact, you may have had a series of failures. It may seem to you today that you might as well quit whatever you are doing. Let me say to you that *God has a law of averages* which will work and be very effective in your behalf, if you make God your Source and fully trust in Him.

God has all power. He can help you step up to bat and knock a home run—not every time. No, for that would not be natural or normal. But He will give you enough home runs so that His law of averages will give you strength and courage to go on and on, day after day.

NEVER GIVE UP!

No situation is too hard for God and you together, for with God "nothing shall be impossible unto you." Hold this thought in your mind continuously.

YOUR GOD-GIVEN KEY FOR TODAY
"I'll Keep On Top By Learning To Trust
God's Law Of Averages."

THURSDAY Key:
IT IS GOD'S POWER HEALING ME

or
How I Learned It Wasn't Something I Did
That Caused A Blind Man To See

Do you find yourself wanting to believe that God can give you the miracle you need but inside there is still some doubt? Do you still doubt that God will reveal himself to you? I know what you are going through for I've faced the same problem and still do.

I remember when I began this ministry in 1947 I had a very difficult time with doubt along a certain line. Oh, I had great faith for some things but I had hardly any faith for other things. The one thing I had the most difficulty in believing for was for God to heal blind people. It was unusual that I had such great faith for virtually all types of people with different types of afflictions to be healed but when it came to blindness something just sort of died within me. It was not that I did not believe God *could* . . . I wondered *if* God *would* use my prayers to help someone who was blind.

Now I wasn't proud of this. I was embarrassed by it. Although there were times I did see God helping blind people through my prayers, it was not often that I did. I think I began to develop sort of a negative attitude.

One night, before a great audience, some friends brought an aged blind man for prayer. As I looked at him something just died in my heart. There I was, I'd been praying so effectively. God was hearing my prayers, and I'm always thrilled when God hears my prayers for anyone or for any need to be met. People were being healed. I was rejoicing. Then I looked up and there was a man who could not see. Inwardly I really did not want to pray for him. And in just a few seconds, I found out he did not want me to pray for him, and that he had come only at the insistence of his neighbors. But I was always willing to pray for any who came, so I stretched forth my hands to pray and he rudely thrust them away. I was stunned. Suddenly before the whole crowd, he said, "Young feller, take your hands off my eyes. I don't believe in this stuff anyway. I don't think God heals blind people today."

There I stood as he just blurted it out before the whole crowd. Somehow I had the presence of mind to say, "Well, prayer is not going to hurt. It might help. Just let me say a little prayer that God will let you see."

I suppose when he got so negative maybe I started getting a little more positive, for he said, "Well, OK, if that will make you feel better."

I prayed a sincere prayer and they led him back to his seat. Later that night I suffered . . . oh, I suffered. I didn't sleep much. I was wondering about my whole ministry. I wondered why God would use me with some and not use me with others. I wondered what it was about blindness that was so difficult anyway. For the Bible says, "With God nothing is impossible" (Luke 1:37). I tossed and turned. I remembered how I was embarrassed and wondered if God really had called me into the healing ministry or if this would be the fatal blow against it.

Before 8 o'clock the next morning there was a rap on the door. It was the chairman of the crusade committee there in Chanute, Kansas. He said, "Brother Roberts, are you awake?"

I opened the door and said, "What's the matter?"

He said, "Do you remember the old gentleman you prayed for last night who was blind?" I thought to myself, *how can I ever forget?*

Then he said, "This morning, in fact just about an hour ago, as the sun started to come up he walked out onto the porch and he could see the sun. He went across the street and shared with his neighbors and they called me. I've just been there and seen him."

"Brother Roberts, He's SEEING."

I said, "I can't believe it. I can't believe it."

"Oh, but he's seeing, I talked to him myself, I saw it. And, Brother Roberts, I'll have him in the meeting tonight."

I said, "Please don't! Please don't . . . unless you're sure!"

He said, "Brother Roberts, God can do anything . . . of all men, you should know that."

I said, "Yes, I know, but I don't always do as well on some things." What I was not realizing was that it was not me anyway. It was *God* doing the healing and I needed to have more faith.

So that night there was a big crowd and they brought him down the aisle. I'm all eyes now, I'm watching. First I'm watching to see if someone is holding his arm. No, he's walking alone and without a cane! He walks right up onto the stage and puts his hand out and says, "How are you, young man?"

And I said, "Fine, how are you?"

And he told me the story of how his sight had come back.

I began to test his eyesight. I had people in the audience hold up different objects and he was able to identify the objects. The man could see. I was standing there still straining to believe it.

Now believe me, I suffered over that. But the good part was that I began to understand. Understanding came as it did to Gideon long ago when God said, "Go in this thy [understanding and you will deliver] Israel" (Judges 6:14).

I began to understand that . . .

GOD IS NO RESPECTER OF PERSONS
AND NO RESPECTER OF DISEASES
AND NO RESPECTER OF HUMAN NEEDS.
HE CAN DO WHAT WE BELIEVE HE CAN DO.

But how does that relate to you and the pain you are feeling? The ache you have in your body . . . in your heart? The hurt you are experiencing in your business or personal life?

It's like this, friend. You and I are only humans. We need somebody bigger than ourselves. That somebody is God. He is the Healer . . . the Miracle-worker. When He touches your life . . .

It will turn you from down to up.

It will bring you into a oneness with your Lord.

It will open your eyes to Jesus' loving concern for you and ALL your needs—

Clothes

Money

Food

New health

Strong and positive attitudes

It is the MAN, JESUS, who heals you. Know it. Believe it. Now say it:

YOUR GOD-GIVEN KEY FOR TODAY

"It Is God's Power Healing Me!"

FRIDAY
Key:
TURNING MY FAITH LOOSE IS MY KEY TO A MIRACLE

or

The Most Negative Man I Ever Met And How He Discovered He Could Receive A Miracle

One of the most negative men I ever met was a dedicated Christian, a hard worker, and a good man. When I met him he was selling home products door-to-door. He had brought his wife and small children to our crusade in Miami, Florida. We had one day off from the crusade so we went swimming in the Atlantic Ocean. He wanted to talk. He started in about how hard it was to make a living and get ahead.

He told what some people had done to him.

He said that his sales were off, people were harder to deal with or sell to than ever before.

He was having problems with some of the people in his church.

Then like a record on an automatic record player he said over and over again, "IT'S NO USE, I CAN'T MAKE IT."

That's when he got my attention. While he was detailing his problems and needs I knew there was nothing I could say or do to help. I had to wait until he ran down and came to the conclusion of being need-centered and said, "It's no use, I can't make it." It was at this moment that I might be able to show him he had sowed seeds of doubt that brought him a harvest of needs, and more needs.

I had not heard him say one positive thing. Not once had he spoken of God, or faith, or giving, or miracles. He wasn't "with it" as Jesus teaches.

He was not living in the *now* but in the *past.* He spoke of bills piling up, of a future looking darker, of people who had let him down, of failure in selling, of needs getting greater. Every breath was a negative one; he was caught up in it, and not aware that he had used the precious moments of our visit wholly in a negative way.

He was not aware of the principles of Seed-Faith. Your needs exist to be met. Jesus teaches that . . .

YOUR NEEDS ARE YOUR CLAIM UPON GOD'S CONCERN FOR YOU AS A PERSON AND HIS MIRACLE-WORKING POWER TO BE PUT TO WORK IN YOUR BEHALF TO MEET THOSE NEEDS

The Bible teaches:

"All that I have is thine" (yours) (Luke 15:31).

"Give, and it shall be given unto you" (Luke 6:38).

"My God shall supply all your need" (Philippians 4:19).

When you ask, expect to receive; expect a miracle. (See Matthew 21:22; Mark 11:24.)

Jesus taught that you are what your believing is. He said, "As thou hast believed, so be it done unto thee" (Matthew 8:13).

FAITH, RIGHTLY DIRECTED, IS THE KEY TO EVERYTHING . . . WHATEVER YOU CAN CONCEIVE AND BELIEVE, YOU CAN DO

Your believing can take opposite forms. It can be faith or it can be doubt.

When you believe God exists, that God loves you, and wants to meet your needs, that God is the Source of your total supply, and therefore should be first in your life . . .

When you believe that all God has is yours, when you start being like God by always giving *first* . . .

When you believe that what you invest with God He will multiply back to you . . .

When you believe you can come to God and He will receive you . . .

THEN YOUR BELIEVING HAS CREATED
FAITH IN YOUR HEART

With faith you do something *first* and thereby make your faith a seed you have planted and release it toward God. In this way you actually demonstrate faith. You release the most positive and powerful thing in the universe—your faith. This is when you are really connected with God and make *contact* with the power that spins the universe and controls all things that affect you.

On the other hand, doubt is just as real, in a negative way, as faith. Doubt (or unbelief) is the REVERSED FORM of faith.

Doubt is believing God doesn't exist.

Or, if you believe He exists, you believe He is not concerned with you as a person; He is not concerned with your needs.

You believe what man can do is more reliable than what God will do. You believe it's not up to God at all but what people do to you, or you do yourself.

You believe your main duty is to look out for number one—self— and you put God second or last in your scale of values and your approach to your needs.

You believe that human forces are sources rather than God.

THROUGH DOUBT YOU BECOME VERY POSITIVE
IN YOUR BELIEVING BUT IN A REVERSED FORM

You are taking your capacity to believe and reversing it in a negative way. You say in effect, "It's no use, I can't make it." You expect no miracles. You say, "If God is love and power and help in time of need, He is certainly not concerned about me."

This is doubt and unbelief. It is bad . . . *very bad* for you. As SEED-FAITH is multiplied back, so is SEED-DOUBT. "Whatsoever a man soweth that shall he also reap" (Galatians 6:7). This refers to both good and bad seed.

This pattern of thinking and believing that you have created over the years keeps God from being real to you. Frankly, He is not real to you at all. Through this act of your believing, more doubt is multiplied back to you.

It's like a driver in a car. With the same hand he shifts to put the car in forward or reverse gear—same car, same gears, same driver—he causes the car to go in a different direction, forward or backward.

The Bible says in Romans 12:3:

GOD HATH DEALT TO EVERY MAN THE MEASURE OF FAITH

This God-given power to believe can create faith or doubt, depending upon the way you choose to believe. You can choose to look to God as your Source of all things, to put Him first in your giving, and expect a miracle. When you do this, **your believing will become an act of faith** which you can release toward God and which will bring you into a state of knowing. It makes you absolutely positive. It is SEED-FAITH.

Releasing this faith from your heart to God will release His mighty power within you. You will be brought to the peak of your abilities and be able to attract good things. You will become part of the solution rather than the problem. It puts your mind on God and His limitless resources rather than on the limited resources of mere mortal man.

On the other hand, you can choose to look to man rather than God as Source, and this act of believing creates doubt in your heart toward God. You can think of what you are going to receive, rather than what you can give. In this negative spirit, you block the flow of God's intervention in your behalf to turn the tide.

Doubt cuts you off from the sources of unexpected supply. God controls both the expected and unexpected source, you know.

That day as we swam in the ocean my friend finally wound down and said, "It's no use, I can't do it."

I looked at him and said, "God didn't make you for this."

He quickly replied, "God didn't make me for what!"

"To use your believing to become completely negative," I said.

He answered, "Why I never thought I was being negative."

I said, "There you have it. You are like thousands who are in the same spot you're in but never consider that they are negative persons. Their belief in God is never used for anything but to be saved and go to heaven. They don't believe that God will meet their needs in this life. They are negative when they should be positively believing God to help them now."

His mouth dropped open.

I said, "You're a long time on this earth. You continually have problems and needs. It's time you recognized that the God who saved your soul, and who will someday take you to heaven, is the God of today. He is God in the NOW . . . in this moment of your existence. He loves you. He's concerned with your concerns. He can give you a whole new life if you will start this moment doing something first."

I didn't think he heard me. While the waves came in and out he stood there looking at me. After a while he said, "Oral Roberts, do you really believe what you are saying?"

"With all my heart," I replied.

"You don't know me," he said. "You don't know what has happened to me."

"Yes, I do," I laughed. "You've spent the last hour or two telling me."

Again he just stood and looked at me. "Let's go sit down on the beach," I suggested.

As we sat down, he said, "Help me."

I felt it when he said it. What a good feeling this is. You can only get help when you are ready and when you ask.

I said, "I want to ask you some questions. God can help you but He must have your wholehearted cooperation." In substance, here's what I said.

"Who do you trust in?"

"Well, God, of course."

"Pardon me, but listening to you I didn't get that idea at all."

"I've been a Christian for a long time."

"I'm sure of that. But you were talking about needs and problems with your job, with people you deal with, with your family, with earthly things that are necessary to your existence. What I mean is, in all these things who do you trust in?"

Slowly, he said, "I guess I have never thought much about it."

You see, he had never thought of God in terms of meeting these needs in his life and family. I said, "I met God first when I learned He was concerned about my body. Through the possibility of healing for my body I became interested in God saving my soul. Then 12 years later when I learned God was interested in prospering His people, of meeting all their needs—spiritual, physical, and financial—I became concerned about all these things too. Out of this has developed this ministry of healing for the whole man."

He said, "Well, before I heard you preach, I hadn't been taught that it is God's will to heal, or that we are supposed to expect miracles. A lot of my religious background has been in don'ts—don't do this, don't do that. I never heard a man say, 'God is a good God,' until I heard you say it. It's almost more than I can take in."

I said, "The same God who is the Source of your salvation and eternal life in heaven is also the Source for your other needs to be supplied. God is concerned about your spiritual development, and He is concerned with your financial needs as you sell door-to-door. He's there too."

"Go on," he said.

"Do you give to the Lord?"

He said, "Oh, yes, I believe in tithing. I give a tenth to my church. I owe this to the Lord."

I said, "But do you ever release your faith when you give to God so God can give to you?"

He said, "Well, when you owe the Lord something, you just pay it."

I saw that he did not connect faith with his giving. It was done as a duty, an obligation, and without faith for a return. Again he had separated God from every part of his life except his being saved and going to heaven. God was back in the past when He saved his soul; He would be in heaven when he died and went there. But where is God in the NOW? Where is God this moment, here, when a man is down and feels he can never get up? Where is God when a man is saved, but is miserable and unhappy and too defeated in his battle with life to take care of his family and fulfill himself? The Scripture, Hebrews 13:8, came to my mind:

Jesus Christ the same yesterday, and today, and for ever.

I thought of the statement of Martha to Jesus concerning raising her brother Lazarus from the dead—"I know that he shall rise again in the resurrection at the last day." Jesus said unto her, "I am the resurrection, and the life" (John 11:24,25).

"I am!"

Jesus didn't say, "I was."

He didn't say, "I shall be."

He said, "I am."

IN EVERY MOMENT JESUS IS THE GREAT I AM—
HE FILLS THE NOW WITH HIMSELF

And that's where He comes to us—we meet Him in the now. Turning to my friend again, I asked, "In your job, your dealing with people, and all that, do you ever expect a miracle?"

He said, "I've only heard about doing that since I came down here. It's a new thought to me."

I said, "Look here. Listen. Do what I tell you from God's Word. I want you to straighten up, square your shoulders, and start a new beginning. I want you to return home looking to God and trusting Him as THE Source of your total supply! I want you to give as a seed you plant and as a point of contact, and I want you to expect God to return it from unexpected sources. And as you go about your work, expect a miracle. I promise you if you will do *these three things* from your heart, and do them day in and day out, God will make you into a new man. You will prosper. Someday you won't know yourself. You may even own your own business. You will be in control of yourself. You will be an effective witness for Christ. You will have influence and fulfillment."

The rest of the day he was quiet. I caught him looking far away several times, and then the day ended.

There was no way I could tell the impact that the Three Miracle Keys of Seed-Faith made on him. As he said a few years later, "I had been down so long, getting up had never occurred to me."

It took months for even a part of SEED-FAITH to soak in and become a part of his thinking. Every now and then a portion of it would become clear to him. Each time though he started putting it into practice.

The most amazing thing to me was when he came to an ORU seminar later in Tulsa. One look at him and I said, "What has happened to you?" He replied, "You should know."

He had come in a new car. He had on a nice looking suit. He grabbed my hand in a positive way. He spoke without hesitating. He acted like a man on a mission.

He had not told me yet that he was no longer selling from door-to-door. Nor did I know that he had started a little company of his own; his sons were in it with him. He had moved into a new home. He no longer was paying his tithes because of the sense of obligation; he was now giving with a joy and gladness, knowing God would multiply it back over and over. He had begun witnessing for Christ. Miracles had been happening. Then he told me that he was at the seminar to get more "ammunition."

Since then he has shared with me on several occasions. He is demonstrating the principles Jesus gave us in SEED-FAITH in a practical way in the city where he lives, his church, his association with other people, and in the partnership he has with this ministry.

You cannot help but be inspired by a man who has come so far upward after he had said, "It's no use, I can't make it."

YOUR BELIEVING CAN TAKE OPPOSITE FORMS—
IT CAN BE FAITH OR IT CAN BE DOUBT.
FAITH RIGHTLY DIRECTED IS THE KEY TO EVERYTHING.
WHATEVER YOU CAN CONCEIVE AND BELIEVE, YOU CAN DO.

When things go wrong . . . and they will! . . . remember that behind every miracle is a struggle of faith. It's a matter of releasing your faith to God. Keep looking for your miracle. It's on the way. Plant this thought in your mind today . . . *all day:*

YOUR GOD-GIVEN KEY FOR TODAY
"Turning My Faith Loose Is My Key To A Miracle!"

SATURDAY

**Key:
I WILL KEEP MY EYES ON GOD
MY SOURCE AND PLANT SEED
FOR MY MIRACLE**

**or
What To Do When Bad Things Keep Happening . . .**

I want to share with you the story of the man Job in the Old Testament. I want you to see Job (pronounced Jobe) and know him— above all, TO KNOW GOD AS HE DID. I want to put Job's story in the NOW to give you a handle for your faith and to help you see how you can face your serious problems . . . for yourself . . . and for your family . . . and feel a knowing inside that you will receive your miracles.

(Read the book of Job, especially the first three or four chapters, also the last chapter, which is chapter 42.)

One day the devil said to God, "I don't like this man. I don't dig him."

God said, "Why not?"

"He's having it too good. He thinks all these things are coming from You. Take them away, give him some bad deals, let people turn against him, let him get sick and feel pain. Then You'll see he's not for real. He doesn't have an honest relationship with You, God. He's pretending to love You because of all the good things that are happening to him."

Ever wonder what the devil tells God about you and me? Does he tell God of our shortcomings and faults, our selfishness and prejudices and fears? Does the devil put us in a bad light when he has a chance?

Well, it wasn't long until one bad thing after another started happening to Mr. Job. It came in like a flood. His children were in an accident. His business fell off and finally went under. He became ill in his body and couldn't work anymore. When he needed her the most, his wife misunderstood and walked out on him. Then his closest friends blamed him for what had happened to him and his family.

With his mind full of anguish and fear, his heart broken, with no one on earth to help him, Job wished he had never been born. He wished he were dead. Sound familiar?

One thing stands out in Job's story. He held on to his faith, to the fact that God was his Source, and that God is good. And that took some doing!

When people read the Bible they don't always see that God is a good God or He is their Source. They don't see these men and women as flesh and blood with serious problems and needs. They don't understand that what they did was to hold on to their faith and to continue to trust in God as the Source of their total supply. Although Job lost a lot, he clung to his faith in God. He discovered in a changing world the only reality, the only enduring thing, is faith in God.

Let's see how he clung to his faith and what the result was.

JOB'S SUFFERING

Everybody has a problem, or he is a problem, or he lives with one. This means everybody suffers at times—he suffers losses, is misunderstood, is forsaken, is all alone.

What's back of it? What causes it?

1. Job suffered as a result of what the devil did to him.

I believe there is a real devil. He's very real. He spoke against Job and caused others to oppose him. It was because of the devil that Job was put through this very severe test.

2. Job suffered as a result of what men and circumstances did to him.

People were envious of Job. Accidents happened to his children and caused their death. It is what some people call the winds of chance, or being a victim of circumstances.

The fact is, these things were beyond Job's control. There was nothing he could do to prevent them. He was struck, blow after blow, until he was utterly alone and helpless as far as man's power was concerned.

3. Job also suffered because of what he did to himself.

While viewing the collapse of everything dear to him, he said, 'For the thing which I greatly feared is come upon me, and that which I was afraid of is come unto me" (Job 3:25).

"The thing I greatly feared . . . that which I was afraid of . . ."

I know this language for I've faced fear all my life. And in every day's mail people say to me, "Oh, Brother Roberts, I'm so afraid such and such is going to happen."

Job put into words what he actually had done to himself. "I feared . . . I was afraid," he admitted.

To me, it's good to admit this. Get it out of your system. Confess it to God. Go on and say it, "God, I'm scared."

Job had believed the worst. He believed terrible things were going to happen—and they did. *This is what constitutes fear, believing the wrong things instead of believing God!*

To sum up Job's suffering, it was a combination of what the devil and men and circumstances did to him, and what he did to himself by fearing.

WHERE ARE YOU TODAY?

Are you in Job's shoes? Wholly or partly? Do you feel deserted and alone? Is the devil really after you?

What about God? How do you feel toward Him?

Well, in spite of all you're going through, you can, through God's help, turn yourself toward God and trust Him as your Source. Don't sweat and fume because certain people and circumstances have let you down. They are not sources . . . but instruments only. As your Source of total supply, God controls the people and things He can use to deliver you out of all your troubles. Cling to your faith; don't give that up. It's the only reality you have left. Do what Job did.

What did Job do?

1. He clung to God, his Source.

As he sat and suffered, he said, "Though God slay me, yet shall I trust in Him. I shall trust my Source . . . My Source is God." Consider that . . .

Job's trust in his wife and family did not prevent something bad from happening to them.

His trust in his associates and friends did not prevent their desertion.

His trust in material possessions did not prevent them from being taken away, leaving him without money and with bills piling up. Therefore, he could not make any of these his source.

Even the fact that he trusted in God did not make him immune to problems and suffering.

What it did do, however, was to give Job an anchor to hold to. By trusting in God as his Source, Job could hold himself steady while everything else was shaking around him.

Now the entire Bible teaches that God is the Source of your total supply. Everything and everybody else is an instrument only. THE BIBLE TEACHES THAT WHEN ALL ELSE FAILS, YOUR DIVINE SOURCE WILL NEVER LET YOU DOWN IF YOU TRUST IN HIM IF YOU CLING TO HIM.

We should not be surprised that people change and fail us, or that circumstances are sometimes against us. They are NOT our source and are not meant to be. We live on earth but OUR LIFE IS IN GOD. Our supply line is between Him and us, not between us and people and things.

2. Job finally put his faith to work by seeding for a miracle. He prayed for those who had hurt him. He forgave them.

To do this, Job had to start giving FIRST. Giving of his love and forgiveness toward others, and doing it first. (This is practicing Key No. 2.)

When Job had been successful and had money, he had given money to the Lord, to the widows and orphans, and to the helpless. Now he has no money left. But he has something he can give and he willingly gives it.

What did he have left to give? He had the ability to pray; he had the feeling for others. These he gave. The Bible says he "PRAYED FOR HIS FRIENDS" (Job 42:10). They were friends who had failed to understand him in his losses. They criticized and blamed him.

How he must have wanted to receive their prayers in his behalf. How he needed to receive. He could have demanded of God that he receive first. He could have said, "Someone pray for me first." Instead, he prayed for them.

Sometimes it costs more to give forgiveness than it does to give money. It surely must have been hard for Job to pray for his friends first and forgive them. There is no record that they accepted his prayer of forgiveness. But they were not his Source. The important thing is what Job DID . . . as it is important to you what you do toward others.

You know God has placed faith, hope, and love in you. All these deeper and finer feelings are God-given. Your ability to pray, to hope, to love, to forgive, are gifts of God. They are real in your life. You've freely received; Jesus tells you to freely give . . . and give first (Matthew 10:8, Luke 6:38).

When Job gave his prayers and forgiveness he put in the seed for God to start multiplying all he had lost back to him. It was the seed he had put in that initiated a new positive action from God in his behalf.

> 3. Job got his miracle. "And the Lord turned the captivity of Job, when he prayed for his friends . . . [God] gave Job twice as much as he had before" (Job 42:10).

Through what the devil and people and circumstances had done to Job, plus what he had done to himself, he had lost everything. By clinging to God, his Source, by seeding for a miracle in opening himself up and giving forgiveness to those who hurt him, and doing it first, Job started expecting a miracle—his miracle—and he got not one but many!

God reversed the trend of what was happening against him. God multiplied back all he had lost—health, family, earnings, faith, love—giving him TWICE AS MUCH. He was twice as well off as before. *This is the OVERFLOW Jesus talks about. "Give, and it shall be given unto you;* GOOD MEASURE, PRESSED DOWN, AND SHAKEN TOGETHER, AND RUNNING OVER, SHALL MEN GIVE INTO YOUR BOSOM" (Luke 6:38). This giving to Job was *overwhelming.* It was when he needed it on earth—in his lifetime—long before he went to heaven.

   This is God supplying all your need ACCORDING TO HIS RICHES (Philippians 4:19). This is God causing the seed sown to multiply beyond what you can ask or think (2 Corinthians 9:10).

Job clung to God, the Source of his supply. In the same way, by trusting in God you can hold yourself steady while everything else crumbles around you. The Bible teaches that when all else fails, your divine Source will NEVER let you down—if you trust in Him, if you cling to Him.

YOUR GOD-GIVEN KEY FOR TODAY

"I Will Keep My Eyes On God My Source And Plant Seed For My Miracle!"

ELEVENTH WEEK

SUNDAY	I WILL PLANT SEEDS OF LOVE AND NOT FEAR
MONDAY	GOD IS ALIVE AND CONTINUOUSLY ACTIVE IN MY LIFE
TUESDAY	NO WEAPON FORMED AGAINST ME WILL PROSPER IF I KEEP MY SPIRIT RIGHT
WEDNESDAY	I'LL KEEP ON TOP BY LEARNING TO TRUST GOD'S LAW OF AVERAGES
THURSDAY	IT IS GOD'S POWER HEALING ME
FRIDAY	TURNING MY FAITH LOOSE IS MY KEY TO A MIRACLE
SATURDAY	I WILL KEEP MY EYES ON GOD MY SOURCE AND PLANT SEED FOR MY MIRACLE

TWELFTH WEEK

Why You Must Struggle And
How To Find The Seed Of An Equal Benefit

SUNDAY

Key:
GOD'S STROKES FOR ME ARE
ALWAYS UPWARD

or
God Will Help You Through Every Struggle Of Your Life

I WAS driving away from Tulsa a few miles down a country road when I looked to my left and there in a pasture a cow was just giving birth to a calf. I stopped my car and watched. I got out of the car and walked up as close as the mother cow would allow me to. When the calf was finally born, it was enveloped in what appeared to be a white plastic shield. Suddenly the little calf gave a big kick and another kick and the shield fell away and the little calf was there. Then it began to struggle to stand up. It tried to raise first one leg and then another. It tried to get up and when it did it fell down. It kept trying to get up and it kept falling down.

Then I saw one of the most marvelous things in nature. The mother cow came over and with her long, tough, bristlelike tongue she began to lick the calf. As she licked it I noticed that she was giving powerful, upward strokes. As she licked the calf she licked it upward. In a powerful way as she began to lick the calf she was also helping it to its feet. As she was licking it she would move it. The little calf would struggle and she would lift it again. She kept on with those powerful strokes until she got the baby calf on its feet. It stood there, all wobbly and trembling and shaky, and again she applied those powerful upward strokes. She never stroked the calf sideways or down. It was always upward. Then as the calf was able to stand and take a step or two the mother cow began to move the calf with her powerful tongue and maneuver it under her body close to her udder where the little baby calf could smell the mother's milk. Immediately the baby calf raised its head and began to nurse. I stood there watching it. After a while it was filled and then I saw something else that was marvelous. The little calf turned and walked away without wobbling or falling. It appeared strong. Suddenly it took off. Have you ever seen a calf run? That little calf ran and jumped and received life exuberantly.

Immediately the Scripture came to my mind—the words of St. Paul where he said:

> *Forgetting those things which are behind . . . I press toward the mark for the prize of the high calling of God in Christ Jesus* (Philippians 3:13,14).

Paul said he was pressing forward—not downward or sideward—but forward. All his life Paul struggled to forget his past . . . the things that he had done wrong. And he felt the powerful urging of God to reach up, to reach out, to go forward.

"ORAL, YOU CAN DO BETTER"

I have a wonderful friend among many other friends. But this friend is different than all others I have on the earth. He stands out because he's a critical guy. He's always criticizing me. Now how could I feel that a critical guy is my friend? Usually when someone is always criticizing you, you wish you'd never hear from him again or see him anymore. But I love this man dearly. I've known him for a long time. I see him very infrequently but he always seems to appear when I need him the most. I mean when I need a good criticism. You see:

EVERYONE NEEDS TO BE CRITICIZED ONCE IN A WHILE

We don't always feel that way about it but that is God's way. We need someone to give us a different kind of stroke. Well, this man has a favorite phrase for Oral Roberts and no matter how well I do or how many accomplishments I make, he has one word to say to me:

"Oral, you can do better."

I remember when we built Oral Roberts University students began coming from everywhere and, my, it was just wonderful. We all knew it was a miracle of God. How thrilled and proud I was. Then my good friend walked up and said, "Oral, you can do better."

We have television specials four times a year on prime time with many well-known guest stars. Each special has been drawing over 50 million viewers. It's a tremendous mission field for the gospel. After we had done such a special in which the ratings gave us an extremely large audience, we were all talking about it and I was thrilled. This fellow happened to see me and he said, "Oral, you can do better."

Once in a while we who preach the gospel feel like we have preached a particularly wonderful sermon. I've never been bothered with this much because I've never preached many sermons that I was completely pleased with. I've always felt like maybe if I'd had it to do over I could preach a better sermon. But on one particular occasion when maybe I did feel that I had preached a rather remarkable sermon, there was this friend again saying to me, "Oral, you can do better."

Now, isn't it wonderful to have a friend like that? I feel God put him in my life. "Oral, you can do better." And that's what the mother cow was saying to the little calf as she stroked it with powerful upward strokes of her thick strong tongue: "Little one, keep on trying, keep on struggling."

You see, if the little calf were to say, "It's no use . . . I've failed . . . I tried but I didn't make it . . . I might as well give up," the mother cow could not help. The calf had to do his part—he had to try . . . he had to struggle . . . to do what may have seemed like the impossible.

All my life I have known struggle so I feel it very deeply when I say that it is absolutely necessary for you to struggle.

STRUGGLE GIVES YOU BACKBONE . . . IT STRENGTHENS YOUR FAITH IN GOD YOUR SOURCE . . . IT HELPS YOU TO OVERCOME GREAT HANDICAPS

For example, I was never able to shake off what my kinfolk said about me when I was growing up. I was a stammerer and a frail child as well. I never thought they believed in me . . . and most did not. They thought my stammering was funny so they teased and tormented me. They probably thought it was only "fun" but to a small boy it was "torment." Perhaps they didn't mean any harm by it but it left an awful mark on my young life. It also gave me a determination to prove them wrong.

The huge tent "cathedral" that we used in the earlier part of this ministry had an immense seating capacity. I was so excited about that big tent and what God was doing that I wanted to take it back to the town where I was raised, Ada, Oklahoma.

I was born five miles out in the country, out in the backwoods, where I lived until I was a good-sized boy. Then Papa moved us to Ada, which is the county seat of Pontotoc County. My grandfather, Mr. Amos P. Roberts, came from Alabama and settled in old Indian Territory in about 1890, several years before Oklahoma became a state. He became a judge in the territory and was held in high esteem by the people. The majority of his offspring still live in Pontotoc County. I suppose there are more Roberts in Pontotoc County than any other family.

So I took the big tent to Ada and stretched it within two blocks of the spot where I was healed of tuberculosis many years before. The population of Ada at that time was only 15,000, and nobody believed we would fill the tent.

But I had a burning desire to go. From the first night God began to pour out His Spirit to save and heal the people and they came from everywhere. They packed and jammed the tent with thousands standing around the edge. It was the largest crowd in the history of that city for anything.

My relatives came in from all over the country. They had known me as a child and now heard I was preaching the gospel and was having great crowds and great meetings. They didn't realize the crowds would be so big, so when they came late they had to stand. They soon caught on and bet. e the meeting was over many of the Roberts kin would come at noon and sit there until the service started at seven-thirty so they would have a good seat.

MAMMA AND PAPA HAD FAITH IN ME

Uncle Willis, who told Papa I would never preach because I couldn't talk, heard of the meeting and came. He thought the world of me, but because he teased me so hard I thought he hated me. I remember one day after a particularly humiliating experience in which he led the crowd in laughing at my attempts to talk, I slipped away and hid under the house. They left about sundown and I crawled out and stood on the back porch of the little log house where I had been born. Barefooted and dressed in overalls, I looked out across the hills of Pontotoc County, Oklahoma, and wondered what was on the other side, and if I would ever amount to anything. Standing there I felt lost and helpless, bewildered and confused, frustrated and afraid. I saw nothing in myself, neither did anyone else, except my father and mother.

Papa remonstrated with my uncle, "Why don't you let Oral alone? God has His hand on him. Some day he will preach the gospel and then you will see."

My uncle laughed and said, "Oral preach? Why he can't even talk!"

Papa said, "Someday you will see."

My uncle thought that was a big joke.

When I returned to Ada, Oklahoma, for a revival crusade in 1948, he came. Uncle Willis had never gone to church much but he stood out there at the edge of the tent with the other people, hanging on to every word I said. At the close of the service he was still standing there. The crowd was still milling around the tent when Papa came upon Uncle Willis. He found him with his face buried in his hands and tears streaming down his face. Papa said, "Willis, what's the matter?"

Uncle Willis looked up and saw it was Papa. He said, "Ellis, I was just standing here wondering if that was the little stuttering boy that I said would never preach."

Papa said, "Well, what do you think now?"

He said, "Ellis, it is the greatest thing I ever saw. I would give everything I have in this world if I had in my soul what he's got in his."

Then he accepted Christ as his personal Savior in that meeting.

After that, he sincerely served God and supported my ministry with his prayers and influence.

So, my friend, if you are struggling today . . . and most of us are with one problem or another . . . don't look on it as a negative thing. Remember that God loves you and He is there with powerful upward strokes . . . if you will just look for Him. To do better, to overcome this problem—this struggle you are going through—you've got to turn yourself upward . . . you've got to respond to God. Like the little calf, you've got to keep trying to get on your feet and you'll discover with the help of God's powerful upward strokes that you can . . . and you will. Begin to open yourself up . . . to let God have His way.

> *First,* be sure you know God is your personal Savior and He is the Source of your total supply. Learn better every day to trust Him as your Source.
>
> *Second,* learn better how to give, to give of your love, of your concern, even of your money.
>
> *Third,* learn better every day how to expect a miracle.

You know, when we expect miracles we are more apt to receive miracles. It's a frame of mind, an attitude of life, in which we are reaching upward. We are looking to God. We are saying, "God, we are trusting in You." And it's like the mother cow with the powerful strokes, stroking the little calf, getting it up, helping it to walk, and to run, and to grow into a normal life. So God picks us up and pushes us with powerful strokes upward and He says to us:

> "FORGET THE THINGS THAT ARE BEHIND AND REACH OUT TO ME FOR THE MIRACLE YOU NEED."

That mother cow and her calf is a real "down-home" illustration. But it's a perfect picture of how God works in our lives so that we grow stronger and learn to know Jesus in a new dimension of understanding and trust.

Even when it appears that someone or something is knocking you down, comfort yourself with these words:

> "GOD'S EVERY STROKE IS ALWAYS UPWARD . . .
> *NEVER DOWNWARD!*"

YOUR GOD-GIVEN KEY FOR TODAY

Again:

"God's Strokes For Me Are Always Upward!"

MONDAY

Key:
I CAN PLANT MY ADVERSITIES AS A SEED AND REAP A BENEFIT!

or

How Recognizing The Seed Of An Equal Benefit Can Turn A Disaster Into Victory

Some time ago I was playing a round of golf with a very important man. I had looked forward to this privilege for I hoped to get in a little witness for my Savior. Well, I did . . . but not in the way I expected.

I stepped up to hit a drive and I hit a bad one. Now I'm a pretty good golfer when I get to play regularly but I had not played in a long time. Anyway, I hit the drive and the ball wound up under a tree.

My friend made a choice comment. He said, "Too bad, Oral." Then he got real serious and said, "Golf is a lot like life. One small mistake and it affects the rest of your whole life."

I heard myself saying, "Yes, golf is sure like life."

Then I thought of what the Bible says and I said, "Wait a minute. Life is not like golf. If God is your Source . . . and if you are giving as a seed you plant as Christ said . . . and if you are expecting miracles, then you can replay the mistakes you make in life."

He said, "What do you mean? Your ball is lying over there under the tree . . ."

I said, "I know I can't replay that stroke. I've got to go over there under the tree and get the ball out the best I can. But God has not left His children like that. He has given us the seed of an equal benefit."

He said, "The seed of *what*??"

I said, "The seed of an equal benefit. In other words, in every mistake you make in life, God has placed another seed. If you know the seed is there and you plant it, then it will be multiplied into something greater, and it will multiply into something greater than the mistake you made."

Then I shared with him a story in the Bible. It was the story of Joseph. He was one of the twelve sons of Jacob, you remember. He was also Jacob's favorite and he was a spiritual boy. He had many dreams because he was very sensitive to the Spirit of God. But Joseph made the mistake of sharing those dreams with his brothers. He told them that in his dream they had all fallen down and made obeisance to him.

This made them angrier than they already were, for they were jealous because their father bestowed special favors on Joseph.

One day Jacob sent Joseph with some provisions for his brothers who were tending the sheep some distance from home. When the brothers saw Joseph coming in the distance they said, "Look, there comes the dreamer. Here's our chance. Let's get rid of him."

While they were deciding exactly what to do, a caravan traveling to Egypt came by and they decided to sell Joseph into slavery.

So Joseph wound up a slave in Egypt . . . far from home. I can imagine that many times he thought about the mistake he'd made in telling his brothers about his dreams. But the Bible says the Lord was with Joseph. And although Joseph had many temptations he kept his eyes on God, his Source. He kept giving.

He landed in prison . . . unjustly accused. There he continued giving and God blessed him. He was put in charge of the other prisoners. He befriended the king's baker and butler who had lost favor with Pharaoh and, therefore, had been thrown into prison. They both dreamed dreams that deeply troubled them, so Joseph interpreted the dreams.

And it was in a dream that Joseph found the seed of an equal benefit. The Pharaoh of Egypt dreamed a dream and he called for all the magicians and wise men in Egypt but none could interpret the dream. Finally the king's butler whom Joseph had befriended and had now been restored to his position, remembered Joseph. And he said to Pharaoh, "There is a man in whom is the Spirit of God. He can interpret your dream."

It was a miracle to Joseph for they brought him out of prison before Pharaoh and he interpreted the dream. And it was part of the overall purpose of God to save Egypt during the time of great famine which was to come. Pharaoh then made Joseph prime minister of Egypt and instructed him to do as the dream had said. Thus Joseph was able not only to save Egypt, but also people from many surrounding countries — including his own family — during the seven years of famine.

IN EVERY MISTAKE, IN EVERY ADVERSITY,
THERE IS A SEED OF AN EQUAL BENEFIT.
IF YOU WILL LOOK FOR IT AND APPLY IT,
YOU CAN GET A BENEFIT THAT IS AS GREAT
AS THE ONE YOU TRIED TO GET OR FAILED TO
GET IN THE FIRST PLACE.
GOD WILL MULTIPLY IT INTO SOMETHING GREATER.

That's hard to do. I'll admit it. But it's absolutely essential to successful Seed-Faith living. Learn to think positively about everything that happens to you . . . even to the point of expressing it . . . like this:

YOUR GOD-GIVEN KEY FOR TODAY

"I Can Plant My Adversities As A Seed And

Reap A Benefit!"

TUESDAY

or
The Biggest Loss I Ever Had And How I Found The Seed Of An Equal Benefit

In September 1950 we took the big tent to Amarillo, Texas. The Amarillo Crusade was great. More than 2,450 people were saved. The miracles of healing were outstanding and people were moved with the presence and power of the Lord.

On the tenth night, a storm struck. The winds came roaring in out of the northwest. I was standing at the pulpit when suddenly the lights went out. I shouted, "Everyone stay seated and keep your mind on God!" They did. In the flash of lightning I saw the entire tent begin to lift toward the sky—it looked like billows of light, then it began to settle, floating down slowly.

"Oh, Lord, save the 7,000 people from harm!" I prayed.

It seemed as if a thousand invisible hands took control of the situation.

I remember a statement I had made in one of my sermons during the meeting. I said, "The storms of life come to everybody—to the saved and unsaved, to those who live in God's will and to those who don't. The only difference is that Jesus is in the Christian's boat, just like He was with the disciples (Luke 8:22-25), and that makes all the difference in the world."

GOD WAS RIDING WITH US THAT NIGHT

The lightning flashed all around us and the winds roared like a freight train. The next thing I knew, the rear of the tent lifted over my head and I felt myself falling backward. I said, "Lord, this is it." I was laid down very gently on the lower section of the platform as if by an invisible hand. I still had the microphone in my hands. I was not hurt. Then I heard several hundred people singing. A man near me began to praise the Lord. I climbed back to the main platform which was still intact.

I looked back at the crowd. The aluminum poles were gently lowering toward the people on the chairs. The big 1,000-pound steel center poles were inching toward the ground. A part of the tent draped over the chairs and I saw people crawling out from under the tattered tent, fighting canvas off their heads. No one panicked.

I BELIEVE THERE WERE ANGELS IN
THAT TENT THAT NIGHT

Every person came out alive. About fifty people were slightly hurt, but none seriously.

I ran from group to group praying with people and praising God for our safety.

Meanwhile the hail was really coming down. People had chairs over their heads to protect them.

The firemen got there, went through the tent, and announced that no one was left under it. A policeman rushed up to me and said, "Reverend Roberts, this is the most miraculous thing I have ever seen."

The newspaper reporters found me. I told them how it happened. One was almost in tears. "Brother Roberts," he said, "God was there." The next morning the *Amarillo Times* crowded the war news off the front page and ran a blazing headline: ESCAPE OF 7,000 CALLED MIRACLE.

The next day I went out to see the wreckage. Poles and ripped canvas lay over the chairs. How anybody could have gotten out alive can only be answered by saying, "This is the greatest miracle I have ever seen." One of the insurance men said to me, "Reverend Roberts, the good Lord had His hand over this place last night." He was right. The Lord had given us a miracle. But as I stood there surveying the wreckage and wondering again if I was through, someone ran up with a telegram that was from one of our partners in Colorado. It read:

"DEAR BROTHER ROBERTS:

YOU CAN'T GO UNDER FOR GOING OVER . . ."

Something leaped in my heart. I looked at the remains of that old tent and for the first time since the storm, tears came to my eyes. I said, "Old tent, you are gone. But I have no regrets. You fought the battle with me and thousands of people have come to Jesus Christ under your shelter . . ."

Then I said to the Lord, "Lord, I have no regrets. I had nothing when I started three years ago but faith. I still have that faith. You protected the lives of 7,000 people in the midst of the storm. No sermon I might have preached could compare with this mighty miracle . . . with Your help, I will begin again. I will secure a bigger tent, one that can withstand the storms . . ."

And this is what we did. I told the people about our plans as I preached on our radio broadcasts. I told them how faith leaped in my heart. I told them how the words of my own sermon came back to me through a telegram: "YOU CAN'T GO UNDER FOR GOING OVER." I told them, "With God's help we're going over," and we did.

But for a little more interesting background on the destruction of the old tent: In 1950 engineers apparently had not yet been able to construct a tent that could survive a hundred-mile-an-hour wind. So apparently the Lord intended that I would be the testing point.

After our tent went down we met with a group of engineers and came up with a plan for a tent that would withstand the storms. It was much larger than we'd ever had before, and of course more durable. In fact, they told us that this tent could withstand the winds better than a brick building.

We took them at their word and ordered the tent. And for the next 15 years we used tents for our crusades that would seat up to 12,000. These tents experienced winds that were even stronger than the Amarillo storm, but they were never blown down.

Out of seeming disaster came THE SEED OF AN EQUAL BENEFIT. And out of it came into my heart a faith that what I was doing was indestructible. Not only was it indestructible—it could not be decreased. It would be MULTIPLIED.

———◆———

What does that say to you in *your* losses? God has bigger things ahead for you . . . ALWAYS! Affirm it with faith, regardless of the circumstances:

YOUR GOD-GIVEN KEY FOR TODAY
"My Losses Will Lead Me To Permanent Gain."

WEDNESDAY Key: GOD NEVER MAKES A MISTAKE IN MY LIFE

or
How To Get Kicked Out Of A Bank And Reap The Seed Of An Equal Benefit

I vividly remember a period during late 1957 and early 1958 when a shortage of funds threatened to stop our ministry entirely.

At that time we were building our first major building—a seven-story headquarters building in downtown Tulsa. A recession struck our nation and we suffered. Lending institutions of the country withdrew many of their commitments, and we were included in the "cutback."

Several months before this, Lee Braxton and I had talked to our banker and he had verbally agreed to loan us one million dollars toward the construction of our building. On the strength of that promise we had gone ahead. We had a payroll to meet and contracts . . . and we ran out of money (we tried to pay as we built) . . . so Lee and I went to the bank for the promised loan. The head man who had personally made the commitment to us looked us right in the eye and said, "I never made you any such loan commitment."

Lee looked at me and I looked at him. Were we dreaming when we had sat in this same office months before and were told that we had a commitment for one million dollars? There was no need to argue, the conversation was over, and we left.

For the next three months I faced absolute defeat. Since we began in this ministry we have never defaulted on an obligation. This is part of the integrity on which this ministry has been built. The outer walls of the building were up and that was all. Now there were no funds left and seemingly we could borrow none.

Lee Braxton and his wife Norma offered their entire estate with no strings attached. Their offer brought tears to my eyes but I turned them down. However, the wonderful spirit of their offer lifted my faith.

One day Manford Engel, our vice-president, phoned me during a crusade. "Oral, I dislike to disturb you during a crusade," he said, "but we are out of funds. May we have your permission to shut down construction of the new building?"

"Manford," I replied, "I have no instructions from the Lord to halt construction. He has told me to build and I must obey."

"Then a miracle must take place immediately," he answered.

The crusade ended and I returned home.

"ORAL ROBERTS' FOLLY . . ."

I went at once to the building site. It was winter and the weather was bad. I stood across the street and looked at what God told me to build. To the physical eyes it was only a skeleton of a building.

The devil whispered, "You are looking at 'Oral Roberts' folly.' This is all the people will ever see as they pass by."

The icy winds whipped around me and I shivered in the cold. But I shut my eyes and ears to the devil's suggestions, pulled my coat collar up around my head, and began to pray.

Suddenly a glowing radiance surrounded my being, for as I prayed I felt the presence of Jesus of Nazareth. All at once it was like a vision before me! The building was finished in gleaming white, the different departments were staffed and workers were sending literature, radio tapes, TV films and letters throughout the world.

Before the vision vanished, God reaffirmed to me that I had been born for this purpose and was raised up for this hour to take the message of His healing power to my generation.

When I opened my eyes the weather was still cold and dreary, the building was still only a shell . . . and I was alone on the street.

Yet I was not alone for Jesus was with me. And a miracle had begun to happen in my heart.

I knew that cold day that a miracle would happen to help us finish the building. No longer did I have the nagging torment of doubt and anxiety.

I KNEW . . . that I KNEW . . . that I KNEW . . . that I KNEW!!!

And the miracle came. I was in the next crusade when Manford called and said, "I have good news! Two things are happening.

First, special contributions for the building are coming in from friends and partners everywhere.

Second, the largest lending institution in Tulsa has extended us a line of credit which, with the contributions coming in, will enable us to finish construction on schedule."

I was happy . . . but not surprised. There had been no question in my mind that the miracle would come . . . it was just a matter of WHEN.

So what looked like disaster turned out to be the best thing that could have happened to us. For when friends learned of our problem they went to the largest bank in town and opened the door for us to go there for a loan. And as I said, the loan was granted. This was *the seed of an equal benefit.* It was time for us to leave the first bank for it was too small to meet our future needs. We did not know that . . . but God did. He had something better for us.

Christianity is very simple when you think about it. It is Christ right in the center of your heart—

helping you to open up . . .

to put God first in your life and in your giving . . .

and to remember . . .

In every mistake you make, there is a seed of an equal benefit—

which means . . . and I want you to memorize this!

YOUR GOD-GIVEN KEY FOR TODAY
"God Never Makes A Mistake In My Life."

THURSDAY

**Key:
I WILL MOVE WITH GOD INTO
NEW DIMENSIONS OF LIFE**

or

How I Turned A NO From Experts Into A YES That Changed My Entire Ministry

In the early '50's, television was a struggling infant. People would cluster around a store window fascinated by this one-eyed genius. Few realized the impact it would make upon humanity.

At that time there were 26 million television sets in the United States and the number was growing every day.

There were predictions that television would overshadow radio. We did not believe this. We were on 300 powerful radio stations in the United States and overseas and were receiving a very good response. However, we felt God was also directing us to use television. We recognized that many would watch a program who would not just listen.

I WANTED TO MOVE WITH GOD

For at least three years, we continued to pray and seek God's will. I was determined that when I made the move it would be divinely ordained of God.

Finally, we believed the time had come. After weeks of hard work, our first television program was premiered on January 10, 1954, on 16 stations. Others were quickly added as time could be cleared and pledges of support were received.

The response was immediate. Overnight, our volume of mail soared. This confirmed our convictions that we were heading in the right direction.

Yet, there was something lacking. The programs, being filmed in a studio, had no live crusade audience to "pull" the message out of me. I felt the people were not getting the real power and impact of the deliverance ministry.

THE EXPERTS SAID IT WAS IMPOSSIBLE TO FILM OUR CRUSADES LIVE

We investigated the possibilities of televising our crusades live. A major television network visited a crusade and told us it could not be done. Rex Humbard of Akron, Ohio, encouraged us to find a way to film directly from the tent. Finally, we located a film company who agreed to try it for $42,000.

THE PEOPLE SAID IT WAS SACRILEGIOUS TO BRING
THE TV CAMERAS INTO THE SERVICES

Besides conquering the mechanical and technical difficulties involved with filming, we had to do a selling job to our audiences. Some felt it was sacrilegious to bring the cameras into the sacred confines of the service. I told them that if they would cooperate by worshiping God and ignoring the cameras, we would have a chance to capture on film the true spirit of the crusade. "If God's anointing is on us here," I said, "it will be on the film. When people view it, it will have the same effect on them as it does on you."

The filming went well. The people were with me 100 percent. The Lord anointed me in a powerful way.

GOD GIVES ME A PLAN

God also gave me a plan—the Blessing-Pact—to finance the television filming. (This was the beginning of my understanding of Seed-Faith.)

I called a special afternoon service and shared this plan with my partners. I told them the Lord had given me a plan to enter into a partnership with each person who would help me to carry on our ministry. This partnership would be called a *Blessing-Pact*.

I pointed out examples of this in the Bible, such as the widow of Zarephath entered into a Blessing-Pact with the Prophet Elijah when she grasped the principle of partnership with God—that it is based upon faith and miracles. She had to do something first, even though it was just a little. Then God performed a miracle for her in return and supplied her needs in abundance.

Then I dropped a bombshell into their thinking. I said, "If I can trust God for the $42,000 to film the crusade, can you trust Him for $100? I am asking 420 people in this audience to make this pledge and in turn let me, as an instrument of God, enter into a Blessing-Pact with you for one year. I will use your gift to win souls; and because of this, I will earnestly pray that the Lord will return your gift in its entirety from a totally unexpected supply."

I promised that if at the end of one year God had not blessed them, I would return their money.

There was an audible gasp in the audience. The audacity of such a plan shook me a little too. But I knew God had given me the plan and I felt it would open the doors of their minds to thinking and believing for bigger things in their own lives.

Approximately 420 stood to accept the challenge and became the first members of the Blessing-Pact.

Once again God vindicated this step of faith. My partners testified by the hundreds how God blessed and prospered them through the

Blessing-Pact. Shortly thereafter we were able to withdraw our guarantee, for God was doing more than we had ever expected.

I could tell you about Blessing-Pact partners who are fruit growers up in Oregon, whose outstanding crops have been the talk of the entire area since they joined the Blessing-Pact; the man from Indiana, who was a local insurance representative when he joined the Blessing-Pact, and in a matter of months was promoted to general agent of northeastern Indiana; or the California botanist who received a call one hour after he mailed his first check to the Blessing-Pact. The county was interested in an old gravel pit he had on his property. They paid him over a thousand dollars for the gravel. I could introduce you to many who have attributed their healing, the salvation of loved ones, and the restoration of broken homes to the Blessing-Pact as the instrument they used to release their faith.

10 MILLION FRONT-ROW SEATS

In February 1955, we televised our first *live* service. Little did we realize that eleven years later we would be on more than 100 television stations, blanketing North America with this message of salvation and deliverance.

Wherever I go I meet people who tell me they accepted Christ while watching the program. Others relate how they were healed. Ministers have shared how seeing an actual healing caused them to restudy Jesus, to reexamine their own ministry. Only eternity will reveal the total results of our television ministry in those early days and as it continues today.

50 MILLION VIEWERS NOW

Under our present television format, begun in 1968, the ratings place our viewing audience for the prime-time specials at above 50 million each, and our Sunday morning ratings as number one over all television programs from 8 to 12 noon. Again, it is a miracle of God.

I've learned something invaluable out of all this experience: *Learn the way God is moving and then move with Him.* And don't be afraid, for God leads you to greater and more wonderful things ahead. You can trust your Source. He will never fail you.

YOUR GOD-GIVEN KEY FOR TODAY

Determine in your heart—

"I Will Move With God Into New Dimensions Of Life!"

FRIDAY

Key:
**GREATER IS HE (GOD) THAT IS
IN ME THAN HE (THE DEVIL)
THAT IS IN THE WORLD**

or

How God Brought Good Out Of Disaster . . . Even When Anti-God Forces Stopped A Crusade That Reached Thousands

The miraculous power of God is a direct frontal attack on the kingdom of Satan to loose the captive, to bring deliverance to the oppressed. In Australia we saw Satan's counterattack.

We went there in 1956 at the invitation of a group of ministers representing the Full Gospel Churches and by the authority of the Australian Government.

The city fathers of both Sydney and Melbourne granted us the use of their beautiful city parks for the big eight-pole tent. The people were hungry for God. It was a most natural setting for a great crusade.

WE WERE ATTACKED BY THE PRESS

But, acting under some strange influence, some of the daily newspapers of the two cities had decided that we would not have successful meetings in Australia. Obviously pre-written stories greeted us as the first crusade opened in Sydney. Later, a few half-truths were sprinkled in to give the stories the appearance of factual reporting. A reporter, who was reproved by a minister for this travesty of reporting, said, *We are not writing what we want to write, but what we are told to write.*

The main body of people who came were eager, open, and ready for the gospel. They represented many of the Australian churches.

During the ten days approximately 75,000 attended. The power of God was seen as hundreds decided to follow Christ. Many testified to miraculous healings.

THE LARGEST ALTAR CALLS IN AUSTRALIA'S HISTORY

The police cooperated splendidly and instructed our workers in the handling of the large crowds. Order was maintained and, with little exception, the people were reverent and impressed. Approximately 3,000 people came forward in ten nights to give their hearts to God. Of the altar calls, our Australian representative said, "We have just seen the largest altar calls in Australia's history."

THE MELBOURNE CRUSADE

The Melbourne meeting started off on an even larger scale than Sydney. It looked as though it might be the greatest opening night of all our crusades. Four hundred came forward for salvation. A nurse who had come hundreds of miles for prayer for deformed feet was marvelously healed.

The next morning (Monday), the Melbourne newspapers launched an all-out attack. Every conceivable ruse was used to mislead the people and keep them away from the meeting.

ANTI-GOD HECKLERS DISRUPTED THE MEETING

On Monday night, heckling started during the service. People yelled out to interrupt during the preaching and prayer for the sick.

By Wednesday night it was obvious that the opposition was organized. Hecklers, who came to the front with the converts, yelled and screamed their defiance. Well-known communist agitators were recognized moving about, stirring up the mob.

From the very start of the crusade the response to the altar calls had been tremendous. But by Wednesday, with the mob defying anyone to accept Christ as their personal Savior, only about sixty brave people came forward. It was then that I realized the mob was not against me, for when they hissed the Word of God and defied sinners to receive Christ as their personal Savior, I saw that they were anti-God and antireligion.

After the service was dismissed the mob surged to the back of the tent to get me, but I had already been rushed off the grounds with a police escort. That night one of our trucks was set on fire and one rope on the big tent was cut. (It was uncanny that a news photographer "just happened" to be present to photograph the vandalism.) That night they "booed" and tried to turn over the car that Evelyn was sitting in because they thought I was in it. When they found I wasn't, they quit.

Later, Evelyn said to me, "Oral, I don't want you to stay. They are going to do something terrible and someone is going to get hurt. I wish you would close the meeting and leave."

I replied, "Honey, as long as the people are getting saved and healed, I can't leave."

THREATS OF PHYSICAL VIOLENCE WERE MADE ON MY LIFE

Several times Evelyn received phone calls saying, "If you want your husband alive, get him out of Australia because we are going to see that he doesn't live if he stays here."

The next day, before I awakened, the team read the early morning headlines:

FIRE SET AT ORAL ROBERTS' TENT . . .
TONIGHT IT IS GOING TO BE BURNED DOWN

It was then that they made the decision to close the crusade, based on Acts 19:30,31:

*And when Paul would have entered in unto the people, the
disciples suffered him not. And certain of the chief of Asia,
which were his friends, sent unto him, desiring him that he
would not adventure himself into the theatre.*

My team did not feel that it was wise to endanger my life further.
Also, they felt that we could not continue the crusade through Sunday
as planned and jeopardize the lives of thousands of innocent people.

When they told me of their decision, they handed me plane tickets
back to America and advised me that the tent had already been
dismantled and was on its way to the ship.

THE GIFT OF WISDOM DEMONSTRATED

Just recently I was talking about the Australia Crusades with
Collins Steele. Collins was in charge of operations at that time and is
still with us today as my administrative assistant. I said, "Collins,
I've never asked you before but what did prompt you and the other
men to close down the crusade? I understand you met around midnight and made that decision, didn't you?"

He said, "Yes, we had a prayer meeting. In fact, we had a prayer
meeting until after midnight. Bob DeWeese and several of the spon-
soring pastors and other team members were there. As we prayed we
decided that we should dismantle the tent and get it on the ship as
quickly as possible. We felt we should take the matter into our own
hands. I really think God was moving through the gift of wisdom, and
guiding us. It was evident that you had done all you could do in
Australia in that location.

"It's true the people were responding well. In fact, there was real
evidence of a hunger for God. But a crowd of about 200 hecklers were
disrupting every service. And the police just stood there with folded
arms. We did all we could to protect the people. And we issued written
orders to the ushers not to lay hands on anyone . . . or to fight back.
Many of them wanted to, you know."

I said, "Yes, I remember one night there was a redheaded Irish-
man who had immigrated to Australia. While the mob was acting up
he jumped up, doubled up his fists, and said, 'Come and get me . . .
I'll take on the whole bunch.' Anyway, you got me out of the country
and probably saved my life."

SEED OF EQUIVALENT BENEFIT

Well, the Melbourne Crusade was over but in many ways it had
a victorious ending. It caught an antagonistic press by surprise. The
full responsibility was thrown into the lap of the newspapers who had
stirred up and supported the mobs. They could not deny their guilt,
for all Australia had been watching their reports.

The greatest good was the fact that it brought to light the power of a communistic minority in Australia. And it underlined the fact that true religious liberty was not known there. It set in motion a drive to get a new law passed to guarantee individual freedom to worship God according to the dictates of one's conscience.

The fact is, we were not the only ones being harassed. Similar mobs had been going into the various churches just like they had come into our tent meetings. Well, the way we were treated by the press and by the mob stirred up the leaders and they got a law on the books to protect religious liberty—*or a seed of an equal benefit.*

Later Billy Graham went there for a crusade and he was able to proceed without such harassment. He wrote me a letter which just broke me up and made me weep. He said he'd met people who had been saved and healed in my crusade and he wanted to encourage me.

It wasn't easy . . . struggle never is. But in the end, because we suffered, people were able to go to church and worship without disruption. And Billy Graham was able to hold a great crusade . . . and the people came without fear that they would be harmed by some mob of dissenters. They knew there would be police protection.

Today our ministry continues in Australia. We maintain an office in New Zealand and other foreign countries. And we are still receiving reports of individuals that were saved or healed in that crusade . . . as well as those who are now being helped through our television, radio, and literature ministries there. PRAISE GOD!

GOD KEEPS HIS WORD

As I am writing this and thinking of those struggles of the past, I know I will face more in the future. You never "arrive." You no sooner get one problem solved than another is there to take its place—at least that's the way it's always been with me. But as I thought on the tougher struggles and the forces that have tried to destroy this ministry, I remembered two prophecies that were prayed over me—each 27 years apart.

The first time was when I was pastoring in Enid, Oklahoma. The year was 1947 and a group of my church members had gathered around to pray for me. One particular couple, a man and his wife, who were very close friends, were a part of the group. Suddenly the woman reached out her hand and touched me and spoke a word of prophecy. The part I remember was:

> *No weapon that is formed against thee shall prosper . . .* (Isaiah 54:17).

To be perfectly honest I hadn't thought of this again until 1974 when I spoke at a conference on the Holy Spirit for a Methodist group in Dallas, Texas. Just before I started to preach, Jack Gray, who was the leader of the conference, asked his wife Revis to offer prayer before my message.

She prayed a beautiful prayer and I felt the anointing of the Holy Spirit flood up within me. And then she paused and I sensed a change in her voice as she began again. She said:

> Hear ye now the Word of God, for thus saith the Lord: No weapon formed against thee will prosper . . . Greater is he that is in you than he that is in the world . . .

The first part of this prophecy is the same as was prophesied in 1947, "No weapon formed against thee will prosper . . . The second part, "Greater is he that is in you, than he that is in the world" is 1 John 4:4. Some of you may recognize the words of this as almost exactly those of the closing theme for our telecasts. But this all happened nearly a year before we even knew such a song existed.

God has been so good and I have tried to follow as He has led. I know there are even greater things in the future . . . and I know too that there will be struggle and even foes rise up against me. But God is faithful to His Word—He has never failed me as long as I am faithful and obedient to His Word and direction.

———◆———

God says, "Resist the devil, and he will flee from you." That means stand up to him. Put your foot down. Use God's Word on him. The devil can't take it . . .

YOUR GOD-GIVEN KEY FOR TODAY

"Greater Is He (God) That Is In (Me), Than He (The Devil) That Is In The World!"

—1 John 4:4

SATURDAY

**Key:
EVERYTHING GOOD I DO IS A MIRACLE SEED I AM PLANTING**

**or
A Stupid Mistake Of Sowing A Bad Seed That Led To One Of The Greatest Seeds I Ever Planted**

In 1964, the year before we opened Oral Roberts University, I was struggling trying to get up buildings, trying to get something going. One day a rich man came out to see me—guess what went through my mind? Well, I'd heard about him—he had a big foundation. I thought, the Lord is really working today!

Well, the man came in and he was telling me about himself. I was so happy I couldn't wait for him to shut up so I could say something to him. But he just talked a blue streak and never did give me a chance. Anyway, after a while he stopped and the first time he stopped I moved right in and began talking about money. Suddenly he jumped up and he almost ran out of the place—he was in such a hurry to leave. I mean, I killed it all. I killed it dead!

After he left, the little voice inside—and I knew it was God talking to me—began to rebuke me. It was not audible but I sure knew someone was talking to me and I'll translate it. He said, *Boy, you sure messed that one up.* I actually felt that coming out of me. Then the voice said, *You don't care anything about him. You are not concerned about him. You are only concerned about what you want.*

I got so low I'd have to climb up on a tree limb to look a snake in the eye. Then something else spoke in me. "Well, you missed it this time but I'm going to give you another chance."

So I had hope. Well, I knew the only thing I could do with my mistake was to give it to God. Do you realize what I just said?

THE ONLY THING YOU CAN DO WITH A MISTAKE IS GIVE IT TO GOD

I sure couldn't give it to anybody else. And I didn't want it myself.

In a few days my secretary said. "There is a lady here to see you." She walked in and she said, "I've come over to help you."

I thought she wanted a job. By this time I mean I was chastened. I wouldn't have asked anybody for anything. She wanted to know what she could do, and I said, "I'm sorry, I don't hire the people."

She said, "I'm not wanting a job. I want to help YOU financially."

I said, "Who are you?" She told me who she was and I recognized that she was more affluent than the fellow who had come in before. And this thought went through my mind: *Oral, if you've ever kept your mouth shut and trusted God, shut up and you trust your Source today.*

This is the truth. I hate to tell that because it makes me look like the fool I was. But I shut up.

She said, "I want to give something. My husband died and left me a large inheritance."

I called my secretary and I said, "Call my wife."

Evelyn came down. I introduced them to each other and then I said to Evelyn, "She wants to give something to us." And my wife said after I explained who the lady was, "You are a widow. You have a large inheritance. You are the kind of person that people take advantage of, and my husband and I don't do that."

We said, "Go back home and if you feel this way in a week, you come back and we'll offer you a Seed-Faith project."

She said, "I don't see why I need to go home, I'm ready. I have my checkbook."

I could feel that thing rising up again. I said in effect, "Lie down!"

You are going to learn something in this story. Because God was finally in control of Oral Roberts. And when He was in control of me I was giving Him my best, and part of giving Him my best was expecting nothing from this woman and protecting her. That was a seed I was planting. So we said, "Go home. If you feel this way in seven days, come back."

So she obviously decided we were strange people, but she went home.

But when she got home she recognized that we were the kind of people she wanted to deal with. She came back in seven days and I offered her the project of building the Prayer Gardens that now surround the Prayer Tower and she said, "I'll take it."

I said, "Do you know what this will cost?"

She said, "No, but I'll take it anyway."

I had a blackboard and I wrote the cost on it. It was quite a large amount, you know, to build a big four-acre sunken garden. That takes a lot of money.

But she said, "I'll take it." She wrote a check for part of it and said, "I'll pay the rest soon." Then she said, "You know, you really surprised me. I was prepared to give you over four times this amount — if you had asked me."

I said, "The reason I didn't ask you for more was because when you were gone I prayed. And the only thing God gave me for you was the gardens."

And she said, "Well, you are nice, you are a nice person. We'll do as God directs."

She was so impressed she got really interested and later became a member of the ORU Board of Regents. Since then she's done three additional great things without anybody asking her. And to think how I could have driven her away by wanting something from her rather than wanting it from God — rather than giving God my best and then asking Him for His best.

I made a mistake — a bad one. But there was a seed of an equal benefit that was even greater than the one I lost. And I found it, planted it, and God did the rest.

◆—◆

A SEED OF FAITH IS ANYTHING YOU DO THAT'S GOOD.

I'm sure that each of us has lost a lot by wanting something for ourselves without regard for the other person . . . by denying God as our rightful Source . . . and failing to put a seed in. See, I put a seed of faith in by being a trustworthy person with her . . . by letting her know I really wasn't seeking something from her . . . by letting her go home and think about it. That was a seed—a seed of real faith.

Remember, a seed of faith is anything you do that's good. It can be a smile, or it can be sitting up with someone all night, or it can be helping someone in distress, or it can be giving money, or it can be giving some of your talent. Whatever the seed is . . . it WILL be multiplied back to you. Give God your best, then ask Him for His best.

Tie this truth to your heart like you tie a string around your finger so you won't forget . . .

YOUR GOD-GIVEN KEY FOR TODAY

"Everything Good I Do Is A Miracle Seed
I Am Planting."

TWELFTH WEEK

SUNDAY   GOD'S STROKES FOR ME ARE ALWAYS UPWARD

MONDAY   I CAN PLANT MY ADVERSITIES AS A SEED AND REAP A BENEFIT

TUESDAY   MY LOSSES WILL LEAD ME TO PERMANENT GAIN

WEDNESDAY   GOD NEVER MAKES A MISTAKE IN MY LIFE

THURSDAY   I WILL MOVE WITH GOD INTO NEW DIMENSIONS OF LIFE

FRIDAY   GREATER IS HE (GOD) THAT IS IN ME THAN HE (THE DEVIL) THAT IS IN THE WORLD

SATURDAY   EVERYTHING GOOD I DO IS A MIRACLE SEED I AM PLANTING

THIRTEENTH WEEK
Greater Is He (God) That Is In You
Than He (The Devil) That Is In The World

SUNDAY Key: I CAN SAY HELLO TO GOD EVERY DAY

or
God Made You The Way You Are . . . Then He Sent His Only Son To Make You Even Better!

WHEN God made man He made him His masterpiece, the crown of His creation.

> *In the beginning God created . . . man . . . in* [*his*] *image* (Genesis 1: 1, 26).

The first thing God did was to make man's physical body . . . the material He used was dust. Then He breathed His own breath into the nostrils of physical man, and man *became*. He *became* something higher —he became A LIVING SOUL.

There is a belief in ancient Hebrew history that on that first day God created man, man recognized who had created him. By the inner light of intelligence and spiritual insight he saw who his Creator was and that in God was his life, his identity, his soul. In that moment he knew what he was and who he was. Seizing life exuberantly he looked up into the face of his Creator, smiled, and said:

"HELLO, GOD!"

And God looking upon His masterpiece—the crown of His creation—warmly embraced him and said:

"HELLO, MAN!"

So from the very beginning there was this intimacy and warmth and knowing between God and man and between man and God.

Man was created immortal, in perfect harmony, peace, love, health, and in communication with God. And in harmony with all creation.

God gave the first man Adam a perfect intellect, with the power to name every living creature (Genesis 2:19). The Hebrews had Adam saying to all these, "Come, you and me, and let us go . . . and accept the kingship of Him who created us." It was . . .

A CELEBRATION OF LIFE!

God gave man many unique gifts:

The Gift of Communication

One was the gift of speech, to talk. In this language man felt a togetherness, the power to talk with God, to communicate with Him from the deepest levels of his being. It was:

"Hello, God!" — "Hello, man!"

The Gift of Enduement of Power

Another gift to man was the power to rise to his highest personal fulfillment and to transmit his powers to the whole world around him, to take dominion and transform and direct it (Genesis 1:26).

There was the capacity for an altogether positive and joyous relationship with God and all creation. This enduement of power made man a responsible being. It gave him the power to choose — the power to acknowledge God as his Creator, or reject Him.

The Gift of The Power of Choice

The power of choice sprang from man's spirit which is the part of him that was made in the likeness of God.

THE DEVIL TESTED MAN

When God gave man the power of choice He had to permit it to be tested. Placing him in a garden called Eden and surrounding him with a perfect environment, God placed everything at man's disposal, including the tree of life. But God prohibited man from eating of the fruit of one tree, the tree of knowledge — knowledge of good and evil. God said:

Ye shall not eat of it . . . lest ye die (Genesis 3:3).

All of a sudden there was a discordant note. The devil approached man (first through Eve) saying, in effect, "God is lying to you. If you eat of the tree of knowledge you shall not die" (Genesis 3:4).

Notice that . . .

the devil did not deny the existence of God,

or deny that man was created by God,

or that man was created as a spiritual being and was a living soul.

What was the devil after?

He was after man's tremendous intellect, his mind. God had created man as spirit, placing the mind under it, so that everything originated in man's spirit, then worked out through his mind, and then his body.

The devil said, "You shall not die . . . but you shall *know*. You will be the master of your own fate, the captain of your own soul . . ."

On the other hand, God was saying to man, "You are a spirit — and your spirit will die, and in dying spiritually you will become mortal, and you will ultimately die physically also."

Eve believed the devil. When she saw the fruit of the tree of knowledge was desirable to the physical senses, she ate and then gave the fruit to Adam, who also ate.

Suddenly they were exposed to their own nakedness (or vulnerability to mortality and death). They were frightened because now they knew for the first time they had lost their first estate with God. They were mortal and would surely die. "Hello, God!" died on their lips and they hid from Him.

There were fear and alienation. The intimacy and communication were broken. God said, "Where are you, Adam? Why are you afraid?"

Adam could only say, "We are naked and we hid."

In other words, they fell from their perfect estate through the sin of disobedience and started trying to cover up. They were no longer real and authentic human beings but phonies, denying their spiritual heritage and knowing the fear of mortality and death.

In that experience of believing the devil and breaking with God, here's what happened: Man deceived his spiritual being and elevated his mind to a point of supremacy over his spirit. And he has been trying to live by his mind and wits ever since — making his intellect an end in itself.

Although man's spirit didn't cease to exist, it was suppressed, put down, disowned, and put in a state of denying God. This has resulted in the awful alienation man feels from God today, his fear of death, his spoiling of God's creation by pollution, war, hatred and violence. But God didn't leave man here.

THE SECOND ADAM

God began to work to redeem and restore man, promising through the seed of the woman a Redeemer (Genesis 3:15). He sent the Law of Moses, the Ten Commandments, the prophets, the nation of Israel . . . but to no avail. Man was still alienated, still straying.

Then He sent His only begotten Son, to be born of a woman, and He became THE SECOND ADAM — the perfect man.

> . . . *and thou shalt call his name JESUS: for he shall save his people from their sins* (Matthew 1:21).
> . . . *they shall call his name Emmanuel . . . God with us* (Matthew 1:23).

The first negative act in creation was by the devil: to get man to reject God and the way He had made him, a spiritual being. When

Jesus came to earth it was full of this negativeness. Even man's language had been confused (Genesis 11:7) and they couldn't understand each other.

God's act to counteract the devil was absolutely positive. It was to conceive by the Holy Spirit the Holy Child Jesus in the womb of a young virgin—Mary. The night the baby was born in the stable at Bethlehem the angels began to sing:

> *On earth peace, good will toward men*... (Luke 2:14).
> *For unto you is born this day*... *a Saviour, which is Christ the Lord* (Luke 2:11).

It was God again saying:

"HELLO, MAN!"

When the angels told the shepherds they came and looked at the Babe of Bethlehem, and in their hearts was the recognition:

"HELLO, GOD!"

And Jesus became a man—so much man, so human it's like He was not God, yet He was so much God it was like He was not man. As He went about healing all who were oppressed of the devil, He was saying, as God:

"HELLO, MAN!"

And all who responded to Him were saying:

"HELLO, GOD!"

THE STORY OF JIM

Not far from where I live in Tulsa, Oklahoma, there was a man whose name was Jim. He had family, position, and a good business. He was a brilliant businessman, but in spite of all this he felt an emptiness in his heart. He began drinking. Finally he got to a place where he was bored with life and just went around day-to-day in a daze.

Then one day in the rush of the Christmas season Jim heard a Christmas carol. It stirred old memories in his heart and he thought, I'd just like to tell God how I feel, but I don't know how to pray.

Nevertheless, he slipped into a church, bowed his head, and said, "Hello, Jesus, this is Jim."

He said it again, "Hello, Jesus, this is Jim."

The third time he said, "Hello, Jesus, this is Jim."

That time he really meant it. He was ready to commit his life to God as his Lord and Savior when something tragic happened. While crossing the street a car ran him down. He was rushed to the hospital and the doctor worked throughout the night and into the next day to save his life.

On Christmas morning Jim was lying in his hospital bed when the minister of the church where he had prayed heard about him and came in. He walked over to Jim's bed and said, "What can I do for you?"

Jim said, "Pastor, I'm so glad you're here because I want to tell you about a wonderful thing that happened to me this morning."

"What happened?" the minister asked.

"Well, I was lying here hurting pretty badly, not knowing if I was going to make it or not, when I became aware of a voice. It was not like a human voice, but more of an inner impression. And it said, 'Hello, Jim, this is Jesus.'

"And again it said, 'Hello, Jim, this is Jesus.'

"And then the third time—'Hello, Jim, this is Jesus.'"

By this time tears were splashing down Jim's cheeks and he said, "Pastor, I can't tell you how good I felt. It was like a heavy burden had been lifted off my chest. I felt so light and free and now I know everything is going to be all right because I know God loves me."

Friend, I want to tell you today, God is smiling at man, at you— through Jesus Christ—warmly embracing each one of us and saying:

"Hello, man."

And you and I can say from the depths of our souls, "Hello, God."

I want you to know that Jesus Christ came to save and restore you to the potential of all God made man to become in the beginning.

As you open yourself to God and receive his Son Jesus as your personal Savior and Lord, He will restore that intimacy and communion and closeness and warmth throughout your entire being. You will be able once again to walk and talk with God, both with your spirit and your mind (1 Corinthians 14:15), just as God intended in the beginning.

Your entire personality will begin to overcome your fears which— because of man's alienation from God—are trying to engulf and destroy you. You will KNOW that . . .

Greater is he (God) that is in you, than he (the devil) that is in the world (1 John 4:4).

You will receive a NEW BIRTH of your spirit and mind as Jesus promised in John 3:5. He will make you a new creation (2 Corinthians 5:17). He will fill you with His Holy Spirit and restore the original enduement of power (Acts 1:8), and you will know who you are, and what you are, and who you are talking to when you say:

"HELLO, GOD!"

Now here's the best part. Why? Because it brings God into your NOW. The moment you know who your Creator is, you enter into the celebration of life every day. That's right, I said every day!

Acts 17:28 says, "In him we live, and move, and have our being."

YOUR GOD-GIVEN KEY FOR TODAY

That means:

"I Can Say Hello To God Every Day!"

MONDAY
Key:
I'LL KEEP PRESSING ON BECAUSE
I KNOW GOD IS WITH ME

or
You Can Make GOOD Things Start To Happen In Your Life!

A great statement was made by the Apostle Paul in Philippians 3:14. I think it's particularly appropriate for the times that you and I live in. He said:

> I press toward the mark for the prize of the high calling of God in Christ Jesus.

Paul said that he *pressed*. He indicated that life is tough and if you don't press you're not going to get through.

Now you'd think a man as close to God as St. Paul was, a man who had such a tremendous calling of the Holy Spirit upon his life, would not find life difficult. You would think that he'd be able to touch God at any moment and he'd be able to go through all of his trials and tribulations without any difficulty. But that wasn't so. Paul faced terrible ordeals. They would come at him from all sides. And in order for him to survive, he had to take his faith, his love, and his hope in God and affirm it with his words, "I press toward the mark." In other words, Paul said, "I put myself into it. I take my will and I stand up inside and I press toward the mark for the prize of the high calling of God in Christ Jesus."

The other day a friend sent me a newspaper story from Denver, Colorado. It was about a little one-armed boy who took part in a calf scramble at one of the big rodeos in Denver. It seems that during the rodeo every year they turn loose a bunch of little calves in the arena. Then little boys run out and those that can catch a calf and hold on to it for a certain length of time, are given that calf to raise for a year. Then one year later the boys bring the calves back, sell them at the auction, and they can keep the money.

All the little boys were excited.

According to this story, this included a little boy who had only one arm. Now nobody believed that a little one-armed boy could wrestle a calf down. It's hard enough for a two-armed boy. But the little boy was standing there on the line and when the man gave the order, all the boys ran. Soon the calves had been grappled and the boys were bulldogging them and pulling them down.

The judges noticed that the little one-armed boy had his arm around the neck of one of the calves, trying to pull it down to the ground. Well, he struggled and struggled.

Meanwhile, the other boys got their calves down and held them long enough so that the calves were theirs.

When they were all through the little one-armed boy and calf were still locked in struggle. The calf refused to be pulled down and the boy refused to turn him loose.

The people began to cheer and to clap. Suddenly, the calf began to jerk the little boy and pull him all over the arena, but he held on for dear life. There was a sudden quietness over the crowd as they watched that little boy being pulled by the calf over the dirt. People began to cry. One big rancher—the paper said—rushed up to the man in charge and said, "Tell him to turn the calf loose. I'll *give* him a calf. Go out there and tell him."

The man ran out and hollered at the little boy and said, "Son, turn the calf loose. There's a big rancher here who is going to give you a calf."

But the little boy, as he was struggling to hold on to the calf, said, "No, sir! I'm going to hold on. This is my calf and I'm going to get him like all the other boys got theirs. This one is mine and I'm going to hold on."

That calf pulled him from one side to the other but he would not turn loose. Finally, he pulled the calf down. The man counted and the little boy passed the test. Then he got up and walked out across the dirt knowing that that little calf was his . . . because he had earned him.

I wrote back to my friend and thanked him and I said in my letter, "That's the kind of spirit that St. Paul was talking about when he said:
I press toward the mark for the prize of the high calling of God in Christ Jesus (Philippians 3:14).

You see, the old devil is looking for a weakness within you and if he can find it that's where he's going to camp. Here's a little boy with just one arm. He hasn't got the chance of a little two-armed boy, but he was tougher. That little boy found out that when he had a will and a fierce determination, one arm was enough.

WE COME TO THE PLACE WHERE WE HAVE TO "PRESS . . ."

Now I want to tell you about one of the great television performers that we meet often at NBC in Burbank, California, and it's Flip Wilson. I know he plays a lot of characters, and people like some of them and dislike others. I want to tell you that in that man's private life he has some real values and I discovered one of them.

Last December when we were making our Christmas television special, we were taping right across the hall from where he was making his show. He came out, saw me, came over, took my hand, shook it and said, "Oral, I'm glad to see you. You played a part in my life not long ago. My brother's wife was taken seriously ill and was facing very serious surgery. I'm close to my brother and sister-in-law and she picked up the phone and called me and said, 'Flip, I'm going under the knife and I'm scared. Flip, I want you to pray. I want you to ask God to be with me.'"

And he said, "Why, sure, sis, I'll pray."

And he said to me, "Oral, I really didn't know what I was saying. Because I'm not as close to the Man Upstairs as I ought to be and I'd like to be. I do believe in prayer and my sister-in-law had asked me to pray. While she was waiting and they were getting her prepared for surgery, I was worried. I knew she was depending on me to pray and I didn't know just how to pray. —

"Sunday morning came and I was sitting at my breakfast table and she was on my mind. I felt like I was letting her down and then your telecast came on the air. You came to your prayer time and you began to pray and I just put my hands down by my plate and I closed my eyes and I listened to your prayer. All of a sudden I knew that you were praying the words that I wanted to pray and you were offering the prayer that I would like to offer to God and I just made your prayer my prayer. When you finished and you said, 'Amen and amen,' I said, 'Amen and amen.' And I felt something inside and I felt it go through me and I felt it go out toward my sister-in-law. Well, she came through the surgery 100 percent OK and everything is perfect."

He reached up and hugged me and said, "Thanks, buddy."

Then he said, "Above all, thanks to God."

And he walked away. Flip had to find that there was a time he had to press.

THERE ARE TIMES WHEN WE HAVE TO PRESS AND HOLD ON AND WHEN WE DO WE DISCOVER GOD WILL MAKE A WAY WHERE THERE IS NO WAY

I believe that with all my heart.

I get mail from people who are desperate and who write me about their needs and it's a thrill to reply to them and tell them God will make a way where there is no way. And then one comes through with an answer that's out of this world. Recently I received a letter from a man who had a great need and with whom I had been corresponding for some time. He said:

Dear Brother Roberts:

I owe my miracle to God but I want to thank you for your counsel and prayers for me during the testing time. Let me tell you what happened.

In 1971 I lost the job I had as an area sales manager for a seed company. It had been a good job and I had worked hard to set a sales record of 25 percent over the previous year. How terribly hard it was for me to go home and tell my family that I had been fired. My ego was shattered. I will admit to you that the next few weeks were miserable. I was depressed and even my health was steadily deteriorating.

Finally, I realized that the world, my life, and my family had to keep moving. I could not give up. (That is, he had to keep on pressing forward.) The seed business was what I knew best, so I started out to look for a job among my old customers. One of them suggested I start my own business but I was in debt and just didn't have any money. Then one night 150 miles away from home, lonely and depressed, I turned on the television in my hotel room and there you were, Brother Roberts, giving a stirring message on Seed-Faith. After the program was ended I wrote you a letter telling you I needed this kind of miracle-working help in my life.

For the next few weeks the idea of starting my own business kept going round and round in my head. I can't tell you that my prayers and yours were answered right away. I wrote several letters to you, Brother Roberts, and every time you wrote back telling me how God wanted to meet my needs and that there was a due season for my life.

Well, finally, with the help of my local bank—people who took a chance and believed in me—I was able to get a business started. The first year I did not do as well as I had expected, but again I wrote to you for prayer and each time your letter said exactly the thing I needed to hear. Then one day very unexpectedly I received a letter from a lawyer who told me I had been left a sizable sum in the will of a great aunt of mine. Now, Brother Roberts, this had to be a miracle, because I had not seen this aunt but one time in my life. Some might say, "Well, it would have happened anyway," but I believe God's due season had come for me. It was truly a miracle because it was exactly what I needed to pay off my debts and put my business in the clear.

The Lord is truly blessing me and I can't thank Him enough. Thank you, Brother Roberts, for your letters of encouragement.

You know, friend, whenever you begin to believe God, you're met with opposition. Struggle is the word. One never achieves anything of real value unless he struggles for it . . . unless he contends or fights for it. He has to be opposed. Criticism, sometimes ostracism, misunderstanding, all kinds of persecution come. These things bring out the best in us. They strengthen us. They test our determination.

If people could just wish their way everybody would have all he needed. Everybody would achieve what his heart cried for. If one could just wish and make it so. But life isn't like that.

A wish is part of receiving our heart's desire. We must have an image of what we desire in our mind. But we must take hold of the proposition and make things happen.

THINGS HAVE TO BE MADE TO HAPPEN

If we want God to meet our needs, we must start thinking toward God. Bringing our thoughts to a climax, making our thoughts a belief . . . our belief into faith . . . our faith into an act. And we must cause that faith to be released, to explode within us, until we make our faith a seed we plant (Matthew 17:20).

At the edge of Tulsa we have some great limestone rocks. One day I was driving by and I noticed that growing right out of the middle of one of these rocks was a beautiful bunch of flowers.

I couldn't understand how they could grow so when I got back I called up Dr. Thurman in our natural science department at ORU. I said, "Dr. Thurman, how can that flower grow right out of the rock?"

He said, "Well, somehow that little seed got inside the rock. Maybe there was a small crevice and it worked its way into it and found a little water or a little moisture and it became a seedbed. The seed began to grow and soon it broke that rock open . . . a little wider and a little wider until it came out on the other side as a flower."

And I thought, how tiny that seed was when it started to grow inside the rock and then how powerful and beautiful it is today as the flower extends from the rock. *The seed had become more powerful than the rock.*

And I tell you that this is just the way your faith works on your needs. Whatever human problem you are facing today—it may be a terrible rock experience—a mountain that you cannot overcome. But if you can get inside that mountain of need with a tiny grain of faith— Seed-Faith—that seed can explode and grow . . . and grow . . . until it has conquered your need.

I don't know the problem confronting you, but I know you have one. Perhaps you have lost your job or had a cut in your pay. Or you are feeling lonely—so lonely you don't know how you are going to get through the days ahead. It could be that something is breaking up your home, or something is wrong in your family. Maybe a daughter or son or grandchild is involved in something that's breaking your heart. Maybe sickness has invaded the life of a loved one. Maybe you are ill yourself. Whatever your problem is, I want to encourage you to

HOLD ON! DON'T GIVE UP!

You can't afford to quit now. God has brought you this far because you've held on. With all your heart, affirm like the Apostle Paul:

YOUR GOD-GIVEN KEY FOR TODAY
"I'll Keep Pressing On Because I Know God Is With Me!"

TUESDAY

Key:
IN EVERY CIRCUMSTANCE I FACE
THERE IS THE REAL LIFE OF MY LORD!

or

I Want To Talk About A Healing—A Total Healing That Most Of Us Count As An Enemy

When you've been ill like I have been in my lifetime, when you've almost lost your life as has occurred to me on several occasions, and then you experienced the healing power of Jesus Christ, both through medicine and prayer, you become aware of the nature of God. You begin to know . . .

GOD IS GOOD . . .
GOD IS CONCERNED ABOUT YOU!

I've read the Bible through scores of times . . . and the New Testament more than 100 times. And I've discovered that there is a thread of healing running all the way through the Bible. I've also learned that there is one method of healing that most of us count as an enemy . . . and that is DEATH.

When our Lord Jesus Christ submitted to death, He conquered it so that death is not what it used to be to the child of God. Now we can say:

> *Death is swallowed up in victory. O death, where is thy sting? O grave, where is thy victory?* (1 Corinthians 15:54,55).

Now death to a Christian is RELEASE . . .

Death is total healing . . .

because of Jesus Christ and His triumph at the Resurrection. He said:

> *Because I live, ye shall live also* (John 14:19).

The Bible also says:

> *Precious in the sight of the Lord is the death of his saints* (Psalms 116:15).

Precious Death. Death has a great value. Our Lord died. His eyelids were closed and He couldn't see because death had come. His limbs were now immovable. His body limp. They buried Him but He arose from the dead. And those eyes saw like they had never seen before . . . those limbs now moved in the power of the Resurrection. He had a new body—an incorruptible, immortal body (1 Corinthians 15:52-57).

The Apostle Paul said:

> *But what things were gain to me, those I counted loss for Christ* (the things I gained, to me were lost but now I take

those losses in order to find Christ that I may win Christ) . . .
that I may know him, and the power of his resurrection
(Philippians 3:7-10).

In other words, Paul was saying, "I want to know Christ in His multiplying power . . . the power that He uses to multiply back to me that
which I have lost."

HOW A FAMILY FACES THE LOSS OF
THEIR 23-YEAR-OLD SON

As I was writing this book there was an automobile accident a
few miles away from the campus. A graduate of Oral Roberts University, the son of some dear partners of this ministry, was instantly
killed. His parents called our Prayer Tower and the prayer partner
taking the call quickly notified Evelyn and me and we got right in
touch with the parents.

The mother was just simply crushed and was crying her heart out,
and the father was crying too. He said, "Brother Roberts, there's got
to be a reason in this."

And so we cried with them and thought about our own children.
We thought about how death comes in sometimes so unbidden.

And the Lord gave me something for them. They are partners of
mine and they are practicing Seed-Faith. Yet, right in the middle of it
all, they had this loss of their precious 23-year-old son.

I said to them, "The only thing you've got left is your Source . . .
you've got God . . . because in death there's nothing and nobody you
can turn to but God."

"Yes," the father said, "we still have God our Source . . . but,
Brother Roberts, the ache, the tormenting grief, the loneliness . . . I
just don't think we know how to cope with it right now."

And I said, "My brother, in death there is nothing, there is nobody
you can turn to but God. But I want to tell you this, *He's concerned.*
He's concerned. He's concerned about you. He's concerned when you
hurt. He's concerned about your grief, your loss, that ache that is
so far down in your heart that you think the very life is being squeezed
out of you . . ."

Speaking in a voice coarse with emotion, the father said, "I can
see that you do know how we feel, Brother Roberts. I guess it will just
take time . . ."

Then I said, "There is something else I want to say to you. I know
the ache is raw right now and this may not mean as much to you right
now as it will when you have time to meditate upon it. But you and
your dear wife have been so faithful to God in your practice of Seed-
Faith. And now this, the most precious seed of your own precious son,
is planted in heaven. Therefore, HEAVEN HAS A BOLDER GRIP

UPON YOU . . . YOU HAVE AN INVESTMENT IN HEAVEN THAT
WILL DRAW YOU CLOSER TO GOD.

"Sometimes life has a way of coming at us and disrupting our best
laid plans and we are apt to let go our hold on God. But knowing that
your son is in heaven will hold you steady."

I could still hear these dear parents weeping over the telephone.
But that is good too. I personally think that just crying your heart out
to God helps wash away the grief that no human reason can touch.
Then I said:

"Remember, not only is your son in heaven, but our dear Savior,
Jesus Christ, is there too and He has sent the Holy Spirit to be your
Comforter NOW. And someday the circle will be unbroken. Heaven
is more precious to you now. You know, we all have that divine appointment and when my time comes, heaven is where I want to be and I
want all my family there. Now, one of your family is already there and
as you await your own homegoing, you can hold on to Him who is
your Source."

Then they both said, "Brother Roberts, it is so hard to give him
up, but it is a comfort to be reminded that we will meet him there.
Keep us in your prayers and we know that our Great Source will fill
that vacancy that seems bottomless right now . . ."

I prayed with them again and I sensed that the precious Holy
Spirit was already soothing their broken hearts with His healing balm.

Now I don't know what you think about a talk like this. I deal
with people all the time who have suffered losses and I too have lost
loved ones. But in every type of loss I've seen in my partners, or have
faced myself, I've discovered that in every loss we can gain Christ
and we can know Him in the power of His resurrection and we can
know Him in the NOW. And we can know Him forever.

Let me tell you . . .

IN THE MIDST OF DEATH THERE IS LIFE

In the midst of that divine appointment of death there is life . . .
because *Christ* is there.

In Hebrews 9:27 we are told:

It is appointed unto men once to die.

We rightly run from death and none of us want to die. We hate death
because it is an unknown . . . because it separates us from those we
love. But there is a time when it's appointed to us to die. And in the
death of a child of God there is release into TOTAL HEALING. Those
limbs that grow old and weary, not able to function, full of aches and
pains, will no longer be that way.

In Revelation 21:4, God says that He'll wipe all tears from our
eyes . . . that there will be no more death . . . there will be

no more sickness . . . there will be no sighing. And we shall see Him face-to-face.

Listen, friend, beyond death is heaven . . . and in heaven there is LIFE—eternal life—and a promise of the resurrection of our bodies.

Here I am right in the bloom of my life and I expect to live until my appointed time. But at that time whatever aches and pains and weaknesses are left in my body, God's going to take care of them. I'm going to have a new body. I'm going to be WITH God. Precious in the sight of the Lord is the death of His saints.

Several years ago I preached a funeral and I was so happy. A lot of people didn't understand why I was so happy. I was happy because that person was where I expect to be some day—WITH GOD!

God wants you to be well. He wants you to be well through His healing power which often comes through medicine or through prayer. God's healing comes in many ways. But healing also comes through death to the child of God. In death, through our Lord Jesus Christ, we are released into TOTAL HEALING . . . into TOTAL IMMORTALITY. Thank God!!

I believe just as death starts now, and ultimately comes as a separation of the spirit and the body, so eternal life begins NOW for the Christian. I believe every time God touches you that disease becomes a little less and life becomes a little more. I believe that through Christ we can have more possession of our faculties, much more of our being through which to live out our days. Through the power of the living Christ within us, we can become all that He wants us to be.

ETERNAL LIFE BEGINS IN THE NOW . . .
GOD'S ULTIMATE HEALING BEGINS IN THE NOW

Now I want to pray with you. I feel that you are going through something. I can feel it while I write this. You're going through something. I'm going to ask you to touch someone near you. The Bible says, "Pray one for another that ye may be healed" (James 5:16) . . . *healed* or that you may be delivered.

Just put your hand out and take someone's hand or wrap your arms around yourself. Just do something that will help you release your faith as I pray for you.

Father, in the name of Your Son, Jesus Christ of Nazareth, I come unto You. I don't come in my name or my strength, but I come in the mighty incomparable name of Jesus, the Son of God, and I ask You for many miracles.

And now, dear friend, I pray for you. I stretch forth these hands that I've given to God. I stretch them forth toward you. And I know that in the midst of your sorrow, in the midst of a loss that you are enduring right now, with your back to the wall, not knowing where to turn, I know who your Source is, and it's God. And through Jesus Christ, our Lord, I pray that you will just let God take over. You will just let go and let God . . . and you will experience the warmth of His presence and God will take hold of your life in a way that you will know that He is moving in your behalf.

So through Jesus Christ, I pray that you'll be healed of that loss . . .

   you'll be healed of that sorrow . . .

      you'll be healed of that sickness and disease . . .

         you'll be healed of that drifting and straying . . .

            you'll be healed of that fear . . .

               you'll be lifted up into the abundant life of Jesus Christ our Lord.

And I believe. I believe it's going to happen. I believe it's starting to happen right now. And I'm expecting many miracles in your behalf.   *Amen and amen.*

YOUR GOD-GIVEN KEY FOR TODAY

Say now:

"In Every Circumstance I Face, There Is The Real Life Of My Lord!"

WEDNESDAY

Key:
WHEN GOD STIRS MY NEST, THERE'S A REASON. I'LL LOOK FOR IT!

or

When Things Get Rough...There's A Reason...And A Way Out

In the Bible God compares himself, in His dealings with us, to an eagle.

   Ye have seen what I did unto the Egyptians, and how I bare you on eagles' wings, and brought you unto myself (Exodus 19:4).

   As an eagle stirreth up her nest, fluttereth over her young, spreadeth abroad her wings, taketh them, beareth them on her wings: So the Lord alone did lead him, and there was no strange god with him (Deuteronomy 32:11,12).

In other words, God says, "As the eagle does certain things, this is the way I will deal with you."

The first thing the mother eagle does is to build her nest in a high place, usually inaccessible. There in the loneliness of the heights she gathers materials, such as briars and sticks, and builds a big nest. Then she covers it over with the soft things that she can find and finally with her own soft downy feathers. She makes it comfortable, snug, and secure.

She lays her eggs and then she hatches her young ones. There they spend the early part of their life while she flies far and near to bring food to them.

The day comes when it is time for the baby eagles to leave the nest and learn to fly. But the nest is so comfortable. The mother's warm body hovers over and near them, protecting them. They are content to stay in the soft nest.

But built into the mother eagle is a way to get her little ones out of the nest. If she doesn't, *they will forfeit their rights to be eagles!* So the mother eagle begins to quietly remove the soft covering and let the little eagles down on the briars where they begin to stir uneasily. They wonder why the world is treating them like this. They become frightened and begin to scream.

Then in the height of their fear, the mother eagle lays her big broad wing down on the side of the nest and clucks to them. The naturalists believe that it is a language through which she speaks to them. My translation is, "Get off the briar and get on the wing."

When the eagles see that soft, powerful wing on the side of the nest, and they themselves are stirring around uneasily on sharp briars, one of them starts climbing out of the nest and getting on the wing. The moment it has fastened its talons on those big broad strong wings, suddenly the mother eagle begins to fly and it hangs on for dear life.

There she goes—up and up, mile after mile—flying, drifting, winging her way across the sky. The little eagle forgets all about everything else except the sheer ecstasy of flight.

Then she brings it back and she puts her wing down. So the little eagle jumps off and gets back into the nest only to find that it is right back on the briars. She puts her wing back down and immediately it climbs off the briar, gets on her wing, and up she goes again. She does this again and again until she takes away the fear.

Then one day, with it on her wings, she is soaring high above the earth. All of a sudden she lurches and knocks it off into the air. The little eagle begins to scream and plummet toward the earth like a bullet, beating its wings and screaming at the top of its voice. Before it hits the ground, the big mother eagle speeds downward with superb accuracy. Spreading out her wings under it, she catches it and up she goes again, high into the sky. She shakes it off and then catches it again and again until it learns to stretch out its wings and fly. Then they go—side-by-side—flying, soaring, and gliding. The mother eagle does this until all the little eagles are into flight.

GOD STIRS MY NEST

I remember it as if it were yesterday. I was in Enid, Oklahoma, in 1947 attending Phillips University, pastoring a small church, raising a family, going through the normal things of life. In that little nest I had a vision that maybe the time had come for me to build a school for God. I picked out a piece of ground—about an acre, not even as big as the Mabee Center at Oral Roberts University. I was thinking in terms of some day building a school on that little spot of ground. People asked me how long I intended to stay in Enid.

I said, "The rest of my life."

Then one day somebody pulled the rug out from under me. The people I'd been close to suddenly became very unfriendly. The best friend I had, whom I'd worshiped with, prayed with, traveled with, played golf with, hunted quail with, suddenly seemed to be my enemy. He didn't hate me but suddenly everything was different.

I NO LONGER FELT AT HOME

I felt like I would smother. It was God pulling that soft cover away from the nest because He knew I had to get out into something bigger . . . because He had something for me to do.

I want to tell you, it's a lonely feeling when people you love and who love you suddenly appear to be your enemies . . . and the place you're in becomes too cramped. The old familiar place is now strange and all the softness is gone and you are down on the briars and you are hurting. There I was.

GOD WANTS TO SHOW YOU HOW BIG HE IS

The Bible also says that the eagle, when she stirs her nest and flutters over her young, *stretches abroad her wings*. That is, she rises six or eight feet above the nest and she stretches out her wings. (Eagles have been captured with a wing spread of over 10 feet.) And the little eagles get a glimpse of how big their mother is. You see, when she comes down and folds her wings around them she doesn't appear too big.

So the mother eagle stretches abroad those wings and the little eagles look up as if to say, "Mother, we never knew you were that big before."

That's how I saw God in 1947. As I got out of that nest and was utterly alone, I began to look to God because there wasn't anyone to look to but God. I began to search His Bible and read it more than I ever had. I began to pray and to miss a few meals and devote myself to seeking God. It wasn't long until God showed me a vision of himself —not something physical—but

I began to realize how big God is . . .

the far sweep of His eternal purpose . . .

the majesty of His presence and power .

Yet, I felt He was closer to me than my breath.

God gave me a dream in which He showed me the human race. I saw them and I heard them. I saw that everybody is sick in some way . . . everybody is crying out inside. My heart felt like it would burst. I wanted to put my arms around the human race and say, "Don't worry, God loves you. God can heal you."

That was God taking me on His wing and showing me His purpose, showing me an acre of ground wasn't big enough for the school He wanted me to build . . . that town wasn't quite the place.

I FOUND THAT GETTING OUT OF THE
NEST ONCE IS NOT THE WHOLE STORY . . .
YOU HAVE TO KEEP ON GETTING OUT OF THE NEST

In the nearly 29 years of this ministry I've thought a dozen or more times that we had reached the zenith . . . that we had fulfilled God's calling. Things would be going great . . . the nest so soft and comfortable. Then suddenly one day I'd find myself on the briars again and I would realize that once again God was laying His wing down and saying, "Get off the briar and get on the wing."

That is, "You weren't made to live in this nest . . . there are heights out there in the unknown that I want to show you. Greater things are ahead."

The next thing the eagle does is to teach the little ones how to *set their wings*. The eagle is one of the few, if not the only bird, that has both a microscopic and telescopic sight. It can see both very close and it can see very far. It has a built-in radar system that can detect a coming storm long before the human eye or the human ear can. The eagle watches and as the winds start blowing in the storm, it simply sets its wings in a certain way. And when the winds come, they strike those wings as they are set and instead of overpowering the eagle, the wind lif.s her until she's above the storm. She's up there where she can stretch her wings and begin to fly. And she stays up there till the storm is over. Then she comes back down to her mountain home.

Now that's a tremendous thing and God says:

"I lead you like that . . . I'll teach you how to climb above the storms of life."

When we are on the wing we can really predict the storms that are coming . . . when bad things begin happening . . . when they start to overwhelm us (and it is the devil's purpose to overwhelm us).

1. We can set our minds toward God. We can remember who our Source is — *God*.
2. We can keep our loving and giving on target, even when losses are striking at us. We can keep on giving out of our need and giving out of our want, giving for our desired results. We can keep on putting the seed in.
3. And we can keep on expecting miracles. We can keep on knowing that God is the everlasting God and His eternal law of sowing and reaping will never change.

We can learn to set our wings so that the storms of illness or storms of opposition or storms of failure striking us will not overcome us. Instead we will feel the power of God lifting us until we're on top.

God never intended us to be on the bottom. He never intended for us to be the tail. He intended for us to be on top and He intended for us to be the head. He intended us to reach heights, to keep on going and never sit down, never lie down, but to keep on climbing.

The final thing the eagle does is probably as important, if not more so than what I have already mentioned. As the eagle grows older she goes off to a quiet place and there *beats off her old feathers*. She just literally beats them off until she appears naked. Then the eagle grows new feathers and stays young till the day she dies.

In Acts 2:17,18, you'll find the prophecy of the baptism in the Holy Spirit, the charismatic experience. It says:

> *Your young men shall see visions, and your old men shall dream dreams . . . and on my handmaidens I will pour out in those days of my Spirit; and they shall prophesy.*

Wouldn't you like, as you get older, to dream and keep on dreaming so that your life never gets old? Your body may get old but your spirit will always be young and your mind will be young. God says, "I deal with you like this."

I read about a great American airline pilot, a crack pilot. He said he almost failed in his solo flight. He was flying a little Piper plane and his instructor watched him. Suddenly the plane began to wobble and dip. The instructor was frightened that the student wouldn't make it back to the ground. Finally the fellow landed it and the instructor ran over and said, "Mister, what were you doing up there?"

He said, "It looks different up there. This little plane looks so small, and I couldn't sit still. I began to jump up and down and hit my head against the ceiling."

The instructor said, "Well, sir, don't you realize that the plane is built to fly itself? You really don't have to fly the plane. All you have to do is move the instruments a certain way. Just rest your full weight upon the seat, move the instruments and the plane will fly itself."

Now, get this inside you—say "God" like you mean it.

O God, I don't have to manipulate You. I don't have to worry about where You are or whether You are going to exist or stand or endure or not. I don't have to worry about life going on in the right way. All I've got to do is just rest my weight upon You, God, and do the things You've told me to do, because Christianity doesn't need any propping up. It'll fly itself. It'll take me where I'm going. It will take me there!!

YOUR GOD-GIVEN KEY FOR TODAY

From now on, say:

"When God Stirs My Nest There's A Reason,

I'll Look For It."

THURSDAY
Key:
I'LL BE AWARE OF GOD'S GREAT RICHES TODAY AND EVERY DAY

or
How You Can Be Rich . . . And In
The Way It Will Benefit You Most . . .

In the Third Week of this book, Saturday, we talked about the rich man who, thinking he "had it made," wanted to tear down his barns and build bigger ones wherein to store all his worldly goods. And if you'll remember, we really laid it on him for his smugness and stupidity in looking to *things* rather than to God as his Source, and he lost not only his earthly possessions, but his eternal soul.

"Well," you ask, "what's that got to do with me? I'm not rich . . ."

This is my point—it's got *everything* to do with you and me. You remember the rich man said, "I'll pull down my barns and build greater, and there will I bestow all my fruits and my goods and I will say to my soul, *soul thou hast many goods laid up for many years, take thine ease, eat, drink and be merry.*" And we say, "Yeah, that's right, a lot of rich folks are like that." But just listen to this. This takes us all in.

> *So is he that layeth up treasure for himself, and is not rich toward God* (Luke 12:21).

You see, we often think that it's only wealthy people who are not rich toward God. (Thank God some of them are rich toward our Lord.) But really you can have only a few pennies in your pocket and not be rich toward God.

What does this story teach you and me in the now of our existence? It means that as we go through life, we often develop a grasping, grabbing spirit. We think only of ourselves. We're trying to pull in everything we can. And some people do it rather well and they get rich. Some people don't do it well at all, but they have the same spirit, the spirit of *getting* for themselves without thought of God or man.

A man took me in his jet plane not long ago and flew me across the country and we sat down at a beautiful lake area and got out of the plane. He took me over and showed me his beautiful home and told me how many hundred thousand dollars it cost. Then with a smile he turned to me and said, "Oral, this is what life is all about."

I can't tell you how I had to hold my tongue. I should have said something, but I was his guest and I didn't want to offend him. But I really felt like winding up and saying, "Brother, if this is all there is to life, riding in a jet plane and having a two- or three-hundred-thousand-dollar home, and really believing this is what life is all about, then I sure have missed it. Because I hear from thousands of people who have enough to eat, who have a nice car, who even ride in jet planes, and they're miserable." And actually the man I was looking at was miserable too. I learned later that his life ended up in divorce and all kinds of problems. And his problems are going to get greater unless he turns his life around and recognizes what life is really all about.

But the same thing is true of people who have just a shack to live in. The same thing is true of people who can't make payments on their worn-out car. It's true of people who don't know where their next meal is coming from. The light company may be about to turn their lights off. That's true of them, because some people really think they can gather it up and take it with them when they die. Well, I'll tell you one thing, friend, I've never seen a Brinks armored car following a funeral procession.

WHAT DOES IT MEAN TO BE RICH TOWARD GOD?

Well, it means that you have a Source for your life. Philippians 4:19 says, "For my God shall supply all your need." You see, God is your Source and when you're rich toward God, you have a Source for your life. When you're not rich toward God, you are your own source. And what a poor source that is. God is your Source. When you're rich toward God, you are making your faith a seed and you're planting that seed, which is giving and giving first. Giving your love and your concern and your money, your prayers, your time, your talent, your friendship— and putting it in as a seed, knowing that God is going to multiply it back. Being rich toward God is knowing that for every seed you plant

God has promised a harvest. The Apostle Paul says, "Let us not be weary in well doing: for in due season we shall reap [a harvest], if we faint not" (Galatians 6:9).

You see, God has a lot of *due seasons* for you, a lot of harvests for you. That's what I call being rich toward God . . .

being able to look to God as your Source,

being able to plant seed,

being able to expect miracles,

to believe that God is going to change

things in your life,

to expect eternal life . . .

That's richness, brother! That's being rich toward God.

Not long ago I read a story about how the ancient Egyptians felt that when they died all their possessions should be buried in the tomb with them. Recently one of those tombs was unearthed in which some person had been buried 2,500 years. And in it were the things he possessed, including a sack of wheat. Wondering about the wheat, they took it out and planted it. And lo and behold — it multiplied! It produced a harvest. After all those years of being in this tomb with the body of this poor person who thought he could take it with him — it was taken out, planted, and multiplied. But until it was planted it just lay there, doing no good.

Have you ever thought about the unplanted seeds in your life? Think about it for a moment. Think of all the mountains in your life you could move if you just started giving out! Jesus said in Matthew 17:20:

If ye have faith as a grain of mustard seed (as a seed you plant), *ye shall say unto this mountain, Remove . . . and nothing shall be impossible unto you.*

He's saying if you plant the seed of faith, if you open your heart and let the love out, you can speak to your mountains and God will move them.

Think of the unmoved mountains in your life. Think what you can do today to start planting seed so that you can speak by the authority of God for those mountains to move — and they will move!

Now I'd like to ask you some questions.

Have you been messing up your life?

Have you been leaving your seeds unplanted?

Are those terrible mountains of need

and problems overwhelming you?

I want you to know that within you are these precious seeds you can plant, these gifts you can give — of your love, concern, or prayer. You could give something maybe I've not mentioned. But God will show you how and what to give. Maybe you're not expecting a miracle because you have no aim in life. God's not your Source. I'd like to take a moment and tell you that I've been through it — and I know if you can make God your

Source that He's going to supply your needs. God's going to make you into a new creature. Would you start giving by just praying this prayer of commitment with me. If you don't know Christ as your personal Savior and Lord, you can know Him now. If you have drifted away and have isolated yourself from God, you can come back now and start all over—start now being rich toward God by giving Him the thing He wants most of all—YOU!

Now I want you to pray this prayer—and mean it!

Father, in the name of Jesus, I repent and I ask You to forgive me and to give me a new spirit, a new nature. Lord, revive my dead spirit, my dead soul.

I want to be saved.

I want to be filled with Your Holy Spirit.

I now commit my life to You.

I release myself to You and truly repent, changing my mind, asking Christ to change the pattern of my life and to give me a new life, and that I will live in God's will forever and ever.

I acknowledge You as my Lord and Savior and give my life as the first seed I plant toward being rich toward You, Lord, knowing that as I follow You, You will multiply it a hundredfold in a great harvest for Your kingdom.

Amen.

Well, thank God for His bountiful love and forgiveness. Nail your prayer down with this affirmation:

YOUR GOD-GIVEN KEY FOR TODAY
"I'll Be Aware Of God's Great Riches
Today And Every Day."

FRIDAY
Key:
GOD'S POWER WILL OVERCOME MY EVERY FEAR
or
How You Can Stop Being Afraid

Recently I went into our Aerobics Building where we have an indoor track (six laps to a mile), where all of us out at ORU walk or jog to get our aerobics points, to build up our bodies and work at being a whole man. As I entered the door there was one of our students who's working his way through school, and part of his duties are to check the ID cards and things like that. He was sitting there doing his job. Also he had his school books and you could tell he'd been studying. As I walked in, he greeted me as usual and then gave me a motion with his hand to come over, which I did. Then he asked me to lean down and he said, "President Roberts, I'm the loneliest and the most frustrated I have ever been in my life, and yet I'm in the best place I've ever been in my life."

And I said, "I know how you feel; I know exactly what that feeling is." So I took his hand and he put his hand on mine, and we planted a few seeds of love together in prayer and I went on and did my jogging.

I came back the following day to jog again and there he was. I said, "How goes it today?"

And he said, "Well, I am much better since yesterday."

And I thought of him being 19 or 20, something like that, with those feelings of loneliness and frustration, and yet being lonely at that age and when you realize that it happens to everyone of us, you know that St. Paul needs to speak to us as individuals in the same way that he spoke to young Timothy (2 Timothy 1:6-8).

He starts off by recognizing Timothy as having been reared by a Godly mother and a Godly grandmother, having known the Scriptures since he was just a little child. Yet Paul recognizes a deterioration in Timothy, a falling apart of his inner man. Being gripped by a terrible fear, Timothy has developed a stomach problem—what's called a "queasy" stomach, where you get sick to your stomach easily.

Now young Timothy, as reliable as he was as a dependable traveler with Paul, and a young man that Paul felt he could utterly depend upon, had problems until Paul had to give him an antidote for his stomach. He has to speak directly to him about these problems that he was encountering. First, Paul said, "Timothy, you have a gift of God within you. You're not alone. God is with you. And His gifts are within you. But those gifts have to be stirred up."

In other words, when the fire burns down into ashes, there're always little live coals in those ashes and you have to brush the ashes away and expose those live coals and take a little kindling and put on top of them and fan them. Soon there's a blaze, and you put a little stick of wood on it, and another stick of wood on it, and another stick of wood, until finally you have a blazing fire. So Paul is saying, "You will get so low until the fire almost dies out. There will be just a few little coals in your heart and they're barely aglow."

I know that's true in my own life. Not long ago I became ill with a respiratory problem. It got way down deep in my chest. Since I was healed back in 1935 of tuberculosis, I've never had a problem like that. And the first thing the devil whispered to me was, "You're taking tuberculosis again." And I wasn't getting well. So I just said to God, "If You don't take this away from me, I want You to take my life. After having ministered to millions of people I don't want to go through the rest of my life like this. I'm not breathing right."

And so there I was asking Him to take away my life. I'm being very honest with you. I come into situations that I don't know what to do, and the burdens get heavy.

I want to tell you that in my Christian life, I'm not on the periphery, I'm out there in the arena. I'm where the hurts of humans are, including my own hurts. And I have discovered that without Scriptures like 2 Timothy 1:6-8, we're not going to make it. We have to live in the now. It doesn't matter if we felt good 20 years ago. If we don't feel good today, we can't remember how good we felt 20 years ago. We want to feel good in the now, don't we?

But I'm so glad that Paul wrote 2 Timothy, because this is God remembering His children. That's exactly what we are—children. I don't think anybody would say that he'd grown up and that he's arrived as a Christian. I'm not going to say it because I don't want to lie.

I'm glad there are Scriptures in the Bible that fit us.

GOD HAS NOT GIVEN US A SPIRIT OF FEAR

Paul is saying:

"You're just about to lose out. You're just about to lose out. You've got to stir up the gift of God within you for God hath not given us the spirit of fear..."

"Timothy, you're frightened. You're afraid. You get this queasy feeling in your stomach. You're shy. You want to run when the battle gets hot."

If you notice the next verse there, he said, "Be a partaker of the sufferings with me." Timothy wasn't doing very good at this point. He liked the meeting when it was going well. But when it didn't go well, Timothy felt a call to go somewhere else. And when Paul reached for him, Timothy was gone. And he was saying to him, "God hath not given you this kind of spirit of fright, to make you get up and run off."

Some of us don't run off physically, we just run off from ourselves and our intellect, or in our spiritual self. We're there physically, but we're not there spiritually. We're not there with our faith. It's as though we're not there at all. You can tell that we're not there because we're not participating. We're not going forward in our Christian experience. We're not positive in our attitude. We withdraw into ourselves, like into a shell. Or if we don't do that, we strike out at people. We say things that we would gladly give anything if we could withdraw, and wish we hadn't said them. And we hurt one another. And usually we do this when we're frightened. And when we're frightened, it's because we have the feeling of insecurity that we can't do what we're supposed to do, or something has happened against us until we give in to it.

Paul was reminding Timothy that God hadn't given him that kind of spirit. When He had placed the gift of the Spirit within him, it did not carry with it the spirit of fear.

ANY FEAR WE HAVE IS NOT A PART OF THE GIFTS OF GOD

It is the same as darkness is the absence of light.

As poverty is the absence of money.

As weakness is the absence of strength.

As sickness is the absence of health.

Fear is the absence of our real faith in God.

When we let down on our faith in God, we feel that fear. Faith of course is stronger than fear in the same way that light is stronger than darkness, and health is stronger than sickness. And strength is stronger than weakness. And financial prosperity is stronger than poverty. So fear is the absence of God, God in His faith, God in His love, God in His power.

Paul is saying, "God hath not given you the spirit of fear, Timothy. He didn't make your stomach get queasy. He didn't make you fall apart inside and make you want to run off when the going gets tough. God didn't do that. For God has given you the spirit of power."

POWER THAT KILLS FEAR

Acts 1:8 says, "Ye shall receive power, after that the Holy Ghost is come upon you." The Holy Spirit is the Spirit of power. The power of God is a Spirit. It is a Spirit of power. And that's the only way you can understand the power of God.

And, friend, that's the power that spins the universe. That's the power that God used to scoop out the beds of the ocean,

to fling the stars from His fingertips,

to sculpture the mountains,

and to hang the earth on nothing.

That's the power that you feel going down your backbone, the power that you feel welling up from inside you, the power you feel that you could just reach up and move mountains.

It's the power you feel inside you that you can lick your weight in a den of wildcats.

It's the power you feel that you can bring down the strongholds of the devil.

It's the power you feel that you can put your marriage back into unity.

It's the power you feel that God can restore your health.

It's the power you feel that God can take away that lust in your
       heart and bring a freedom and purity in your body and spirit.
It's the spirit of power. And it's the power of God who is a Spirit.
And when that power possesses us, there's no way we can be afraid.
We can face anything.

Here's what I want you to do now. Reread this last section, "POWER
THAT KILLS FEAR." Let these mighty truths sink in—sink in deep.
And every time you feel fear begin to grip your insides, read it again
and again and again. I tell you, friend, it'll turn your life around.

YOUR GOD-GIVEN KEY FOR TODAY

Say: **"God's Power Will Overcome My Every Fear."**

SATURDAY

Key:
I BELONG TO GOD—
THE DEVIL CAN'T HAVE ME

or
How To Bring Healing To Yourself And Your Loved Ones By Getting Mad At The Devil And Resisting Him

Did you know that your body is a temple of the Holy Spirit? We
usually don't know it, so this Scripture starts with a question:

> *What? know ye not that your body is the temple of the Holy
> Ghost which is in you, which ye have of God, and ye are not
> your own?*
> *For ye are bought with a price: therefore glorify God in your
> body, and in your spirit, which are God's* (1 Corinthians 6:19,20).

So your body isn't merely the temple of your own human spirit, though
it is that. But it is also the temple of the Holy Spirit. And the Holy
Spirit puts a dignity and a glory in your body. It makes you God's
property. You belong to God!

Now, there is nothing to compare with the price that God paid for
you, the jewel of His kingdom, the apple of His eye. He so loved you
that He gave His only begotten Son. He gave Him freely so that you
wouldn't perish but that you might have eternal life. And when you
receive Christ as your Savior, your body becomes the temple of the
Holy Spirit. You belong to God. Do you believe it? Then resist the devil.
I mean, get mad at him!

Hate sickness and disease.
>Reject satanic power.
>>Reject evil thoughts.
>>>Bring yourself close to Christ.
>>>>Keep your body clean.
>>>>>Stop polluting your body.

That body is a temple. And you don't do damage to a temple. You say, "Well, I'll quit my smoking and my drinking."

Well, stop your overeating too. Quit damaging yourself. I'm talking to myself too. Everything I say to you, I say to me. None of us is exempt from the gospel. The gospel holds us all on the same line with our Lord. We belong to Him. Our bodies are sacred. We should protect our minds and our bodies from bad thoughts and quit throwing off negative thoughts to other people. Quit telling them how bad they look, how sick they look. Quit sympathizing. Start having compassion.

AM I STILL IN THE HEALING MINISTRY?

People ask me if I'm still in the healing ministry. Is God still God? There's your answer to that. I change my methods and I may still be changing my methods five years from now. I'm not married to methods. I'm married to my principles, which are in God my Source.

Just the other day I prayed for a pastor of a Presbyterian Church who is also chaplain at a Presbyterian junior college. I've known this man for years. He loves this ministry and Oral Roberts University. When I learned he had developed paralysis and other complications I just had to pray with him. When I finished praying for him we were both crying like children, and the Holy Spirit gave me a word of prophecy:

"You won't know yourself in three weeks.
>You'll feel like skipping from hill to hill.
>>And you will move out of sympathy into compassion."

Now I didn't know what I was saying except by the word of prophecy. Later I understood and I shared it with him because he didn't know what I meant. I said, "Sympathy is a human feeling. It's a good feeling but it doesn't do people much good. You sympathize too much with people and they get sicker. They get more self-centered. But compassion is to rid the person of sickness. Compassion gets you down under the load and you have the power of God with you so you can help rid a person of sickness. When you come into compassion, you hate the disease. You are now going to resist that disease. You are going to say, 'Disease, you have no part in me because I am the temple of the Holy Spirit. Disease, you have no part in my life because I belong to God. Disease, take your hands off my body because my body is God's.'"

He thanked me and I thanked him for letting me say it to him. And the occurrence of that experience is why I'm talking to you like this.

DON'T DIVIDE GOD'S HEALING POWER

Respect your doctor. Respect medicine. *Don't divide God's healing power.* Some people will pray and never take advantage of medicine, and some will take medicine and never pray. I don't know about them, but I take it all from God myself. If God wants to heal me through a doctor, I say, "Thank you, God, for sending that doctor across my path."

If God wants to heal me through prayer, I say, "Thank you, God, for sending that prayer."

Or if He wants to heal me through both, I don't care—I just want to get healed!

THE HEALING POWER OF OUR LORD JESUS CHRIST CAN TAKE MANY FORMS

Sometimes people are helped in their sicknesses by good words said to them, by a helping hand, a pat on the shoulder, a smile, or somebody coming over and saying a word of love to them. That's God's healing power too.

Sometimes we find doctors who seem to have an uncanny gift from God to diagnose and to prescribe the right kind of medicine, or the right kind of surgery, or the ability to recommend the right climate. I'll tell you, when it works it's a tremendous blessing from God.

Then sometimes there are people who seem to be directed by the Lord to know *how* to pray. They know how to touch God for a person's healing. What a blessing that is! So don't fragment or divide God's healing power—just know that God is the Source of our total supply. God is the Source of our entire healing. I thank God for the human instruments—doctors, people that pray, climate, and things of nature, but God is the Divine Source. So I say, "Thank You, God, for healing me any way you choose."

HOW GOD'S ANOINTING POWER HELPS YOU

God anointed Jesus of Nazareth with the Holy Ghost and with power: who went about doing good, and healing all that were oppressed of the devil; for God was with him (Acts 10:38).

Now let me share with you why it's important for you to be anointed. What is the anointing anyway? I don't know that I can tell you what it is, but I can tell you what it's not. I know that when I'm anointed my soul can't stand still, and miracles happen. And when I'm *not* anointed I *can* stand still, and nothing happens. It is a kind of electric warm feeling that I experience going through me. And it's good. Friend, if it's good, it's God. If it's bad, it's of the devil; and that's a pretty good way of determining whether it's of God or not. When I feel this anointing that comes upon me from time to time, I'm different. I have more of God. He works through me better. I can preach better. I love with a stronger love. I love until I want to put my arms around the whole human race. I love until I want to rid them of every torment and doubt and sickness and fear and demon. I want them to be well. That's the kind of love I feel when I'm anointed of God. I know this—whatever your calling in life is, God's anointing will make it better and make it stronger.

And then, I have a hatred of the devil. I hate him. I would wring his neck if I could. I would kick him out of existence. I would rend him to pieces. I would cast him head down into the bottomless pit and if he tried to dig out he'd just dig deeper. I mean, I get mad at the devil. I'm sick of the devil. I'm sick of his sickness. And I hate the kind of fear he puts upon me, or upon you. I hate everything about him. I don't like him.

I HATE ANYTHING NEGATIVE

Most people don't even know how negative they are. It's so easy for the devil to put negative thoughts in our minds. It's so easy for a conversation like this to be carried on:

"I'm never going to get well."

"Well, you look better."

"Well, I'm not."

"But, you look like you feel better."

"Well, I always feel the worst when I feel the best, because I know how bad I'm going to feel when I start feeling bad again."

The devil makes you look like an accident going off to happen. He makes you act like you've been drinking vinegar and eating sauerkraut and crab apples and hanging onto the weeping willows and living in the mully-grubs and your face looks as long as a mule's.

But when you have this love that is a result of God's anointing, it puts a spring in your step, a light in your eye, and a shine on your face. God is your Father, Jesus is your Savior, and the Holy Spirit your Comforter. Oh, friend, when you have this anointing, you don't hate people, but you hate the things that are wrong with them. You never hate a sinner, but you hate sin. You never hate a sick person, but you hate sickness.

I'll never forget an incident that happened in 1947 when I was a young pastor and just starting out in the ministry. I got a call to pray for a sick woman. When I got in the house there was another minister over in a corner praying, and moaning, and sympathizing—"O God, what a dreadful thing this is . . ." and on and on. And I guess I got mad at the devil. Something exploded in me and I walked over to the bed and laid hands on the woman and rebuked the devil. I said, "Devil, take your hands off God's property!" and she came out of that bed rejoicing. I left and the other minister was still over in the corner moaning and sympathizing. He didn't know a miracle of healing had happened. I remember that like it was yesterday. Well, that is what I am like when I feel God's anointing.

Now let me tell you what I'm like when I don't feel His anointing.

As I said, I was just starting out in the ministry. I was pastoring a church, going to college, trying to take care of my family, and my people were calling me day and night asking me to pray for them. On this particular occasion I had been out all day and just about all night. Now it was 4 o'clock in the morning and I had gone to sleep. Sure enough, the phone rang. Evelyn answered. "Oh, Mrs. Roberts, my wife's nose is bleeding and I'm afraid she'll bleed to death if Brother Roberts doesn't come right away."

Evelyn woke me up but by this time I was so tired I didn't even know where I was. Evelyn said, "Honey, Mrs._____is about to die."

I turned over and said, "Let her die."

The next morning when I woke up Evelyn told me what I had done. I said, "I didn't do that."

She said, "Yes, you did. You certainly did."

So I went over just as fast as I could to that lady's house. But by that time, the doctor had already been there and stuffed her nose full of gauze and she was all right. Anyway, I wanted to tell you both sides of me. I'm afraid I'm not anointed one hundred percent of the time.

WHO HEALS—MAN OR GOD?

Several years ago in one of our crusades a woman said, "Brother Roberts, pray hard for me, I'm really sick."

How *hard* I pray doesn't make any difference. It's how God touches you that makes the difference. I never have exalted myself in the matter of praying for the sick. I've never believed that I had to pray a long time. That's saying the man—God's instrument—has too much to do with it. If I thought that would work, I'd do it—but it just won't work. If God Almighty doesn't do the healing, it isn't going to be done.

It's the same in medical science. When a surgeon performs an operation, using every resource available, the body still will not heal until God gets in there and makes that body of yours respond to surgery. What I'm saying is, you belong to God. You are the temple of the Holy Spirit.

YOU ARE GOD'S BELOVED!

Above all, you've got to love yourself, but hate the thing that's wrong with you. And you've got to love your neighbor, just like you love yourself, and hate the thing that's wrong with him. You can't hate him and you can't hate yourself. You've got to have love for yourself and you've got to have love for someone else. You've got to believe in yourself and you've got to believe in other people and that makes you vulnerable. Often I believe in people and they let me down. Often they believe in me and I let them down. But we still have to believe, even though we are let down at times. We still have to keep that belief up or we'll become cynical. In general, newspapers are cynical. What they are looking for is not good news. They are looking for something bad. You know why? Because the newspapers reflect you and me. We like bad news.

I was thrilled recently when I opened our Sunday morning *Tulsa World* newspaper and the front page headline was about a man's healing of cancer in a Methodist Church in St. Joseph, Missouri. It was headline news right on the top of our front page. I appreciated that and I told the editor I appreciated it. I was so tired of bad news and I was glad to know the newspaper recognized somebody got healed of cancer through prayer.

Now, that ought to be a lesson to you and to me. Let's start hating bad news and loving good news. I come to you with good news. You know what I want for you? I want you to be well. I want you to prosper. And I want you to be right with God spiritually. And I base that on 3 John 2.

> *Beloved, I wish above all things that thou mayest prosper and be in health, even as thy soul prospereth.*

What's the first word? "Beloved." Say it. Say, I'm beloved of God." Look up and tell Him, "God, I'm Your beloved. I'm going to quit hating myself. And, God, You want me to prosper and be in health, even as my soul prospers."

Now, don't you feel better? That's got healing in it, friend! Healing for *you*, the person, your total self. And the whole of God's power is back of His wish for you to be well and have your needs met. That verse was one of my first discoveries in 1947, and it's my wife's favorite now.

What do I want for you? I want you to be well. Friend, this is why we exist. This is why God called us. We didn't build Oral Roberts University just to be building. We built a place to be filled with the Holy Spirit and to operate upon God's authority. We want to minister healing and see people get deliverance for body, mind, and soul and learn how to prosper, learn how to do the will of God. That's what we want.

When I touch people in prayer I touch them with my heart. And when I lay hands on someone to pray, I try not to think about my hands. I try to think about the hands of Jesus. I really do. Oftentimes I have my eyes shut and I'm visualizing His hands. Because I tell you the truth, if I can do that, if I can just visualize His hands on you, I can see the disease going.

A NEW EMPHASIS

When praying for a person I often say:
> *Devil, take your hands off God's property!*

I've started emphasizing this point recently because I feel the devil is causing too many bad things to happen all over the world. He's attacking people with all kinds of sicknesses and torments, with hunger, with unemployment, with loneliness, with a feeling that nobody cares, with war. And people need to hear a voice saying:

"Devil, you're a defeated foe.

Our Savior defeated you on the cross."

They need to hear someone say:

Greater is He (God) that is in you, than he (the devil) that is in the world (1 John 4:4).

The Holy Spirit has been dealing with me to come right out and say this stronger than I've ever said it before.

I belong to God. Devil, in the name of Jesus, take your hands off God's property—ME!

Now some people get frightened and don't have the nerve to say that. They feel they might be saying it in their own power. But every time you say those words in Jesus' name, you're giving the devil a command that's really straight from the Lord!

IT APPLIES TO LOVED ONES

This can also be applied to your business, your home, your loved ones, and friends . . . all those close to you.

I've heard Evelyn many times speaking in the name of Jesus, and saying, "Devil, let us alone." And she would go to the kitchen door and open it and tell him to get out of our house. You see, a lot of people don't understand the devil is a personality . . . evil personified.

Another thing Evelyn did, especially when the children were growing up, was when one of them was sick or something was wrong, she would pray for him and I would hear her say, "Devil, you're not going to do this to my child." And this was scriptural. Acts 16:31 says, "Believe on the Lord Jesus Christ, and thou shalt be saved, *and thy house.*" God has promised us our household.

I constantly ask God to help my loved ones. And when I'm praying for them, I command the devil to take his hands off my children, my grandchildren, off my friends, or off some partner I'm praying for, because I believe that's the kind of prayer the devil understands. When you belong to God and you know it, and you let the devil know you know it, it makes all the difference in the world!

There are FIVE main things in today's reading I want you to grab hold of and make them a part of your everyday life:

1. GOD STILL HEALS TODAY
2. DON'T DIVIDE GOD'S HEALING POWER
3. YOU ARE GOD'S PROPERTY

4. YOU BELONG TO GOD
5. GREATER IS HE (GOD) THAT IS IN YOU THAN HE (THE DEVIL) THAT IS IN THE WORLD.

YOUR GOD-GIVEN KEY FOR TODAY

Now say:

"I Belong To God—The Devil Can't Have Me."

NOW, LET US (JUST THE TWO OF US), YOU AND ME, TALK ABOUT THIS BOOK

If you were my own brother or sister, I would say to you what I'm going to say to you now . . . you haven't got much time!

I don't know how old you are, but that really doesn't matter where God is concerned. He doesn't count time like you and I do. But RIGHT NOW is the only time you have for sure. The older you get the faster time goes by.

Right now as I write this book, I'm 57 years old, and I just can't believe it. I almost get dizzy when I think how fast the time has passed since I began this ministry nearly 29 years ago—and how much more God has called me to do. And I believe He will give me the time to finish what He has called me to do.

Now, you have finished reading this book. I think I know how you must feel . . . just like I felt after I read it through. There's so much here, you may feel confused. You don't know exactly what to do about it.

Let me suggest three things:

1. You can choose to do nothing. If you lay this book aside and don't memorize and follow the keys to miracles that I have set down here according to the Holy Bible, then the book has probably been a waste of your time.

2. You can choose to say, "That's really great stuff, and it might work for some people, but not for me." If you do this—you'll miss the miracles and abundant living through Seed-Faith living that God intended you to have.

3. You can choose to take the advice I've given in this book. Learn to live in the "keys." I have staked my life on them. And God has done just exactly what He said He would do.

Regardless of what you do for a living I can guarantee you upon the authority of God's Word that if you will study this book—take each of these subjects one day at a time—at the end of 13 weeks you will be a different person. You will be surprised at yourself. Your friends will notice the difference in you—your business associates, your family. And I KNOW by the time you have *repeated* this 13 weeks four times in a year, EVERYONE will see the difference in you, both in your spiritual and material life. Best of all, you will see and feel the difference.

In this book I have given you the very heart of what I have learned from God through experience in this ministry. For the past 10 years I have been telling this to the students at Oral Roberts University. I have tried to write this as I speak it to them, to the lay seminars at ORU, to the audiences where I speak all over America, and to individuals with whom I come in contact. It is as the Spirit works through me. And it's for you . . . and your loved ones . . . with all my love.

Well, here it is. I pray you have been helped by it. Now start through it again and you'll get more, more, MORE!

Your partner always,

Oral Roberts

THIRTEENTH WEEK

SUNDAY	I CAN SAY "HELLO" TO GOD EVERY DAY
MONDAY	I'LL KEEP PRESSING ON BECAUSE I KNOW GOD IS WITH ME
TUESDAY	IN EVERY CIRCUMSTANCE I FACE THERE IS THE REAL LIFE OF MY LORD
WEDNESDAY	WHEN GOD STIRS MY NEST THERE'S A REASON—I'LL LOOK FOR IT
THURSDAY	I'LL BE AWARE OF GOD'S GREAT RICHES TODAY AND EVERY DAY
FRIDAY	GOD'S POWER WILL OVERCOME MY EVERY FEAR
SATURDAY	I BELONG TO GOD—THE DEVIL CAN'T HAVE ME

MIRACLE OF SEED FAITH, one of Oral Roberts' most popular books, is also available in a Spire edition.

You are invited and encouraged to write Oral Roberts for prayer or for information regarding his ministry at Oral Roberts University. Simply address your letter:

Oral Roberts
Tulsa, Oklahoma 74171

Your letter will be most welcome and you will receive a prompt and positive written reply.

If you have a special prayer request, you are encouraged to call the Abundant Life Prayer Group at (918) 492-7777. Call anytime, day or night, and a trained prayer partner will answer your call and pray with you.